Globalized E-Learning Cultural Challenges

Andrea Edmundson
eWorld Learning, USA

 **Information Science Publishing**

Hershey • London • Melbourne • Singapore

Acquisitions Editor:	Michelle Potter
Development Editor:	Kristin Roth
Senior Managing Editor:	Jennifer Neidig
Managing Editor:	Sara Reed
Copy Editor:	Susanna Svidunovich
Typesetter:	Cindy Consonery
Cover Design:	Lisa Tosheff
Printed at:	Yurchak Printing Inc.

Published in the United States of America by
      Information Science Publishing (an imprint of Idea Group Inc.)
      701 E. Chocolate Avenue
      Hershey PA 17033
      Tel: 717-533-8845
      Fax: 717-533-8661
      E-mail: cust@idea-group.com
      Web site: http://www.idea-group.com

and in the United Kingdom by
      Information Science Publishing (an imprint of Idea Group Inc.)
      3 Henrietta Street
      Covent Garden
      London WC2E 8LU
      Tel: 44 20 7240 0856
      Fax: 44 20 7379 0609
      Web site: http://www.eurospanonline.com

Library of Congress Cataloging-in-Publication Data

Globalized e-learning cultural challenges / Andrea Edmundson, editor.
    p. cm.
  Summary: "This book's purpose is to inform educators and instructional designers of issues and cultural misunderstandings that could hinder the effective transfer of knowledge when e-learning is exported to other cultures. Addressing these cultural challenges will enhance the effectiveness of e-learning, thereby supporting the societal benefits of increased access to education at a global level"--Provided by publisher.
  Includes bibliographical references and index.
  ISBN 1-59904-301-7 (hardcover : alk. paper) -- ISBN 1-59904-302-5 (softcover : alk. paper) -- ISBN 1-59904-303-3 (ebook : alk. paper)
  1. Virtual reality in education--Cross-cultural studies. 2. Internet in education--Cross-cultural studies. 3. Distance education--Computer-assisted instruction--Cross-cultural studies. 4. Multicultural education--Computer-assisted instruction. 5. Intercultural communication. I. Edmundson, Andrea, 1955-
LB1044.87.G59 2006
371.3'58--dc22
                            2006015166

British Cataloguing in Publication Data
A Cataloguing in Publication record for this book is available from the British Library.

Globalized E-Learning Cultural Challenges

Table of Contents

SECTION V:
Conclusion

Foreword

All those who are involved in creating e-learning materials for international audiences should read this book. It is an honest attempt to come to grips with the multitude of challenges that this field provides, and a treasure trove of clever ideas.

E-learning can be a matter of instruction to individuals. Ten years ago, when I created e-learning applications to teach novices from around the world to work with office software, the students from hierarchical societies especially loved the patience of the software: They could run any movie as often as they would, and it did not become angry or impatient. Those with poor English liked the written transcripts. Those with previous computer experience simply skipped the sections with which they were familiar.

Culture certainly had an influence, but by and large this was only through the practices with which the students were or were not familiar. To some, operating a keyboard was the first adventure. To many, I suppose, the example of a pizza restaurant in the Excel course was novel. I was not aware of any major problems or misunderstandings, though.

The notion that every individual is unique and might therefore require a unique interface to his or her learning materials has become popular in individualistic societies. A lot of literature has appeared on learning styles. More recently, since the advent of the Web, cultural differences have also become salient to designers of educational materials. But how large a role should they play? It turns out that many tasks have an ideal interface, regardless of whom you ask to perform these tasks. For showing the molecular structure of a protein, a 3-D picture surpasses a text; but for carrying out a chemical experiment, a procedural text surpasses a picture. For other tasks it is not so clear-cut, and learning styles enter the picture. To complicate life for the designer, conventions in maps and pictures, and above all use of language, may differ across cultures. So this area of e-learning design poses manifold challenges. Many of them are addressed in this text.

E-learning can also be teamwork. Five years ago, I was involved in e-learning team projects across Europe and Asia. This involved virtual classroom sessions between Hong Kong, French, and Dutch students who had never met face to face. Did cross-cultural problems occur? Some said no, culture was not an issue at all. Other teams claimed that they could not work with the foreigners, and that the team failed due to cross-cultural problems. My analyses of virtual classroom sessions during project definition showed that both personality and culture were important. The French typically wanted to detail the topic further to start with, the Hong Kong males wanted to get down to work, Hong Kong females tended to be concerned with a good atmosphere and to use emoticons a lot, while the Dutch were concerned with the quality of communication, and some of them tried to be funny. In some teams, depending on, among others, mutually-accepted leadership, this mix led to disaster, while in others the team members had a splendid time. The unhappy teams came up with typical complaints: For instance, Hong Kong participants said the Dutch did not stick to the rules and were blunt. In short, if teamwork is involved, cultural differences between team members can lead to violent crises. But other factors might also carry some of the blame, most notably personalities, team composition, and supervision.

So how important to e-learning is culture? Very. But in most cases, you do not wish the participants to notice. They want to do a course with as little hassle as possible. That is a course designer's predicament. This book provides some clues. In my opinion, when group work is involved, a course designer or course leader cannot always avoid conflicts such as the ones mentioned just now. A good debriefing is crucial, so that the participants learn from the episode rather than just building prejudice. A general awareness of the importance of cross-cultural skills would, in fact, be a desirable pre-condition for participating in such a course.[1]

Cross-cultural challenges are part of today's life. An e-learning course never stands alone. To a learner from a different cultural background than the instructor's, an e-learning course also acts as a window on another culture. The material may contain many clues about the social assumptions of the society in which it was created. Along with the material, the student may be faced with additional practices such as how to subscribe, and how to be supervised and graded. All these elements of learning can be quite valuable for the learner, even though they are not in the terms of reference. What is more, they cannot be customized away. And I would put it even more strongly: They *should* not necessarily be customized away. People in general, and learners in particular, are very good at making their own translation from what an e-learning tool offers into what they need from it.

E-learning is also a branch of applied information systems design. If you are in the process of inventing something and you wish to know whether it is any good for the audience, the proper thing to do is to go find representatives of your audience and have them try out your concepts.

This book testifies to the creativity of instructors. A multitude of thoughts and practical suggestions are assembled in this book. As the field matures, some ideas will be more widely-adopted than others. One size will never fit all, though. The e-learning field will reflect the width of subjects and educational methods that it embraces, as well as the creativity of instructors worldwide. May this book be a source of inspiration!

Endnote

[1]   Consider Gert Jan Hofstede, Paul Pedersen, and Geert Hofstede (2002) *Exploring Culture: Exercises, Stories, and Synthetic Cultures*, Intercultural Press, a book for both instructors and students, to get hands-on experience with cross-cultural situations.

Gert Jan Hofstede

Preface

Like many authors, I generated the idea for this book when I was unable to find the information I needed for my work. As the CEO of eWorld Learning, I have many roles and, correspondingly, multiple concerns. From the perspective of my role as an educational consultant and manager of educational projects, how could I best guide my clients in the creation of accessible and viable e-learning? As an instructional designer, I had different concerns. How would I design instruction for educators and learners in other cultures? If I were offering e-learning to non-American, or even non-Western, audiences, could I adapt e-learning to their needs? Would I need to design differently, or would/could students adapt to a Western style of teaching or learning? In addition, as an instructor for online universities, I wanted information about the learning environments in countries outside of the United States: To what types of educational systems were they accustomed? How did they, as members of different cultural groups, prefer or expect to learn? What instructional strategies would be most effective for a globalized, multicultural group of learners?

Useful information was available, but often in disciplines or fields of expertise other than education. I could find substantial information about the effects of culture in business and communications. I could also find research on the effects of culture on various aspects of people's lives and/or their work. I could find authors who *postulated* on how this information and cultural research might be applied to e-learning; however, there were few personal accounts and scant empirical research, especially in the field of e-learning, to answer questions adequately. In addition, much of the research with which we are familiar was conducted by Westerners. Would results be valuable to members of cultures? Did the research reflect the perspectives of learners and educators in non-Western cultures?

When I originally proposed this book to the publisher, the table of contents closely resembled the literature review for my research study, *The Cross-Cultural Dimensions of Globalized E-Learning*. However, as chapter proposals began to arrive, the table of contents morphed into the version you see now. I received chapter submissions from authors of many cultures and countries. I received proposals on topics previously overlooked by at least my blossoming view of where and how culture might have an impact on e-learning. Some of these challenges could have been anticipated, and within disciplines, they were. The language issues were obvious to linguists, and computer code issues were obvious to computer programmers. However, such concepts had not previously been assembled together and treated as essential components of success-ful e-learning. This book should serve as a tool for "consciousness-raising" for con-sumers and producers of e-learning, educators, instructional designers, trainers, fac-ulty, and university administrators, challenging them to address the many cultural as-pects of e-learning. Gert Jan Hofstede, co-author of *Exploring Culture: Exercises, Stories, and Synthetic Cultures*, with Gert Hofstede and Paul B. Pedersen, introduces the book. I have placed the chapters into four sections, leading the reader from broad perspectives of globalized e-learning to practical considerations.

Section I:
The Big Picture: Culture and
E-Learning from Global Perspectives

In the first chapter, *The Meaning of Culture in Online Education: Implications for Teaching, Learning, and Design*, Chun-Min Wang and Thomas C. Reeves present a review of the literature on cultural dimensions in online education and draw implica-tions for design and research in this area. Bolanle Olaniran, in Chapter II, *Challenges to Implementing E-Learning in Lesser-Developed Countries*, discusses how global-ized e-learning has implications for communications, culture, and technology in both developed and lesser-developed countries, all of which must be addressed in order for successful implementation to occur. In Chapter III, *Designing Quality Online Educa-tion to Promote Cross-Cultural Understanding*, Youmei Liu discusses the relationship between cultural value systems in education and how cross-cultural online education can promote the development of social capital by improving cultural awareness and social competency. In Chapter IV, *African Education Perspectives on Culture and E-Learning Convergence*, Wanjira Kinuthia uses examples from an African perspective, illustrating that increasing awareness of cultural aspects is crucial to making instruc-tional decisions. In Chapter V, *Intercultural Dimensions in the Information Society: Reflections on Designing and Developing Culturally-Oriented Learning*, Nektaria Palaiologou promotes the development of non-culture-centric online e-learning that incorporates values that support global citizenship.

Section II:
Western Philosophies and Theoretical Foundations in E-Learning

In this section, Western authors raise various questions about the theoretical foundations of e-learning. In the globalized environment, where the majority of e-learning producers are from Western cultures, but the largest growing consumer groups are Eastern, we need to determine whether we can use (or impose) Western learning theories and paradigms in other cultures. In Chapter VI, *Theorizing and Realizing the Globalized Classroom,* Steve McCarty discusses the characteristics, criteria, and conditions that constitute a successful "globalized" classroom, including constructivist approaches. In contrast, in Chapter VII, David Catterick asks, *Do the Philosophical Foundations of Online Learning Disadvantage Non-Western Students?* Lyn Henderson, in Chapter VIII, *Theorizing a Multiple Cultures Instructional Design Model for E-Learning and E-Teaching,* proposes a theoretical *model of multiple cultures* that provides the rationale and strategies for creating and adapting e-learning resources for various cultural contexts.

Section III:
Language and Semiotics

The tasks of addressing language differences and the potential need for translation both seem to be obvious challenges, but the authors in this section take us beyond the concepts of simple translation. In Chapter IX, *How to Globalize Online Course Content,* Martin Schell shows us how English, being the most common language used in e-learning, needs to be "globalized", stripped of idioms, colloquialisms, and other biasing characteristics, in order for it to be understood among learners for whom English is not a first language. Meng-Fen (Grace) Lin and Mimi Miyoung Lee, in Chapter X, *E-Learning Localized: The Case of the OOPS* (Opensource OpenCourseWare Prototype System) *Project,* describe how volunteer translators are translating English courseware into Chinese and simultaneously "localizing" it for learners. In Chapter XI, *What Can Cave Walls Teach Us?* Ruth Gannon Cook and Caroline M. Crawford remind us of another dimension of language, semiotics (the use of symbolism), and how semiotics affect comprehension in Web sites and e-learning courses. Lastly, Katherine Watson in Chapter XII introduces us to the concept of *Electronic Paralanguage: Interfacing with the International,* explaining how immersion in the language environment online can actually lead learners to a better understanding of the culture itself.

Section IV:
Addressing Issues of Cross-Cultural Instructional Design

In this section, authors who are practitioners, or who have conducted research studies on some of the challenges identified in previous sections, present practical information and advice on designing instruction for the e-learning environment. In Chapter XIII, *Adapting E-Learning Across Cultural Boundaries: A Framework for Quality Learning, Pedagogy, and Interaction,* Catherine McLoughlin challenges us to use flexible and pluralistic instructional design to provide learning experiences, activities, and forms of communication that are congruent with the learners' cultural values, belief systems, and preferred styles of learning. Then, two somewhat opposing approaches to designing e-learning are introduced. Jane Eberle and Marcus Childress, in Chapter XIV, *Universal Design for Culturally-Diverse Online Learning*, propose that, using principles they delineate, we can design one course that is suitable for all cultures. In contrast, in Chapter XV, *Beyond Localization: Effective Learning Strategies for Cross-Cultural E-Learning*, Patrick Dunn and Alessandra Marinetti propose adaptation strategies that supersede localization techniques to accommodate the needs of different cultures. Then I, in Chapter XVI, *The Cultural Adaptation Process (CAP) Model: Designing E-Learning for Another Culture,* illustrate how to use the model, within the framework of a needs assessment, to determine if and how e-learning may need to be adapted for other cultures. Next, two authors address important aspects of communication in today's globalized e-learning: In Chapter XVII, Rita Zaltsman presents research findings on *Communication Barriers and Conflicts in Cross-Cultural E-Learning*, and in Chapter XVIII, Datta Kaur Khalsa discusses *Multi-Cultural E-Learning Teamwork: Social and Cultural Characteristics and Influence.* Lastly, in Chapter XIX, *Modern Technology and Mass Education: A Case Study of a Global Virtual Learning System*, Ahmed Ali presents a case study in which e-learning was implemented from European countries to Africa, and discusses its effectiveness, including feedback from the students themselves.

In the conclusion, in Chapter XX, *The Treasure Trove*, I provide a brief overview of the state of globalized e-learning and cultural challenges, based on concepts raised in seminal research and in this book. We are in the early stages of discovery and change. Speaking for all contributors to this book, we hope you enjoy the journey.

How to Use This Book

Here are few suggestions on how to use this book:

1. Take advantage of the authors' reference lists to locate seminal research studies on cultural dimensions and other aspects of culture that may have an impact on e-learning.

2. Be open to the concepts offered throughout the book; they come from several different disciplines, and thus, should be treated as potentially useful in new domains.

3. Use the book to begin to identify the critical challenges *you* or *your organization* may face and begin to seek practical ways in which to address them.

4. None of the concepts presented in this book are "set in stone", and we can expect new developments continually and in the near future.

5. Lastly, we are working with human beings and, while we can make reasonable generalizations about members of cultures and groups of people with similar attributes, we must respect members of all cultures as individuals and thus, use the concepts presented in this book accordingly.

Andrea Edmundson
eWorld Learning, USA
February 2006

Acknowledgments

I appreciate the time, support, and professional experiences of all those who helped make this book a reality. Foremost, I thank all of the authors for their creative perspectives, hard work, diligence, and their dedication to their profession and to the advancement of globalized e-learning. In addition to writing chapters, many of them also donated their valuable time as peer reviewers: Nektaria Palaiologou, Katherine Watson, Steve McCarty, Datta Kaur Khalsa, Youmei Liu, Marcus Childress, Jane Eberle, Patrick Dunn, Martin Schell, Wanjira Kinuthia, Meng-Fen (Grace) Lin, Mimi Miyoung Lee, David Catterick, Bolanle Olaniran, Rita Zaltsman, and Chun-Min Wang. In particular, Ruth Gannon Cook and Caroline Crawford went beyond the call of duty with their assistance, especially when they sensed any note of desperation in my voice!

Several professional colleagues and friends also offered their time voluntarily as external reviewers of the book chapters, often responding to my request for a fast turnaround: Pier Junor-Clarke (Georgia State University, USA), Sanjaya Mishra (Indira Gandhi National Open University, India), Gert Jan Hofstede (Wageningen University, The Netherlands), Curtis Bonk (Indiana University, USA), Vivian Wright (University of Alabama, USA), Victor Quiros (Our Family Services, USA), Xu Di (Walden University, USA), Linda Crawford (Walden University, USA), Gaye Bumsted-Perry (Maricopa Community College, USA), and John Petroff (Professional Education Organization International, USA). In addition, I would like to thank Gert Jan Hofstede for writing the book's foreword. He is frank, funny, and foremost, a professional!

Thanks to my development editor, Kristin Roth, for providing timely information and feedback, and for commiserating with me when I got "whiny."

I also thank my friends and family for their unflagging support and encouragement. In particular, thanks to the Lunch Bunch, Annette Carapellucci, Marie Wesselhoft, and Valerie Grindle, for our monthly "encouragement" sessions! And, lastly, I am especially appreciative of my husband, Victor, who supports and encourages my passions unquestioningly.

Section I

The Big Picture:
Culture and
E-Learning from
Global Perspectives

Chapter I

The Meaning of Culture in Online Education:
Implications for Teaching, Learning, and Design

Chun-Min Wang
University of Georgia, USA

Thomas C. Reeves
University of Georgia, USA

Abstract

Individual online learning courses and even entire online degree programs are increasingly a part of the mainstream in higher education. Steadily-improving online delivery systems and an emphasis on globalization have encouraged more and more higher education institutions to try to reach diverse learners around the world. In light of the growing population of learners from various cultural backgrounds engaged in online education, there is an urgent need to understand how culture affects online education. This chapter presents a review of the literature regarding cultural dimensions in online education, and draws implications from this literature for design and research in this area.

Introduction

Online education has experienced dramatic growth in higher education around the globe, but especially in the United States of America (USA). Six years ago, Harasim (2000) proclaimed that online education was no longer peripheral or supplementary, and that it had become an integral part of mainstream higher education. In 2003, more than half of all institutions of higher education in the USA offered at least one fully-online or blended course (Sloan-C, 2004). College and university students in the USA increasingly view online components of their courses as commonplace as textbooks and other traditional resources.

The computers and networked technologies that enable online education do not simply represent a change of the medium for implementing traditional teaching and learning activities. Instead, these technologies, integrated with innovative pedagogical methods such as inquiry-based learning (Olson & Loucks-Horsley, 2000) and authentic tasks (Herrington, Reeves, Oliver, & Woo, 2004), provide instructors and their students with unprecedented opportunities to teach and learn in more powerful ways.

Online education has opened the way for educators to reach learners "beyond brick and mortar" campuses (McIsaac, 2002), including many people who would otherwise not have access to higher education. Potential participants in online higher education are not just from the USA; they can be from many other countries, via the Internet. Of course, the USA is by no means the only online education provider, as Australia, Canada, the United Kingdom, and other countries compete with the United States to be the provider of choice for English-language online courses and programs. One trend is clear: With the growth of globalization, the students enrolling in e-learning programs have become increasingly diverse with respect to culture.

A foundational principle underlying online education as an alternative instructional delivery system is that it can be designed in a manner such that the educational opportunities provided are responsive to the needs of different types of students, including special accommodations for the world in which diverse students work and live (Palloff & Pratt, 1999). For example, online education can be designed in such a way that learners can work at their own pace; those who need more time to complete a course or unit of instruction than a regular academic term (e.g., semester or quarter), perhaps because of work or family commitments, may take more time without penalty in some online education models. Alternatively, online education models may be tailored so that those learners who might wish to and are able to accelerate their learning may accomplish the goals of a particular course of study in a faster time than traditionally expected.

Given the increasingly heterogeneous nature of groups of learners in online education, we must give much more consideration to how we can accommodate learners from different cultural backgrounds. Although few would disagree that cultural factors are important in theory, there is surprisingly little published literature concerning the cultural aspects of online learning and teaching, and there are even fewer research-based studies (Gunawardena, Wilson, & Nolla, 2003). The lack of research related to culture in online education can be partly explained by difficulties related to both identifying appropriate methodologies and finding adequate resources for this kind of research, but may also be explained by the lack of agreement about the concept of culture (Straub, Loch, Ev Aristo, Karahanna, & Srite, 2002). With the ultimate goal of providing practical guidelines for teachers, learners, and designers to build culturally-sensitive online learning environments, this chapter first explores the meaning of culture. How should culture be defined? What are the dimensions of culture? After clarifying the nature of culture, this chapter then describes some of the cultural issues that must be faced in online teaching and learning. Finally, this chapter provides a set of practical principles for teachers, learners, and designers regarding the cultural aspects of online education, and suggests some directions for future research.

What is Culture?

It is impossible to provide an answer to the question, *"What is culture?"* that would satisfy everyone. Taking a dialectical perspective in his book, Nuckolls (1998) actually argued that defining culture is a problem that cannot be solved because the values underlying any specific definition consist of motivations that are closely bound up with the dynamics of cultural ambivalence. Nonetheless, anthropologists, as scientists conducting scientific and humanistic studies of man's present and past biological, linguistic, social, and cultural variations, have made the most extensive attempts at the thorny task of providing an answer regarding what culture is. The first official definition of culture found in the literature was from British anthropologist Sir Edward Tylor (Kroeber & Kluckhohn, 1952). In his book, *Primitive Culture*, Tylor defined culture as "that complex whole which includes knowledge, belief, art, morals, law, custom, and any other capabilities and habits acquired by man as a member of society" (Tylor, 1871, p. 1).

Since Tylor's seminal work, many definitions of culture have found their way into the scholarly literature. In the early work done by Kroeber and Kluckhohn (1952), they identified 164 different definitions of culture across various disciplines. Although giving a specific definition of culture may be helpful while communicating with a particular group, given the huge number of definitions of culture, it is difficult, if not impossible, to pick one appropriate definition, because different scholars define culture based on their own research interests and experiences. Fortunately, among the many definitions found by Kroeber and Kluckhohn, a broad consensus on two points has emerged, as described by Danesi and Perron (1999): "(1) culture is a way of life based on some system of shared meanings; and (2) culture is passed on from generation to generation through this very system" (p. 22).

Instead of synthesizing the myriad definitions of culture and perhaps adding yet another definition to the debate, this chapter prefers to focus more on how culture is viewed in society and the everyday practices of members of a society or community. Bodley (2000) suggested looking at culture in three aspects: What people think? What people do? And what people produce? He categorized these aspects as mental, behavioral, and material. Using Bodley's constructs, researchers studying culture may focus on the underlying mental rules people follow, their daily life behaviors in a society, or the products people

Table 1. Key aspects, features, and functions of culture (Adapted from Bodley, 2000)

Aspects	Features	Functions
Mental	Patterned	Regulation
Behavioral	Symbolic	Maintenance
Material	Shared	Survival and reproduction
	Socially transmitted	Fitness-enhancement
	Ethnocentric	Communication (Hall & Hall,
	Conservative	1990)
	Normative	Problem solving (Straub et al.,
	Dynamic	2002)
	Historical	

produce. For example, Danesi and Perron (1999) attempted to demonstrate the meanings of culture through a semiotic analysis that involved observing people in different social contexts and analyzing various aspects of culture such as language, metaphor, and art. Their research helped the conceptualization of culture evolve from a vague concept to a more concrete one based upon the critical analysis of visible products such as television and advertising. Their work emphasizes the close relationship between culture and our daily life.

Bodley (2000) also points out the value of analyzing culture with respect to its features and functions. He regards culture as socially transmitted and as learned, and recognizes that it has important features such as shared values and symbol systems. At the same time, culture encompasses important functions such as maintaining the stability of society and educating people to follow social rules. Table 1 presents some key ideas of culture derived from the work of Bodley and others.

Cultural Dimensions

In an attempt to understand culture more deeply, other researchers have tried to deconstruct the meaning of culture, and present culture in terms of multiple dimensions. Among these cultural schemas, Geert Hofstede's (1979, 1980, 1982, 1984) five national culture dimensions is the most frequently-mentioned framework in the literature.

The comparative study done by Hofstede for an international company is mentioned frequently in journals and books. A Google Scholar (http://scholar.google.com) search for Hofstede's book, *Culture's Consequences: International Differences in Work-Related Values*, published in 1980, indicates that more than 2,000 articles and books cite his book. These citations are found in publications from many fields such as management, international marketing, social psychology, communication, and education. Hofstede (1984) proposed four national culture dimensions at the early stage of this study based on a large-scale empirical study involving thousands of participants from more than 40 nations; he added the fifth dimension later, based upon the findings of a Chinese Value

Survey (CVS) conducted around 1985. The five national culture dimensions are defined as:

- **Power Distance (PDI):** "The extent to which the less powerful members of institutions and organizations accept that power is distributed unequally" (Hofstede, 1984, p. 419).

- **Uncertainty Avoidance (UAI):** "The extent to which people feel threatened by ambiguous situations, and have created beliefs and institutions that try to avoid these" (Hofstede, 1984, p. 419).

- **Individualism vs. Collectivism (IDV):** "It reflects the position of the culture on a bipolar continuum. The one pole, Individualism, is defined as a situation in which people are supposed to look after themselves and their immediate family only" (Hofstede, 1984, p. 419). In contrast, Collectivism is defined as "a situation in which people belong to in-groups or collectivities which are supposed to look after them in exchanges for loyalty" (Hofstede, 1984, p. 419).

- **Masculinity vs. Femininity (MAS):** Masculinity is defined as "a situation in which the dominant values in society are success, money, and things" (Hofstede, 1984, pp. 419-420). In contrast, Femininity is defined as "a situation in which the dominant values in society are caring for others and the quality of life" (Hofstede, 1984, p. 420).

- **Long-term vs. Short-term orientation (LTO):** The fifth dimension identified by Hofstede deals with Virtue rather than Truth. Interestingly, this dimension was found through the questionnaire designed by Chinese scholars, and was not found in the questionnaire designed by Western scholars. This orientation "is related to the choice of focus for people's effort: the future or the present" (Hofstede, 2001, p. 29). For example, values associated with Long-term orientation are persistence and thrifty; values associated with Short-term orientation are protection of one's "face" and respect of traditions.

According to an early analysis of Hofstede's work done by Søndergaard (1994), Hofstede's work in the literature have been applied by other scholars and practitioners in different ways, including nominal quotations, reviews and criticisms, empirical usages of the five-dimensional framework for research, and citations that take his work for granted. The primary reason that Hofstede's work has become an influential classic work is because his work was supported by hundreds of both qualitative and quantitative studies in different disciplines, and by large replications (Søndergaard, 2002). However, Hofstede's work is also criticized by many researchers. For example, McSweeney (2002) argues that Hofstede's work was based on some false assumptions underlying the measurement, and thus his national cultural descriptions are invalid and misleading. These false assumptions include the assumption that an analysis of sub-national populations can represent the whole national culture, and further that the average of individual opinions drawn from specific situations can reveal the general nature of national cultures. In addition, Baskerville (2003) argues that nations are not the best units for studying culture, because any one nation often includes multiple cultures. Fang

(2003) also argues that Hofstede's fifth dimension is philosophically flawed in interpreting Chinese culture, and thus the usefulness of this "new dimension" is dubious.

These criticisms, as points out by Søndergaard (2002), can be summarized into five points: (1) inappropriate instruments to measure culture; (2) nations is not the best unit for studying culture; (3) participants from one company cannot represent entire national cultures; (4) the data is old and obsolete; (5) four or five dimensions cannot tell the whole story. These criticisms are fundamental and must be answered, and not surprisingly, Hofstede has responded. For example, Hofstede's (2003) reply to Baskerville's (2003) criticism was "true, but they (nations) are usually the only kind of units available for comparison and better than nothing" (p. 812).

Instead of continuing the debate about Hofstede's work, the purpose in this chapter is to suggest that this model provides one example of a way of looking at culture through various dimensions. This chapter wishes to help readers develop a conceptual framework related to their own experiences. There are, of course, other ways of looking at culture in terms of multiple dimensions. For example, Edward Hall (1981, 1990) made distinctions between high- and low- context cultures with regards to the different demands for contextual information among cultures. Hampden-Turner and Trompenaars (2000) identified six linear binary oppositional dimensions of culture. Educators, researchers, and practitioners have a responsibility to be aware of these different ways of looking at culture and to build their own conceptual framework to both apply and evaluate these cultural dimensions in their own situation.

Thus far, this chapter has discussed culture from two different approaches. One way is to look at the similarities among cultures by exploring the universal definitions of culture as well as the commonalities among different cultures. The other way is to look at the dissimilarities among cultures by investigating the cultural dimensions that various scholars have devised to analyze cultural differences. Neither approach is inherently good or bad, but as Rose (2005) argues while discussing cultural studies in instructional design, more work is needed to make sense of these various cultural perspectives in practice. How do these perspectives inform our understandings about culture with respect to our interest in online education? What have researchers in the field of online education done to apply the cultural perspectives in practice? Next, this chapter outlines the development of studies related to cultural issues in online education.

Cultural Issues in Online Education

Research in online education is generally impoverished with respect to theory, and the limited theoretical underpinnings used in online education research largely ignore culture as a significant factor. Few online education researchers have incorporated cultural dimensions into their investigations, and there is an even greater lack of research investigating the connections between cultural dimensions and the design of more effective online education. In this section of this chapter, cultural issues in online education related to pedagogical concerns and instructional design are presented, and the limited research which has been done in this area is reviewed.

What are Cultural Issues in Online Education?

To begin, it is important to clarify what is meant by cultural issues in online education. Joo (1999) pointed out some cultural issues that arise when using the Internet in classrooms:

- **Content of materials:** Some content in certain subjects such as history, religion, or politics might be very sensitive in different social contexts.

- **Power of multimedia:** Although multimedia can increase students' motivation, instructors must be careful that the multimedia does not reinforce cultural stereotypes.

- **Writing styles:** In some languages, words and grammar are used to convey different level of politeness. In online learning environment, the usage of informal language may cause uncomfortable feelings for non-native English speakers.

- **Writing structures:** The ways in which ideas are presented and constructed should be examined. Some translated texts can appear obscure to non-native English speakers.

- **Web design:** Different cultures can also reflect different orientation in Web design. For example, Arab-language speakers usually read from right to left.

We can notice that the observations in Joo's (1999) work were mainly focused on language differences among different cultures, along with some reminders of the awareness of cultural sensitivity in instructional materials and the multimedia which is being used. However, there is no clear attempt to link these observations to cultural perspectives as we discussed previously. The conclusions remain in the primitive stage. In contrast to Joo's (1999) article, Bentley, Tinney, and Chia (2005) look at this issue in a more holistic way in which they incorporate not only language and technology, but also learning styles and cultural dimensions with considerations of local and global levels. Based on their literature review and cross-cultural educational experience, they provide eight educational value differentials for understanding cultural issues in Internet-based learning (Bentley et al., 2005):

- **Language differential:** Language and culture are interrelated. It is hard to understand one without knowing the other. In preparing an online learning environment for learners with different cultural backgrounds, simple sentences should be used and slang should be avoided.

- **Educational culture differential:** Different cultures place different values on education. Teachers and course designers should be sensitive to these differences while offering courses for worldwide adult learners.

- **Technical infrastructure differential:** Not every global learner has the same technical infrastructure such as broadband. It is inappropriate to believe that learners from other places will be able to access complex simulations and streaming video as quickly as many Americans can.

- **Local versus global differential:** Some cultures emphasize the local context, whereas others encourage a global perspective. Instructors and designers must strive to understand their target audience's perspective.

- **Learning style differential:** Students learn how to learn based on their cultural background. For example, certain American training programs that emphasize competition do not fit the learning style of other cultures.

- **Reasoning pattern differential:** People from different cultures can have different thinking patterns with respect to problem solving, and also have different views of objectivity.

- **High- and low-context differential:** High- and low-context cultures have different demands for concrete versus abstract information, and this might cause problems when they meet online.

- **Social context differential:** Learners respond to new information based on the social context they encounter. The interaction between social context and learners' high- or low-context cultural background, albeit complex, should be considered.

Later in this chapter, the ideas from Bentley et al. (2005) are integrated with the recommendations provided by other researchers, to make a list of principles for teachers, students, and designers for constructing and implementing culturally-sensitive online education.

Pedagogical Concerns in Online Education

The pedagogical choices made by instructors and designers in online education are one of the most important concerns for researchers and practitioners alike. Many researchers have argued that the most important shift from traditional classrooms to online learning environments should involve the change of pedagogies (Hase & Ellis, 2001). Clearly, teachers' beliefs and attitudes about teaching and learning play an important role in implementing new technologies in the classroom (Warschauer, 1998). Pedagogical dimensions such as the nature of the tasks (academic or authentic) and the role of the teacher (didactic or facilitative) inevitably influence the learning experience in the online environment (Reeves & Reeves, 1997). In an ongoing longitudinal study, Pan, Tsai, Tsai, Tao, and Cornell (2003) have tried to reveal the elements embedded in Confucian pedagogy and Western pedagogy, and determine whether there is symbiosis or asymbiosis for these different pedagogies. From their draft report, some preliminary results can be applied to the design of online learning environments. For example, one principle they espouse is to "encourage Asian students to not work together in the same project groups, thus provide the Asian students with direct opportunities and challenges in using English" (p. 324). In addition to addressing pedagogical concerns in online education, another important factor that needs to be considered is the instructional design embedded in online education.

Cultural Considerations in Instructional Design

For starters, Henderson (1996) reminded us that instructional design is a product of culture, and thus it needs to take culture into consideration. As she described:

Approaches to instructional design not only reflect differing world views, but they consist of values, ideologies, and images that involve inclusions and exclusions that act in the interests of particular cultural, class, and gendered groups. Instructional design and the designer are inextricably tied to their societal context and thus infused with the cultural, class, and gendered influences resulting from the subtle and intricate interplay of these factors. (p. 87)

In addition, McLoughlin (1999) proclaimed, somewhat idealistically, that the need to ensure the coverage of every culture is important in the beginning of adopting an instructional design model. A sound instructional design needs to consider not only the designers' cultural background, but also that of the learners. However, challenges arise under this ideal situation when the core pedagogical values in one culture are culturally inappropriate in another (Reeves & Reeves, 1997). This dilemma can often cause uncomfortable feelings among learners, and sometimes it will result in serious misunderstandings. For example, the color of text in an online learning environment is critical to Chinese students (Tu, 2001). Chinese interpret red text as a warning, but the instructor or instructional designer from another culture may use red just to emphasize certain content. While some scholars have merely discussed the importance of cultural factors in instructional design, others have sought to embed cultural considerations into the instructional design models that already exist. For example, Branch (1997) proposed ways that cultural pluralism can be accommodated in many current instructional design models. However, although incorporating cultural contexts into old instructional models may be a good way to start, the online learning environment is so new and unique in education that many old assumptions about instructional design should be carefully examined in the new environment. After this examination, some assumptions may be abandoned, and others may be modified. More design-based research studies are needed to build the foundation for a robust framework to guide further development in this area (Bannan-Ritland, 2003).

Research in This Area

An extensive survey of the literature by Macfadyen, Roche, Roche, Doff, Reeder, and Chase (2004) revealed four different research orientations regarding culture and education in cyberspace. Generally, these research orientations focus on studies related to: (1) the interactions in an online course which involved culturally-diverse adult learners; (2) the access to the Internet among different groups; (3) the assessment criteria applied in online education; and (4) the design of virtual learning environments to accommodate the needs of culturally-diverse learners. As noted above, there is surprisingly little published literature on the cultural aspects of online learning and teaching, and there are even fewer research-based studies (Gunawardena et al., 2003). Thus, it is a hopeful sign that several recent international conferences, for example, the *Cultural Attitudes towards Technology and Communication Conference* (http://www.it.murdoch.edu.au/catac/) have been dedicated to investigating this issue. Ideally, more and more researchers will get involved in this area in the future.

Indeed, designers of online education, as well as the instructors who implement online education, should strive to be models of cultural sensitivity, but the level of challenge in this endeavor, especially as online learning communities become truly global, should not be underestimated. In the next section, this chapter presents guidelines for building culturally- sensitive online learning environments, as well as principles for constructing and implementing culturally-sensitive online education.

Building Culturally-Sensitive Online Learning Environments

Cultural sensitivity issues are important in instruction, regardless of whether one is teaching in a classroom, online, or through some sort of blended approach. Protheroe and Turner (2003) pointed out that the overall aim of culturally-sensitive instruction is to "facilitate the ability of all students to meet high standards, using approaches best suited to meeting students' individual needs" (p. 2). Protheroe and Turner (2003) further addressed other key characteristics that a culturally-sensitive instruction should have. For example, "there is no single best teaching method that will effectively reach all students at all times" (Protheroe & Turner, 2003, p. 3). As a result, the teacher needs to adjust his/her instruction in response to the students' needs. Of course, the purpose of culturally-sensitive instruction is not to duplicate the learning environment from the learners' home culture. Rather, the purpose is to build mutual accommodation and respect for the culture of others in order to reach academic success (Protheroe & Turner, 2003).

While thinking of culturally-sensitive online education from a global perspective, it is important to realize that cultural issues must be considered in virtually any type of online education. To better comprehend the nature of cultural differences within a specific online context, here are some questions that should be addressed:

- From where are the online courses originating?
- Who has designed these courses?
- Who are the students that are taking them?
- Who are the teachers that are teaching them?
- What is the nature of the content and to what degree is the content subject to different cultural interpretations?

- What is the nature of the pedagogy used in the design of the courses, and to what degree does the pedagogical design accommodate cultural differences?

As more and more higher education institutions in the USA begin offering online courses and seeking larger global audiences (Sloan-C, 2004), the complexity of accommodating cultural differences will increase. Consider an online English course designed for and provided to Chinese students in China. Cultural issues may arise not only from translation problems, but from the pedagogical assumptions as well. How can differences in contextual expectations be handled appropriately? Should the cultural values inevitably embedded in the contexts be minimized or simply acknowledged? How can the course be designed and implemented in a way that Chinese students feel comfortable participating in an active manner, when their enculturation may have prepared them to be more passive in instructional contexts?

Consider a different situation, one in which an online course is offered by an American university to students from multiple cultures located all over the world who differ widely in their English language abilities. Class communication in this multiple cultures situation will be difficult, but it could also enable a special learning opportunity. Several strategies that could be used in this situation have been identified by researchers. For example, in a cross-cultures synchronous online learning environment, a common language like English can be used for joint activities, but preparation and follow-up activities can be organized locally in their native language (Van den Branden & Lambert, 1999).

Based on a literature review, the following lists of suggested principles are compiled for constructing and implementing culturally-sensitive online education. These principles are mainly derived from several resources: (1) the work done by McLoughlin and Oliver (2000) in which they designed an online learning environment for indigenous learners in Australia; (2) the work done by Collis (1999) to discuss the cultural issues in the development of Web sites for course support; (3) the recommendations made by Bentley et al. (2005); as well as other empirical studies done by various researchers. These principles are categorized into separate lists for teachers, students, and designers.

Principles for Teachers

- Adopt an epistemology that is supportive of multiple perspectives, so that students from different cultural background will feel comfortable enough to share their opinions (McLoughlin & Oliver, 2000).

- Create flexibility in learning goals, tasks, and modes of assessment so that learners from different cultural backgrounds can choose those best suited to their educational needs (Collis, 1999; McLoughlin & Oliver, 2000).

- Design authentic learning activities and tasks aligned with the learners' existing skills and the values of their own community in order to motivate them to develop practical skills needed in their contemporary society (McLoughlin & Oliver, 2000).

- Ensure different forms of support within and outside the community, such as creating an online discussion forum for learners to communicate ideas and share experiences (Bentley et al., 2005; McLoughlin & Oliver, 2000).

- Create online journals to manage self-directed learning so that learners can have a better sense of their own learning status (Collis, 1999; Ku & Lohr, 2003; McLoughlin & Oliver, 2000).

- Attempt to increase students' self-confidence and motivation early in the course by providing necessary scaffolding (Ku & Lohr, 2003).

- Design activities that enable small groups to give feedback to the members of those groups (Ku & Lohr, 2003).

- Discuss embedded values explicitly and honestly in class (Bentley et al., 2005; Chen, Mashhadi, Ang, & Harkrider, 1999).

- Encourage students to keep writing in an online class and to lower their internal editor when composing their messages (Schallert, Reed, & D-Team, 2003).

- Provide clear guidelines for online communication to avoid unnecessary confusion (Tu, 2001).

- Clarify the level of English skills required in the courses, and use simple sentence structures (Bentley et al., 2005).

- Avoid slang, colloquialisms, and local humor when possible (Bentley et al., 2005).

Principles for Students

- See taking online course as an adventure, and strive to adapt to the new environment (Bentley et al., 2005).

- Have an open mind to try new things (Bentley et al., 2005).

- Join study groups and social groups (Bentley et al., 2005).

- Seek English as a Second Language (ESL) help (Bentley et al., 2005).

- Talk to the instructor about your concerns (Bentley et al., 2005; Schallert et al., 2003).

Principles for Designers

- Provide communication tools for social interaction, such as bulletin boards (McLoughlin & Oliver, 2000).

- Provide a wide variety of combinations of supplementary media and resources for learners and instructors to expand their knowledge, such as links to resources on the Internet (Collis, 1999).

- Minimize technical demands because some students might not be familiar with using computers and related technologies (Collis, 1999).

- Allow different communication configurations such as allowing students to send private messages to someone, or to the whole class anonymously (Collis, 1999).
- Be realistic about what instructors can and will do. Do not create useless functions or additional work for teachers (Collis, 1999).
- Make the course materials available for students to preview and review (Bentley et al., 2005).

The principles listed above are only general guidelines for teachers, students, and designers for building culturally-sensitive online learning environments. They are intended to be helpful, but they are insufficient. Other suggestions are to conduct a needs assessment about your audience as thoroughly as possible to guide the design process and maintain flexibility throughout the whole process of implementation. In any case, it must be acknowledged that much more research is needed to provide a stronger basis for prescribing design principles for students, teachers, and designers involved in online education.

Future Studies

It would be desirable to illustrate the relationship between cultural dimensions and design principles. Unfortunately, this relationship across the sets of principles compiled above is not very obvious. Interestingly, some of the empirical studies which this chapter used to compile the principles actually mentioned either Geert Hofstede's or Edward Hall's concept of culture in their literature reviews. Then, why do the results look so piecemeal? One problem is that these studies lack a "thick description" (Geertz, 1973) of these cultural accounts. Without profound narratives to make the cultural context of online education represented in these studies more concrete to both the researchers and practitioners, the applications of the studies in other situations are inevitably limited. In addition to a weak connection between theory (cultural dimensions) and practice (design principles), another problem is that we lack a robust theoretical framework for investigating cultural considerations in online education. Regarding this cultural complexity, Gunawardena and McIsaac (2001) wrote that "the challenge is to develop theory to explain how new construction of knowledge occurs through the process of social negotiation in such a knowledge-building community" (p. 364). As noted previously in the chapter, there is still a lack of research investigating the connections between these cultural dimensions and online education. The challenge for researchers in this area is to incorporate these already-identified cultural dimensions into an integrated theoretical framework. Lacking a sound theoretical framework, it is difficult to establish a robust agenda for future research. The cultural-dimensions frameworks described above provide a starting point, but new approaches to dealing with cultural issues in online education are needed. Gunawardena et al. (2003) stated that "future researchers need to conceptualize identity issues in cross-cultural studies to go beyond simplistic stereotyping and use qualitative methods to understand how people define themselves" (p. 771).

In the future, we need more cross-national research to understand and compare the effects of online learning across different cultures. Future studies are also needed to determine how the perceptions of online learning environments differ for international students located in the host country from the perceptions of students residing in their native country (Tu, 2001). Additionally, online learning usually requires a shift of pedagogies. Thus, research is needed to focus on how different pedagogies are perceived in different cultures. The aim of such research should be to find the similarities and differences among different pedagogies in light of various cultural backgrounds, and seek ways to incorporate different pedagogies into online education without creating cultural problems.

Perhaps educational researchers should adopt perspectives from other fields such as sociology to establish more robust foundations for their research. In any case, cultural differences in the increasingly global learning environment are a fact (Van den Branden & Lambert, 1999), and it is necessary to delve much more deeply into the experiences of learners from different cultural backgrounds to see what is going on when they are learning online. Lauzon (1999) argues that one of the main challenges as we enter the new millennium will be "learning to live with difference" (p. 274). However, both history and the current state of world affairs indicate that living with difference is easier said than done. If it is ever to be accomplished, education must take the lead. Within the broader field of education, online education may well have the greatest potential for enabling people to develop tolerance and learn to live with difference. But this potential will only be realized if we as researchers and developers take the kinds of issues raised in this chapter much more seriously.

References

Bannan-Ritland, B. (2003). The role of design in research: The integrative learning design framework. *Educational Researcher*, *32*(1), 21-24.

Baskerville, R. (2003). Hofstede never studied culture. *Accounting, Organizations and Society, 28*(1), 1-14.

Bentley, J. P. H., Tinney, M. V., & Chia, B. H. (2005). Intercultural Internet-based learning: Know your audience and what it values. *Educational Technology Research & Development, 53*(2), 117-127.

Bodley, J. H. (2000). *Cultural anthropology: Tribes, states, and the global system* (3rd ed.). Mountain View, CA: Mayfield Publishing.

Branch, R. M. (1997). Educational technology frameworks that facilitate culturally pluralistic instruction. *Educational Technology, 37*(2), 38-41.

Chen, A.-Y., Mashhadi, A., Ang, D., & Harkrider, N. (1999). Cultural issues in the design of technology-enhanced learning systems. *British Journal of Educational Technology, 30*(3), 217-230.

Collis, B. (1999). Designing for differences: Cultural issues in the design of WWW-based course-support sites. *British Journal of Educational Technology, 30*(3), 201-215.

Danesi, M., & Perron, P. (1999). *Analyzing cultures: An introduction and handbook.* Bloomington, IN: Indiana University Press.

Fang, T. (2003). A critique of Hofstede's fifth national culture dimension. *International Journal of Cross Cultural Management, 3*(3), 347-368.

Geertz, C. (1973). Thick description: Toward an interpretive theory of culture. In *The interpretation of cultures: Selected essays* (pp. 3-30). New York: Basic Books.

Gunawardena, C. N., & McIsaac, M. S. (2001). Distance education. In D. H. Jonassen (Ed.), *Handbook of research for educational communications and technology: A project of the Association for Educational Communications and Technology* (pp. 355-395). Mahwah, NJ: L. Erlbaum Associates.

Gunawardena, C. N., Wilson, P. L., & Nolla, A. C. (2003). Culture and online education. In M. G. Moore & W. G. Anderson (Eds.), *Handbook of distance education* (pp. 753-775). Mahwah, NJ: L. Erlbaum Associates.

Hall, E. T. (1981). *Beyond culture.* Garden City, NY: Anchor Books.

Hall, E. T., & Hall, M. R. (1990). *Understanding cultural differences.* Yarmouth, ME: Intercultural Press.

Hampden-Turner, C., & Trompenaars, A. (2000). *Building cross-cultural competence: How to create wealth from conflicting values.* New Haven, CT: Yale University Press.

Harasim, L. (2000). Shift happens: Online education as a new paradigm in learning. *Internet and Higher Education, 3,* 41-61.

Hase, S., & Ellis, A. (2001). Problems with online learning are systemic, not technical. In J. Stephenson (Ed.), *Teaching & learning online: Pedagogies for new technologies* (pp. 27-34). Sterling, VA: Stylus Publishing.

Henderson, L. (1996). Instructional design of interactive multimedia: A cultural critique. *Educational Technology Research and Development, 44*(4), 85-104.

Herrington, J., Reeves, T. C., Oliver, R., & Woo, Y. (2004). Designing authentic activities in Web-based courses. *Journal of Computing in Higher Education, 16*(1), 3-29.

Hofstede, G. (1979). Value systems in forty countries: Interpretation, validation, and consequences for theory. In L. H. Eckensberger, W. J. Lonner, & Y. Poortinga (Eds.), *Cross-cultural contributions to psychology* (pp. 389-407). Lisse, The Netherlands: Swets & Zeitlinger.

Hofstede, G. (1980). *Culture's consequences: International differences in work-related values.* Beverly Hills, CA: Sage Publications.

Hofstede, G. (1982). Dimensions of national cultures. In R. Rath, H. S. Asthana, D. Sinha, & J. B. H. Sinha (Eds.), *Diversity and unity in cross-cultural psychology* (pp. 173-187). Lisse: Swets and Zeitlinger.

Hofstede, G. (1984). Hofstede culture dimensions — An independent validation using Rokeach value survey. *Journal of Cross-Cultural Psychology, 15*(4), 417-433.

Hofstede, G. (2001). *Culture's consequences: Comparing values, behaviors, institutions, and organizations across nations* (2nd ed.). Thousand Oaks, CA: Sage Publications.

Hofstede, G. (2003). What is culture? A reply to Baskerville. *Accounting Organizations and Society, 28*(7-8), 811-813.

Joo, J. -E. (1999). Cultural issues of the Internet in classrooms. *British Journal of Educational Technology, 30*(3), 245-250.

Kroeber, A. L., & Kluckhohn, C. (1952). *Culture: A critical review of concepts and definitions*. Cambridge, MA: Peabody Museum.

Ku, H.-Y., & Lohr, L. L. (2003). A case study of Chinese students' attitudes toward their first online learning experience. *Educational Technology Research & Development, 51*(3), 95-102.

Lauzon, A. C. (1999). Situating cognition and crossing borders: Resisting the hegemony of mediated education. *British Journal of Educational Technology, 30*(3), 261-276.

Macfadyen, L. P., Roche, J., Doff, S., Reeder, K., & Chase, M. (2004). *Communicating across cultures in cyberspace: A bibliographical review of intercultural communication online*. Piscataway, NJ: Transaction Publishers Distributor.

McIsaac, M. S. (2002). Online learning from an international perspective. *Educational Media International, 39*(1), 17-21.

McLoughlin, C. (1999). Culturally responsive technology use: Developing an on-line community of learners. *British Journal of Educational Technology, 30*(3), 231-243.

McLoughlin, C., & Oliver, R. (2000). Designing learning environments for cultural inclusivity: A case study of indigenous online learning at tertiary level. *Australian Journal of Educational Technology, 16*(1), 58-72.

McSweeney, B. (2002). Hofstede's model of national cultural differences and their consequences: A triumph of faith—A failure of analysis. *Human Relations, 55*(1), 89-118.

Nuckolls, C. W. (1998). *Culture: A problem that cannot be solved*. Madison: University of Wisconsin Press.

Olson, S., & Loucks-Horsley, S. (Eds.). (2000). *Inquiry and the national science education standards: A guide to teaching and learning*. Washington, DC: National Academy Press.

Palloff, R. M., & Pratt, K. (1999). *Building learning communities in cyberspace: Effective strategies for the online classroom*. San Francisco: Jossey-Bass.

Pan, C. -C., Tsai, M. -H., Tsai, P. -Y., Tao, Y., & Cornell, R. (2003). Technology's impact: Symbiotic or asymbiotic impact on differing cultures? *Educational Media International, 40*(3/4), 319-330.

Protheroe, N., & Turner, J. (2003). *Culturally sensitive instruction*. Arlington, VA: Educational Research Service.

Reeves, T., & Reeves, P. (1997). Effective dimensions of interactive learning on the World Wide Web. In B. H. Khan (Ed.), *Web-based instruction* (pp. 59-66). Englewood Cliffs, NJ: Educational Technology Publications.

Rose, E. (2005, March-April). Cultural studies in instructional design: Building a bridge to practice. *Educational Technology, 45,* 5-10.

Schallert, D. L., Reed, J. H., & D-Team, T. (2003). Intellectual, motivational, textual, and cultural considerations in teaching and learning with computer-mediated discussion. *Journal of Research on Technology in Education, 36*(2), 103-118.

Sloan-C. (2004). *Entering the mainstream: The quality and extent of online education in the United States, 2003 and 2004.* Retrieved May 23, 2005, from http://www.sloan-c.org/resources/entering_mainstream.pdf

Søndergaard, M. (1994). Research note: Hofstede's consequences: A study of reviews, citations and replications. *Organization Studies, 15*(3), 447-456.

Søndergaard, M. (2002). 'In my opinion'—Mikael Sondergaard on 'cultural differences'. *European Business Forum.* Retrieved September 6, 2005, from http://www.ebfonline.com/main_feat/in_depth/in_depth.asp?id=288

Straub, D., Loch, K., Ev Aristo, R., Karahanna, E., & Srite, M. (2002). Toward a theory-based measurement of culture. *Journal of Global Information Management, 10*(1), 13-23.

Tu, C. -H. (2001). How Chinese perceive social presence: An examination of interaction in online learning environment. *Education Media International, 38*(1), 45-60.

Tylor, E. B. (1871). *Primitive culture.* London: John Murray.

Van den Branden, J., & Lambert, J. (1999). Cultural issues related to transnational open and distance learning in universities: A European problem? *British Journal of Educational Technology, 30*(3), 251-260.

Warschauer, M. (1998). Online learning in sociocultural context. *Anthropology and Education Quarterly, 29*(1), 68-88.

Chapter II

Challenges to Implementing E-Learning in Lesser-Developed Countries

Bolanle Olaniran
Texas Tech University, USA

Abstract

The integration of communication technologies and the Internet has created an explosion in the use of e-learning both locally and globally. The beneficiaries of this new media integration are organizations at large, in both developed and lesser-developed countries. For instance, globalized organizations have been able to develop training programs that serve their needs. However, global e-learning raises some implications, which include communication, culture, and technology, that must be addressed before successful implementation and outcome can occur.

Challenges to Implementing E-Learning and Lesser-Developed Countries

As communication technologies and the Internet continue to merge, organizations continue to integrate them within their activities and corporate practices. One of the key benefits of such integration includes learning and curriculum development, which is otherwise referred to as e-learning, and more appropriately referred to as global e-learning. Because of the trend toward globalization of research and development (R&D), there exists the need for uniform and customized training. On a more comprehensive scale is the need for employees' continued training, which circumvents traditional college training and requires participants to be in a specific location in order to access and participate in learning. It is not surprising that online universities (e.g., AIU Online, Capella University, Devry University, Kaplan University, University of Phoenix, Walden University, and Westwood College Online) are thriving and attractive to corporate travelers and expatriates. Notwithstanding, as corporate e-learning solutions continue to explode and gain popularity in the sphere of global e-learning, challenges exist from cultural standardization rather than differentiation. Standardization creates problems for learners who are culturally different from the culture that developed the learning content.

The major advantage of e-learning remains cost savings. However, for e-learning to produce desired results, there should be some kind of accounting for effectiveness of the learning program. Effectiveness of e-learning cannot be assessed outside of its cultural underpinnings. To this end, the current chapter examines cultural implications of global e-learning and education. It explores significant challenges created by learning preferences and adoption of innovation using the Hofstede's REF (1983) dimensions of cultural variability. Finally, the chapter provides recommendations for implementing successful global e-learning programs.

As the Internet goes global, so does e-learning (Van Dam & Rogers, 2002). However, the e-learning programs mostly emphasize organizational goals in terms of how and what organizational leadership intends to accomplish in their respective region and employees. In essence, users of e-learning often ignore cultural implications and insights that employees or customers have in controlling how they learn and the learning process as a whole. Specifically, consumers of e-learning (e.g., purchasers, instructors, students, and end-users) are expected to work with curriculum designed in and for another culture.

Internet Usage and E-Learning

There is a correlation between Internet usage and global learning penetration and adoption in any given society. In Asia, Internet usage was expected to increase from 64 million in 2001 to 173 million by 2004, but the most recent data on internet usage in Asia show an actual figure that reflects a jump to 323.76 million—a 405% increase from the 2001 figure, and a 87 % increase above projected figure (Internetworldstats, n.d.). A 65.8% increase is reported for Japanese Internet use while a 357.8% jump was recorded for Chinese between 2000 and 2005, which represents a jump from 22.5 million to 103 million users (Internetworldstats, n.d.). In spite of the tremendous increase in the number of users, the overwhelming predominance of English is considered a major deterrent that limits Internet usefulness for most countries and regions (Barron, 2000). For instance, when the number of Internet users is compared with actual population figure, it reveals that there are still a lot of potential users to reach. The Internet world statistics, for example, puts the total Internet usage for China at 7.9% of the country's population figure.

Culture and E-Learning

In order to realize the aim of e-learning as an educational tool, it is essential to accommodate the learning needs of different cultures in order to promote equitable learning outcomes for targeted students, and to promote education and technological literacy that improve socio-economic opportunities in developing nations (Dede, 2000; Henning, 2003; Selinger, 2004). Attention to geographic cultures and implications for diffusion of technological innovation is warranted. But first it is important to look at the dimensions of cultural differences. One useful model in exploring cultural differences includes Hofstede's dimensions of cultural variability (Hofstede, 1980). The four dimensions of cultural variability are power distance, uncertainty avoidance, individualism, and masculinity (Hofstede, 1980, 1983, 2001; see also Dunn & Marinetti, 2002, overview of cultural value orientations and cultural dimensions). These four categories result from data collected from 50 countries and three world regions (Hofstede, 1980, 1983). Past research uses these four dimensions to operationalize cultural differences and their effects on uncertainty reduction in intercultural communication encounters (Gudykunst, Chua, & Gray, 1987; Olaniran, 1996; Olaniran & Roach, 1996; Roach & Olaniran, 2001, 2004; see also www.worldvaluessurveys.org). A brief description of the four dimensions includes the following.

Power distance is "the extent to which the less powerful members of institutions and organizations accept that power is distributed unequally" (Hofstede & Bond, 1984, p. 418). Uncertainty avoidance describes "the extent to which people feel threatened by ambiguous situations and have created beliefs and institutions that try to avoid these" (Hofstede & Bond, 1984, p. 419). Individualism-collectivism acknowledges the fact that in individualistic cultures, "people are supposed to look after themselves and their family only," while in collectivistic cultures, "people belong to in-groups or collectivities which are supposed to look after them in exchange for loyalty" (Hofstede & Bond, 1984, p. 419). Masculinity-femininity refers to cultures "in which dominant values in society are success, money, and things," while femininity refers to cultures "in which dominant values are caring for others and quality of life" (Hofstede & Bond, 1984, pp. 419-420). One of the challenges to dimensions of cultural variability is that comparisons are "relative" and "restricted" to two cultures or regions. Notwithstanding, these dimensions can still serve as a starting point for educational providers in global e-learning contexts. It is noted that cultural drivers of people play a significant role in learning, while representing the foundation for which global e-learning platforms must be based (Henning, 2003; Van Dam & Rogers, 2002).

Van Dam and Rogers (2002), using Hofstede's dimensions of cultural variability, consider design elements and actions for adaptation of e-learning. Within uncertainty avoidance dimension and e-learning, issues of security and risk are of primary concern. For instance, the e-learning is expected to be seen in a high-risk environment (i.e., low uncertainty avoidance culture) as something intriguing and potentially fun, motivational and interesting; while in a low security environment (i.e., high uncertainty avoidance culture), it can be perceived as dangerous and risky. Power distance, which is a measure of inequality in a given culture, suggests that in high equality culture (low power distance), the expectation is that knowledge is shared or distributed equally across an organizational structure. In a high status culture (high power distance), however, the expectation calls for "telling" strategies where the knowledgeable are required to teach whatever needs to be learned. Individualism then suggests that in high independence culture, there is a sense of controlling one's destiny as far as career and work choices go (i.e., freedom to choose). But in collectivistic culture (group oriented), the success of the group is more important. The masculine-feminine dimension describes the idea of work-life balance where work-focused countries require achievement and recognition, that is, people "live to work" (masculine culture), whereas in a "life-focused" culture, work-related issues, including learning, must be performed within the context of life, in essence, people "work to live" (feminine culture).

Value Preferences and Technology

Despite decentralization and opportunity for increased participation, facilitated by technology in certain cultures, most cultures still remain high context and power distant (e.g., African countries, Japan, South East Asian countries). In a high-context culture, information is internalized in the person or situations, while power-distant cultures recognize or accept the fact that power is not evenly distributed (Hall, 1976; Hofstede, 1980). These cultural categories have implications for implicit and explicit communication tendencies and the general propensity to use technology in global education and e-learning. Therefore, cultural factors tend to influence how individuals use or view communication technologies, and interpretations drawn from messages through them. Specifically, Devereaux and Johansen (1994) argue that it might be difficult to get people to use certain technology such as the computer-mediated communication (CMC) systems in power-distant cultures where status dictates every aspect of interpersonal communication. Others (Ess, 2002), however, have argued that the "soft deterministic" effect of technology, implying that every culture tends to find ways to adapt technologies to their cultural communication patterns. For instance, in the African culture, where significant emphasis is put on relationships, it was found that when e-mail was used for local communications, organizations habitually followed the e-mail with the telephone as a back-up medium to ensure that the message had been received (McConnell, 1998), and had the desired effect (Olaniran, 2001). Following through with a more traditional medium may be less cultural than McConnell suggests, however. No scholars disputed the fact that cultural differences affect technology adoption and use. Japanese designers acknowledge the effect of culture that not all types of communication can be supported by communication technology such as the CMC systems (Heaton, 1998).

Heaton (1998) contends that if communication technologies are to be useful in Japan, it is important that a familiar sense of atmosphere or feeling must be conveyed through the system. Her research on computer-supported collaborative work (CSCW) systems in Japan suggests that it is problematic for groups to use computers without first meeting face-to-face to establish a trust environment (see also Barron, 2000; Mason, 1998).

The challenge in what a technology innovation such as e-learning can offer, and the hindrance by traditional (local cultural) approach, is not to be taken lightly. People fear new things despite the fact that change itself is a constant in human life. Moreover, in high power-distance cultures, people tend to see a technology system as threatening to their traditional learning methods. The perceived threat creates anxiety about technologies, and consequently, the ensuing negative reactions to using these technologies. For instance, Henning (2003) provides a synopsis of sample effects of culture in response to online courses and information. The encounter synopsis looks at interaction with technology between two teachers in South Africa. She found a high level of anxiety among e-learners. In addition to the physical distance to cyber café, and not having computer facilities at their schools, home, or village, the students' struggle with technology is vividly apparent in the following statements:

When I wrote my first discussion posting I was so afraid. Would this get to others? Will they laugh, what will Prof say? ... I feel I have not the same control as before. I type and I read and I am scared to click because when I do that I feel I am falling down. (Henning, 2003, p. 308)

From this example, one can see the terrifying feelings that emerge from the feeling of loss of control emanating from the attempt to adapt to the new mode of learning. The feelings of anxiety are real to the people from this culture, because they have certain expectations of how learning ought to occur. Henning interprets this information and concludes that these individuals face confusion with who is in charge of the learning environment (i.e., the teacher or the student). Furthermore, the scenario also points to another problem that needs to be addressed by e-learning content providers who are usually from industrialized and economically-developed countries (EDCs) and low power-distance culture: These providers often stress the convenience of online learning and, more importantly, the freedom to put learners in control of learning. Yet in the above scenario, participants point to the need for instructors to perform their job and teach by telling. This case illustrates an example of what we can expect from learners in high power-distance cultures, especially when using a technology system that focuses on a different (i.e., low power distance) learning preference.

Attention to differences in the oral tradition of certain collectivistic cultures and the non-oral tradition's emphasis among individualistic cultures has different implications for e-learning. For instance, e-learning in oral tradition cultures might be better to allow for more interpersonal interactions where students and instructors get to explain ideas to one another. On the other hand, the concept of self-paced independent focus for e-learning might succeed in non-oral tradition cultures. Cultural differences can influence the use or choice of technologies in e-learning. The use of PowerPoint in both nonoral and oral cultures provide supports for the above recommendation. For example, it was reported that some instructors from the United Kingdom (i.e., non-oral culture) succeeded in e-learning contexts when using PowerPoint presentations, while their counterparts from the United Arab Emirates (UAE) saw PowerPoint presentations as extra work that did not fit into oral cultures where students explained ideas to one another about what they read (Selinger, 2004). Specifically, Selinger (2004) reports one student claimed that he does not like e-learning because he prefers to work from a book and from talking with people.

The fact that most of the teachers' toolboxes, provided by the content provider and based on cultural differences, are considered irrelevant by instructors from cultures different from those of the content providers; this adds support to the argument that the needs of the end users should be incorporated into the e-learning course design. This prompts one to ask, "What use is an e-learning toolbox when information provided is not useful to those who need it to do their duties?" Selinger (2003) finds that instructors from about half of the countries participating in the evaluation of the Cisco global e-learning program hardly use the materials available on the teachers' site, and have to develop or adapt the contents to their own eclectic cultures. A more effective strategy would be to resolve problems before the course, by asking the instructors about their requirements and students' preferences, instead of after the fact.

Language

Central to cultural challenges in globalized or e-world learning is the issue of language, since the majority of Internet content is in the English language (Barron, 2000; Van Dam & Rogers, 2003; Wilborn, 1999). Non-English speaking individuals may feel that technology has nothing to offer them since they cannot understand the content. Even in situations where people speak or understand English, its use is limited to certain contexts such as e-mail and entertainment. For instance, it is not uncommon for people in other cultures to restrict their English usage to work, school, or formal business settings, and using the local language and dialects for most of their daily communication encounters. Furthermore, scholars acknowledged that learning a second language in school is quite different from simply learning a foreign language itself (Collier, 1995). Moreover, as much as 36% of online users indicated that they would prefer a language that differs from English (Van Dam & Rogers, 2003). In a study of the global e-learning program offered by Cisco in the English language, students who use English as a second language indicated that they prefer their instructors to first overview the contents of the chapter before readings were assigned (Selinger, 2004). In a global e-learning curriculum, it may also help to note that even when curriculum is made available in languages other than English, there are differences within languages. For example, in the Cisco scenario mentioned above, French and Spanish versions of its e-learning course were provided. Unfortunately, the French version was the Canadian French, and the Spanish version was the South American Spanish, both of which differ from their European versions, thus creating problems for students from France and Spain, and necessitating the need to provide contents and services in localized language.

A scholar addresses the non-participation by the Japanese in online education by attributing it to their language (Kawachi, 1999). Specifically, the Japanese language, which is developed early in life, is conducive to right brain learning modality (i.e., visual and memorization skills) when compared to left brain (i.e., analytic and argumentation skills) which is required by online content (Kawachi, 1999). The limited English proficiency in Japan is attributed to why the Internet is used primarily for searching and printing-out information for reading or translating off-line, and for entertainment and games (Kawachi, 1999).

In relation to the difficulty in language, it is suggested that the potential for information overload exists because non-native speakers read at slower speed than native speakers read. For instance, Chinese-English bilinguals read English at 255 words per minute, compared to Chinese at 380 words per minute (Chambers, 1994; Wang, Inhoff, & Chen, 1999). Kawachi (1999) speculates that the English reading rate for Japanese is slower than the figure for Chinese, given the Japanese English proficiency and learning style. In Europe, the language barrier is seen as a hindrance to the rapid adoption of e-learning. The language barrier results in an increased call for "native-language" content development for local companies who are unwilling to adopt English (Barron, 2000). Unfortunately, language barriers often result in national or cultural pride, which further put U.S. companies at a disadvantage in competing with home-grown developers and content providers.

The need to be part of a group rather than an independent person is imminent when different cultures view or use e-learning. For instance, people from collectivistic cultures tend to seek the connections or look for signs or symbols that provide them a general sense that they connect with others. Henning (2003) found that when some of her participants view Web pages for information, the participants claim that all they see are words and graphics. The participants had no sense of someone else being on the other side to "invite them into their homes", and they could not physically interact with them. Simply put, the personal feel and connection with other learners is not present, and participants' lack of interaction affects willingness to participate in e-learning environments. Although theories such as "tie strength" and "transactional distance" are suggested as solutions to the obvious deficit in e-learning, the apprehension about participation persists and is reflected in instructors' willingness to not have learners' initial e-learning course experience graded or evaluated. Learners express the need for trial run and assurance to know that they are doing well, but more importantly, someone to encourage them that everything will be all right as noted in the next statement from a teacher participating in an e-learning environment:

I have learned something, but not a lot. What I think they [instructors] should do is to teach us how to behave in this sort of set-up before we do a course. I mean not just computers, but the real e-learning thing. By the time I got used to it, it was too late and I think I will fail this one. I still dream of a book and a neat study guide and I am not happy with professor…she thinks we are Americans who breathe through the lungs of the Web. (Henning, 2003, p. 310)

In another example, Henning noted a participant longing for his friend to come into the discussion, just like coming into a house so that they can work on the project together. Henning reports that the learner did not want his peer to complete the project, but to provide a rescue from a very bad experience or "oppression." This analogy clearly illustrates the fact that there are different expectations among learners in individualistic and collectivistic cultures about learning, and these expectations are transferred to e-learning settings.

In general, the challenge is that there does not appear to be a technological and cultural fit in the diffusion of some Westernized technology (Green & Ruhledder, 1995; Mesdag, 2000). Specifically, from the global e-learning standpoint, the learning content needs to match the needs of users. Thus, the key to resolving cultural problems with technology use, especially in any global e-learning environment or curriculum, is to recognize cultural differences and associate technology use with the prevailing cultural values, structures, and activities within these different environments.

Access and Propensity to Use Technology

The propensity to use any communication technology starts with access to technology and the willingness to use it (Olaniran, 1993), and e-learning is no different. A study on attitude and perceptions of e-learning finds easy accessibility as one of the top motivating factors. Forty-seven percent report accessibility of participants, while course relevance to future career and user friendliness follow at 29% and 24% respectively (Vaughan & MacVicar, 2004). A factor contributing to technology access in less economically-developed countries (LEDCs) is "technology transfer." Bozeman (2000) argues that technology transfer is based on cost and benefits, and usually the transfer exists only when the benefits outweigh the costs. The rate of technology transfer is significant in the race to bridge the digital divide between developed countries and LEDCs. Since major communication technology advances occur in economically-developed countries (EDCs), there is disparity in access to this technology in LEDCs when compared with EDCs. With global e-learning, the implications extend beyond mere access attributable to lack of financial capabilities to pay the cost, especially when organizations provide technologies to employees. The access problems create challenges with frequency of use and lack of comprehension of basic commands and protocols to be successful and to facilitate adoption that result in renewal—continued use of the technology (Olaniran, 1993). Furthermore, due to lack of adequate infrastructure and failure to transfer technology to LEDCs, most organizations subcontract their e-learning needs to third- party vendors. Some employees may have to travel several miles to access required e-learning curriculum, which does not bode well in motivating potential users to adopt the technology.

The lack of technological infrastructure could derail any e-learning program regardless of how lofty its goal might be. In addition to how different cultures use or react to different technology media, certain infrastructure, such as high-speed Internet access, are simply not commonplace elsewhere around the globe. Selinger (2004) alludes to this problem with the level of frustration expressed by some e-learning participants in South Africa. One participant expressed:

Did they not know that I had no electricity? Did they not know that I had no telephone line? Did they not know I could hardly type? ... First, we stayed over in Joburg for an extra day, when we could, because that was the only way we could get to computers. (p.311)

The above scenario is not unique; there are significant portions of the world population that have never made a phone call or used the Internet. Therefore, lack of critical technological infrastructure will hinder the deployment of e-learning. Consequently, lack of access to computers, transportation, and convenience in accessing technological infrastructure are conditions that must be considered before any successful deployment of e-learning can materialize.

When technology is available, the propensity or motivation to use it is an internal one. There has to be a willingness or motivation on the part of potential users to use the technology (Olaniran, 1993; Storck & Hill, 2000; Vaughan & MacVicar, 2004). However, the motivation is also tied to cultural norms. Some LEDC cultures adopt technology only as long as it does not conflict with their cultural norms (Heaton, 2001), while others simply adopt technology without considering the impact. Also, one research study reported that older generations may have the tendency to resist new technology because of complacency with old ways of doing things (Wheeler, 2001). In general, the reliability and effectiveness of the communication taking place over the information technology medium has been called into question (Daft, Lengel, & Trevino, 1987; Mitra, 1997; Vaughan & MacVicar, 2004).

Culture and Implications for Implementing Global E-Learning

While the move toward globalizing e-learning is driven by the need to reduce educational cost and the drive to improve efficiency (Pargman, 1998; Sproull & Kiesler, 1991), it has been found that efficiency and cost advantage showed no significant predictive value on usage or social or cultural effects once technologies have been deployed (Pargman, 1998). Nevertheless, it is possible to implement effective and successful global e-learning, such that individuals from LEDCs are receptive to adopting the technology systems and implied structural changes. Successful adoption process would be facilitated only when it is done in a way that takes the idiosyncrasies of cultural factors into consideration both when designing and implementing the technology (Ess, 2002). By doing this, the implementation strategy would enhance the propensity to adopt communication technologies, leading to embracing them for global e-learning and curriculum dissemination. Therefore, attempts to develop a successful global e-learning program that encourages people to use information technologies accompanying e-learning must incorporate the cultural characteristics of the given nation into the design. Another advantage to this approach is that consideration for the cultural characteristics can be a persuasive mechanism for motivating people, and, consequently, speeding up the adoption process.

Adoption Concerns

According to Sitkin, Sutcliffe, and Barrios-Choplin (1992), CMC technology has symbol-carrying capacity such that the users often are presumed to have specific status in using it. This argument appears to have validity, as computers and telephones in certain societies put people who own or use them in the elite category of the society. Few cultural implications are presented to help in this regard. First, people in harmonious or collectivistic cultures are members of a "social network," where conflicts are handled in a non-confrontational manner despite the contexts. Second, the hierarchical structure of a culture makes the use of technology a status symbol. Third, oral tradition in certain cultures use planned and organized face-to-face meetings, visits, and the telephone as primary modes of interaction, while e-learning (or e-mail based on written tradition) are problematic and are hardly ever used (Barron, 2000; Nulens & Audenhove, 1999).

By themselves, the above criteria do not necessarily imply that these technologies will be rejected automatically by a culture. However, they convey the fact that a re-orientation that is built around the adaptation of technology within the cherished values and societal norms of a culture is a necessity for organizational vendors and e-learning providers. For example, the need for individuals in a collectivistic culture to maintain close contact with families and loved ones is a common thread that can serve as a selling point to get the people in collectivistic cultures to adopt technology. Perhaps preference for close contact is one of the reasons that the need for personal contact with teachers and students during learning was stressed by users in e-learning environment (Henning, 2003; Vaughan & MacVicar, 2004).

Blending Needs

While the needs of organization and e-learning content providers are essential, the needs of end users (i.e., cultural perspectives and learning styles) must be taken into consideration in the design and development of the technology. To such an end, Vaughan and MacVicar (2004) indicate that e-learning, as in any learning, is doomed to fail when it fails to focus on learners. For example, developers need to take into consideration access to infrastructure and accruing costs. High Internet access charges often hinder students from accessing e-learning curricula outside class. When this is the case, provisions must be made for learners to access the Internet at work or campus sites. Access and usage must be allowed even when it means spending significant amounts of class time on assignments so that students can familiarize themselves with the curriculum and the technology. Similarly, in situations where students need to work together in groups in order to resolve problems, it would be ideal for the e-learning instructors to allow learners to have each other's contact information (e.g., instant messenger where available), and also those of their instructors (if appropriate). Increased access to their peers and their instructors would help students to avoid the feeling of being lost from the start.

Change Agents and Their Roles

E-learning content providers (in-house or third-party) need to realize that they are cultural change agents and, thus, need to make the change process for e-learners as painless as possible. In essence, providers must make sure that the change aligns with specific cultures in order to successfully accomplish their goals. One way of accomplishing this goal is to recognize that, while the curriculum contents may be universal in their goals, the process for accomplishing those goals must be particularistic. The need for modification in how exercises and assignments are structured for end users is warranted. For instance, different instructor toolboxes can be made available depending on countries, languages, and culture types.

Furthermore, teachers of foreign languages can also serve as leaders who often facilitate the change process and help by using the e-learning curriculum as a tool for teaching foreign languages (e.g., English). After all, end users planning on working in the information technology area usually are in organizations where English is spoken, and there is little need to learn another language (Selinger, 2004). The advantage of this method is "redundancy reinforcement," a principle considered necessary for successful diffusion of innovation in order for novel users to become continued users (Olaniran, 1993). However, foreign language acquisition should never be considered as a substitute for making e-learning contents available in local cultures' languages.

The use of translation software has been suggested (Selinger, 2004), but this software is not readily available across contexts and, more importantly, it is still lacking in precision and accuracy. A valuable approach is to collaborate with other change agents who can help organizations from EDCs with their e-learning projects to convey information and persuade end users that the use of technology (i.e., e-learning) would help to achieve other valuable goals such as learning English or other foreign languages (which could also be necessary to advance students' respective careers). The goal of education and partnering in reducing the digital divide should be to prepare students and teachers to master new skills that current programs may not address. One of these skills includes the ability to collaborate with a diverse team of people in both face-to-face and distance environments in order to achieve different tasks and goals. Making technology available to students and teachers would help them acquire and develop the technological skills and knowledge (Dede, 2000), that are necessary in today's globalized economy.

Facilitating Technology Use

Another proposed benefit to getting users to use technology that could be adapted to e-learning environment is the need to allow students to use technology for reasons other than the designated purpose (Olaniran, 1993, 1994, 1995), as long as it does not violate legal or ethical uses. For instance, if users are allow to send and receive personal e-mails, or browse the Internet for personal reasons, the time spent using the technology to access information could indirectly help students overcome their fears in using e-learning technologies. Research indicates that up to 70% of job-related learning is informal, and driven by individuals rather than acquired from instructors in a structured environment or class (Center for Workforce Development, 1998; see also Brussee, Grootveld, & Mulder, 2003).

User Support

Critical and readily available supports must be a component of any e-learning program. In the adoption process, it is frustrating for individuals to feel flustered, with no help during moments of need. Consequently, e-learning will be better served, especially in culturally-diverse environments, to provide communication tools and social settings, such as virtual classroom for peer supports, as well as fostering competent management in planning, implementation, learner tracking, and certification issues (Brussee et al., 2003). Provision of support is important in the sense that it can improve and perhaps facilitate knowledge transfer even when learners or participants are spread across the globe. The reason for good technological support is that the social setting, or virtual classroom, provides a support group where learners can attempt to discuss or resolve complex problems on their own. Therefore, the more readily available the user support, the easier a user can figure-out the technology and help other students in doing the same.

Instructors' Roles

Teachers need to understand their specific and changing roles in the e-learning environment. First of all, the "one size fits all" teaching is not going to be successful with different cultures and different learning styles. In individualistic cultures where students tend to seek greater control in their learning, the instructor's role would have to shift towards that of a learning facilitator and a coach (Brussee et al., 2003; Selinger, 2004), meaning that instructors only come in as needed. On the other hand, in a collectivistic and a high power-distance culture, instructors must help provide the initial structure, and take a more active role in explaining e-learning contents, and only after that can they use group collaborations where students are able to work on complex problems. Even then, the instructors in a collectivistic culture would have to be available to guide individuals or groups along tasks toward goal accomplishment.

Learning Environment and the Choice of Media

Perhaps one of the greatest struggles in e-learning across cultural contexts that one needs to be prepared for is the need to cultivate learning in a cultural environment, with the provision of a stronger blend of the familiar social environment and the virtual technology environment. In order to do this, the physical world of learners needs to coincide with the tools, signs, and symbols of the e-learning world. To this end, it is suggested that simple visual materials such as icons, sounds, and menus can be replaced with localized words or symbols. In addition, the discussion tool does not have to adhere to a strict structure, but to offer an alternlate and innovative way of presenting learning content (Selinger, 2004; Van der Westhuizen & Henning, 2001). In essence, students should be allowed to have inputs on the structure and format of e-learning as much as possible. Similarly, the social environment in which learning takes place contributes to the students' motivation to learn. The choice of communication media represents another area where significant deliberation must be given. For example, while videoconferencing provides more cues and offers participants opportunities to see other learners (through synchronous interaction), it is more difficult to implement in contexts where high-speed broadband access are not available. At the same time, videoconferencing activities have been found to reduce active participation. Videoconferencing has a tendency to be more formal than the classroom because interactions are stifled, and students are more reluctant to ask questions (Brussee et al., 2003; Malpani & Rowe, 1997). Mailing lists or bulletin boards, on the other hand, offer a low bandwidth alternative but are difficult to set up for synchronous interaction, and are considered lacking in a "personal feel," which may reduce participation level.

The choice and selection of the technology medium ought to be done with significant consideration for different cultures. For instance, it has been shown that in Korea and Japan, e-mail usage is common in peer interaction, but not in superior-subordinate interactions (i.e., power distance). Thus, learner preference is shown for alternative media such as the phone, the fax, and the face-to-face when communicating with superiors, in order to acknowledge and convey respect (Lee, 2002; Olaniran, 2004). Western cultures do not share similar perceptions of respect, and thus do not perceive the use of e-mail between subordinates and superiors to be rude. In essence, the role of culture and the complexity it can create in e-learning and other virtual collaboration work cannot be over-emphasized.

At the same time, the choice of technology medium for disseminating e-learning curricula points to the fact that "technology for the sake of technology" is not a sufficient criterion for motivating learners' and end users' interest in acceptance of, and satisfaction with, e-learning. Rather, it is better when the technological innovation in learning context supports communication and interaction between learners, and builds a social climate that fosters knowledge exchange (Brussee, 2003) and retention of learning, in order to secure the commitment of and the acceptance from users. Gallagher (2003) echoes a similar claim when he argues that people need to take the center stage, while other issues, such as content and technology medium, should take on supportive roles. Similarly, the SMART model of technology planning for delivery of management education suggests the need to assess user needs against the available technology infrastructure to implant or to provide e-learning (Hamlin, Griffy-Brown, & Goodrich, 2003).

Beyond internal organizational technology needs, technology planning for management education and e-learning should reflect global environments and contexts. In essence, the challenge is not whether e-learning is potentially useful or that the trend to use e-learning will continue to grow or to have wider acceptance, but how e-learning fits into specific organizations' strategies, and whether e-learning providers are using the technologies in a way that is feasible and can help them and their participants (employees, students, and target audience) accomplish organizational goals. On this note, the recommendation is that the implementation of e-learning and accompanying technologies be instituted with a long-term view where acceptance and use are based on ongoing simultaneous process (Cummings & Buzzard, 2002; Wankel & DePhillippi, 2003).

Conclusion

Certainly e-learning is evolving, whether it is intended to supplement traditional face-to-face learning or be used to replace traditional learning altogether within organizations. Regardless of the aim or purpose, it is paramount that providers tailor e-learning use to the client, and pay attention to differences in cultural learning styles and the preferences of its end users. Yes, we live in a global world where product standardization seems to be the norm. Notwithstanding, the idea of a "one size fits all" learners' approach across different cultural contexts is not feasible. Moreover, the lack of attention to different cultures could be the ultimate deciding factor between success and failure. This chapter argues that cultural contexts matter, that the dimensions of cultural variability have implications on the decision to introduce e-learning technology, and stresses the need for e-learning providers to incorporate these cultural differences into their planning. E-learning technologies must be about the learner. Attempting to seek the learner's commitment during planning is crucial to user acceptance, to user satisfaction, and to continued use of the innovation object. This chapter adds to the scholarly dialogue the role of culture values in the adoption process of technological innovations, especially those developed in a different culture. The arguments explore and provide specific problems and challenges facing potential users of e-learning technology. The chapter offers some recommendations for organizations using e-learning, and porviders of e-learning technologies, as well as ideas for facilitating successful adoption.

Finally, e-learning is not a cure-all; e-learning is a means to an end. Therefore, while the potential for e-learning is enormous among emerging markets and developing economies, careful planning and attention to the idiosyncrasies of cultures is necessary in order to realize the potential benefits of e-learning, and this information must be communicated to any e-learning content providers, whether organizational in-house or subcontracted third-party vendors and platforms.

References

Barron, T. (2000, September). E-learning's global migration. *Learning Circuits*. Retrieved August 26, 2005, from http://www.learningcircuits.org/2000/Sep2000/barron.html

Brussee, R., Grootveld, M., & Mulder, I. (2003). Educating managers, managing education: Trends and impacts of tomorrow's technologies. In C. Wankel & R. DePhillippi (Eds.), *Educating managers, with tomorrow's technologies* (pp. 1-16). Greenwich, CT: Information Age Publishing.

Center for Workforce Development (1998). The teaching firm: Where productive work and learning converge. *Report on research findings and implications*. Newton, MA: Education Development Center.

Collier, V. P. (1995). Acquiring a second language for school. *Directions in Language & Education*, *1*(4). Retrieved May 4, 2005, from http://www.ncela.qwu.edu/pubs/directions/04.htm

Cummings, D., & Buzzard, C. (2002). Technology, students, and faculty: How to make it happen! *Techniques, 77*(8), 30-33.

Daft, R. L., Lengel, R. H., & Trevino, L. K. (1987). Message equivocality, media selection, and manager performance: Implications for information systems. *MIS Quarterly, 11*, 355-366.

Dede, C. (2000). A new century demand new ways of learning. In D. T. Gordon (Ed.), *The digital classroom* (pp. 171-174). Cambridge, MA: Harvard Education Letter.

Devereaux, M. O., & Johansen, R. (1994). *Global work: Bridging distance, culture, & time*. San Francisco: Jossey-Bass.

Dunn, P., & Marinetti, A. (2002). *Cultural adaptation: Necessity for global e-learning*. Retrieved May 4, 2005, from http://www.linezine.com

Ess, C. (2002). Cultures in collision philosophical lessons from computer-mediated communication. *Metaphilosophy, 33*(1-2), 229-253.

Gallagher, J. (2003). The place and space model of distributed learning: Enriching the corporate-learning model. In C. Wankel & R. DePhillippi (Eds.), *Educating managers, with tomorrow's technologies* (pp. 131-148). Greenwich, CT: Information Age Publishing.

Green, C., & Ruhleder, K. (1995). Globalization, borderless worlds, and the tower of Babel: Metaphors gone awry. *Journal of Organizational Change Management, 8*(4), 55-68.

Gudykunst, W. B., Chua, E., & Gray, A. J. (1987). Cultural dissimilarities and uncertainty reduction processes. In M. McLaughlin (Ed.), *Communication yearbook: Vol. 10* (pp. 457-469). Beverly Hills, CA: Sage.

Hall, E. T. (1976). *Beyond culture*. New York: Doubleday.

Hamlin, M. D., Griffy-Brown, C., & Goodrich, J. (2003). From vision to reality: A model for bringing real-world technology to the management education classroom. In C. Wankel & R. DePhillippi (Eds.), *Educating managers, with tomorrow's technologies* (pp. 211-238). Greenwich, CT: Information Age Publishing.

Heaton, L. (1998). Preserving communication context: Virtual workspace and interpersonal space in Japanese CSCW. In C. Ess & F. Sudweeks (Eds.), *Cultural attitudes towards communication and technology* (pp. 163-186). Sydney, Australia: University of Sydney.

Heaton, L. (2001). Preserving communication context: Virtual workspace and interpersonal space in Japanese CSCW. In C. Ess (Ed.), *Culture, technology, communication: Towards an intercultural global village* (pp. 213-240). Albany: State University of New York Press.

Henning, E. (2003). I click therefore I am (not): Is cognition "distributed" or is it "contained" in borderless e-learning programmes? *International Journal of Training and Development, 7*(4), 303-317.

Hofstede, G. (1980). *Culture's consequences*. Beverly Hills, CA: Sage.

Hofstede, G. (1983). Dimensions of national cultures in fifty countries and three regions. In J. Deregkowski, S. Dziurawiec, & R. Annis (Eds.), *Expiscations in cross-cultural psychology* (pp. 335-355). Lisse, Netherlands: Swets & Zeitlinger.

Hofstede, G. H. (2001). *Culture's consequences: Comparing values, behaviors, institutions, and organizations across nations*. Thousand Oaks, CA: Sage.

Hofstede, G., & Bond, M. (1984). Hofstede's culture dimensions: An independent validation using Rokeach's value survey. *Journal of Cross-Cultural Psychology, 15*, 417-433.

Internet Usage in Asia. (n.d.). Retrieved December 31, 2005 from http://www.internetworldstats.com/stats3.htm

Kawachi, P. (1999, April 19-21). *Language curriculum change for globalisation* (mimeograph). Paper presented at the 34th Annual RELC Seminar—Language in the Global Context: Implications for the Language Classroom. Singapore: SEAMEO RELC. Retrieved from ouhk..edu.hk/cridal/gdenet/Teaching/Design/EATL11A.html

Lee, O. (2002). Cultural differences in email use of virtual teams a critical social theory perspective. *Cyberpsychology & Behavior, 5*(3), 227-232.

Malpani, R., & Rowe, L. A. (1997). Floor control for large-scale MBone seminars. *ACM Multimedia*, 97. Retrieved May 4, 2005, from http://bmrc.berkeley.edu/research/publications/1997/137/qsbmm97.html

Mason, R. (1998). *Globalising education: Trends and applications*. London: Routledge.

McConnell, S. (1998). NGOs and Internet use in Uganda: Who benefits?. In C. Ess & F. Sudweeks (Eds.), *Cultural attitudes towards communication and technology* (pp. 104-124). Sydney, Australia: University of Sydney.

Mesdag, M. V. (2000). Culture-sensitive adaptation or global standardization: The duration of usage hypothesis. *International Marketing Review, 17*, 74-84.

Mitra, A. (1997). Virtual commonality: Looking for India on the Internet. In. S. G. Jones (Ed.), *Virtual culture* (pp. 55-79). London: Sage.

Nulens, G., & Audenhove, L. (1999). The African information society: An analysis of the information and communication technology policy of the World Bank, ITU, and ECA. *Communicatio: South African Journal of Research and Theory, 25*(1-2), 28-41.

Olaniran, B. A. (1993). An integrative approach for managing successful computer-mediated communication technological innovation. *Ohio Speech Journal, 31*, 37-52.

Olaniran, B. A. (1995). Perceived communication outcomes in computer-mediated communication: An analysis of three systems among new users. *Information Processing & Management, 31*, 525-541.

Olaniran, B. A. (1996). Social skills acquisition: A closer look at foreign students on college campuses and factors influencing their level of social difficulty in social situations. *Communication Studies, 22*, 72-88.

Olaniran, B. A. (2001). The effects of computer-mediated communication on transculturalism. In V. Milhouse, M. Asante, & P. Nwosu (Eds.), *Transcultural realities* (pp. 83-105). Thousand Oaks, CA: Sage.

Olaniran, B. A. (2004). Computer-mediated communication in cross-cultural virtual groups. In G. M. Chen & W. J. Starosta (Ed.), *Dialogue among diversities* (pp. 142-166). Washington, DC: National Communication Association.

Pargman, D. (1998). Reflections on cultural bias and adaptation. In C. Ess & F. Sudweeks (Eds.), *Cultural attitudes towards communication and technology* (pp. 73-91). Sydney, Australia: University of Sydney.

Roach, K. D., & Olaniran, B. A. (2001). Intercultural willingness to communicate and communication anxiety in international teaching assistants. *Communication Research Reports, 18,* 26-35.

Sitkin, S. B., Sutcliffe, K. M., & Barrios-Choplin, J. R. (1992). A dual capacity model of communication media choice in organizations. *Human Communication Research, 18,* 563-598.

Sproull, L., & Kiesler, S. (1991). *Connections: New ways of working in the networked organization.* Cambridge, MA: MIT Press.

Storck, J., & Hill, P. A. (2000). Knowledge diffusion through strategic communities. *Sloan Management Review, 41*(2), 63-74.

Van Dam, N., & Rogers, F. (2002, May). E-Learning cultures around the world: Make your globalized strategy transparent. *E-Learning,* 28-33.

Vaughan, K., & MacVicar, A. (2004). Employees' pre-implementation attitudes and perceptions to e-learning: A banking case study analysis. *Journal of European Industrial Training, 28*(5), 400-413.

Wang, J., Inhoff, A. W., & Chen, H. (1999). *Reading Chinese script: A cognitive analysis.* Marwah, NJ: LEA Publishers.

Wankel, C., & DePhillippi, R. (2003). Introduction: Emerging technological contexts of management learning. In C. Wankel & R. DePhillippi (Eds.), *Educating managers, with tomorrow's technologies* (pp. vii-ix). Greenwich, CT: Information Age Publishing.

Wheeler, D. (2001). New technologies, old culture: A look at women, gender, and Internet in Kuwait.' In C. Ess (Ed.), *Culture, technology, communication: Towards an intercultural global village* (pp. 187-212). Albany: State University of New York Press.

Wilborn, J. (1999). The Internet: An out-group perspective. *Communicatio: South African Journal of Research and Theory, 25*(1-2), 53-57.

Chapter III

Designing Quality Online Education to Promote Cross-Cultural Understanding

Youmei Liu
University of Houston, USA

Abstract

This chapter focuses on four main areas: (1) the relationship between cultural value systems and education, (2) the influence of cultural values on assessment systems, (3) the use of technology to facilitate cross-cultural communication, and (4) online education promoting the development of social capital. It argues that in order to design an effective curriculum that can be applied in a cross-cultural learning environment, both instructors and students need to be aware of diverse cultural value systems and their characteristics. This cross-cultural understanding and the creation of social capital can be developed through effective communication with the assistance of technology.

Introduction

The advent of Web technology has brought learning to a global scale through online education. That students from all over the world attend virtual classes is no longer a newborn phenomenon. Many higher educational institutions hasten to catch up with this new trend, offering degree programs and courses online to meet the needs of many non-traditional students. The growth is not only likely to continue but to accelerate (Salman, 2000). According to the federal government's National Center for Educational Statistics (NCES), "by 2009-10, online courses are projected to account for 31% of all course enrollments at the postsecondary level" (Eldson & Pittman, 2001, p. 4). However, this trend is not just a fashion: "As we move further into a society dominated by technology and communication, both educators and students will increasingly use e-learning to minimize the costs of educational products and services" (Partow & Slusky, 2001, p. 70). Due to the dynamic nature of distance learning (anywhere, anytime), "Web-based electronic delivery is fast becoming the dominant mode of instruction" (Edelson & Pittman, 2001, p. 3). At the same time, institutions and faculty members are facing new challenges to maintain and improve the instructional quality in this international online classroom. In order to design an effective and cultural-inclusive (Kenneth & Zeichner, 1992) curriculum that can be applied in a cross-cultural learning environment, instructors need to be aware of diverse cultural value systems and of their characteristics. "It is not possible, in the view of some scholars, to create a model of the good teacher without taking issues of culture and context into account (Cole & Griffin, 1987; Delpit, 1988). We need to understand the value differences regarding educational systems to create a learning environment in which "all students felt valued and capable of academic success" (Cummins, 1986; Olsen & Mullen, 1990).

This chapter promotes cross-cultural understanding in an online learning environment. Through online learning communities, both instructors and students from different cultural backgrounds can reduce cultural misunderstanding and build mutual respect and trust to improve the quality of education. Cross-cultural online education provides students with a global context in which students can improve their cultural awareness and gain social competency to accommodate the changes in the global community. Web technology can be used effectively to expand the learning community, to facilitate interaction and engagement in community activities, and to promote mutual understanding and trust. One of the most important issues raised in this chapter is that cross-cultural online education is a great venue to develop social capital on a worldwide scale. In a cross-cultural learning community, students from different cultural backgrounds share values, information, and knowledge with each other. Meanwhile, they also build up a strong social networking, which furthers the exploration and utilization of social resources in benefiting mankind in the most efficient way.

This chapter provides a comparison of value differences between Eastern cultures and Western cultures. The terms "Asians", "Eastern cultures", and "Easterners" are used alternatively to indicate East Asian countries, such as China, Japan, Korea, and the countries close to China and influenced by Chinese culture. "Westerners" and "Western cultures" are used to indicate North Americans influenced by European value systems.

The author of this chapter has more than 15 years' teaching experiences in higher-education institutions in both China and the United States. There are some generalizations through the author's experiences, most of which are supported by research studies. But, by no means can these generalizations be applied to different cross-cultural scenarios. As Nisbett (2004) pointed out, "the cultures and subcultures of the East differ as dramatically from one another as do those of the West" (p. xxii). The author's intention is to share personal experiences with readers and raise some critical issues in cross-cultural online leaning for public discussion.

Cultural Difference

"Cultures are not static; they are always evolving as people respond to new conditions and influences. The relationships between ethnic groups and the dominant culture also change and vary over time and place" (Ramsey, Williams, & Vold, 2003, p. 68). Cultures have a bearing on people's communication and behavioral patterns. Each culture has its distinctive way of living as reflected in social interactions, in determination of status, in religious belief, and in political viewpoints, as well as in levels of civilization and of economic development. The difference can be as simple as how people greet each other. For example, "How are you?" in Asian countries is a genuine question calling for a thoughtful reply; however, in Western countries, it is just a casual daily greeting to which the only polite replies are "fine", "great", or the like. Rackl (2002) gave two examples of using this casual greeting. "For most people, asking an acquaintance 'how are you?' don't really want to know an answer;" (para. 3) and "another irksome aspect of the 'how are you?' situation is that, in many cases, the person who asks the question does not stick around to wait for the answer" (para. 3). A friendly smile to a member of a different gender could cause serious problems in Eastern cultures. The word "love" can be used casually in Western culture to express one's fondness of another human or of anything else, but in Eastern culture the word love can only be used very seriously to indicate human emotional affection. Liu (2001) described her first experience in a different culture that "the beliefs, values, norms that govern my social behavior no longer seemed to function well in new environment" (pp. 8-9).

The relationship between students and teachers in schools also varies from culture to culture. In Asian countries, the teacher is regarded as an absolute authority. Azimi (1998) described the relationship between teacher and students in Afghan schools, "teachers are treated with respect, students may have to stand up when they enter" (para. 5). In Western countries, for example, in America, "teachers are supposed to treat the students as basic equals and are expected to be treated as equals by the students" (Azimi, 1998, para. 8). In Western culture, it is perfectly all right for a teacher to say "I don't know" to a student's question, but in Eastern culture, any teacher who speaks this way risks losing the respect of the students. In Western countries, students can challenge or even debate with their teachers on controversial issues. "Students may make uninvited interventions in class and argue with teachers, express disagreement and criticism in front of the teachers" (Azimi, 1998, para. 8). In Eastern countries, students barely even ask any questions beyond lectures. Liu (2001) cited an example in her research, "a Korean student spoke up in class mainly to show that he had done assigned readings" (p. 71). Kuwahara (2005) reflected a similar issue in her study that Asian "students have a difficult time asking questions in the classroom for fear that they may insult the teacher" (para. 9).

Generally speaking, society and family exert much more pressure on children's education in Eastern cultures where education means social status and family honor. "Social constraints are in general greater on both Chinese and Japanese than on Westerners" (Nisbett, 2004, p. 72). Kaneko (2004) listed one of the family roles is to give children pressure of learning due to high aspiration and competition in Japan. Besides, in Eastern cultures, particularly in China, education is associated with family honor. "Academic achievement and upward mobility are not viewed by Asian parents as personal matters but part of their children's obligation for the maintenance of the family" (Shen & Mo, 1990, para. 4). They often consider their children's schooling directly related to the family's integrity: High achievement brings honor and prestige to the family, failure brings shame (Lee, 1989). "The individual works not for self-benefits but for the entire family" (Nisbett, 2004, p. 15). Eastern students are expected to follow rules, and to memorize learning content. The Chinese, along with the Japanese, are often detail-and precision-oriented (Oxford & Burry-Stock, 1995). They practice very hard for high grades. "Poor grades are viewed as culturally unacceptable behaviors" and "parents would do whatever they think effective to avoid failure" (Shen & Mo, 1990, para. 4). In school, Eastern students tend to wait for the assignments or project requirements; they normally do not initiate activities on their own, do not respond to or involve themselves actively in learning activities unless such activities are required and given credit. Some classroom activities seem as a pure waste of time to Asian students. They think that the activities are less awarding than lectures; while in Western culture, especially in business schools, teamwork and collaboration are promoted. Students are encouraged to be innovative and creative.

Cultural Characteristics and Social Value System

Social Structure and Values

Cultural characteristics are strongly influenced by the social value system. In Eastern culture, ever since recorded history began, the hierarchical structure of the society mattered enough to be recorded. For example, in China, this value system deeply rooted in the Confucius educational theory: Those who work with their heads will rule, while those who work with their hands will serve. Confucius promoted equal education, which was considered "a path of upward mobility to anyone who could survive the rigors of study and examinations" (Beck, 2000., para. 7). Exams have been the stepping-stones to success ever since. Western people sometimes ridiculed the high prestige and importance in which examinations were held by Asian students.

In a perfect hierarchical society, there is no equality; each person is either above or below any other given person. "Equality of treatment is not assumed nor is it necessarily regarded as desirable" (Nisbett, 2004, p. 49). The traditional Chinese moral system clearly spelled out the relationship between officials and ordinary people, parents and children, older generation and younger generation. Ordinary people have to listen to those with power and authority without any interposition of their own opinions. This value system still has a strong influence in Eastern countries today. "Unfortunately, feudal traces, especially clannishness and nepotism, continue to hold Asian societies back, preventing them from becoming true meritocracies, where individual citizens are able to grow and thrive on the basis of their abilities" (Mahbunani, 2002, p. 31). In Western cultures, individuality, democracy, freedom of speech, self-advancement, and equal human rights are promoted. Nisbett (2004) has made the following generalizations about most Westerners:

1. Each individual has a set of characteristic, distinctive attributes;

2. People are largely in control of their own behavior;

3. People are oriented toward personal goals of success and achievement;

4. People strive to feel good about themselves;

5. People prefer equality in personal relations; and

6. People believe the same rules should apply to everyone. (pp. 47-48)

Even though there are still some social rankings in Western cultures, people at least have some understanding about treating each other equally and fairly. These differences create a daunting challenge to Eastern students in cross-cultural learning environments in affecting their judgment about others and their level of participation in class activities. It affects their relationships, interactions, and their communication with instructors and with other students. Levine, Oded, Connor, and Asons (2002) did a research study on peer response in student group activity. They found out that students from Asian countries tend to see the teacher as "an absolute authority figure who must evaluate student work" and students "hesitate to accept peers' criticism and to prefer teacher's criticism instead" (para. 50). They tend to be more submissive to the people who are in an authoritative position and to follow them without questioning. Sue and Kirk (1972) stated that many Asian students are less autonomous, more dependent on authority figures, and more obedient and conforming to rules and deadlines. This is one of the reasons that Eastern students more often learn passively for they regard themselves as being controlled externally by their instructor.

Cross-Cultural Racial Issues

Racial discrimination is a bigger barrier for Eastern students than for Western students. The European's colonization of Asia in the 16th century made Asians began to believe that Asians were inferior to the Europeans and even now "many Asian societies are still struggling to break free (this mental colonization)" (Mahburani, 2002, pp. 22-23). White people have racial privileges in Eastern countries. In Asian societies, the racial issues have seldom been addressed since the culture is normally dominated by its own race and ethnic group and not as diverse as that in the United States and some other Western cultures. One Chinese college student based the racism on the availability of black people and said that "there is no racism in China because there are no black people" (Anonymous, 2003, para. 7). But according to David Szykulski (2003), a multiracial Canadian teacher in China, "all I ever experienced were racial taunts, blatant discrimination, and general loathing from the majority" (para. 1). Yu Hai (2003), a sociology professor, believed that "a long-standing Chinese tradition of discrimination according to 'status' has created an atmosphere conducive to racial prejudice" (para 8). Asian students are not even aware that this could be a serious issue when studying in a cross-cultural learning environment. Asian people tend to relate skin color to aesthetics, civilization, wealth, human evolution, and even to personal hygiene. Asians respect and even look up to Caucasians, but look down upon black people. On the contrary, in the United States, for example, racial issues have been a part of the history, such as the quest for racial educational equality: "in 1954 the Supreme Court unanimously ruled in Brown v. Board of Education of Topeka that racial segregation in public schools was unconstitutional" (Thattai, 2001, para. 15); intergroup education movement of the 1940s and 1950s-education reform related to diversity is viewed as essential for all students (Banks, 1993); ethnic/single-group studies: "to raise consciousness about a group by teaching its history, culture, and contributions, and how it has worked with or been oppressed by the dominant group in society" (Towson University, n.d., para. 18); and multicultural education movement from 70s up till today, a movement designed to empower all students to become knowledgeable, caring, and active citizens in a deeply-troubled and ethnically-polarized nation and world (Banks, 1993). These historical movements have made people more aware of racial issues and individual rights. Eastern students' skin-color preference will make the racial issue prominent in the cross-cultural learning environment. "Dark-skinned foreigners are more likely to face obstacles than white, as many Chinese see them as inferior" (Yu, 2003, para. 10).

Cultural Stereotypes and Communication

Cultural differences are generalized for the convenience of communication, but, more often than not, the generalization becomes a stereotyped concept that turns out to be the hindrance for mutual communication and understanding. People are likely to associate an individual with unwarranted assumptions concerning his or her cultural background, economic and political status of the country in the world, and make pre-judgments about him or her even before getting to know this person. These pre-judgments are the origin of "prejudice." The individuality is lost in the stereotyped bias. "What we should not lose sight of is that variation within cultural groups is often greater than variation between groups" (Murrell, 1990, p. 50). On the other hand, most individuals tend to be proud of their own culture and its heritage no matter what their original country is. For example, Chinese students are proud of their long historical civilization, but in the eyes of advanced countries, China is a third-world, developing country, poor and backward.

Everyone is unique even though he or she bears his or her cultural signature. Race, culture, ethnicity, and religion must be seen as "dimensions along which individuals and samples vary, rather than as categories in which individuals can be classified" (Phinney, 1996, p. 919). Phinney (1996) also pointed out that individuals within any group may differ considerably in terms of how much they identify with, believe in, and express the cultural values of their group and how they negotiate between their group and the dominant society. Respect for each individual as a valued entity is very important since such mutual respect forms the basis of a student's ability to hear others and form meaningful opinions. No matter what kind of wealth a person or a country possesses, such wealth should never become grounds for prejudice and discrimination against those of other countries or cultures. Despite the best efforts of mutual respect, however, every student will experience more or less identity crisis in the cross-cultural learning environment.

Cultural Values and Education System

Besides the above diversities in cultural characteristics and value systems, the educational systems between Eastern and Western countries differ drastically since "Westerners and East Asians maintained very different systems of thought for thousands of years" (Nisbett, 2004, p. xvi). In most Asian countries, education is centralized and controlled by the government. The central educational ministry or department makes education policies, develops curricula, and assigns textbooks or at least approves the textbooks to be used in schools at all grade levels. For example, in China, a school has never had the authority to develop its own curriculum. In some schools, teachers are required to study the curricula from the Educational Ministry. Each curriculum provides detailed standards and learning objectives for a given subject area with very limited choices of textbooks. In quite a few schools, teachers may not even know about the central curricula, but teach whatever material they are supplied. In such a case, there is no need for teachers to write a syllabus. Teachers walk into the classroom with a textbook and an attendance book. Both the instructional methods and student learning styles are monotonous. The majority of teachers teach in pretty much the same way. They lecture with very little interactions with the students, almost no classroom activities, and even less after-class activities. Students listen to the teachers, busily take notes, and do a lot of homework afterwards. They also normally study on their own. Because of the legacy of the Confucian exams, high marks in school remain critical to future job success, and student competition is fierce. Teachers and students work very hard towards the same goal—high test scores. Teachers teach for the test; students learn for the test. Eastern students find it very difficult to adjust themselves to a globalized learning community in which they are expected to work collaboratively and cooperatively with students from different cultural backgrounds.

In Western higher education systems, students enjoy the flexibility of selecting their major areas and changing their majors if they wish. But Oliver (1999) observed that "Japanese students find the flexibility and numerous choices offered in the U.S. system of higher education extremely confusing" (p. 29). The Eastern educational system offers students only one opportunity to choose their major area of study, and they stick to this area for the rest of their life. Graduate schools will not accept students from different majors. Employers normally will not hire somebody who has not majored in a specific area. College teachers never teach the courses across their fields. The advantage of this system is that students are concentrating deeply on one majoring area and become very well trained in that selected field; but the flaw of the system is that students tend to ignore other areas and limit themselves to a narrow spectrum of knowledge. The challenges they will face are not only in their own learning style, but also the need for extra readings to catch up to common knowledge bordering their majoring area. In Western cultures, instructors freely select the materials they teach. There is very little across-the-board uniformity in the teaching content and teaching method. Every instructor teaches differently and uniquely in accordance with his or her individual personality and interests. For example, one teacher may choose to offer a shallow presentation with many links to related disciplines; another may offer a very narrow presentation, which treats his or her own specialty deeply; another may stir the surface, offering neither breadth nor depth; another may be able to offer meaningful depth while also presenting some links to other studies. Students must be aware of the proclivities of teachers and choose accordingly. Asian students need to adjust to the flexibility of the teaching styles.

Diverse Learning and Communication Styles

Eastern and Western students also have different learning processes, interaction patterns, and communication styles. Nisbett (2004) has made an analysis of group behavior of Easterners and Westerners, that Easterners are much more trusting of in-group members (friends and family) while Westerners "tend not to make as great distinctions between in-group and out-group" (p. 51). A study conducted by Freeman and Liu (1996) suggests that Asian students tend to ask fewer questions either from instructor or from other students than do Western students. In online learning interactions, Asian students tend to rely heavily on the posted instructions, while Western students tend to be peer-oriented learners. They believe in interactions among students (Liang & McQueen, 1999). Most Asian students are silent learners, and are afraid of making mistakes and being ridiculed by classmates (Tsui, 1996), while Western students are more expressive. In their study, Kim and Bonk (2002) found out the Eastern and Western students have different communication patterns: Western cultures tend to be low-context (direct, explicit, unambiguous communication) along with the high-low-context continuum, and most Asian cultures tend to be high-context (indirect, implicit, and reserved communication). Gudykunst and Matsumoto (1996) summarize that low-context communication is prevalent among members of individualistic cultures, while members of collectivistic cultures use predominantly high-context communication. Kim and Bonk's (2002) study also finds that student communication styles influence their collaborative behavior; they suggest that "activities for social interaction are recommended in the early stage of online collaboration in order to facilitate active participation of the learners from high-context communication cultures" (para. 91).

Curriculum and Instruction for Cross-Cultural Online Learning

Computer technology has globalized education without geographic limits. This globalization has put new trials to the existing education systems and instructors as well as on students. The traditional face-to-face curriculum no longer fits into this setting. "A school curriculum not only reflects but is a product of its time" (Oliva, 2001, p. 29). The multi-cultural learning environment has created new challenges for curriculum development and for instructional delivery. In 1990, Geneva Gay proposed a broad interpretation of curriculum that "if we are to achieve equally, we must broaden our conception to include the entire culture of the school-not just subject matter content" (p. 61). Even this concept is no longer broad enough. Curriculum needs further expansion to include cultures in the global sense. Research studies have indicated that the major issues in planning, designing, and delivering online learning now include the given fact of globalized learning and the resultant cultural diversity of students (Chute & Shatzer, 1995; McIsaac & Gunawardena, 1996).

The curriculum has been interpreted from very broad perspectives depending on an individual's philosophical beliefs (Oliva, 2001). It could be just the teaching content; it could include everything in the school system. Based on the purposes it serves, one of the definitions is that "curriculum is transmission of the cultural heritage" (Oliva, 2001, p. 6). Kim and Bonk (2002) also stressed that "culture plays an important role in cognitive development of learners through social interaction and discourse" (para. 7). The development of curricula for cross-cultural learning environments must consider the cultural differences and diverse value systems as well as the different education systems to be served. The rich diversity can benefit learning only when the curriculum and instruction are well designed and organized with the integration of different cultural value systems. Ramsey, Williams, and Vold (2003) pointed out that, "effective multicultural education must be grounded in an understanding of its relation to other social and political movements and in an ability to make curriculum developmentally-appropriate or accessible" (p. 14). Curricula should be designed to provide a learning environment conducive to students' understanding of different cultural values, acceptance of individuality, and adaptation to the global learning community. In order to achieve this objective, the environment should include "(1) respect for personality; (2) participation in decision-making; (3) freedom of expression and availability of information; and (4) mutuality of responsibility in defining goals, planning and conducting activities, and evaluating" (Knowles, 1980, p. 67). It is also very important to build a trust and trustworthiness between instructors and students as well as between students and students. Brookfield (1990) believed the building of such trust to be essential for meaningful learning. Grant (1978) stated that curricula for cross-cultural learning should be: (1) "appropriate, flexible, unbiased, and incorporate the contributions of all cultural groups; (2) the different languages of cultural groups are seen as assets, not deficiencies; (3) institutional materials are free of bias, omissions, and stereotypes; are inclusive, rather than supplementary; and show individuals from different cultural groups portraying different occupational and social roles" (p. 47).

Cross-cultural curricula should be designed to support student learning through the integration of collaborative learning in online learning community, which will promote cross-cultural understanding, increase students' awareness of global mentality, enable each student to think out of his or her own cultural sphere, and will bring the best out of each culture to maximize the benefit of education to the global community. The diverse interactions, collaborations, and communications should be integrated in teaching activities. Veenman, Denessen, Akker, and Rijt (2005) state in their research study that, "students do not naturally develop constructive interactional patterns without instruction" (p. 120). Instructors need to provide students with explicit instructions on how to conduct collaborative learning. This detailed instruction should include the goal, objective, role, specific task, timeline, expectation, and participation. This is especially necessary and important for Eastern students since they have had hardly any collaborative learning experiences. Collaborative learning can be encouraged and supported through "reflective interaction" (Harasim, 1989, p. 52). Bannon (1995) suggested that cultural barriers can be alleviated when the need for collaboration and the nature of the joint activity is made clearly evident to the students. Collaborative learning in an online learning community can help students reduce their anxiety level, which is very important for first-time online learners, whose frustration affects their motivation and their participation in class activities. Bannon (1995) and Jaffee (2001) suggested using social interaction among learners to share their concerns to encourage participation. Slavin (1995) stated that when the conditions of role equality have been met, relationships between students of different ethnic groups improve. It will be very beneficial to students in collaborative learning if instructors could help students identify the major differences between Eastern and Western cultures regarding social systems, cultural values, social behaviors, and various viewpoints. Students will be consciously aware of the differences, and get prepared ahead of time. Nisbett (2004) illustrated four distinct dimensions to compare Easterners and Westerners:

1. Insistence on freedom of individual action vs. a preference for collective action;

2. Desire for individual distinctiveness vs. a preference for blending harmoniously with the group;

3. A preference for egalitarianism and achieved status vs. acceptance of hierarchy and ascribed status; and

4. A belief that the rules governing proper behavior should be universal vs. a preference for particularistic approaches that take into account the context and the nature of the relationships involved. (pp. 61-62)

A learning environment should be designed to encourage students to extend their learning to the local community and business to increase the value of their knowledge through applying it in reality. With extended community learning, students will have an opportunity to do a reality-check in the real world using the knowledge they have learned. Students will be able to discover their strengths and weakness so that they may make improvements where needed. Students "need to test-run their knowledge and skills in an out-of-school setting before carrying the full mantel of citizen" (Bacon, 2004, para. 3).

This will also give the instructor a chance to validate the curriculum by setting appropriate and practical learning objectives that will meet societal needs. In community learning, students can become better team players and can improve their personal skills to work independently, collaboratively, and cooperatively. Students' interest in learning will be raised to a new level through active engagement with real-world projects, which "moves students beyond immediate interests and present knowledge into a larger world" (Luther College, 2003, para. 6). The instructor and the students can invite field experts to share knowledge and business strategies with students. It will provide students an opportunity to start connecting with and transforming the social network even before they step into society. By participating in real-world projects and activities, students can increase their sense of responsibility for community services and can contribute publicly. Students become "resilient enough to confront and evaluate the changing society in which they serve" (Luther College, 2003, para. 6). Real-world community learning is a great way to assess student learning and check student ability to solve real-life problems at the same time they can improve their skills in communicating with people, their flexibility in adapting to reality, and their creativity in applying knowledge. This integration process will benefit the instructor in teaching more effectively, will benefit students in their careers and lifelong learning, and will benefit the public in social capital development. Bacon (2000) concludes the following:

Students who graduate from school with a strong academic experience and firsthand exposure to the machinery of our society and world are more likely to vote, participate in civic discourse, and think critically about the political and economic issues that connect us with the world beyond our borders. (para. 3)

Another very important part of designing a curriculum for the cross-cultural online learning environment is the inclusion of a nurturing upstanding human being with the standards, morality, and integrity to promote positive social change, equal human rights, mutual respect, and global peace. Even though there are more cultural differences than we can imagine, the many human commonalities can help us bridge the cultural gaps and promote mutual communication. Instructors can take advantage of these commonalities and infuse them into the process of online education. People are more or less group-oriented no matter in what cultural environment they grow up, and "people themselves establish public relations between people in their nature" (Abishev, 2003, para. 3). Instructors could set up discussion groups of special topics relating to social issues, human rights, cultural standard of morality and equality, and so forth. Students who have the same interest in the topic can exchange opinions and ideas with each other. This project itself is an exemplary model of promoting equal human rights, freedom of speech, and mutual respect. Another example of human commonality is creativity. According to Noam Chomsky, the human innate organizing mechanism is a constituent element of human nature, which is something biologically given and unchangeable. Instructors can create a cultural challenging environment to encourage students' critical thinking and bring out each student's creativity to minimize cross-cultural conflicts and promote world peace.

To engage students in cross-cultural learning, both instructors and students need to understand how cultural values affect students, and how students learn from the values and act on them. Students need to develop their understanding, attitudes, identities, and behaviors related to different dimensions of society. Through this process, "the individual develops competencies for perceiving, believing, evaluating, and behaving in different cultural settings and becomes more responsive to the conditions of all humans, the cultural integrity of the individual, and diversity of the society" (National Council for Accreditation of Teacher Education, p. 14). Mezirow (1978) stated that learning is more than the accumulation of new knowledge, added on to existing knowledge; it is a process where many basic values and assumptions by which we operate are changed through our learning process, change our ways of working together with people, and understand the importance of human relationships in a globalized community, distinguishing, separating, and understanding diverse cultural values and personal values.

Cultural Values and Assessment Systems

Assessment systems are different in different cultures. In some cultures, assessment outcome is closely connected to the student's future career; in some others, assessment is considered as the measurement of learning, a closure to a course. Different cultural values will affect people's attitude toward learning and assessment. In Eastern cultures, education is seen as the source of material needed for life-instrumental value, and few people would view education as an improvement of individual quality and enrichment of life experience. In Western culture, people tend to think education has intrinsic value, which is crucial to the quality of personal inner life. In any cross-cultural online learning environment, the assessments should be designed to balance these two different attitudes towards assessment to benefit students no matter what previous system they have experienced.

Differences and Limitations of Assessment Systems

In Eastern cultures, the assessment system tends to ignore student's social competency. For generations, educational systems in China, Japan, and Singapore have put "a premium on academics and a rigorous testing system" and the "current practices limit opportunities for creativity and innovation" (Riley, 2000, para. 19). The strong competition in test scores skews the attention of both students and instructor to overemphasis on the test achievement. High test scores mean everything: entering top schools, obtaining high-salaried jobs, a high quality life, a high social profile, even a possible entrance into the political arena. In short, it is a path to advancement above others. School assessment is designed to help students to achieve high test scores. Lee affirmed (2005) in his paper that in East Asian countries, Confucian values pursue learning in order to obtain socio-political privileges; the values have caused a severe educational competition and have become the main factors promoting unhealthy private education and accelerating social inequality. This is true at all school levels, from kindergarten to higher educational institutions. Chu (2005) stated that educators in Asia consider grades the top priority. The assessment is based purely on textbook knowledge, designed in the format of quizzes and exams. One of the teaching objectives in school is to teach students test-taking skills. Students memorize text content, regurgitate class notes, and do homework consisting entirely of answering a large number of quiz questions. Students are rarely assessed on their communication skills and social competency. The final grades are based on the test scores. The biggest problem with this assessment system is that education trains students to be excellent test-takers, but it deprives students of their creativity, innovation, and social competency. On the other hand, in Western cultures, for example in America, education "consists of a much more hands-on, balanced education experience; emphasizing not only social skills but also developing strong and complete vocational skills" (Chu, 2005, para. 6). Learning is assessed through different assessment formats based on varying teaching methods. In addition to traditional assessment method, students can be also assessed by group projects, class activity participation, discussion message postings, peer-to-peer review, and even self-assessment. Since the projects and activities take up lecture and exercise time, American students' test scores are not as competitive as those of Asian students.

Assessment Design for Cross-Cultural Online Learning

Both systems have advantages and disadvantages. Students from Asian countries have solid foundations in their subject knowledge. The challenge that instructors will face in designing online assessment in cross-cultural learning environment is how to accommodate different assessment systems. The testing format in Asian countries cannot comprehensively and fairly assess a student's competency in mastering knowledge. It disregards students' different learning styles and multiple intelligences (Gardner, 1993). It cannot bring the best out of a student. On the other hand, in Western cultures, assessment is not viewed as seriously as in Eastern cultures. When students are accustomed to their own assessment system, they will not see its limitations. If students cannot see the value of an assessment, it will not be as pedagogically beneficial to them and to society as it is supposed to be. In turn, the toughest issue in the process of designing an assessment is how to balance these two extremes, to design an assessment system that can benefit both Eastern and Western students, and to fairly judge the student learning outcome.

In order to make students consciously understand the importance and necessity of different assessment formats, instructors can design class activities to help students see the value and the practical application of a given assessment. One of the ultimate goals of education concerns seeking a professional career. Here is an example of career-seeking role-play activity. As homework, assign students to design an interview requirement list and a test based on their own assessment system, and to use them as hiring standards to interview students from different cultural backgrounds. Then the students will write reports on their interview results and post these reports to the online discussion forum.

The instructor encourages other students to offer comments and feedback on these interview reports from different perspectives. The analysis and reflection will help students see the limitations of each assessment system, to identify knowledge and skill gaps, and to gain a better understanding of the importance of mastering different skills and knowledge for the global job market.

Well-designed assessments should align with learning objectives. In cross-cultural online learning, instructors can use different assessment formats to assess different perspectives of learning, such as knowledge acquisition, collaborative learning, individual skills, and social competency (George Institute of Technology, n.d.). All online projects and activities should be assessed and credited to motivate student participation. There should also be an incentive in the grading system to encourage prompt response, timely submission, and quality work. The assessments need to focus on the learning process (formative) rather than on the end product (summative). The commonly-used summative assessment is online testing, which can assess effectively student knowledge acquisition, especially the automated features in Course Management Systems, such as WebCT and Blackboard. Students can get to know their test scores and respond to results and the instructor's feedback right after they submit the test. Quite a few activities can be used to assess collaborative learning, such as online role-play, graded discussion topics for group projects, problem solving, information sharing, group debating, online group presentation, peer review and evaluation, and others. Instructors can use online rubrics to clearly state the assessment standards, which will motivate students to strive for the best; it will guide them through the collaborative learning process and make sure students are following instructions and producing quality work, especially for Eastern students who have no experiences of collaborative learning. Individual skills can be further improved through individual writing assignments, reports and essays, self-assessment exercises, case studies, and online research in addition to the online tests and collaborative learning.

Student-Centered Assessment: E-Portfolio

Another learning assessment format that will help students develop multiple skills is the designing and developing of electronic portfolios. E-portfolios are a student-centered assessment activity, which involves student participation in selecting the content and student reflection on the product. Students are engaged in meaningful performance tasks (Burke, 1999). E-portfolio helps students track and organize their learning and provides them an opportunity to re-evaluate their learning experiences. E-portfolio emphasizes on metacognition and self-evaluation (Burke, 1999), so the process requires students to engage actively and reflectively as well as to think critically. E-portfolio can also promote community learning and collaboration between peer-to-peer, student-mentor, student-instructor, and student-employer. They can help each other with collaborative efforts to promote teamwork, and improve organizational and communication skills. Through e-portfolios, students can make a meaningful connection of what they have learned with societal needs.

Designing and developing e-portfolios is a relatively new assessment format for both Eastern and Western students. It is necessary for instructors to provide step-by-step guidance on how to start the project. Students need to be clear in the first place that e-portfolio is not a haphazard collection of artifacts, but rather a reflective tool that demonstrates growth over time (Barrett, 2000). Instructors can help students analyze selected materials regarding relevance, quality, and practical value, and provide students with feedback for further improvement. Students are encouraged to share different perspectives to help each other to grow as a team rather than competing individually. The collaboration can promote team spirit and cross-cultural understanding. Danielson and Abrutyn (1997) specified the process for developing an e-portfolio: *collection – selection – reflection – projection – presentation*. Instructors may need to develop a simple tutorial on how to proceed with each step, how to select a technology to design e-portfolio, how to save, review and evaluate the collected artifacts, what would be the effective way to present them, and how to publish e-portfolios onto the Web. Instructors may try to find out if technical help is available among students, so that students can help one another to improve the efficiency.

The purpose of assessment is more than a test of how much students remembered from textbooks and lectures; it should measure a student's capability to perform effectively in a globalized society with diverse skills of communication and collaboration, which will benefit a student for his or her entire lifetime. Assessment is an effective way for the instructor to get feedback on student learning and to determine further improvement of the instructional quality. It will also help the instructor validate the curriculum and learning content in multi-cultural learning environments to meet the expectation that global values and international awareness be incorporated into curriculum content in implicit and explicit ways (Australian Flexible Learning Framework, 2003).

Technology Facilitating Cross-Cultural Communication

Effective communication is the only assurance of online instructional quality. This issue is especially prominent in the cross-cultural learning environment. Communication is more than a superficial language exchange or skillful use of a computer; it requires the understanding of different cultural value systems. The instructor has to assume multiple titles to be an effective role to facilitate and promote the mutual understanding of students and improve the quality of online learning. Successful online learning depends on a teacher's acquisition of new competencies and becoming aware of its potential to inspire the learners (Salmon, 2002).

The Essence of Cross-Cultural Communication

The essence of cross-cultural communication is about our paradigms and paradigm shifting. Hiemstra (1991) states that "our behaviors and attitudes are shaped by the paradigm we know, believe in, or have directly experienced," "the way we see, perceive, or understand the world around us" (p. 9). Kuhn (1970) explained the paradigm shifting as significant advancement from breaking with the old or traditional way of thinking. Communication and culture reciprocally influence each other (Gudykunst & Ting-Toomey, 1996). Quality communication will improve the effectiveness of online education, promote cross-cultural understanding, and speed up the curriculum reformation. Cross-cultural communication will benefit both instructors and students in increasing individual awareness of cultural traditions and experiences (Ramsey & Williams, 2003). We often get to know our own culture through the eyes of people from different cultural backgrounds since we are so accustomed to the way we live and the system we believe in; this will be a valuable, if also perhaps a "painful self-reflection" (Hiemstra, 1991, p. 8) experience. Effective cross-cultural communication is the sharing, understanding, and appreciation of different value systems instead of imposing one's culture on the other. "We cannot simply have our way, not even when we believe our way to have the 'happiness of mankind' as its promise" (Niebuhr, 1952, p. 74).

Online Activities Facilitating Cross-Cultural Communication

Effective use of activities can improve the quality of online learning, promote cross-cultural communication, and develop awareness and appreciation for different cultural value systems. These activities can help students learn skills to function in the social and economic mainstream (Ramsey, William, & Vold, 2003). Sisco (1978) suggests three "R" activities to build strong relationships through asking "Who are we?", "Who am I as the instructor?", and "Why are we here?" In the virtual learning environment, students' feelings of isolation are one of the biggest barriers for communication. When students introduce themselves, it can help them get to know each other. Students can achieve this by posting self-introduction messages to the discussion board, or creating simple Web pages to include their pictures if they like. Most probably, some students already have personal Web sites to share with the class. The instructor can also post messages to show personal belief and sincerity of working together with students to build a trusting relationship with them. This is an opportunity for both the instructor and the students to establish a common understanding of the course objectives, expectations, and standards, and more importantly, to develop a virtual learning community based on mutual respect and trust. Through these activities, three types of relationships (the 3 Rs) will be built as concluded by Heimstra and Sisco (1990): relationships with classmates who help, support, and share resources with each other; relationships with the instructor, built on mutual trust, respect, and credibility, and relationships with content materials and resources of the course.

It is not an easy task to break one's belief system, or paradigm. For example, Asian students' racial bias will be a big hindrance for mutual respect. In one of the activities on Edchange Multicultural Pavilion proposed by Gorski (2005), Respect Activity, students will talk about respect from their own perspective and share with each other to learn to appreciate other's opinion even if they do not agree with it. Students learn to listen to each other, and try to understand different cultural value systems. "The community is built through an understanding of how the group perceives respect, and how they negotiate its meaning" (para. 3). People feel comfortable communicating with each other when there is mutual respect. Community members need to respect different opinions and need to respect different cultural value systems. "Respect is an acknowledgment of the inherent worth and innate rights of the individual and the collective" (Living values, para 1). Being more appreciative of diversity and less judgmental of differences creates a respectful environment in which community members are likely to help and support each other.

A cross-cultural learning community can only be sustained successfully through sharing and understanding. Sharing means more than to offer one's own values and thoughts, but also in addition, to offer the willingness to listen and understand others. To be patient in listening to other community members will greatly improve communication quality and work efficiency. Students need to detach themselves from their own value system, to be less self-defensive, to try to understand different viewpoints, and to understand people from their perspective. "Listening is often times much more productive when working to communicate effectively" (Fowler, n.d., para. 8), and listening attentively can prevent conflict and misunderstanding (Fowler, n.d.). This will give students an opportunity to increase their knowledge from students of different cultural background, and improve their personal characters as well. "Good listening is an intellectual and moral virtue of high importance," and "by means of good listening, one's own and other's character are brought to awareness, scrutinized, and revised" (Beatty, 1999, p. 281). Through sharing with each other, students "will have a better understanding and appreciation for the diversity within the group" (Gorski, 2005, para. 3).

In an online learning environment, Web technology such as online video conferencing, synchronous chat and Whiteboard, instant messaging, discussion forums, email, Web sites, and CMS can be used effectively to expand the learning community, to facilitate interaction and engagement in community activities, and to promote mutual understanding and trust.

Solution to Cultural Misunderstanding

Online communication is different from face-to-face communication. People do not receive instantaneous feedback, and the online feedback does not include the seeing of facial expressions and physical gestures, and the hearing of tones of voice. "There is great potential for conflict when people from cultures having different orientations must deal with each other" (Nisbett, 2004, p. 64). Setting up an authentic online communication forum can help the community achieve successful and quality communication. The online netiquette and policy is very important. This proactive approach can prevent possible misunderstanding. If any misunderstanding occurs, the instructor needs to play a dominant role in helping students find solutions or common ground to negotiate the situation. Misunderstandings can be caused by many variables: cultural values, religious beliefs, political views, or language expressions. Dworkin (1993) believed that religious/spiritual notions lie at the heart of our cultural disagreements. Religious and spiritual beliefs are either group-oriented or individual-oriented. Kreeft (2002) noted that "religion is the strongest force in the world, and the strongest motivation there is" (p. 28). He further states that persuasive arguments or political-legal maneuvers alone will not be sufficient to win the culture war. Students need to come to a mutual understanding that there is no winning battle for personal, religious, or spiritual belief. Cross-cultural learning environments provide us with a valuable opportunity to promote cultural awareness, and to get to know the differences existing in the world, an opportunity to understand people with a genuine and good intention. This process may involve some reconciliation and compromise, which is absolutely normal and nothing to be ashamed of.

In addition to individual belief issues, cultural "routines" may cause misunderstanding-critical incidents. People might say or do the things that would unintentionally hurt others from different cultures. For example, certain conversation topics are very common in one culture, but are regarded as offensive in a different culture. Eastern people ask others about their age, personal income, marital status, and family background as part of daily dialogue, but such questions might offend Western people as intrusions on their personal privacy. Eastern people would feel very uncomfortable or even insulted if sex or even sexually-related words are mentioned, while such language is very common in the conversation of Western people. For example, even the word "sexy," which is used as a compliment in Western culture, would imply wanton sexuality to Eastern ears. These kinds of verbal mishaps occur accidentally. It is impossible for anyone to know everything about different cultural values, belief systems, and cultural customs. We are sure to make mistakes here and there accidentally, but these need not become the barriers to cross-cultural communication. Learning to communicate effectively in a cross-cultural environment requires that the instructor and the students be willing to offer time and mutual efforts. We cannot guarantee avoiding mistakes, but as long as we are willing to open up to other cultures, willing to trust and understand people, we can help each other jump over the communication hurdles. Students need to learn how to explain the misunderstanding rather than defend themselves. One of the online activities can be used to promote mutual understanding and reduce cultural conflict. Instructors can set up a "casual chat corner" on the discussion board, and make it anonymous if necessary. Students can post the things they like to do, or they hate to do, their favorite activities within their culture, and so forth. Instructors can also create puzzle game exercises to help students identify cultural characteristics to improve their cultural awareness. This kind of activity can help loosen up the intense learning environment and make learning fun.

Nisbett (2004) analyzed the differences between Westerners and Easterners in cognition: how people think, affected by culture and philosophy. He presents examples of five domain areas in which Westerns and Easterners would do differently: *Science and Mathematics, Attention and Perception, Causal Inference, Organization of Knowledge and Reasoning.* According to Nisbett, Westerners tend to use abstract principles, rules, and logic to look at the nature and apply to all cases while the Easterners tend to contextualize the nature, pay attention to the relations and variables of the object, and apply the rules to address each individual case. "To set aside universal rules in order to accommodate particular cases seems immoral to the Westerner. To insist on the same rules for every case can seem at best obtuse and rigid to the Easterner and at worst cruel" (p. 65). This might cause conflict and result in different viewpoints from students with Eastern or Western perspective. Instructors could take advantage of the differences and lead a meaningful discussion or even debate on the different viewpoints to find out why the differences occur and how to deal with them instead of objecting them without understanding. Instructors could also help students identify the uniqueness of each perspective, compare the strength and weakness, and signify the application values in different cultural settings. This could be a very good opportunity for students to learn to look at the nature more comprehensively and learn different approaches to solve problems.

Online Education Developing Social Capital

Online education is more than just knowledge transfer via wire. It is a great venue to develop social capital on a worldwide scale. Social capital is the key to the successful development of a sustainable learning community. Even though the definitions of social capital are varied and multi-dimensional, the basic meaning is clear: the use of collective power and resources to improve and benefit society and individuals through strong relationships and active interactions. With the availability of Internet technology, the meaning and significance of social capital has been further expanded. E-learning creates "new information-sharing educational database all over the world, and it has already caused a significant cultural shift in public educational institutions" (Partow & Slusky, 2001, p. 72). The community is no longer constrained within limited geographic areas since online education is expanding to every corner of the world, so the social capital inventory is expanding worldwide as well. The successful establishment of a social network and infrastructure through online education will maximize the benefit of social capital to the global community.

Effective communication is vital to the development of social capital since social capital addresses the issues associated with human relationships in communities, neighborhoods, and groups. Social capital has indispensable significances for learning communities, especially cross-cultural online learning communities. "High social capital is crucial for creating successful virtual learning environments" (Daniel, Schwier, & McCalla, 2003, para. 5), since communities with high social capital have constant interaction that helps develop trust and reciprocity between community members (Narayan & Pritchett, 1997). In such an environment, community members are likely to share values, information and knowledge, and mutual understanding as well as to help each other. This promotes the exploration and utilization of social resources in benefiting the communities in the most efficient way. Daniel, Schwier, and McCalla (2003) defined social capital for virtual learning communities as a "common social resource that facilitates information exchange, knowledge sharing, and knowledge construction through continuous interaction, built on trust and maintained through shared understanding" (para. 14). A cross-cultural learning community can benefit from social capital in the following respects:

1. Students can build a trust-based relationship with each other to promote interaction and engagement in learning.

2.   Students can share information, personal experiences, and knowledge with each other to facilitate the achievement of learning objectives, so as to save time and resources and to improve time management skills.

3.   Students can improve their personal character, can become more considerate of the community's interest, can become more understanding, and can become less selfish.

4.   Each student can increase his or her senses of responsibility, accountability, and commitment.

5.   Students can establish mutual understanding and can share common interests among cultures through bonding, bridging, and linking (Woolcock, 1998).

6.   Students can increase their work efficiency and can save resources through well-coordinated cooperation.

Developing social capital directly involves the relationship and interaction of each individual within the community. The vital elements for a sustainable community are all related to each individual's personal character, his or her understanding of shared trust, norms and values, and commitment and accountability to the community. Bourdieu (1996) considers social capital to be an attribute of an *individual in a social context*. The four major components of social capital as accentuated by Nahapiet and Ghoshal (1998) are: trust, norms, obligations, and identification. In order to take full advantage of social capital and to sustain the learning community, online community members should:

1.   Learn to trust each other, be open with each other, and share true thoughts with community members. Only in a safe and non-threatening environment can students be more creative and contributory and be willing to engage in learning activities. Trust is the central variable (Daniel, Schwier, & McCalla, 2003).

2.   Learn to understand different value systems; self-interest and the formation of cliques sometimes create barriers to developing an extended community. People who have the same beliefs and interests tend to tie together to protect these beliefs and interests while sacrificing justice and fairness. In an online learning environment, community members could be from any part of the world with varying political, religious, and cultural values, so if everyone tries to fight for his or her own righteousness, no one can benefit from social capital.

3.   Learn to be responsible and committed; be responsible for individual behavior, for shared norms, and for values. The trust-based reciprocal relationship depends on the commitment of each community member. In any group-learning project, each member should take proactive action on his or her own part to ensure the quality of the project.

4.   Learn to be independent, dependent, and interdependent in a community learning environment. Peer support in community learning is very important. Community members need to work collaboratively and need to be interdependent on each member's experiences, best practice, and knowledge to achieve the best learning results.

Conclusion

This chapter has discussed the issues related to the designing of online learning in a cross-cultural environment. The online education is becoming diverse and continually changing with the dynamic student body from all over the world. The diversity and changes have posed challenges to traditional educational systems on curriculum development and instructional delivery. The effective design of curriculum and online instruction to include cross-cultural diversity become the only solution to improve the quality of online education. Online education is not only a channel for students to learn new knowledge, but it also bridges the gaps of cross-cultural awareness and understanding. A cross-cultural learning community sets up an exemplary model to promote global communication and world peace based on mutual trust and respect. It establishes the worldwide network for the development of social capital to benefit mankind. "In this shrinking globe of ours, as East and West come closer, many ancient civilizations will rub together in a direct fashion never seen before in human history" and "the future lies in the fusion of civilization" (Mahbunani, 2002, pp. 16-17).

References

Abishev, K. (2003, August 8-9). *On meaning of human being in the world.* Paper presented at the 2003 International Conference on The Dialogue of Cultural Traditions: Global Perspective. Retrieved on September 30, 2005, from http://www.crvp.org/conf/Istanbul/abstracts/Kazhimurat%20Abishev.htm

Anomymous (2003, April 17). *Racism in China.* Retrieved on September 23, 2005, from http://app1.chinadaily.com.cn/star/2003/0417/cu18-1.html

Australian Flexible Learning Framework. (2005-2006). *Supporting flexible learning opportunities.* Retrieved on June 15, 2005, from http://flexiblelearning.net.au

Azimi, A. (1998, October-December). Culture, family, school: Where does East meets West? An educational model. *Lemar-Aftaab, 1*(6). Retrieved on September 18, 2005, from http://www.afghanmagazine.com/oct98/articles/education.html

Bacon, N. (2004, summer). From outside in: How out-of-school programs enrich student learning. *New Horizons for Learning, X*(3). Retrieved on September 28, 2005, from http://www.newhorizons.org/strategies/character/bacon.htm

Banks, J. (1993). Multicultural education: Development, dimensions, and challenges. *Phi Delta Kappan, 75*(1), 20.

Bannon, L. J. (1995). Issues in computer-supported collaborative learning. In C. O'Malley (Ed.), *Computer supported collaborative learning* (pp. 267-281). Berlin: Springer-Verlag.

Barrett, H. (2000). Create your own electronic portfolio. *Learning & Leading with Technology, 27*(7), 14-21

Beatty, J. (1999). Good listening. *Educational Theory, 49*(3), 281-298.

Beck, S. (2000). *Confucianism and the Chinese scholastic system*. Retrieved on June 8, 2005, from http://www.csupomona.edu/~plin/ls201/confucian2.html

Bourdieu, P. (1996). On the family as a realized category. *Theory, Culture & Society, 13*(1), 19-26.

Brookfield, S. D. (1990). *The skillful teacher*. San Francisco: Jossey-Bass.

Burke, K. (1999). *How to assess authentic learning*. Arlington Heights, IL: Skylight Professional Development.

Chomsky, N. (1971). *Human nature: Justice versus power*. Retrieved on September 30, 2005, from http://www.chomsky.info/debates/1971xxxx.htm

Chu, L. (2005, March 7). American, Asian schools hold different education standards. Message posted to *The Campanile*. Retrieved on September 30, 2005, from http://voice.paly.net/view_story.php?id=2692

Chute, A. G., & Shatzer, L. S. (1995). Designing for international teletraining. *Adult Learning, 7*(1), 20-21.

Daniel, B., Schwier, R., & McCalla, G. (2003). Social capital in virtual learning communities and distributed communities of practice. *Canadian Journal of Learning and Technology, 29*(3). Retrieved on June, 19, 2005, from http://www.cjlt.ca/content/vol29.3/cjlt29-3_art7.html

Danielson, C., & Abrutyn, L. (1997). *An introduction to using portfolios in the classroom*. Alexandria, VA: Association for Supervision and Curriculum Development.

Dworkin, R. (1993). *Life's dominion: An argument about abortion, euthanasia, and individual freedom*. New York: Vintage.

Edelson, P., & Pittman, V. (2001). *E-learning in the United States: New directions and opportunities for university continuing education*. Retrieved on September, 16, 2005, from http://www.sunysb.edu/spd/dean_papers/newdelhi.pdf

Fisher, R. (2003). Racism in China. *Shanghai Star*. Retrieved on September 23, 2005, from http://app1.chinadaily.com.cn/star/2003/0417/cu18-1.html

Fowler, K. (n. d.). *Communication in your organization*. Retrieved on February, 16, 2005, from http://www.mindtools.com/CommSkll/CommunicatingInAnOrganization.htm

Freedman, K., & Liu, M. (1996). The importance of computer experience, learning processes, and communication patterns in multicultural networking. *Educational Technology Research and Development, 44*(1), 43-59.

Gardner, H. (1993). *Multiple intelligences: The theory in practice*. New York: Basic.

Gay, G. (1990). Achieving educational equality through curriculum desegregation. *Phi Delta Kappan, 72*(1), 61-62.

George Institute of Technology. (n.d.). *Online learning: What to assess and what tools to use*. Retrieved on September 27, 2005, from http://www.assessment.gatech.edu/eReports/slide_shows/Online_Learning_Assessment.pdf

Gorski, P. C. (2005). *Awareness activities: Getting started – respect activity*. Retrieved on June 19, 2005, from http://www.edchange.org/multicultural/activities/activity1.html

Grant, C. A. (1978). Education that is multicultural: Isn't that what we mean? *Journal of Teacher Education, 29*(1), 45-49.

Gudykunst, W. B., & Matsumoto, Y. (1996). Cross-cultural variability of communication in personal relationships. In W. B. Gudykunst, S. Ting-Toomey, & T. Nishida (Eds.), Communication in personal relationships across cultures (pp. 57-77). Thousand Oaks, CA: Sage.

Harasim, L. (1989). On-line education: A new domain. In R. Mason & A. R. Kaye (Eds.), *Mindweave: Communication, computers and distance education* (pp. 50-62). Oxford, UK: Pergamon Press.

Hiemstra, R. (Ed.). (1991). *Create environments for effective adult learning.* San Francisco: Jossey-Bass.

Hiemstra, R., & Sisco, B. (1990). *Individualizing instruction: Making learning personal, empowering, and successful.* San Francisco: Jossey-Bass.

Jaffee, D. (2001). Asynchronous learning: Technology and pedagogical strategy in a distance learning course. *Teaching Sociology, 25*(4), 262-277.

Kaneco, M. (2004, December 11-12). *Education-economy link in Japan—"J-mode".* Paper presented at the 3rd International Symposium on Educational Policy and Reform in a Global Age Cross-Cultural Perspectives. Retrieved on September 20, 2005, from http://www.p.u-tokyo.ac.jp/coe/sympopaper/kaneko2004in3.pdf

Kim, K. J., & Bonk, C. J. (2002). Cross-cultural comparisons of online collaboration. *Journal of Computer-Mediated Communications, 8*(1). Retrieved on March 21, 2005, from http://www.ascusc.org/jcmc/vol8/issue1/kimandbonk.html

Knowles, M. S. (1980). *The modern practice of adult education: From pedagogy to andragogy (Rev. ed.).* New York: Cambridge University Press.

Kreeft, P. (2002). *How to win the culture war: A Christian battle plan for society in crisis.* Downers Grove, IL: InterVarsity Press.

Kroeber, A., & Kluckholm, C. (1952). Culture: A critical review of concepts and definitions. *Papers of the Peabody Museum of American Archeology and Ethnology, 47*(1), 1-223.

Kuhn, T. S. (1970). *The structure of scientific revolutions* (2nd ed.). Chicago: University of Chicago Press.

Kuwahara, K. (2005, November 10-11). *Understanding Asian ESL students: Translating school cultures.* Paper presented at the California 2005 CATESOL State Conference. Retrieved December 10, 2005, from http://www.catesol.org/Kuwahara.pdf

Lee, A. (1989). A socio-cultural framework for the assessment of Chinese children with special needs. *Topics in Language Disorders, 9*(3), 38-44.

Levine, A., Oded, B., Connor, U., & Asons, I. (2002). Variation in EFL-ESL peer response. *TESL-EJ. Teaching English as a Second or Foreign Language 6,* 3.

Liang, A., & McQueen, R. J. (1999). Computer assisted adult interactive learning in a multi-cultural environment. *Adult Learning, 11*(1), 26-29.

Liu, J. (2001). *Asian students' classroom communication patterns in U.S. universities.* Westport, CT: Ablex Publishing.

Living values. (n.d.). Retrieved on June 21, 2005, from http://www.livingvalues.net/values/respect.htm and http://www.livingvalues.net/values/honesty.htm

Luther College (2003). *Valuing diversity: Promoting educational excellence—A strategic plan for the Luther Diversity Center.* Retrieved on September 28, 2005, from http://diversity.luther.edu/strategic_plan/plan/

Mahbubani, K. (2002). *Can Asians think: Understanding the divide between East and West.* Vermont, Southroyalton: Steerforth Press

McIsaac, M. S., & Gunawardena, C. N. (1996). Distance education. In D. H. Jonassen (Ed.), *Handbook of research for educational communications and technology* (pp. 403-437). New York: Macmillan.

Mezirow, J. (1978). Perspective transformation. *Adult Education, 1978*(28), 100-110.

Murrell, P. (1990). Making uncommon sense: Critical revisioning professional knowledge about diverse cultural perspectives in teacher education. In M. Diez (Ed.). *Proceedings of the Fourth National Forum of the Association of Independent Liberal Arts Colleges for Teacher Education* (pp. 47-54). Milwaukee, WI: Alverno College.

Nahapiet, J., & Ghoshal, S. (1998). Social capital, intellectual capital, and the organizational advantage. *Academy of Management Review, 23*(2). In E. Lesser (Ed.), *Knowledge and social capital: Foundations and applications* (pp. 119-158). Boston: Butterworth-Heinemann.

Narayan, D., & Pritchett, L. (1997). *Cents and sociability: Household income and social capital in rural Tanzania.* Washington, DC: World Bank.

National Council for Accreditation of Teacher Education. (1977). *Standards for the accreditation of teacher education.* Washington, DC.

Niebuhr, R. (1952). *The irony of American history.* New York: Charles Scribner's Sons.

Nisbett, R. (2004). *The geography of thought.* New York: Simon & Schuster.

Oliva, P. (2001). *Developing the curriculum* (5th ed.). New York: Priscilla McGeehon.

Oxford, L., & Burry-Stock, A. (1995). Assessing the use of language learning strategies worldwide with ESL/EFL. *Strategy Inventory for Language Learning (SILL) System, 23*(2), 153-175.

Partow, P., & Slusky, L. (2001). Distance learning as e-commence. *USDLA Journal, 15*(10), 70-77

Phinney, J. S. (1996). When we talk about American ethnic groups, what do we mean? *American Psychologist, 51,* 171-183.

Rackl, K. (2002). *Repeated insincerity ruins daily greetings.* Retrieved on September 18, 2005, from http://www.ithaca.edu/ithacan/articles/0201/24/opinion/1repeated_ins.htm

Ramsey, P. G., Williams, L. R., & Vold, E. B. (2003). *Multicultural education: A source book* (2nd ed.). New York: RoutledgeFalmer.

Riley, R. (2000). *The growing importance of international education.* Retrieved on September 28, 2005, from http://www.aacc.nche.edu/Content/NavigationMenu/ResourceCenter/Services/International/The_Growing_Importance_of_International_Education.htm

Salmon, G. (2000). *E-moderating: Teaching and learning online.* London: Sterling

Shen, W., & Mo, W. (n.d.). *Reaching out to their cultures — Building communication with Asian American families.* Retrieved on September 20, 2005, from http://www.ncela.gwu.edu/pathways/asian/cultures.htm

Sisco, B. R. (1987). Adult learning process. In K. E. Plank (Ed.), *Mountain states journeyman and apprentice instructor training seminar curriculum manual* (2nd ed.). Laramie: University of Wyoming Press.

Slavin, R. E. (1995). Cooperative learning and intergroup relations. In J. A. Banks & C. A. M. Banks (Eds.), *Handbook of research on multicultural education* (pp. 628-634). New York: Macmillan.

Sue, W., & Kirk, A. (1972). Psychological characteristics of Chinese-American students. *Journal of Counseling Psychology, 19,* 471-478.

Szykulski, D. (2003). Racism in China. *Shanghai Star.* Retrieved on September 23, 2005, from http://app1.chinadaily.com.cn/star/2003/0417/cu18-1.html

Thattai, D. (2001). A history of public education in the United States. *Journal of Literacy and Education in Developing Societies, 11.* Retrieved on September 26, 2005, from http://www.servintfree.net/~aidmn-ejournal/publications/2001-11/PublicEducationInTheUnitedStates.html

Towson University. (n.d.). *The intersection of race, gender, and class: An overview and guide to teaching.* Retrieved on September 26, 2005, from http://www.cofc.edu/~winfield/socy354/intersections.html

Tsui, A. B. M. (1996). Reticence and anxiety in second language learning. In K. M. Bailey & D. Nunan (Eds.), *Voices from the language classroom* (pp. 145-167). New York: Cambridge University Press.

Veenman, S., Denessen, E., Akker, A., & Rijt, J. (2005). Effects of a cooperative learning program on the elaborations of students during help seeking and help giving. *American Educational Research Journal, 42,* 115-151.

Winfield, I. (n.d.). *The intersection of race, gender, and class: An overview and guide to teaching.* Retrieved September 26, 2005, from http://www.cofc.edu/~winfield/socy354/intersections.html

Woolcock, M. (1998). Social capital and economic development: Toward a theoretical synthesis and policy framework. *Theory and Society, 27*(2), 151-208.

Yu, H. (2003). Racism in China. *Shanghai Star.* Retrieved on September 23, 2005, from http://app1.chinadaily.com.cn/star/2003/0417/cu18-1.html

Zeichner, K. (1992). *NCRTL Special Report: Educating teachers for cultural diversity.* East Lansing: Michigan State University.

Chapter IV

African Education Perspectives on Culture and E-Learning Convergence

Wanjira Kinuthia
Georgia State University, USA

Abstract

Culture affects individuals' responses to learning and instruction. It also influences the acceptance, use, and impact of e-learning environments because instructional approaches are entrenched in a context of beliefs, expectations, and values within the context of its application. Advances in e-learning are prompting a debate as to whether or not the tools and technologies are culturally neutral, inclusive, and representative. The aim of this chapter is to provide a background for understanding the links between cultural content and context and e-learning. The discussion relates instruction to technology in the face of dynamic socio-cultural issues and changing instructional systems. In doing so, challenges and exemplars from the African perspective are presented.

Introduction

One of the purposes of e-learning is to emerge learners into a culture where they are introduced to technology in order to understand it and to be able to participate in it at some level. Technology stands alongside ways that culture is represented, and with recent and rapid advancements in e-learning technologies and paradigms, the debate on culturally-appropriate instructional development continues. One argument proposes that e-learning tools are all encompassing, while another perspective maintains that there are many unresolved cultural issues in the design and delivery of instruction. For example, the delivery medium shapes the meaning of the message depending on where it is conveyed (Chen, Mashhadi, Ang, & Harkrider, 2000).

The discussion that follows provides an introspective of Africa's complex cultural structures, instructional implications of e-learning, and challenges faced when integrating e-learning within culturally-specific content and nuances. It is not the intent of this chapter to discount the role of inherited or formal instructional models in Africa. Rather, the purpose is twofold: (1) to provide a conceptual framework for understanding the links between different cultural contents and contexts and the development of e-learning; and (2) to rationalize the relevance of e-learning in these socio-cultural contexts.

The chapter is organized thus: First, the concepts of culture and e-learning are presented based on their usage herein. Next, a theoretical base for e-learning is presented followed by a discussion of relevance, complexities, and applications in both general and specific socio-cultural contexts. This forms a basis for the section on recommendations and trends. The chapter is written from the perspective that culture is dynamic and that there is no single all-encompassing model that ensures design of total culturally-inclusive and sensitive learning environments. It should be noted that while a persuasive argument for convergence of e-learning in cultural contexts is presented, it is conceded that doing so is not a seamless process. It is, however, argued that increasing awareness of diverse cultural aspects is crucial to making instructional decisions. Moreover, given that culture is a dynamic phenomenon, it is important to approach this chapter from both historical and current situational perspectives.

Culture and E-Learning: Definitions and Complexities

Defining Culture in Instruction

Culture as noted by Collis (1999) influences the acceptance, use of, and impact on instructional resources. From anthropological, sociological, and educational perspectives, the term "culture" is broadly viewed as the beliefs, philosophies, traditions, values, perceptions, norms, customs, arts, history, experiences, and patterns by individuals and groups (Chen et al., 2000, p. 200; Collis, 1999, p. 204). The groups may be identified by race, age, ethnicity, language, national origin, religion, or other social categories. This warrants the understanding of learners, their learning styles, and perception of learning. The very definition of culture, therefore, suggests that members of a group have the latitude to transform their environment. In doing so, they use sets of tools that they create, and disseminate knowledge in their own unique way.

For the purposes of this discussion, the definitions by Collis (1999, p. 204) and Mabawonku (2003, p. 118) are adopted. Mabawonku refers to culture as the definitive, dynamic purposes and the tools (values, ethics, rules, knowledge systems) that are developed to attain the group goals. The groups are characterized by their cultural products (skills, artifacts, and technology). Collis classifies the cultural variables that interact and influence each other on four levels: societal, personal, organizational, and disciplinary. Additionally, culture influences instruction at five levels: institutional, instructional content, instructors, and learners. It is conceded in this article that the definition of culture is broad and does not fit all cultural groups.

A discussion of culture is incomplete without mention of indigenous knowledge, which is the unique, traditional, local knowledge that is part of the cultural heritage and histories used to preserve a way of life and serve social interests. These knowledge forms are cumulative and represent generations of experiences (Dei, 2000, p. 72; Grenier, 1998, p. 1). Almost 300 million indigenous peoples live in over 70 countries and represent 4% of the world's population. In Africa, this number accounts for 30 million nomadic peoples. Other statistics estimate that there are 14.2 million indigenous people in Africa (Education International, 2005, para. 4; Maybury-Lewis, 2002, pp. 8-10). It should, however, be noted that Africa, by its sheer size and nature, has too many unique and potential ethnicities, indigenes, and cultural groups. Moreover, the concept of "indigenous" is complicated and identities are too tangled. Thus, indigenous knowledge is cultural knowledge in its broadest form and is pertinent to people's understanding of themselves, their world, and the influence on education (Dei, 2000).

Historical and Contemporary Influences in Education

Although some cultural features are visible in instructional systems, the transfer of knowledge has been influenced by historical events and economics constraints, and foreign dependencies that seek "advancement" but fail to consider the contexts in which they are transplanted. This brings us to a discussion of the history of colonization, inherited education models, and their effect on instruction. There are similarities in the way that formal education systems expanded within Africa in that the same principles were exported through the hegemony of colonial relationships in the 19th century. Following World War II, there was tremendous economic expansion that translated to educational expansion (Morrison, 1995). However, the motives were political, and education was regarded as a social overhead rather than as an investment (Mammo, 1999). Over time, indigenous knowledge has been replaced by formal education and technology. Ultimately the same educational principles of education now exist between African and Western countries, with the difference being the timing of their emergence as dictated by political and economic conditions (Morrison, 1995).

Today primary and secondary education in post-colonial Africa has spread considerably, although higher education opportunities are still limited (Dei, 2001). Moreover, some groups have been excluded from participation, for example, the Maasai of Kenya and Tanzania, the San of Southern Africa, and the Efe of Central Africa (Maybury-Lewis, 2002). Education International (2005) reports that indigenous communities rank at the bottom of indicators of educational achievement, a phenomenon further complicated by attempts to localize the relevance of instruction and organizing knowledge. As part of its commitment to promote education for all (EFA), Education International (2005) is raising awareness about critical education issues for Indigenous Peoples. Educational International (2005) and Semali (1999) report on the factors that have impeded access to quality education as follows:

- Lack of retention and achievement efforts for indigenous learners
- Culturally-inappropriate testing and labeling of indigenous learners
- Racial and economic segregation in schools and society
- Discrimination against indigenous communities in public spending
- Failure to incorporate indigenous instructional methodologies
- Lack of resources and appropriate curriculum to support indigenous education programs
- Limited involvement of indigenous peoples in curriculum and program development
- Insufficient effort to teach non-indigenous communities about indigenous cultures
- Lack of political motivation
- Planning on macro levels that ignore local needs
- Inappropriate research methods

Trends in Technology Adoption

The merge between instruction and culture is often overlooked, and challenges are encountered in its facilitation, recognition, and validation for several reasons: (1) an underlying fear that introduction of cultural content is potentially identifiable with the dominant group; (2) recognition that groups with differing opinions can create conflict; (3) acknowledgment that introduced systems of education may not allow for cultural differences; and; (4) the limits of oral knowledge transition to literate forms. Conflicts arise when approaches, standards, and values among different groups differ, and those who resist change are ultimately subordinated economically, politically, and socially. This has in part been brought on by socio-cultural differences that underlie a lack of consensus as to what constitutes knowledge (Semali & Kincheloe, 1999). Using cases in Ethiopia, Ghana, Nigeria, and Tanzania, Dei (2000), Lewis (2000), Mammo (1999), and Semali (1999) explore the obstacles that have resulted from lack of local capacity to assimilate, adapt, and/or create technology and why these knowledge structures have not been systemically incorporated or taught in formal settings.

Increasingly as noted by McLoughlin (1999), technologies are being described as cognitive tools that transform, augment, and support engagement among learners. This creates many variables that impact design processes. Therefore, to successfully integrate e-learning, it is important to understand the history and perception of technology in instruction in the African context. For the purposes of this discussion, e-learning refers to the application of new information and communication technologies (ICT) to deliver instruction. It ranges from the use of software such as television, video, CD-ROM, to learning management systems that utilize email, discussion forums, and the Internet to deliver distance learning, instructor-led, or computer based instruction. E-learning utilizes networks for delivery, interaction, and facilitation, and can be either synchronous or asynchronous (Klein & Ware, 2003). When introduced to indigenous populations, it bring along mass media, popular culture, and global languages such as English, which can potentially class with local cultures. Likewise, the same technologies provide them with new tools that can be used to preserve and promote their language and culture (Liberman, 2003).

Depending on availability and access, perceived benefit, and economic capacity, many countries in Africa have attempted to take advantage of new technologies. For instance, in the Zimbabwe case discussed by Lewis (2000), technology education assumed new status after independence, but has taken on different names at different times and phases. However, a challenge facing education systems is the discord between efficient and effective utilization of existing ICT and the ever-growing demand for more and better access to education. While its potential is well acknowledged, limited infrastructure, technological capacity, funding and sustainability of resources, and human resources and expertise is limited. For many, this presents the equity dilemma that translates to the so-called "technology gap" or "digital divide" (Lewis, 2000, p. 166; Sonaike, 2004, p. 41). Poor infrastructure, regulatory policies and frameworks, and unequal distribution have also subsequently resulted in inadequate access to affordable telephones, broadcasting, computers, and the Internet.

The International Telecommunications Union (ITU) (2005) estimates that the total population in Africa was 825.45 million in 2003 and that there were 9.98 million Internet users on 9.45 million computers in 2004. The figures rose to 12.8 million and 10.8 million, respectively, in 2003. A report in Mmegi Business Week (September 8, 2005), for instance, reports that Africa's cell phone industry is booming, with subscriber numbers expected to hit 100 million by the end of the 2005, up from 40 million in 2002. While this is arguably one of the continent's biggest business success stories, there are less than one in 10 people own a phone and even fewer with access to the Internet.

Other issues result from reliability of the equipment. Vecchiatto (2004), for instance, discusses the issue of computer dumping in Africa, noting that United Nations Education, Scientific, and Cultural Organization (UNESCO) statistics indicate that about 50% of the 7.5 million computers in Africa could be second-hand. These resources are usually donated by charity organizations and companies wishing to replace equipment or obtain tax breaks. While many of the resources may be unreliable, yet they are the reality because it helps to keep the costs down.

Contextualizing Culture in Instruction and E-Learning

McLoughlin and Oliver (2000, p. 61) ask a pertinent question: "Is cultural pluralism possible in instructional design?" In truth, culture permeates learning, and during the design process, there needs to be a dialog on the socio-cultural facets of task design, communication, problem solving, and organization of information to meet the needs of diverse learners. Instruction that acknowledges and incorporates multiple cultural perspectives regardless of the instructional content may thus qualify as culturally pluralistic. Paradoxically, it can also be argued that the uniqueness of indigenous knowledge in a particular culture does not necessarily imply that everyone who belongs to that culture shares the same knowledge base, and to blend local knowledge into formal education fallaciously assumes that the bodies of knowledge are easily definable and ready for extraction and incorporation (Semali, 1999).

Dilemmas in Incorporating E-Learning

One of the complexities of e-learning is that it is often inappropriately transferred without sufficient recognition of the recipient's cultural setting (Chen et al., 2000). Kearsley (1990) points out that those resources that are designed without instructional strategies in mind are less likely to be culturally inclusive, flexible, and modifiable, and are consequently less successful. Moreover, an e-learning environment that is adaptable to many contexts is more likely to be accepted. Musoni (2005) proposes use of ICT in all stages of education, training, and human resources development. This would ensure that ICT policy in the education sector would go a long way in ensuring the roadmap for the development of ICT teaching and learning programs for the continent's institutions of learning.

E-learning casts learners in particular roles and re-organizes the framework for learning with access to resources. It is important to note that while members of a culture may develop a technology, that technology in turn shapes the users. Challenges also arise when the core pedagogical values in one culture are inappropriate in another. For instance, electronic performance support systems (EPSS) are often designed based on the customs and requirements of a particular culture or organization. In order to be successfully adopted in other settings, the EPSS requires modification of technical and social facilities for successful adoption in another culture (Collis, 1999; Kearsley, 1995).

While the above-mentioned aspects may be intended to enhance support or communication, design features may inadvertently be understood. In response to emerging post-apartheid governance and policy in South Africa, Butcher (2004) reports on initiatives in Cape Town to identify the needs regarding the ICT Empowerment Charter. The charter intends to address the impact of historical imbalances in South Africa by promoting the transformation of the ICT sector. Several areas have been identified, including language as a factor in achieving empowerment. One aim is to acknowledge the impact of different cultures and languages as a barrier to the achievement of economic empowerment and bridging the digital divide.

Incorporating E-Learning

Overarching Approaches

Henderson (1996) cautions against using educational paradigms that attempt to incorporate diverse cultural groups at the expense of a meaningful learning experience. First, she discusses inclusive curriculum that imports the social, cultural, and historical perspectives of different cultural groups, yet undermines the dominant culture. Next, she examines the inverted curriculum paradigm that incorporates learners' cultural aspects, but fails to provide them with mainstream cultural experiences. She also talks of the culturally uni-dimensional paradigm which excludes cultural diversity with the assumption that all learners have the same educational experiences. To counter these dilemmas, Henderson proposes a *multiple cultures model* of instructional design, one that is characterized by multiple cultural realities, variability, and flexibility.

Kearsley (1990) outlines a three-step approach for developing technology-enhanced learning environments: First, cultural conversion is necessary to customize the content, instructional strategy, or user interface so as to fit different culture. The extent of changes will depend largely on the type of e-learning. Next, the content may have to be translated into another language. Finally, the instruction may have to be localized to adapt it to the needs of a particular culture. These three steps all require collaboration with content and technical experts as well as the prospective users.

A fundamental aspect of developing learning materials is ensuring appropriate design from the onset (Kearsley, 1990). However, many design aspects are not culturally neutral; color for instance, may have religious or political significance in some cultures. Additionally, references to gender roles or political and religious positions will most likely be contextual. Perhaps the most important measure of cultural strength is the use of local language, and knowledge of these languages offers more economic opportunities. Unfortunately, little emphasis is often placed in passing down traditional language (Lieberman, 2003). Many aspects of language and communication such as humor and idioms are also culturally relative or specific. This means that interface and content design should take into consideration the content layout, menus, images, color, symbols, and text layout because these elements influence the intended messages. In response to these nuances, there are several initiatives aimed at localizing e-learning resources.

In some cultures individual achievement is valued, but in most African cultures, team participation and consensus is valued just as much, if not more (Semali, 1999) Therefore, instructional strategies that include individualized computer-based drill and practice or tutorials in collaborative learning environments may be less ineffective, while activities that require inquiry-based collaboration may be better received.

Guiding Questions and Recommendations

To guide the instructional design process it is helpful to address the questions by posed by McLoughlin and Oliver (2000):

- Does the instruction address differences in learning styles of the learners?
- Is the course culturally biased, and does the instruction need to be revised to incorporate the learners?
- Does the instruction incorporate the use of culturally-sensitive intervention strategies such as teaching and learning strategies, assessment, collaboration, and conflict resolution?
- Does the course design encourage meaningful communication?
- Does the course design allow for opportunities for establishing cross-cultural collaboration?
- Does the course design identify strategies that optimize cultural diversity and sensitivity of the learners?

The use of e-learning in any society reflects the prevailing attitudes about technology. In Africa where access to technology is limited, there is less motivation to adopt e-learning. A design-principles checklist, as suggested by Collis (1999) and McLoughlin and Oliver (2000), is also helpful in the development of culturally-inclusive micro-level e-learning:

- Adopting epistemologies that support multiple perspectives.
- Developing authentic learning activities that build on existing knowledge, values, and skills of learners.
- Offering an assortment of tools that can be combined for different communication modes.
- Developing flexible tasks and tools that include shared work space discussion, and other collaborative tools.
- Providing instructional support within and outside of the learning community.
- Assigning responsive student roles and responsibilities.
- Providing flexibility in learning goals, outcomes, and assessment modes.
- Planning for flexibility and adaptation, hence allowing a variety of supplementary media and resources.
- Designing courses with a variety of roles for both instructors and learners, and being realistic about what they can and will accomplish.
- Designing courses so that use of e-learning materials is minimally impeded by poor infrastructure.
- Designing with organizational flexibility such that courses of different lengths, offered at a variety of times, and with different types and levels of prerequisites and assessment can be supported.

To help learners acquire critical thinking skills, educators should: (1) address cultural inclusion where learners are exposed to processes that acknowledge the sources of empowerment accomplished through open discussions with other learners, guest speakers, and access to resources; (2) seek advocacy and support networks to promote local educators; (3) address pertinent issues at a political level that define guiding principles, objectives, goals, action plans, and resources; and (4) seek an understanding of probable outcomes, and change agents responsible for executing action plans must also be considered (McLoughlin & Oliver, 2000).

Pedagogical, instructional, and communicative approaches to synthesizing different knowledge structures should allow learners to produce and control knowledge about themselves and their communities (Semali, 1999). This necessitates a systemic change process; one that incorporates synthesized, multiple, collective, and collaborative dimensions of knowledge when considering the possibility, viability, and desirability of e-learning, it is important to: (1) develop curriculum that respects and promotes cultural values, philosophies, and ideologies; (2) establish fair and equal evaluation and assessment; (3) establish parameters and ethics of research in instruction and culture; and (4) adopt education standards that account for cultural differences.

Current and Future E-Learning Trends

Generally, access, interconnectivity, immediacy, and interactivity of e-learning resources are limited in most learning contexts, yet they are all integral elements in the technology adoption process. In countries such as Zimbabwe and Tanzania, radio is still a primary medium in non-formal instruction and distance education (Arias & Clark, 2004). However, there are various examples of successful integration of e-learning that is delivered via a variety of other media. These learning environments take advantage of Web resources and CD-ROM that are used to present cultural information and chat rooms in indigenous languages (Lieberman, 2003).

The University of Benin, Nigeria, holds a digital festival organized by Broadband Technologies©, Intel©, and Microsoft© (Ikhemuemhe, 2004). The festival is aimed at demonstrating e-learning and is intended to be an annual ICT festival which would rotate amongst educational institutions of higher learning across Nigeria. Kenyatta University in Kenya is another example of such efforts; it houses the African Virtual University, as well as the Culture Village, an outfit that blends Western and local cultures. Here, learners are presented with opportunities to explore both technical and cultural dimensions.

Mosha (1999) presents the example of how the Chagga community of Tanzania has assimilated learning opportunities into everyday interaction and teachable moments. By describing the instructional process and its fundamental virtues, Mosha proposes that introduced instructional systems should give equal emphasis to both technical and cultural knowledge to attain holistic status. In the case of Senegal presented by Sylla (2004), a discussion revolves around an initiative that uses new technologies to provide pastoralists in the Sahel with information about resources in the transhumance zones, and to track and monitor the course followed by selected shepherds and their flocks from one point to another in the forestry-pasture zone in order to develop livestock production, and to encourage environmental sustainability. However, the setbacks of the project in these rural areas include low literacy rates, network failures, and power outages, owing to dependency on solar energy, and lack of equipment maintenance.

The Association for Progressive Communications, for instance, reports on the Aid Lands Information Network—Eastern Africa (ALIN-EA), which successfully completed a one-year pilot phase of the Open Knowledge Network (OKN) East Africa project in 2004. OKN is a global initiative linking marginalized communities and facilitating information sharing through ICT, and it aims at promoting the creation and exchange of local content by local people in local languages. It provides a forum for rural people to network and share ideas on indigenous practices in agriculture, health, nutrition, and general development-related information.

The challenges of implementing e-learning interventions in Africa span a culture of participation, information sharing, and open discussion that should not be assumed to exist in all settings. Change often involves a "top-down" approach making commitment to change or adopting new procedures a challenge to potential users (Arias & Clark, 2004). Using the bottom-up approach of knowledge sharing, the network encourages documentation and dissemination of local knowledge beyond the precincts of community boundaries. Although most of the problems have been solved, the main challenges faced during the piloting phase were software and technical issues, inadequate writing skills, lack of e-mail and Internet facilities, inadequate awareness creation and dissemination strategies.

As noted by Benjamin (2000), there has been increased interest in the use of telecenters as a means of addressing limited access to ICT throughout the continent. With more than 9000, Senegal has the largest number of telecenters. Other services are offered by Africa Online, with a great presence in Kenya and Ghana. The centers offer e-mail, Internet, fax, photocopying, printing, and telecommunication services. Other projects are donor-funded; for example, the Nakaseke Multipurpose Community Telecenter (MCT) in Uganda and the International Development Research Centre (IDRC) funded projects in Mozambique.

The Balancing Act News Update (2004, September) reports on the LugandaICT Translations, a Ugandan-based organization, launched the first ever-indigenous local language software in Uganda. It is projected that the software in Luganda, a dialect spoken by over 80% of Ugandans, will be potentially used by over 50% of the country, especially in rural areas where there is a shortage of information access and low literacy levels. This software, named Kayungirizi Web browser, is available for download from the Internet, making it easier for local communities to surf the Internet and access information on health, agriculture, education, and news.

The Open Swahili Localization Project (Kilinux) is a similar Swahili program based in Tanzania. The organization has launched Jambo OpenOffice, a free package similar to Microsoft© Office program. Kiswahili is spoken by an estimated 100 million people in East Africa, of whom 10% have access to computers (Phomeah, 2004). The aim of the project is to avail computers at grass-roots levels, primary schools, and universities. Phombeah (2004) also discusses the rollout of Swahili Microsoft© products, in response to complaints that young people in Eastern Africa are losing their native tongues. The Microsoft© programs are also aimed at encouraging literacy campaigns and attracting more computer users. Although the different Swahili dialects pose a challenge, other languages are in the process of being customized, for example Hausa, Yoruba, and Amharic. This initiative follows the South African translation of computer software into indigenous South African languages (REF).

A report in the IT Web (January 20, 2005) discusses the collaboration between Partners in Learning (PiL) and Microsoft©. The two organizations are working together to bring technology into the classroom in ways that are locally relevant. The implementation framework of PiL begins by addressing the technological skills of teachers and educators. Once they have the requisite skills, they in turn will lead training courses and enhance the experiences had by their students.

Interest in cultural knowledge has grown beyond anthropological documentation. However, as pointed out by McLoughlin (1999), little research is available on the implications of cultural inclusivity in instructional design. Research should, however, set out to make connections between local people's understandings and practices and those of outside researchers (Grenier, 1998). Research should also aim to contribute to long-term positive change and promote cultural inclusivity, calling for appropriate research approaches that recognize socio-cultural constraints (Sillitoe, 1998). Information sharing and mutual decision-making is crucial to rationalizing what research may have to offer; otherwise, local participation is likely to have limited impact. Grenier (1998) and Sillitoe (1998) best summarize it when they state that facilitating meaningful communication between e-learning researchers and local cultural groups encourages reciprocal flow of ideas and contextualizes cognitive, social, cultural, and pedagogical elements in instruction.

Conclusion

Learning is the appropriation of cultural practices and the development of an identity within those practices. Likewise, knowledge and learning are grounded in historical, cultural, and social frameworks where interpretation and perceptions vary according to the learner's context. E-learning is infused with cultural meaning and nuances, and instructional approaches must therefore be relevant to the users; it should also not be assumed that e-learning is in great demand by all. To be successfully integrated, it is necessary to work toward synthesis of the different knowledge systems. E-learning, therefore, should be a continuous search for jointly- negotiated advances rather than as a top-down imposition, one that seeks systematic accommodation of cultural knowledge and aspects in research and application on technological interventions. It can be argued that instructional processes that address the needs of multiple cultural groups are bound to be more effective and meaningful to learners. Thus, transferring and sharing of knowledge should not be about coming up with technological fixes to (their) problems, or passing along ICT for (them) to adopt. It should be about acknowledging that these local groups have their own effective knowledge, resources, and practices management systems. An effective learning environment goes beyond the use of ICT; culturally-mediated social interaction is a part of the learning process.

As it is, Africa is faced with many challenges, and education is expected to be an effective tool in coping with these predicaments. In doing so, instructional decisions must be consistent with learner values, perceptions, communication styles, and learning outcomes that apply within a particular cultural context and evaluated for the appropriate cultural content. Incorporating cultural knowledge into e-learning paradigms assumes that coexistence of different knowledge structures is conceivable, and that while the paradigms may be in conflict, they can complement each other.

References

Africa warned on "half-hearted" telecoms overhaul (2005, September 8). *Mmegi Business Week, 22,* 138. Retrieved September 17, 2005, from http://www.mmegi.bw/2005/September/Thursday8/9332070451392.html

ALIN-EA. (2004, November 13). *Local content, local people, local languages: ICTs used to promote exchange of indigenous knowledge.* Retrieved September 16, 2005, from http://www.apc.org/english/news/index.shtml?x=28548

Arias, S., & Clark, K. A. (2004). Instructional technologies in developing countries: A contextual analysis approach. *TechTrends, 48* (4), 453-455, 470.

Balancing Act News Update (2004, September 17). *Uganda gets Web browser translated into Luganda, 225.* Retrieved September 16, 2005, from http://www.balancingact-africa.com/news/back/balancing-act_225.html

BBC News Africa (2004, December 9). *"Jambo" to open source software.* Retrieved September 16, 2005, from http://news.bbc.co.uk/1/hi/world/africa/4078753.stm

Benjamin, P. (2000, November/December). *African experience with telecenters.* Retrieved September 17, 2005, from http://www.isoc.org/oti/articles/1100/benjamin.html

Butcher, N. (Ed.). (2004, October 01). Members of South African Civil Society meets to discuss input to information and communications technology (ICT) empowerment charter. *The SANTEC Weekly Newsletter.* Retrieved from http://mailman.unisa.ac.za/pipermail/santecnewsletter/2004/000004.html

Cavallo, D. (2000). Emergent design and learning environments: Building on indigenous knowledge. *IBM Systems Journal, 39*(3-4), 768-781.

Chen, A., Mashhadi, A., Ang, D., & Harkrider, N. (1999). Cultural issues in the design of technology-enhanced learning system. *British Journal of Educational Technology, 30*(3), 217-230.

Colllis, B. (1999). Designing for differences: Cultural issues in the design of www-based course-support sites. *British Journal of Educational Technology, 30*(3), 201-215.

Dei, G. J. (2000). African development: The relevance and implications of "indigenousness". In G. J. Dei, B. L. Hall, & D. G. Rosenberg (Eds.), *Indigenous knowledges in global contexts: Multiple readings of our world* (pp. 70-86). Toronto, ON: University of Toronto.

Education International (2005, May 21). World day for cultural diversity. *Indigenous Education is part of Education International's Education for All Challenge.* Retrieved September 16, 2005, from http://www.ei-ie.org/en/news/20050517a.htm

Grenier, L. (1998). *Working with indigenous knowledge: A guide for researchers.* Ottawa, ON: International Development Research Centre.

Henderson, L. (1996). Instructional design of interactive multimedia. *Educational Technology Research and Development, 44*(4), 85-104.

Ikhemuemhe, G. (2004, September). *Technology giants promote e-learning through the universities.* Retrieved September 16, 2005, http://allafrica.com/stories/2004091501 25.html

International Communication Union. (2005). Retrieved September 16, 2005, from http://www.itu.int/ITU-D/ict/statistics/index.html

IT Web. (2005, January 20). All African News. *Microsoft, Ugandan government bring tech to education.* Retrieved September 16, 2005, from http://www.itweb.co.za/sections/business/2005/0501200730.asp?S=All%20Africa%20News&A=AFN&O=FRGN

Kearsley, G. (1990). Designing educational software for international use. *Journal of Research on Computing in Education, 90*(23), 242-250.

Klein, D., & Ware, M. (2003). E-learning: New opportunities in continuing professional development. *Learned Publishing, 16*(1), 34-46.

Lewis, T. (2000). Technology education and developing countries. *International Journal of Technology and Design Education, 10*, 163-179.

Lieberman, A. E. (2003). Learn Link. *Taking ownership: Strengthening indigenous cultures and languages through the use of ICTs.* Retrieved January 2, 2005, from http://learnlink.aed.org/Publications/Concept_Papers/taking_ownership.pdf

Mabawonku, A. O. (2003). Cultural framework for the development of science and technology in Africa. *Science and Public Policy, 30*(2), 117-125.

Mammo, T. (1999). *The paradox of Africa's poverty: The role of indigenous knowledge, traditional practices, and local institutions: The case of Ethiopia.* Lawrenceville, NJ: The Red Sea.

Maybury-Lewis, D. (2002). *Indigenous peoples, ethnic groups, and the state* (2nd ed.). Boston: Allyn and Bacon.

McLoughlin, C. (1999). Culturally responsive technology use: Developing an online community of learners. *British Journal of Educational Technology, 30*(3), 231-245.

McLoughlin, C., & Oliver, R. (2000). Designing learning environments for cultural inclusivity: A case study of indigenous online learning at tertiary level. *Australian Journal of Educational Technology, 16*(1), 58-72. Retrieved December 19, 2004, from http://www.ascilite.org.au/ajet/ajet16/mcloughlin.html

Morrison, T. R. (1995). Global transformation and the search for a new educational design. *International Journal of Lifelong Education, 14* (3), 188-213.

Mosha, R. S. (1999). *The heartbeat of indigenous Africa: A study of the Chagga educational system.* New York: Garland.

Musoni, E. (2005, September 8). All Africa Global Media. *ICT, the only solution to bypass the West.* Retrieved September 16, 2005, from http://allafrica.com/stories/2005090803 70.html

Phombeah, G. (2004, June 17). *Microsoft to launch in Kiswahili.* BBC News Africa. Retrieved September 16, 2005, from http://news.bbc.co.uk/1/hi/world/africa/ 3816717.stm

Semali, L. (1999). Community as classroom: Dilemmas of valuing African indigenous literacy in education. *International Review of Education, 45*(3-4), 305-319.

Semali, L. M., & Kincheloe, J. L. (1999). Introduction: What is indigenous knowledge and why should we study it? In L. M. Semali & J. L. Kincheloe (Eds.), *What is indigenous knowledge: Voices from the academy* (pp. 3-57). New York: Falmer.

Sillitoe, P. (1998). The development of indigenous knowledge: A new applied anthropology. *Current Anthropology, 39*(2), 223-252.

Sonaike, S. A. (2004). The Internet and the dilemma of Africa's development. *The International Journal for Communication Studies, 66*(1), 41-61.

Sylla, C. (2004, August). Science in Africa. *A cyber shepherd at work in the Sahel.* Retrieved September 16, 2005, from http://www.scienceinafrica.co.za/2004/july/ cybersheperd.htm

Vecchiatto, P. (2004, November 10). Mambo Open Source. *Africa still a PC dump.* Retrieved September 17, 2005, from http://cinsa.info/portal/index2.php?option= content&do_pdf=1&id=390

Chapter V

Intercultural Dimensions in the Information Society:
Reflections on Designing and Developing Culturally-Oriented Learning

Nektaria Palaiologou
University of Piraeus, Greece

Abstract

Nowadays, it is a common ascertainment that information and communication technologies (ICTs) and networked learning are not easy to access for many people in non-Western societies and for those who belong in etho-cultural minority groups. As a result, one of the major drawbacks in networked learning programs is miscommunication amongst culturally-diverse participant users, which, to a great extent, is due to the lack of services that meet the needs of various socio-cultural groups of people. In addition, there is great need for multi-language Web sites (such as educational programmes, curricula, and software) in order to emphasise the importance of culture as a dimension which should be incorporated in modern ICT implementations. A literature review approach is followed so as to review statements and studies in the joint field of ICTs.

Introduction

In the decade of 1995-2005, the rate of investment in *ICTs in different sectors, such as the market economy,* healthcare, and education, *of the national agenda is considered to be an important indicator of a country's* broader economic development and growth.

Nevertheless, reality shows that *ICTs* not only do not offer the expected outcomes as a tool for the economic growth for all people, but at the same time they exclude access for many people. Especially, they do not meet the needs of many who are settlers of the non-Western world block. As a result, the potential offered by *ICTs,* and specifically the cultural expression through *ICTs,* both emerge as key factors in a global world.

In this direction, numerous studies reveal the impact of culture on ICTs development (Boist, 1996; Tan, Wei, Watson, Clapper, & McLean, 1998; Walsham, 1996), the role and consequences of national culture to everyday life (Hofstede, 1991; Hofstede & Pedersen, 1999), and the impact of technology and culture in the process and outcomes of different cultural groups towards decision-making in organisations (Calhoun, Teng, & Cheon, 2002).

Taking all the above aspects into consideration, the main objective of this chapter is to highlight intercultural communication and activities as important dimensions in the use of ICTs and Web-learning on an equal rights basis for all people, independently of their colour, race, language, social class, and religion. First, the role of culture on ICTs and education in general is emphasised, in order to specify the needs that arise in a global society, by making a synthesis of characteristic statements and studies' outcomes which one can read in the relevant literature. Following on, the role of instructional design in the development and promotion of communication, mutual respect, tolerance, and understanding with the aid of ICTs is reflected by offering some hints about the development of e-learning addressed to students with different ethno-cultural background, aiming at the construction of a new citizen, the *homo "interculturalis".*

It is hoped that this contribution will provide brainstorming opportunities for those educators and scholars who make efforts to find ways and tools for overcoming the cultural differences during the educational process with the aid of *ICTs* and bringing people with various ethno-cultural backgrounds and national identities together.

Cultural, Multi-Cultural and Inter-Cultural Global Societies: Theoretical Paradoxes

This section arises from the common belief that throughout the route of mankind's history, culture is functioning as a system of values and norms that serve the society's equilibrium.

Definitions of Culture

Culture is a concept often discussed in the academic literature from different disciplines. A variety of definitions of "culture" have been proposed from the angle of anthropology, sociology, and archaeology. In brief, definitions of culture have originated in three general fields: anthropology, ethnography, and social-political empowerment. Most of these have been made with a rationale that what we call culture is neither predictive nor quantitative, but rather descriptive and/or comparative.

To begin, a definition of culture found in early anthropological literature is that it is the "knowledge, belief, law, morals, and customs" that are passed on from one generation to another within a particular society or group of people (Tylor, 1871, p. 46). Given that "culture is one of the two or three most complicated words in the English language" (Williams, 1983, p. 87), one can understand why scholars across the disciplines have not yielded yet a simple or uncontested approach of its content. The term "culture" is used to represent distinct and important concepts in different intellectual disciplines and systems of thought. Street (1993) states that "culture is not a thing", but it is often "dressed up in social scientific discourse in order to be defined" (Macfadyen, 2004, p. 7).

The definition of culture most commonly found in the literature of science and engineering (Cobern, 1991; Waldrip & Taylor, 1995) is that of Geertz (1973) who indicates that:

The concept of culture I espouse ... is essentially a semiotic one. Believing... that man is an animal suspended in webs of significance he has spun, I take culture to be those webs, and the analysis of it to be therefore not an experimental science in search of law but an interpretive on in search of meaning. (p. 3)

Geertz's definition is one that suggests that a person's knowledge of his world is essentially mediated by signs, and it is the structure of these signs which establishes reality for an individual or a group. In seeking to identify cultural effects, one is therefore looking for contexts in which individuals from different countries or groups will respond in different ways to, or provide different interpretations for, the same sign.

In the same direction, Hofstede (1991) states that culture is a "collective phenomenon"; it is learned, not inherited. In other words, we could describe culture as a repository of values, customs, and achievements which one generation leaves as a "testament" to its descendants. As an example, we can refer to the ancient Greek culture which reminds us not only of the glory of the ancient Greeks' attainments but, mainly, of their contribution to the evolution of mankind in the fields of science, moral philosophy, and values.

The word "culture" becomes much more complicated in its content, when combined with the prefixes "multi", "inter" or "trans". A typical example is the use of the terms "multicultural education" or "intercultural education"; the first depicts the mosaic of different ethno-cultural identities that exist in societies, while the second is used to describe the mutual communication and interaction among various ethno-cultural groups, which implies not only the existence but the co-existence of different individuals (Palaiologou & Evangelou, 2003). As Gundara (2003) clearly illustrates, the word "multiculturalism" or "social diversity" is used descriptively, not as programmatic or policy term. By contrast, the term "intercultural" is used as a programmatic term. Firstly, there is the common sense notion that many West European societies have become multicultural. The assumption is that it is the post-World War II immigrants, especially those from the Commonwealth who migrated to Britain, who have caused diversity, leading to a loss of national identity.

There exists a link between the notion of culture and multiculturalism and the ensuing effect of multiculturalism on society. In this direction, Giroux's (1990) understanding of culture is one that is widely accepted in education. According to him, culture is reduced to a type of monumentalism, in other words, to the artefacts of a people/nation, and the pedagogy through which it is expressed is organised around the process of transmission and the practice of moral and political regulation; the latter raises questions whether, nowadays, education accomplishes its role as a means of transmitting values, ethos, and cultivating apart from transmitting solely information and knowledge. In Western societies, multiculturalism has become a highly politicised issue. As D'Souza (1995) states, the debate about multiculturalism is not over whether to study other cultures, but how to study the West and other cultures.

Among various definitions about culture, essentialist models that focus on shared patterns of learned values, beliefs, and behaviours are also included, as well as social constructivist views that regard culture as a shared system of problem-solving or of making collective meaning (Macfadyen, 2004; Macfadyen, Roche, & Doff, 2004). Culture is a common system of shared meanings that form a framework for problem solving and behaviour in everyday life. Individuals communicate with each other by assigning meaning to messages based on their prior beliefs, attitudes, and values. Since people from different cultures often have different beliefs, attitudes, and values, normal human misunderstandings that occur in interactions between people of the same culture are aggravated by the wider differences in intercultural interaction. The key to effective communication is to know what kind of information people from other cultures require and in what form (Hall & Hall, 1990).

In this chapter, culture is considered to be a descriptive term, which includes thoughts, speech, behaviour, and artefacts that could be learned and transmitted from one society to another.

The Local, the Global and the "Glocal"

One of the fundamental questions in this contribution is whether culture in modern information societies is seen as a *threat* and/or an *opportunity* for cultural diversity. Accordingly, in this section, the main question is whether nowadays culture is functioning as an obstacle or as a communication vehicle in global societies. Another question is whether there exists one "online culture" or "cyber-culture" or "global culture." The question following will reveal that the impact of culture in societies bears various stances or attitudes associated with one's attitude towards the ICTs.

In the research field, the studies of the Dutch researcher Geerd Hofstede (1980) about the culture's consequences have had an enormous influence on the oncoming research tradition in the domain of intercultural communication. Concisely, Hofstede throughout his studies (1980, 1984, 1991) investigated the relationships between employees and managers in forty different cultures. On a cultural basis, he identified four dimensions of culture such as power/distance, uncertainty/avoidance, individualism/collectivism, and masculinity/femininity. These dimensions are all based on the position that cultures are homogenous national cultures that do not change in time. Hofstede's model is a schematic presentation of depicting the world in some very simple categories that we can recognise in everyday life. From this point of view, Hofstede's efforts are of great value for offering an immediate explanation of how the communication in management is influenced by culture in the field of management and business administration. Moreover, from a practical point of view, many modern organisations are using the intercultural concept underlying Hofstede's aforementioned dimensions as an axis for developing training scenarios addressed to their employers' needs.

In the same direction, one can wonder whether software developers aim at what is defined as "cultural maintenance" information, which encompasses the values of the target group and the group's preferred cognitive style (both instructivist and constructivist styles) by including the target group in the design of decision-making (McLoughlin, 2000).

As Macfadyen (2004) very aptly points out, the rhetoric of the "global village", an utopian vision of a harmonious multicultural virtual world, has tended to overlook the more problematic social interfaces of cyberspace: the interface of individual with cyber-culture(s) and the interface of a specific culture with other cultures. Current intercultural communications research has focused primarily on instances of physical (face-to-face) encounter between cultural groups, for example, in the classroom or in the workplace, and other sections of intercultural communication, such as communication through the Web, have been ignored; virtual environments are an increasingly-common site of encounter and communication for individuals and groups from multiple cultural backgrounds.

The concept of "glocal," which has been recently found in fields such as economics, sociology, and architecture, is used as a refinement of the concept of "global" and as a more descriptive term for what is happening during communication in the Web today. It incorporates the dimension of culture pointing out, at the same time, the importance towards the communication process in the cyberspace. Global culture should not be considered as "unified" or as a "socialising institution" into which local cultures integrate, but as a contradictory phenomenon, which entails a dialectical relationship between the global and the local (Koutsogiannis & Mitsikopoulou, 2004). To describe this process, Robertson (1995) has coined the term "glocalisation", which describes "the universalization of the particular and the particularization of the universal" (Koutsogiannis & Mitsikopoulou, 2004, p. 4). This view of "glocalisation" assumes a dynamic negotiation between the global and the local, with the local appropriating elements of the global which are of use, while employing at the same time strategies to retain its identity (Koutsogiannis & Mitsikopoulou, 2004).

Throughout his studies, Macfadyen (2004) and Macfadyen, Roche, and Doff (2004) found that cyberspace itself has a/many culture(s), and is not culture-free. Cultural gaps can exist between individuals, as well as between individuals and the dominant cyber-culture, increasing the chances of miscommunication; electronic communication across cultures, though it complicates further intercultural understanding, at the same time it presents distinctive challenges as well as opportunities to course planners.

Modern societies, groups, and sub-groups have to find a communication path within the boundaries of each state. They have to accommodate actions that impart legal, economic, and cultural contingencies upon local and small communities and impinge upon their resource bases. This also sets the local "*stage*" and turns local community processes into open system processes, where resources are contextualised in monetary economics and internal regulators are geared towards world-market's economic values and norms (Dascalopoulos & Vernicos, 2002); otherwise, we will be led to a taxonomy of "first" (dominant and superior) and "second" and "third" cultures (the subordinate ones).

Online Intercultural Communication, the Virtual, and the Cyber-Culture

Communicating in the cyberspace is a complicated issue itself. In the literature review of studies on cultural differences, "cyberspace" is understood as the virtual "places" in which human beings can communicate with each other, and that are made feasible by Internet Technologies, whereas the "Internet" refers more explicitly to the technological infrastructure of networked computers that contribute to digital communications world-wide. The term "cyber-culture" is a social space in which human beings interact and communicate and can be assumed to possess an evolving culture or set of cultures (cyber-cultures) that may encompass beliefs, practices, attitudes, modes of thought, behaviours, and values.

Dascalopoulos and Vernicos (2002) mention that as the cultural and the action sub-systems interact, they simultaneously form specific sets of collective behaviours and organisational patterns among people. This results in information inputs that are, in turn, gathered by culturally-determined organised patterns (structures) during problem-solving processes. As a result, information is culturally appraised as to whether it reinforces or calls for adaptation of the regulatory functions. This is a very interesting approach comparing the global culture of the Web with those cultures and parts of a community that form a system.

Findings of Reeder, Macfadyen, Roche, and Chase's study (2004) show that participation rates in the Web differ as far as cultural background is concerned, by gender and by role, as well as that online interaction is dominated by facilitator-learner exchanges (rather than by peer-to-peer communications). In this study, individuals (N = 453) received about the same number of responses from about the same number of people when these sub-groupings were compared. This means that in spite of receiving the same number of postings from a similar group of people, certain subgroups of participants were more likely to interact (or re-post beyond the required minimum) than others. In other words, we could argue that only certain groups were more likely to continue an online conversation.

McLoughlin and Oliver (1999) mention that the use of ICTs by indigenous Australians is very limited, and aboriginal Australians are a minority group in higher education. Increased support for indigenous use of ICTs and an emphasis on the development of information literacy skills is part of the equity and access provision in Australian universities. They refer, as a case study, to the Edith Cowan University in Western Australia which in 1998 successfully obtained funding to launch its pre-university bridging courses on the World Wide Web to cater for indigenous students wishing to undertake a pre-tertiary course. Online learning environment and content were intended to enhance the participation of indigenous learners in technology-based learning approaches, and to increase their academic success through increased proficiency and awareness of computer technology.

In the same direction, Macfadyen (2004) and Macfadyen, Roche, and Doff (2004) are referring to multiple studies that either present statistical data about the English language and Western dominance of the Internet (Keniston & Hall, 1998) or show that the "...humanist traditions of Islamic and Arab high culture" (Anderson, 1995, p. 15) are absent from the world of cyberspace because they are literally drowned out by the cultural values attached to the dominant language and culture of cyberspace as it is currently shaped.

Ferris (1996), Morse (1997), and Knupfer (1997) report that the gendered culture of cyberspace has tended to exclude women from this virtual world, which is another important social issue.

Concisely, cultural differences emerge during the communication process in the net. The ways one expresses his/her feelings and ideas to someone or to a cultural group other than his own is associated with his/her own cultural identity.

For example, concerning the attitudes of Greek people towards the use of the Web, Dragona and Handa (2000) in their study (pp. 63-64) analysed the Greek reaction towards the use of the Web in terms of the following two points: (a) the cultural imperialism of imposed foreign rhetorical and visual structures, (b) technological pressures causing English to emerge as the dominant foreign language; and (c) the relationship between the Web and the Greek cultural Web. They also remark that there is a cultural imperialism in the Web. Consequently, hypertext may not reflect a universal mode of cognition, but it may, instead, be a mode of thinking that reflects cognitive constructs and connections that are particularly English. As such, the grammar of the Web encodes English linguistic and semantic structures.

Dragona and Handa stress that the Greek response to this linguistic and cultural imperialism is influenced by its rich culture and history. Greece has "Hellenized" other conquering cultures, and Dragona and Handa's studies of online correspondence and Greek Web sites uncovered a Hellenizing of the Web. Greeks are beginning to employ the Web as an economic tool and a mask offering the world the "Greek face" it expects while manipulating the Web in a way that preserves Greek privacy from being overrun by yet another in a long series of conquerors, albeit a technological instead of an armed one (p. 63). Just as some Greeks are developing their online literacy practices as a means to Hellenize the Web, many more Greeks are relying on their own cultural Web, their own communities and families, to continue to provide the entertainment and information that the Web, a series of machines, provides. For the Greeks, the Web's penetration of the culture is limited by an active resistance to its colonization and by a cultural practice that relies more on humans than on machines for interaction (p. 64).

A benchmark problem in the online communication process is to take into consideration those factors that constitute obstacles for the "interaction" in the cyberspace and, mostly, their role towards an effective communication process. In his study, Zheng (2005) defines the factors that can prove to be obstacles/barriers during the online communication. These could be: (a) reducing communication by written communication (no gesturing, talking, looking, and other para-verbal cues), (b) writing affords time and effort, (c) communicating in a foreign language (in an international context, English is often the common language), (d) asynchrony, lack of quick feedback, (e) limitations of provided medium, (f) struggling with technology due to a lack of technological competence, (g) attributing meaning in electronic communication.

Finally, Ess (1998) argues that the lack of an adequate theory of culture prevents the analysis of the complexities of virtual classrooms and communities.

Until now, one can realize that the risk of cultural misunderstanding through Web communication is high and, thus, cultural communication becomes a very complicated issue. As a result, the question raised is whether there might be a possibility of reaching a global predictability for cultural behaviours and attitudes, at a particular time and in specific contexts. This is a matter under investigation for all those interested in the field of ICTs studies.

Therefore, when the design of a "culturally-sensitive" model with the aid of ICTs is suggested, it may be important, for either educators or designers, to have in mind a diverse range of users, especially when expecting the access by a target group of different socio-cultural background users.

Review of the Concept "Information Culture"

There is apparently no consensus yet on the meaning of the term "information culture" and one can find different insights from different authors. There is, however, a need for a deeper, more synthesised and theorised conceptualisation. Nevertheless, a practical definition of "information culture" incorporates: the general capability, views, norms, and rules of behaviour, with regard to accessing, understanding, and using information in a social collectivity (Zheng, 2005). This definition takes into consideration two stances. Firstly, information culture cannot be "created" or "established" (Sen, 1999, 1980; Zheng, 2005). It has always existed, as one dimension of culture, national, or organisational. Information culture can be conceptualised at multiple levels of society, institutions, and individual actions. It is deeply rooted in historical and social settings, yet is constantly evolving over time. Information culture of an organisation can be cultivated, developed, or shaped, subject to appropriate management and institutional formulation. The second stance of this definition argues that technology is part of the resources human beings draw upon to shape their information culture. How technology is used reflects, and is at the same time constrained, by the information culture within which it is located. On the other hand, information culture exists with or without information technology. In short, in this term the concept of information culture focuses on information rather than technology (Zheng, 2005).

Based on the paradox that technology could be seen as more or less neutral in global societies, it could be compared to a tool utilised more by those in power than those in disadvantage. On the other hand, technology is socially constructed and defined through the ways people shape tools to their needs rather than the characteristics of the tool itself. In this direction, we discern four main possible scenarios concerning the use of technology in modern society according to which the use of technology can range from *control and repression* to *emancipation*; and the collective mind-set can range from an *atomistic, entrepreneurial* one to a collective *network mentality*. These possible scenarios are the following ones: (a) *Boring disease*, a "Big Brother" type pessimistic vision characterised by control technologies and the breakdown of social cohesion, (b) *Cyber-polis*, a scenario characterised by co-operation and collaboration but under the control of technical systems, (c) *Liberation*, a Silicon Valley-type model characterised by hyper-competition based on technology opportunities, and (d) *Eco-cyber*, the scenario closest to our vision of an inter-cultural, networked society (European Parliament, 2001).

As far as the infusion of the cultural factor in Web sites is concerned, Collis and Remmers (1997) and McLoughlin and Oliver (1999) have defined two categories of sites that have cross-cultural implications: (a) sites made in one context and culture and visited by a particular audience; and (b) sites designed specifically for cross-cultural participation.

Theorists have argued for a cultural dimension in the design process and the need to provide "culturally-sensitive" learning environments (Collis, 1999; McCahill, 1998). Flexible delivery of educational resources must take into account different cultural variables and recognise the specific learning needs, preferences, and styles of learners. In the designing of instruction, there may be a tension between the need to ensure access for a multicultural student population, while at the same time taking into account the need for localisation to satisfy different cultural learners' cognitive styles and preferences (McLoughlin & Oliver, 1999).

Henderson suggests (McLoughlin & Oliver, 1999) three identifiable approaches, all of which are limited with respect to cultural dimensions of learning and pedagogy, such as: (a) the inclusive or perspectives approach which imports the social, cultural, and historical perspectives of minority groups, but does not challenge the dominant culture and is therefore cosmetic, (b) the inverted curriculum approach which attempts to design an instructional component from the minority perspective, but fails to provide the learners with educationally-valid experiences as it does not admit them into the mainstream culture, (c) the culturally one-dimensional (mono-cultural) approach which excludes or denies cultural diversity and assumes that educational experiences are the same for both minority and indigenous students.

McLoughlin (1999) gives examples of Web design that may be open to different cultural interpretations. Email, chat, and other forms of peer dialogue may impose expectations to communicate which, depending on the culture, may impose burdens on participants. Lectures are accepted differently by different cultures. Hypermedia organisation could create problems for students with strong task orientation.

Another important issue is the new social and economic conditions in modern multi-cultural societies. Economic integration, the global market, and advances in transporta-tion and telecommunication have broken down geographical barriers and isolation. Nowadays, the world is more global and mobile than ever before. Globalisation is associated with ICTs, business enterprises, and cultural needs of workers and people. International companies, when expanding their operations abroad, must balance be-tween prospects of growth and the risk to invest in unfamiliar markets. Successful companies, managers, employers, and employees are those who take into consideration the growing global needs and utilise them. Both ICTs and the cultural diversity are key components of European policy (European Parliament, 2001) in the legislative and funding budgets.

Referring to the global software economy, Edmundson (2003) notes that the software developed in the U.S. often contains only European humans, while other countries often include characters from two or more cultures. As an alternative, animations can be used, if it is recognisable to the majority of the cultures who will use the software. Sometimes, the characters and settings in educational media could be familiar to both Eastern and Western audiences from urban, developed countries; thus, less educated or exposed participants may not comprehend certain images or icons, but again, it depends on the intended target audience.

In our era, the main problem in minimising the gap between the information society and the multicultural society still remains the lack of finding a common denominator between cultural and information society policies, and this is the most difficult part. The role of education in teaching the respect, mutual understanding, and empathy is very important for the cohesion and peace in societies.

Hofstede, Pedersen, and Hofstede (2002) use the didactic triad of awareness of cultures as the set of social rules of a society, followed by knowledge of cultural patterns and then by skills in cross-cultural interaction. Their "synthetic cultures", extreme representa-tions of Hofstede's (1981) dimensions of culture, were created to serve as vehicles for the knowledge and skills steps. As each synthetic culture is sketched out, the authors mention the "obsessions" of each of the ten cultures (e.g., people in the individualist culture are obsessed with freedom), the core distinctions, the golden rules, and the concepts that are positive and negative in each culture. Furthermore, the models of Trompenaars (1997) and Hall (1997) are among the most popular regarding the effect of cultural issues on user interface design.

All the above necessitate the re-vamping of the old Greek concept of "*Paideia*" (meaning *Education*) or the German notion of "*Bildung*" so as to develop interactive and intercultural aspects within complex schools and their communities. If this process is not undertaken through academic and formal political or citizenship and human rights education as well as through active citizenship engagement, the underclass or pauperised groups of whatever nationality or religion will activate their own separatist "politics of recognition". Such a situation could heighten notions of fragmentation and divisions with political consequences. Even if these groups are statistically small, they cannot be written off as having no political consequences (Gundara, 2003).

Suggestions for Instructional Design: The Cultural Learning Objects (CLOs)

What are the implications for designing culturally-sensitive environments, learning models, and scenarios? In this section, those factors and parameters that software developers, curricula designers, and educators should take into consideration for supporting and promoting intercultural understanding and empathy for people of non-dominant cultural groups are presented as dominant factors in the design of learning objects, educational curricula, and software. Also, another important issue for educators is to develop culturally-dependent methods for the assessment of the attainments of their immigrant or minority students.

Based on the author's experience and on the relevant literature review, pedagogical strategies and learning models with an intercultural approach might include: (a) culture-specific and culture-general knowledge, (b) Positive attitudes towards ethno-culturally different students, (c) skills, language and social, which promote students' intercultural communication and cooperation. Proponents of intercultural appropriateness and effectiveness approaches advocate integration of a variety of educational theories and training methodologies through multi-dimensional approaches.

Among the skills that will be developed through such a model are the following ones: (a) self-awareness, (b) cultural awareness, (c) human relations and cooperation with people other than those of our own culture. An intercultural taxonomy of learning goals, content, and methods offers an alternative to disparate teaching and training models.

According to Hammerly (1982), a cultural-based second/foreign language learning can cover three areas by giving: (a)information about native speakers' society, history, and geography of their country so that learners get an understanding of the world view that native speakers have of themselves and their own country (information culture), (b) information about attitudes, values, and so forth, so that students can acquire particular patterns of speaking behaviour associated with cultural behaviour that are appropriate in the community of the target language (behavioural culture), and (c) information about artistic and literary accomplishments so that students can acquire a completed view of the target language (achievement culture).

In theory, the above areas could shape the axis of a basis of a repository of learning objects (LOs) in online education, where all students with different ethno-cultural background could have access to the same information but in culturally-acceptable ways; in this manner, students could find information about a variety of cultural issues and, at the same time, they could offer their own contribution. In general, LOs are defined as digital entities deliverable over the Internet (McGreal, 2004), meaning that any number of people can have access and use them simultaneously (as opposed to traditional

Figure 1. The intersection between "culture" and "LOs"

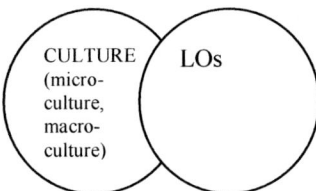

instructional media, such as an overhead or video tape, which can only exist in one place at a time). In future, we are aiming at constructing a repository of LOs in tertiary education where all students with different ethno-cultural background can have access; in this way students can find information about a variety of cultural issues and at the same time they can offer their own contribution. The model of "personalised learning" will be followed (Sampson, Karagiannidis, & Kinshuk, 2002).

Taking into consideration the existing theories of cultural-based and blended learning, the designing of LOs can be enriched by information about the target culture. These learning objects are named "cultural LOs" (Figure 1).

Conclusion

"Global culture" should be viewed as *a human right*, on a basis of *equal rights* for all people, independent of their colour, race, language, or religion. As educators, we regard this "access for all" as a first-priority demand of our era, which leaders of the Web should realise and implement in praxis. There are many factors inherent in intercultural communication that can enhance or adversely affect the success of training courses and programs. The role and power of mutual understanding and communication is very important for the cohesion and peace in societies. A *non-culture centric* online environment should incorporate values that support global citizenship education and promote human rights education in a democratic context.

References

Boist, M. H. (2000). *Information space: A framework a qualitative study of the information culture in for learning in organizations, institutions and the Finnish insurance business.* London: Routledge.

Calhoun, K. J., Teng, J. T. C., & Cheon, M. J. (2002). Impact of national culture on information technology usage behaviour: An exploratory study of decision making in Korea and the USA. *Behavior & Information Technology, 21*(4), 293-302.

Cobern, W. W. (1991). *World view theory and science education research.* NARST Monograph no.3. Manhattan, KS: National Association for Research in Science Teaching.

Dascalopoulos, S., & Vernicos, N. (2002). *Culture in a system's approach.* Retrieved from www.aegean.gr/culturaltec/dasc/bio.html

Dragona, A., & Handa, C. (2000). Xenes glosses: Literacy and cultural implications of the Web for Greece. In G. E. Hawisher & C. L. Selfe (Eds.), *Global literacies and the World-Wide Web* (pp. 52-73). London; New York: Routledge.

D'Souza, D. (1995). *The crimes of Christopher Columbus.* Retrieved from http://www.cyad.com/cgi-bi/Upstream/CrimesofChristopherColumbus.htm

Edmundson, A. (2003). Decreasing cultural disparity in educational ICTs: Tools and recommendations. *Turkish Online Journal of Distance Education-TOJDE, 4*(3).

Ess, C. (1998). Cultural attitudes towards communications and technology. In C. Ess & F. Sudweeks (Eds.), *Proceedings of First Looks: CATaC '98* (pp. 1-17). Sydney, Australia: University of Sydney.

European Parliament. Directorate General for Research (2001). *Cultural diversity and the information society* (Final Study No. PE 297.559). Brussels.

Geertz, C. (1973). *The interpretation of cultures.* New York: Basic Books.

Giroux, H. A. (1990). *Curriculum discourse as postmodern critical practice.* Geelong, Victoria, Australia: Deakin University Press.

Gundara, J. (2003, June 15-18). Higher education programmes intercultural education. *Unesco Conference on Intercultural Education,* Jyväskylä, Finland.

Hall, E., & Hall, M. (1990). *Understanding cultural differences.* Yarmouth, ME: Intercultural Press.

Hammerly, H. (1982). *Synthesis in second language teaching.* Blaine, WA: Second Language Publications.

Hofstede, G. (1991). *Cultures and organizations: Software of the mind.* New York: McGraw-Hill.

Hofstede, G. (1994). *Cultures and organizations: Software of the mind: Intercultural co-operation and its importance for survival.* London: Harper Collins Publishers.

Hofstede, G. J., & Pedersen, P. B. (1999). Synthetic cultures: Intercultural learning through simulation games. *Simulation and Gaming, 30*(4), 415-40.

Koutsogiannis, D., & Mitsikopoulou, B. (2004). The Internet as a glocal discourse environment. *Language Learning and Technology, 8*(3), 83-89.

Macfadyen, L. P. (2004). *Internet mediated communication at the cultural interface.* Retrieved from http://homepage.mac.com/leahmac/LM/Docs/C63Macfadyen.pdf

Macfadyen, L. P., Roche, J. & Doff, S. (2004). *Communicating across cultures in cyberspace: A bibliographical review of online intercultural communication.* Hamburg, Germany: Lit-Verlag.

McGreal, R. (2004). *Online education using learning objects.* Falmer Press.

McLoughlin, C. (1999). Culturally responsive technology use: Developing an online community of learners. *British Journal of Educational Technology, 30*(3), 231-245.

McLoughlin, C. (2000). Cultural maintenance, ownership, and multiple perspectives: Features of Web-based delivery to promote equity. *Journal of Educational Media, 25*(3), 229-241.

McLoughlin, C., & Oliver, R. (1999). Instructional design for cultural difference: A case study of the indigenous online learning in a tertiary context. In J. Winn (Ed.), *ASCILITE '99: Responding to Diversity. Proceedings of the 16th annual conference of the Australasian Society for Computers in Learning in Tertiary Education* (pp. 229-238). Brisbane: Queensland University of Technology. Retrieved June 28, 2006, from http://www.ascilite.org.au/conferences/brisbane99/papers/mcloughlinoliver.pdf

Palaiologou, N., & Evangelou, O. (2003). *Intercultural education: Pedagogical teaching and psychological dimensions (in Greek).* Athens, Greece: Atrapos.

Reeder, K., Macfadyen, L. P., Roche, J., & Chase, M. (2004). Negotiating culture in cyberspace: Participation patterns and problematics. *Language Learning and Technology, 8*(2), 88-105. Retrieved from http://llt.msu.edu/vol8num2/reeder/default.html

Rodrigues, E. J. (2004). Technology importation and the strategy of informality: The heterogeneous enactment of an American computer-based learning project at public schools in Brasil. In C. Ess & F. Sudweeks (Eds.), *Proceedings of CATaC'04 (Cultural Attitudes Towards Communication and Technology)* (pp. 57-171). Sydney, Australia: University of Sydney.

Sampson, D., Karagiannidis, C., & Kinshuk (2002). Personalised learning: Educational, technological, and standardisation perspective. *Interactive Educational Multimedia*, special issue on *Adaptive Educational Multimedia, 4,* 24-39.

Sen, A. (1999). *Development as freedom.* New York: Knopf.

Tan, B. C. Y., Wei, K. K., Watson, R. T., Clapper, D. L., & McLean, E. R. (1998). Computer-mediated communication and majority influence: Assessing the impact in an individualistic and a collectivistic culture. *Management Science, 44*(9), 1263-1278.

Trompenaars, F., & Hampden-Turner, C. (1997). *Riding the waves of culture: Understanding cultural diversity in business.* London: Nicholas Brealey Publishing.

Tylor, E. B. (1871). *Primitive culture.* London: John Murray.

Vygotsky, L. S. (1978). *Mind in society.* Harvard, MA: Cambridge University Press.

Waldrip, B., & Taylor, P. C. (1995). Understanding students' cultural background: A prerequisite of effective teaching. *PNG Journal of Education, 31*(1).

Walsham, G. (1996). *Cross-cultural software processes*. Informs Conference.

Zheng, Y. (2005). Information culture and development: Chinese experience of e-health. *Proceedings of the 38th Hawaii International Conference on System Sciences*.

Section II

Western Philosophies and Theoretical Foundations in E-Learning

Chapter VI

Theorizing and Realizing the Globalized Classroom

Steve McCarty
Osaka Jogakuin College, Japan

Abstract

This chapter examines what criteria, conditions, or characteristics actually constitute a globalized classroom. A graduate course on online education taught in Japan is presented as a case in point. Online mentoring and educational technologies spanning six countries are described. Explanatory frameworks include globalization, constructivism as a cross-cultural pedagogy, cultural attitudes toward the adoption of online technologies, transformative learning, and empowerment. Voluntary feedback from the graduate students, mostly translated from Japanese, provides evidence such as: (a) that mainstream Western constructivism has some universality to be readily accepted by Japanese students, (b) that unfamiliar online information and communication technologies (ICT) are also welcomed, (c) that a positive form of globalization can occur in such a class, and d) that their learning was transformative and empowering. The theoretical framework accounts for the changes which students reported in their attitudes and practices. Thus the class provides a model for realizing the globalized classroom.

Introduction

This chapter addresses such questions as: What actually constitutes a globalized classroom? Is it some ideal future goal, a potential state that is achievable today, or has it already been realized? What criteria or conditions, including educational technologies, would facilitate or characterize a globalized classroom? What breadth or diversity of cultural perspectives among the participants would qualify as global? What quality of learning experiences by students would result from or correspond to a globalized classroom? Since globalization can be positive or negative, when students and educators are from different cultures, what kind of pedagogical considerations can assure a positive form of globalization as the outcome of a course?

Lest the globalized classroom be reduced to a mere slogan or label, the factors involved need to be clarified with greater precision. This chapter aims to contribute to a theoretical framework of explanatory concepts augmenting existing literature, and grounded in a case of teaching online education to graduate students in Japan. Issues focused upon will include cross-cultural pedagogy, particularly testing the universality of the constructivist paradigm across cultures. Explanatory concepts proposed for their suitability to the globalized classroom and corresponding student experiences will include globalization, transformative learning, and empowerment. By the above criteria, the intensive course in online education, particularly the voluntary feedback from the graduate students, mostly translated from Japanese, will bear on the extent to which a globalized classroom has already been realized.

Case of the Tsukuba Course on Online Education

In Japan's Science City of Tsukuba just north of Tokyo from February 16-20, 2004, the author taught an intensive course at the national University of Tsukuba entitled Online Education in Theory, Practice, and Applying the Internet to English Education. The graduate students were majoring in English as Foreign Language (EFL) pedagogy. Three of the eight learners were already English schoolteachers and were at the Graduate School of Education for further studies.

With considerable preparations at a distance, the physical and virtual learning environments were designed. Complex planning involved securing a networked computer classroom that had not been used before for such courses, ensuring that the necessary hardware and software would be available, including having technical support staff install java runtime software necessary for the Internet voice technologies.

Professional Networking Enables Online Mentoring

The lecturer arranged with colleagues in four countries to serve as mentors on online education during the week and particularly at certain times for live chats and audio-conferences. This networking was a natural extension of international mentoring projects among educators in the World Association for Online Education (WAOE) (www.waoe. org/) (McVay Lynch, 2004). In other words, there was a ready-made distributed community of practice available to tap expeditiously, with fellow officers of a virtual organization who had proven reliable over years of collaboration willing to share online education expertise with a voluntaristic ethic.

Learning Management Systems Enhanced with Voice Technologies

Portland State University in the U.S. hosts WAOE (pronounced "wow-ee") as an international public service, so the instructor could arrange to use their WebCT platform combined with their HorizonLive conferencing system from New York for this course. NetSpot in Australia also offered their WebCT platform to demonstrate Wimba Internet voice technologies. Given access to the designer interface of the two WebCT course shells, the lecturer decided which tools would be used, how the interface would appear to the students, and how the various venues could be navigated through links. The mentors and technologies made the course widely distributed in space and media, blending online activities with f2f instruction, involving six countries and demonstrating experientially how online education can open the classroom to the world.

The cohort of graduate students had received a colorful flyer with the course description and a chart of concepts surrounding online education for brainstorming in class. Online education is defined as distinct from distance education and e-learning in McCarty (2004). As the course approached, the graduate participants were confirmed, and the lecturer received their e-mail addresses as requested. Their names were forwarded to Portland and Adelaide so the students could receive user names and passwords for the WebCT course platforms and the HorizonLive virtual classroom. The lecturer then sent them a suggested assignment, to read some of the many articles in English and Japanese linked from a Web page prepared for this purpose at <www.waoe.org/president/tsukuba>. The students were also asked to bring earphones with a microphone for the voice technologies, which all of them did.

Of the eight students, one had made a home page before, while the others had experienced e-mail and Web browsing, so the course activities were nearly all new experiences for them. One virtue of Web-based technologies is that, while being challenging for the designer, they are generally not difficult for students to navigate. Having the instructor's computer screen visible via a projector and screen throughout the week-long course allowed the students to follow step-by-step instructions with a growing sense of accomplishment. Some techniques for effective computing were introduced, such as making screen shots and pasting them into a word-processing document, with a view to their final reports. Training in online educational technologies proceeded smoothly, as hands-on experience is essential to empower learners with information and communication technologies (ICT).

One of the first activities was making their own home pages with that function of WebCT. The mentors were also registered to use the student interface of the virtual learning environments, while the instructor used the designer view that shapes the interface which the participants see. The mentors also made home pages, so students could become familiar with them before the interactions. Students could see photos of the mentors to visualize during synchronous text chats and audio-conferences as well as when using the asynchronous discussion function (text BBS) of WebCT and the Wimba Voice Board (audio BBS). Internet video-conferences would demand even greater bandwidth for each participant, and it was telling that the mentors in Brazil and Malaysia could access the text chat function but not the sound data of the audio-conferences. The British and Americans could be heard clearly, and students said that their English was a bonus of target language communication on top of the content. In order for the mentors to visualize the students, the latter were asked to take each others' photos with their Internet-enabled mobile phones and e-mail the photos to the instructor's Web mail in the U.S. Then almost immediately the photo files could be uploaded to the students' home pages. The students were asked to consider where the data had actually traveled, wired and wireless, criss-crossing the Pacific Ocean nearly instantaneously.

A Fully Hybrid Course Suited to the Host Culture

As the course was both *on* online education and taught *utilizing* online education communication tools, the media reinforced the message. However, Japanese culture privileges face relationships and solidarity rituals of everyday f2f communication. Thus a fully hybrid approach was most suitable, that is, utilizing a classroom with the instructor there throughout the course, plus a constant Internet connection for each student and opportunities for authentic interaction with informants at a distance. Substantive discussions of online pedagogy, as will be evidenced hereinafter, helped the learners correct their own preconceptions about distance education and transform their attitudes toward online education.

Accountability of Online Education to Support Hypotheses

Aside from the course work, five graduate students agreed to compose a collective report in Japanese detailing the course activities over the five days and their impressions thereof. A diary to record new learning experiences and observations out of piqued interest, not graded, that was voluntary and in their native language, can be considered a most authentic reflection on the course from the learners' standpoint developmentally. For a full translation of their report into English and more information on the Tsukuba course, see McCarty (2005b).

Digital technologies allow for much of the course to be preserved as research data, so in many ways the classroom is opened to the world. By the same token, courses with an online dimension can also be more *accountable* than traditional f2f classes. While only a small selection of students' bilingual writings and transcribed speech from Internet voice technologies can be presented in this limited space, the case of this course may demonstrate certain repeatable conditions hypothesized to constitute a globalized classroom. The students' testimonies may provide evidence to support hypotheses that: (1) the learning, including new technical skills, was transformative and empowering, (2) the constructivist approach was readily accepted culturally, (3) the course constituted a positive form of globalization, and (4) a globalized classroom was realized.

Globalization and the Learners' Cultural Identity

Characteristics Constituting a Globalized Classroom

While the subjects of globalization and culture in general are too vast to even outline in this limited space, certain questions can be addressed in scaffolding the notion of a globalized classroom. What could a globalized classroom mean concretely? How does it differ from similar terms used almost interchangeably? What kind of globalization is taking place, and how is the cultural identity of learners affected? The notion of a globalized classroom needs to be fleshed out with specific conditions and technological affordances. Besides the testimonies of learners later in this chapter, some representative literature on globalization, constructivism, transformative learning, and empowerment can also ground the discussion bearing on the hypothesis that an entirely positive form of globalization can take place in the intercultural classroom.

This chapter aims to substantiate the notion of a "globalized classroom," but why not a more familiar formulation such as "global class?" "Global" is often used interchangeably with "international," exaggerating the importance of one or two contacts across national borders. To be called global, a project should involve a multicultural cross-section of the world, with representatives of transitional and developing as well as developed countries. Meeting those criteria were volunteer mentors in the Tsukuba case who were located in England, the U.S., Malaysia, and Brazil. Australia was also represented, as the location of the voice-enhanced WebCT learning management system utilized as one of the course platforms. So the technologies as well as people involved were widely distributed in space and media, which globalized the classroom.

Then why "classroom" instead of "class?" Distributed online education is not synonymous with distance education, where there would not necessarily be a classroom. The instructor was with the students the whole time, and occasionally there were f2f activities planned, such as sitting in a circle to analyze results of the author's global online education survey (McCarty, Ibrahim, Sedunov, & Sharma, 2006). In this case the students did form a class as well, but the vital need is to clarify what is meant by "globalized."

Intercultural Sensitivity for a Wholly Positive Form of Globalization

Globalization itself can be positive or negative, with exploitive winners and exploited losers possible, so evidence must also be brought forward to assert that online education, if conducted not to change the culture of the learners but to empower them with new ideas and technical skills, is a winning proposition for the learners and therefore a positive form of globalization.

As the Foreign Minister of Finland (Tuomioja, 2003) stated in an address at the University for Peace in Costa Rica:

What has given a new impetus to the process of internationalisation is the development of new technologies, particularly information and communication technologies ... Globalisation is not only unavoidable but a process which, on the whole, opens up more positive prospects than new threats ... The most important challenge related to globalisation is the fact that the increase of wealth and prosperity is being distributed more unequally than before. (p. 21)

2001 Economics Nobel Prize Laureate Joseph Stiglitz writes that "poverty has soared" in most transitional countries, while "East Asia's success was based on globalization" (2002, p. 214). "Caring about the environment, making sure the poor have a say in the decisions that affect them, promoting democracy and fair trade are necessary if the potential benefits of globalization are to be achieved" (p. 216).

While the above authors emphasized economic inequalities and opportunities, Fareed Zakaria includes further aspects of globalization even while reporting from the Davos Economic Summit:

While the war on terrorism has dominated headlines, the great engine of globalization has kept moving, rewarding some, punishing others, but always keeping up the pressure by increasing human contact, communication, and competition. For almost every country today, its primary struggle centers on globalization issues: growth, poverty eradication, disease prevention, education, urbanization, the preservation of identity. (Zakaria, 2004)

Applying some of these considerations to teaching in a different culture, practices would need to be beneficial and empowering to the learners, in their own view, while not threatening their sense of cultural identity. The above passages also help make the distinction clearer between "global," implying a worldwide or representative *scope* of geographic and cultural diversity, and "global*ized*," implying the *dissemination* of technologies and ideas that could be given or taken in a value-laden manner, and that could cause positive or negative effects depending on motives and execution. As Zakaria (2004) observed above, few cultures are rejecting globalization out of hand, but most are wary of its potential threats to the existing social order and cultural identity. A resident in a different culture can ensure more positive results by respecting the local ways of thinking, gaining cultural literacy, and studying the local language, which demonstrates a commitment to meeting the culture halfway.

In the annual globalization index (Kearney, 2004) and cultural globalization index (Kluver & Fu, 2004), the highly ranking countries tend to use English and are influenced by foreign ways in return for economic benefits. Even so, if asked, few would agree that their cultural identity was at risk. Increased choices, provided they are voluntary, tend to be invigorating, not dispiriting. The increased information available has generally been empowering to the public in the more globalized societies.

Be that as it may, Japan has managed to remain one of the largest beneficiaries of systemic globalization without its citizens being decidedly globalized, in terms such as engaging in intercultural communication or adjusting their collective practices to international norms. The reciprocity that binds Japanese to one another is evidently out of its compartment when non-Japanese are involved. Defining themselves by contrast with foreign cultures reinforces the group solidarity of insiders, but it creates frictions with outsiders. Cultural contrasts reassure them of their unique ethnic identity, excusing them from emulating other cultures or mastering foreign languages to bridge the gap. Western cultures and communication styles do indeed contrast with Japan's traditionally re-served, indirect, self-controlled, other-oriented social organization of peer groups emphasizing commonalities. It is not that Japanese people are as similar to each other as they act, particularly in companies; Camus noted the great effort it takes individuals to conform. Most Japanese still do not aim to be individualistic, however, so they cannot be understood from such a viewpoint. In their social system, they tend to find that their happiness stems from their devotion to their peer group or family, and the momentum of harmonious customs tends to relieve them of the need to think for themselves or question the way things are. From the outside it could be described as ethnocentrism, whereas to insiders it is having things safe and secure and not wanting the boat to be rocked. One could also observe that tribalism is nearer the surface in Japan than it is in other developed countries.

For the purposes of this chapter, the upshot of the above observations is that Japanese culture is not threatened by anything a visiting lecturer could say or do, and a public setting such as a national university is decidedly immunized from outside influences. Even so, while being respectful of another culture as a guest, an educator must not take a monolithic or static view of the culture. For what would it indicate if no friction occurred when a lecturer opened the classroom to the world, communicated bilingually but mostly in English unlike other courses, and introduced one new concept or technology after another in a decidedly constructivist manner? Could learners have been chafing at some aspects of their own country's educational system, being taught about English in Japanese by professors who were distant or remote not technologically but hierarchically in terms of social distance? Could the different approach along with the new technologies be embraced by learners as a breath of fresh air, agreeable to their own aspirations? The palpable enthusiasm of normally reserved graduate students in their testimonies toward the end of the intensive course will call for considerable depth of explanation.

For the scope and purposes of this chapter, a working definition of globalization is that individuals and local communities are now susceptible to, or can leverage to their advantage, international forces affecting them in many ways, including the availability of new educational opportunities. Globalization offers individuals not only unprecedented access to information, particularly through the Internet, but also to widen their social circles by interacting with people around the world online. That in turn often leads to offline friendships, concrete scholarly collaboration, and professional development.

Constructivism for Online Education Across Cultures

Constructivist, student-centered learning, facilitated in a somewhat Socratic manner of promoting discovery by the students, is a mainstream pedagogical approach in native English-speaking countries that is closely associated with the use of educational ICT that calls for more student initiative than in more traditional settings. For the purposes of this chapter, constructivism refers to a moderate form of this mainstream paradigm, particularly in view of the expectations of non-Western students for clear and continuous guidance from a teacher who is present and supportive. However, even in the West this constructivism has been more *contemporaneous with* than *necessary to* education utilizing ICT. Thus, all the more so, the universality of the constructivist paradigm in online education remains to be tested in non-Western cultures. Japan, for instance, has deliberately undergone modernization without Westernization and maintains a cultural common sense quite in contrast to that of Western cultures. Yet if the graduate students by their own testimony welcomed windows opening to the world from their customarily monocultural, hierarchical, teacher-centered, instructivist, and nearly hermetically-sealed Japanese educational environment, then it would be permissible for the instructor to aim to realize the globalized classroom.

The stronger the version of constructivism, the more exceptional the assumed roles of teachers and students are from a global viewpoint, which should be the default context. Most institutional cultures in Africa, the Mideast, Russia, Asia, and elsewhere tend to be more instructivist, teacher-centered, and authoritarian than Western countries in their educational systems, which establishes the expectations of students toward any teacher. In those countries, ICT is or could be readily introduced without constructivism or other student-centered approaches. The universality of constructivist approaches remains to be tested across cultures as to whether or not it actually enhances learning and the uptake of new technologies for empowerment. Observations of the Tsukuba learners and their own words will bear on the issue of whether or not there were latent cultural attitudes through which the graduate students could readily welcome a constructivist pedagogical approach, with Thailand arguably providing a counterexample.

Constructivism is used in this chapter to describe the pedagogical approach, aside from Internet training and imparting of necessary information, whereby the Tsukuba graduate students were guided to reflect on their preconceptions and socially create their own new knowledge. Literature below will mainly serve to clarify what forms of constructivism in conjunction with educational ICT that the author finds useful across cultures. Two authors summarize constructivism, with a view to designing learning experiences, as follows:

Constructivist epistemology assumes that learners construct their own knowledge on the basis of interaction with their environment. Four epistemological assumptions are at the heart of what we refer to as "constructivist learning":

1. *Knowledge is physically constructed by learners who are involved in active learning.*

2. *Knowledge is symbolically constructed by learners who are making their own representations of action.*

3. *Knowledge is socially constructed by learners who convey their meaning making to others.*

4. *Knowledge is theoretically constructed by learners who try to explain things they do not completely understand.* (Gagnon & Collay, 2000, para. 3)

Cultural Receptivity to Constructivist Pedagogy

Similarly the Tsukuba graduate course was designed to have the students learn experientially by doing, and to brainstorm toward their own conclusions, even at the risk of their not fully grasping every concept to which they were exposed. Socially-constructed knowledge through peer collaboration is quite natural to Japanese learners from elementary school before the education race gets more competitively individualized, which may partly explain why the graduate students readily embraced this approach.

[S]ome cultures may lean toward instructivist methods while others will be based upon constructivist methods; this polarity in approach also runs across nationalities and organizations. Similarly, while rote learning may have gone out of favor in Western education systems, but it is quite prominent in Asian contexts. It still has a proven viability depending on context. (Mason, 2003, para. 20)

"Instructivist," as discussed by Mason (2003), for the purposes of this chapter refers to the nearly worldwide teaching tradition that, from the recent viewpoint of constructivism, is considered an authoritarian, teacher-centered, information-transmission paradigm. But given the progress that was made before constructivism, it would be rather extreme to disregard that paradigm in all circumstances. In the Japanese case as mentioned, the educational system has both sides: instructivism when the achievement is graded, and constructivism with an affinity to group project work when the learning goals involve socialization.

Constructivism and Instructional Design

Constructivism does not directly translate from theory into practice when it comes to e-learning:

Constructivism is the dominant theory of the last decade (but) is a learning theory and not an instructional-design theory. Therefore, instructional designers must attempt to translate constructivism into instructional design through a more pragmatic approach that focuses on the principles of moderate, rather than extreme, constructivism and makes use of emergent technology tools. This shift could facilitate the development of more situated, experiential, meaningful, and cost-effective learning environments. (Karagiorgi & Symeou, 2005)

That is, constructivism needs to be recontextualized for what is increasingly called "Webagogy":

Webagogy is the art, craft, and science of using networked technologies, including the World Wide Web and email, to support teaching and learning. Inherent in the idea of Webagogy is that carefully considered pedagogy is being implemented with technology—the pedagogy comes first. (Ells, 2000, para. 1-2)

A leader in theorizing online education asserts that technology is available to put constructivism into practice:

Vygotsky's ... ideas have been expanded in Lipman's (1991) community of inquiry and Wenger's (2001) ideas of community of practice to show how members of a learning community both support and challenge each other, leading to effective and relevant knowledge construction. Wilson (2001) has described participants in online communities as having a shared sense of belonging, trust, expectation of learning, and commitment to participate and to contribute to the community. ... the capacity for students to create their own learning paths through content that is formatted with hypertext links is congruent with constructivist instructional design theory that stresses individual discovery and construction of knowledge ... Education is not only about access to content, however. The greatest affordance of the Web for educational use is the profound and multifaceted increase in communication and interaction capability that it provides. (Anderson, 2004, paragraphs 24, 31)

In the Tsukuba graduate course, the instructor did maximize the communication opportunities through computer conferencing with mentors abroad, which the learners found most valuable (McCarty, 2005b). While the Web (WWW) provides interactive functions along with the world's biggest library by far, actually the audio-conferencing with virtual classroom software utilized the voice over Internet protocol (VoIP) as well as the Web.

Testing the Universality and Ethics of Approaches Across Cultures

While the potential to bridge theory with practice seems clear, the theories still need to be tested for their universality in various cultures. The British authors below, where "tutoring" refers to teaching adults, sum up a number of key cultural and ethical issues that should be considered by international e-learning practitioners:

In a global learning community our key question is: "How do we maximize the diversity and respect for cultures while tutoring online?" Culture is a complex concept defined by attitudes, values, and patterns of behavior. Ethics are negotiated and agreed rules of behavior for group interaction and communication. Culture is expressed in the online environment through the form, structure, and choice of language or images. In order to work and learn successfully in a culturally-diverse online community, we must be aware of our own culture and how we present ourselves in the online environment through what we say and how we say it. Different cultures have very different values underlying the production and transmission of knowledge. Constructivism is the predominant pedagogy used in online learning, involving the active participation of the learner in discussions and knowledge construction. The expectations of the tutor-student relationship can vary from extremely formal master-student relationships to learner-centered approaches that encourage autonomous student learning. The diversity of learners in the online community demands an inclusive approach that respects differences and promotes understanding. (Labour, Juwah, White, & Tolley, 2000)

Transformative Learning and Empowerment as Explanatory Concepts

Perspective Transformation as a Sufficient Outcome

Mezirow (1991) started the movement to aim for transformative learning in adult education based on Gregory Bateson's four categories of learning, and he formulated the following learning theory:

"Zero learning" involves extending a pre-existing habitual response (meaning scheme) to cover additional facts ... Learning I includes learning about our own habitual responses ... Learning I would include thoughtful action without reflection ... Learning II involves learning about contexts (meaning schemes). The premises based upon which we learn may become changed during this stage, although we are unaware of such changes, and consequently we learn how to learn in a different way ... Learning III

involves transformations of the sort that occur in religious conversion, Zen experience, and psychotherapy. These are perspective transformations through which we can become aware that our whole way of perceiving the world has been based on questionable premises. (Mezirow, 1991, pp. 90-91)

The above framework provides a starting point, but it does not seem to describe the full range of learning possibilities that would be expected of a taxonomy. Although mentioning Zen Buddhism adds some multicultural legitimacy, there is no formal education that can legitimately make Learning III an explicit goal. Even the study of religion as an academic discipline does not aim to encourage students to undergo religious transformations. To join a cult is transformative, but that only shows that transformation in itself is not necessarily to be encouraged. Teaching practices that clash with the culture of students can harm them psychologically. If such teaching occurred where the instructor was a guest in a different culture, critical pedagogy would term it imperialistic. For the purposes of this chapter, education could best aim for Learning II, but perhaps more broadly conceived.

There seem to be many possibilities between Learning II and III that could qualify as transformative learning. Why are learners necessarily unaware in Learning II that their premises have changed? When one becomes aware of dropping a certain bias, it is an important change, but it need not be so life-changing as Learning III. Learning how to learn in a different way also seems to describe empowerment by ICT through a class like the Tsukuba one in a concrete sense as well as in learning theory. Furthermore, "perspective transformations" need not change a learner's entire outlook to be transformative. If graduate students including schoolteachers could turn from skepticism to enthusiasm toward online education, a greater transformation of perspective could scarcely be aimed for as a learning goal.

Mezirow and his followers have expanded upon the above framework in ways that demystify the higher goals and may be useful for designing learning experiences. Critical reflection can change:

meaning schemes (specific beliefs, attitudes, and emotional reactions). Perspective transformation is the process of becoming critically aware of how and why our assumptions have come to constrain the way we perceive, understand, and feel about our world; changing these structures of habitual expectation to make possible a more inclusive, discriminating, and integrating perspective; and, finally, making choices or otherwise acting upon these new understandings. (Mezirow, p. 167)

Imel (1998) summarizes further work in this school of thought with a view to the pedagogical implications:

Perspective transformation explains how the meaning structures that adults have acquired over a lifetime become transformed. These meaning structures are frames of reference that are based on the totality of individuals' cultural and contextual experiences and that influence how they behave and interpret events (Taylor, 1998). The teacher's role in establishing an environment that builds trust and care and facilitates the development of sensitive relationships among learners is a fundamental principle of fostering transformative learning (Taylor, 1998). Loughlin (1993) talks about the responsibility of the teacher to create a "community of knowers," individuals who are "united in a shared experience of trying to make meaning of their life experience" (pp. 320-321). As a member of that community, the teacher also sets the stage for transformative learning by serving as a role model and demonstrating a willingness to learn and change by expanding and deepening understanding of and perspectives about both subject matter and teaching (Cranton, 1994). (Imel, 1998)

The subject-object structure of the above argument fits more closely with individualistic cultures than with collectivistic ones, yet the Japanese custom of peer group reflection at all educational levels happens to fit the pedagogical approach of constructivism, though it arose independently.

Since the advent of the Internet, evidence has been painstakingly accumulated regarding the potential and tentative outcomes of online education as ICT dissemination grows worldwide. In this chapter, the focus is on the globalized classroom and some of its prominent dimensions in terms of the kinds of learning, cross-cultural considerations, and technologies involved. The above passages suggest that teaching can foster transformative learning not only with the efficiency of new technologies but also with a timeless humanism, intercultural sensitivity, and a moderate constructivist pedagogy. If the instructor overpowers the students as an authority and source of education, the students may remain dependent, receiving and giving back information that they think is expected. But if the instructor is also an inquirer and fosters a process of discovery in the learners, the risk of less material covered or misconceptions remaining is out-weighed by the authentic process of growth among the students that continues, independent of the instructor, long after the course. Thus, episodes of transformative learning may not be as important as the cumulative effects of empowering changes in attitudes, new technical and learning skills, affective rewards, and practical benefits of what learners discover. Particularly in a sensitive cross-cultural context, perspective transformation constitutes a sufficiently ambitious pedagogical goal or learning out-come.

Empowerment of Learners as a Positive Individual Form of Globalization

Empowerment would seem to provide a suitable explanatory concept to describe the results of learning about and through online education or the uptake of ICT generally. However, like transformative learning, the concept of empowerment has some disciplinary and cultural baggage, having arisen in certain contexts of inequality such as workplace hierarchies. The United Nations (2002) does recommend ICT to disadvantaged women explicitly for their empowerment. Overcoming space and time to some extent with ICT, and gaining access to vastly more information and informants online is surely empowering to most learners qualitatively as well as quantitatively. Increased productivity as well as knowledge and skills recognized in societies nearly worldwide constitute empowerment for learners regardless of age or sex. The vast majority of humans are disadvantaged or situated in an unequal socio-economic structure, but ICT literacy and technical skills empower learners with the optimal ability to level the playing field themselves, which is better for all concerned than outside intervention where the people "saved" do not necessarily grow to meet their next challenge. Knowledge is power, but more precisely, it is knowledge in action at the initiative of the individual that manifests empowerment. Performance specialist Diane Howard calls this empowerment "enhanced by technology" (2002) when pedagogy is well matched with ICT. "Enhanced" is similar to "empowered" but at the same time argues against the common misconception that distance education intrinsically can never be equal to, or more valuable than, f2f education. F2F is fine for those who can afford the time out, but for the vast majority of humanity the Web is opening up unprecedented opportunities for lifelong learning and therefore empowerment.

Empowerment provides another possible explanatory concept with which to weigh the skills and attitudes of students before and after such a course. There are many forms of power: weapons, money, position, knowledge, technical skills, connections, even beauty or love. For the purposes of this chapter, which is largely about e-learning in terms of content and media, empowerment is used to mean the acquisition of useful learning and productive skills, particularly through online ICT, the learners' own release from constraining preconceptions through greater awareness, particularly about distance communication and online education, the widening or internationalization of the learners' social and intellectual horizons, and the amplification of their voices afforded by ICT skills, new knowledge, and relationships. Insofar as the individual learner benefits from a globalized classroom practically and in terms of personal development, empowerment represents a positive individual form of globalization.

Cultural Attitudes and Preconceptions of Non-Western Learners

An analysis of where the students were coming from may help provide a baseline for student statements indicating attitudinal changes. These in turn bear on the hypotheses that the approach and course conditions described in this chapter facilitated the learners' experience of a globalized classroom, transformative learning, empowerment, and a positive form of globalization. At the same time, the results will represent one case of online educational technology and constructivist pedagogy being tested for their universality across cultures.

Distinguishing Online Education from Distance Education

As alluded to earlier, the students could not overcome all their preconceptions, but the progress was their own. They tended, for example, to see only the discussions with mentors as online education, a common misconception conflating online education with distance education. Actually, because the students were using the Internet throughout the course except when sitting in a circle for a change of pace to clarify concepts and world trends, nearly the whole course was online education in media as well as content. Having the instructor with the students in person is to be desired whenever possible, and having the course in hybrid form takes nothing away from its being online education. But the instructor stepped aside in this respect, as the students were in the midst of a process of discovery. In accord with moderate constructivism, to feed answers would have taken the wind out of the learners' sails. The international communication from their classroom in Japan, and the technologies that supported it, were most exciting to the graduate students.

As the students asked one question after another to the mentors about online education in practice, it became clear not just that they were curious and had little previous knowledge of the field, but that they had been skeptical about its value for education, thinking of it mostly in terms of distance education. In Japan more than in Western countries, frequency of meeting f2f is a measure of closeness and correlates with career advancement. At least two Japanese white-collar workers will often go to visit another office where a telephone call or email would suffice for Westerners. In other words, the form, in terms of non-verbal communication or action, is more important than the content. In a similar vein, gift-giving manifests not materialism but rather symbolic communication. Japanese people bow even on the telephone because relatively elaborate non-verbal rituals accompany the verbal rituals in their everyday f2f communication. Add to that the importance of maintaining face, and there is considerable cultural resistance to remote communication. Such people need to find out that a computer does not necessarily isolate them but can expand their social sphere as well as their intellectual horizons.

Constructivism Faces Cultural Obstacles in Thailand, unlike Japan

Researchers in Thailand surveyed virtual education delivery (VED) with intercultural communication methodology and arrived at results reminiscent in most ways of similar studies in Japanese culture with respect to English education. But it appears that student-centered constructivism faces more obstacles in Thai culture than in Japanese culture:

According to Hofstede (2001):

Thai cultural issues which can be viewed as barriers to knowledge sharing are high power distance, high uncertainty avoidance, and collectivism. High power distance ... refers to the acceptance of a hierarchical authority system with an emphasis on status differentiation and unequal power distribution. Thai subordinates usually accord respect and feel obligations to their superiors as a father figure. This might obstruct the process of transferring knowledge through university networks, such as email or discussion boards, since students are not encouraged to express their ideas to solve problems, and lecturers are unlikely to oppose any ideas or opinions expressed by senior administrators. (Burn & Thongprasert, 2005)

High power distance is alluded to elsewhere in this chapter based on student statements about regular faculty members. In terms of social hierarchy, the monocultural classroom in Japan could almost be considered a form of distance education. Even outside of Asia, in a large lecture hall format with graduate students intermediating with undergraduates, the social distance is considerable, and proximity f2f in the same room alone does not guarantee a student-faculty relationship.

Thai people are characterized as having high uncertainty avoidance (Hofstede, 2001). This refers to being threatened by ambiguous situations and trying to avoid challenging experiences. Thais seek certainty in their relationships and are normally reluctant to be the cause of discomfort to others ... an attitude whereby an individual tries to restrain his own interest or desire, in situations where there is the potential for discomfort or conflict, and where there is a need to maintain a pleasant relationship. (Burn & Thongprasert, 2005, para. 24)

It seems counter-intuitive at first that most Japanese people, known for employing ambiguity, would also rate high in uncertainty avoidance. But in all-important relationships, like the Thais, they need to know where they stand in the group and what is expected of them. Ambiguity, often used to gain maneuvering room, is a defense that at the same time threatens others with uncertainty. Thus students need very specific guidance and usually do not appreciate open-ended classwork.

Thai culture is recognized as collectivist rather than individualist. The sense of collectivism in Thai people is strong as a consequence of their living in extended families (Hofstede, 2001). Thus, the dependency relationship between the person and in-groups is stronger than in out-groups. They usually hold views and opinions respecting the group, and this plays a vital role in their learning styles. (Burn & Thongprasert, 2005)

This collectivism is similar to Japan except that Japanese society is not organized around familial relations so much as categorical peer groups at work, school, in play or interests. That may account in part for the common phenomenon of salaried workers putting their company before their family. More specifically, it is their peer group within the company that they feel they must not break from, let down, or be ostracized by. Companies also succeed to an extent in instilling a sense of family that conveniently obliges workers to their superiors.

Both students and staff found "Bhun Khun" [high power distance] to be a significant inhibitor to knowledge sharing in an online environment with a teacher-centered approach being far preferred as a learning style. This extended even further within the university relationships between instructors and administrators, with instructors stating that they would not dare question any decisions made by the hierarchy and similarly would not admit to any problems with ICT usage. ... students did not adopt a self-learning, self-paced approach as allowed by VED [Virtual Education Delivery] and wanted structure and control—specifically being told what to think. Staff also felt less comfortable with not being in control and found the VED threatening. Finally, students found that their preferences for group activity facilitated learning online whereas staff found this again a major inhibitor ... Staff found that their collectivist approach ... prevented them from pursuing individual learning styles, raising questions or presenting novel ideas. (Burn & Thongprasert, 2005, paragraphs 60-62)

Modernization and East-West Biculturalism

The Thais at this stage evidently maintain a more purely non-Western way of thinking than the Japanese because of less exposure to Western influences. While the Japanese have tried to retain their traditional culture, in their modernization drive since the 19th century, they have not wanted to miss any technologies or methods that might help them compete with the West. Since the Western artifacts and ways they adopted could not be completely decontextualized from their cultural background, it could be observed that the Japanese have inadvertently become bicultural to an extent. This may help to explain data such as the Tsukuba graduate students' testimonies indicating receptivity to constructivism as well as instructivism. The more globalized societies mentioned above, such as Singapore, are without a doubt more bicultural than Japan in this sense. The unsung heroes of globalization include millions of Asians who are acquiring English as their second language and, inadvertently or voluntarily, becoming East-West biculturals to some degree in the process.

The Japanese graduate students also said things directly to the instructor that have contributed to this analysis. For example, they lamented that other classes were taught in Japanese despite their EFL major and relative fluency in English, at one of the most prestigious graduate schools in Japan. Keeping all of the above observations in mind as representing the starting point of the students, there were obstacles to be surmounted toward their appreciation of online education, so it was remarkable how positive their final reports turned out to be. Quotations and translations in the next section will endeavor to cite what students wrote that bears on the questions raised in this chapter. The globalized classroom on the one hand, and transformative learning and empowerment on the other hand, may turn out to be external and internal aspects of the same overall picture.

Testimonies of the Learners Pertinent to the Hypotheses

Content, Pedagogical Approach, and Learning Outcomes

The globalized classroom and perspective transformation were not explicit or direct goals of this intensive course on the theory and practice of online education. Thus it is intriguing that learning outcomes call for such explanatory concepts as transformative learning and empowerment. Causal factors for these learning outcomes could be sought basically in the efficacy and timeliness of the content for learners in this particular cultural context, and in the pedagogical approach.

Utilizing a moderate constructivist approach, goals were for the graduate students to understand the discipline of online education and to be able to use its technologies for their own study and career purposes. Thus students were encouraged to construct knowledge of how online education could be applied to teaching EFL in Japan. Given the status quo of prior knowledge and the educational system, this actually challenged them to innovate. One who was already a public schoolteacher of English spoke exactly as transcribed below in a message posted to the Wimba Voice Board in Australia:

Through this intensive course on online education, I have found some new possibilities for Japanese students to learn English. First, online education can provide the participants with the opportunities of not only input but output. For example, chatting gives a good chance to improve writing skills, and teleconferencing is a good chance to improve fluency in speaking. The activities like these are really important for Japanese students because they have little chance to use English in their daily life. English is not a second language to the Japanese. Second, they can learn English at their own pace according to their own English level. Online education can become less threatening and more comfortable way of learning to some students than face-to-face situation. Generally speaking, Japanese who are learning English are not confident in their communication skills. And there are many Japanese who are shy. Online education can give them a good preparation for face-to-face communication.

As a teacher himself, the graduate student focuses more on the students' foreign language development than on the corresponding authentic international communication. He still privileges f2f communication, as mentioned in connection with Japanese cultural attitudes, so online education needs this remarkable justification of cognitive transfer washing back to offline society. Yet there is the implicit realization that computers are not information-processing machines that isolate users but are turning into devices for communication.

The voluntary report in Japanese that five students wrote was intended to record the class activities over five days, but the graduate students spontaneously added sections of their impressions, not unlike the Japanese custom of holding group reflection meetings after a big project or school course. Some changes they underwent can be discerned from the comments they volunteered in the following excerpts from their report (all translations from Japanese by this author; with "we," "our," etc., referring to the graduate students):

"Nearly all the participants had only experienced email, Word and Excel, etc., so it was our first time to make a home page, chat, audioconference, and more. Copying Web pages into Word documents will prove to be extremely useful even after this course. ... Rather than being suddenly hit with high-level content, we were guided step-by-step through basic Internet functions and can recall almost no difficulties in learning. It was the first time for almost all of us to make a home page, so a bit of confusion was observed at first, but by the second half of the session everyone was used to the functions, including some useful tips, and had arrived at their own home pages with unique characteristics. ... Prof. McCarty had lunch with us and was joking about noodles here vs. where he lives. Although it was the first day there was an extremely frank atmosphere."

Frankness is considered uncharacteristic of formal gatherings in Japan, but is common among friends or peers, so the students seemed to welcome a liberating element in contacting the outside world or an instructor from a Western culture in this case. During that lunch, students characterized their regular professors as remote, so there is a certain social distance that cannot be bridged for all the proximity in the f2f classroom. Evidently, online and intercultural communications are not subject to the same inhibitions.

The following comment was about their first experience of a text chat room with several mentors, using the WebCT chat function:

Of course when many people are participating there are limitations such as difficulty in finding needed messages, but in this case we found ways to avoid such problems. We also received the chat log file to go over again at our leisure. Compared to a BBS, chat has strengths and weaknesses, so it is difficult to say which is better. But both BBS and chat have good points, and contemporary junior and senior high school students would like this type of communication. It would provide a way to get accustomed to English while having fun.

Fun is so rare in East Asian classrooms that this suggestion may be heretical, but it points to a yearning to transform educational practices in the relatively slow-changing institutional culture of Japanese public schools.

After sitting in a circle discussing online education survey results from around the world compared to the situation in Japan, the following was reported:

We had hardly heard of online education before this course, but this discussion provided a good opportunity to think about it. This takes nothing away from f2f education, of course, which is suitable especially for younger students. But online education has numerous strengths, so combining f2f with online education is certain to be much more effective. It was keenly felt that this should be a nationwide topic of discussion from now on.

In relatively conformist Japan, most schoolteachers are moreover in the conservative civil service, so the graduate students must have gained a strong conviction to be willing to try to persuade the nation to consider adopting online education. Japanese people tend to mask their emotions, precisely because they are so important and affect others, so expressions of superlatives are uncommon, yet they appear again below:

This was a first experience of audioconferencing, and although approaching it nervously, one could shed timidity and exchange opinions, so it was extremely meaningful ... Using a BBS is markedly more efficient that than the traditional blackboard, chalk and notebook, and there are various applications, so it was felt that it should by all means be used in mainstream educational institutions ... In this class we engaged not only in practical activities like chat and audioconferencing but also in the theoretical side characteristic of the typical class. We also received very important feedback from student-student exchanges. The teacher brought the discussion together in the form of augmenting our own views, so the progression of the discussion was easily understandable. There were some difficult theoretical issues, but explanations were illustrated by very helpful examples. The great potential online education holds has left a lasting impression.

The above feedback shows that not only online technology but also constructivist pedagogy can be readily accepted in this non-Western culture, providing some evidence for their universality. The "lasting impression" comment also points to transformative learning and empowerment brought about by technological and pedagogical dimensions of the globalized classroom.

The graduate students expressed more positive comments and gratitude, plus the following conclusions:

Having had almost no prior knowledge of online education, this intensive course was very useful for grasping the big picture ... Education through the Internet had seemed to be something personal and closed off from others, but it turns out to be surprisingly interactive. It is useful in expanding the individual's narrow world. Provision of online education opportunities in Japan, with students participating unreservedly, is to be anticipated.

A female graduate student aside from the five who wrote the above report volunteered an email message in English on February 19, 2004, writing that in this course she discovered that virtual organizations could be a resource. Furthermore, mandated for English schoolteachers by the Japanese Ministry of Education, the course of study says that communicative competence is important if we live in Japan. Given that, this system does meet requirements presented for EFL education in Japan. Due to this course, I find that we can use online education to give learners a chance to **communicate** *(or interact) as well as to develop their proficiency ... Especially, I enjoyed many practical tasks! So, I want to keep studying this.* (emphasis in original)

Although Japanese students are often seen as passive, the above student actually did not need the course credits and her feedback was not sought, so her enthusiasm was entirely genuine. Her message indicates that she was empowered as a teacher and learner to continue exploring online education after the course. Her emphasis on the social dimension of learning through virtual organizations and other interactions shows that she has internalized elements of constructivism in her approach to pedagogy as a future teacher. Her emphasis on authentic communication alludes to the lack thereof in the usual English language classroom in Japan. This provides some indication that she has experienced a globalized classroom. She wants to discover more, through online education, and not just for herself: She wants EFL teaching in Japan to move in this direction.

Further Research and Future Trends

Besides the many practical and theoretical issues raised by such an unprecedentedly distributed course across cultures, a vast amount of written material was electronically archived, and much more could be transcribed from audio-conferences and voice board messages. The scope for research, analysis, and accountability is also much greater in classes utilizing cutting-edge online technologies than in the traditional f2f classroom. Either book-length monographs will be needed for each such course, or else the dimensions involved need to be carefully divided into installments. More details of the Tsukuba course, illustrations of the virtual learning environments utilized, and the graduate students' complete report translated into English with annotations are described in McCarty (2005b), while e-learning concepts and definitions are the focus of two other articles (McCarty, 2004, 2005a).

The topic as well as the approach of this course will remain a rarity for some time because of the conservative educational culture in most non-Western institutions. Online education as an elective graduate course in an EFL pedagogy program probably found its opening in terms of educational technology and content-based English education, by analogy with courses such as global issues taught in English. Instructors and researchers will have to seek such openings unobtrusively in a cross-cultural climate where instructivism may be the norm rather than constructivism, where f2f communication is privileged over distance communication, and where online education suffers from misconceptions, budgetary limitations, vested interests in the status quo, or technophobic fear of the unknown among decision-makers.

Yet, citing the evidence of the Tsukuba course, further attempts to improve the pedagogy and technology utilized across cultures can proceed with more confidence. Both the extent of initial skepticism and the degree of subsequent enthusiasm among the learners were surprising in this first attempt. As global information and ICT spread along with a diminishing attachment of young people to f2f communication, such opportunities will increase. There is a science of research and teaching methodology, but teaching itself and intercultural communication involve the art of negotiating values as well as meanings. For a guest or resident instructor abroad, or teaching online across cultures, even a sense of best practices should not preclude sensitivity to the host culture, because the receptivity of learners and their surrounding community determines the success of the approach.

The Tsukuba graduate students were reassured by the constant presence of the instructor that f2f teaching was not being downgraded. Even in a distance education course in such a culture, at the beginning there should be hands-on orientation in a computer lab, where a final exam may also take place. Having met an instructor or mentor in person even once makes a big difference to learners. After such an orientation, text discussions or audio-conferences would be quite sufficient to connect the communication to the students' memories of the instructor. Similarly, if an intensive course such as the one in Tsukuba were conducted more than once a year, it may not be necessary to travel the long distance after the first session. This is an approach to recommend to other cross-cultural practitioners of online education in the future.

Conclusions on Online Education and the Globalized Classroom

Within the frameworks outlined above are grounds for evaluating the changes described by graduate students in the Tsukuba course on online education. Then if the pedagogies as well as technologies are found to work across cultures to the satisfaction of the learners, the classroom becomes a seat for a positive form of globalization. The classroom, once viewed as a closed and static location, may be seen as moving toward becoming a node in a global network. Communication among world citizens is rapidly becoming less limited by geography, transportation, language barriers, and nationalism enforced by governments. The Internet, through a process of disintermediation, has unleashed direct and borderless networking among like-minded individuals, opening up new possibilities for educational innovation as well. Besides unprecedented access to information, learners can contact online instructors, tutors, mentors, subject matter experts, and technical specialists, or network with those who have similar interests, including virtual organizations for mutual support. Knowledge and skills introduced in the case of a globalized classroom go with the graduates into their communities and workplaces, compounding the empowering educational benefits.

Online education, as a new field that a community of practitioners is turning into an academic discipline, is constituted largely of concepts and technologies, many of which were brainstormed and experienced in the intensive graduate course. These technologies have rapidly become available worldwide to overcome space and time. If everything worked to perfection in one graduate course, it is not to discount the challenges to be faced, especially in widespread implementation. But the technologies can be adopted in incremental steps along with teacher training to move from f2f-only education to online education. In this case the instructor was able to remain with the students throughout the course for maximum learner support and interaction, which is generally more effective than distance education alone. Yet the course was online nearly the whole time. While the Internet connection for each student is a sufficient condition for online education, it was combined with distance education by having mentors in several other countries join the class via written and spoken asynchronous and synchronous online communication tools. These are some of the conditions by which a globalized classroom was arguably realized.

A globalized classroom is open to the world, connected to the global network, involving learners or peers, teachers, or mentors, from different cultures in communication, whether f2f or at a distance. The classroom, usually monocultural, closed and seldom observed by peers in the case of Japan, is opened to the world in terms of both global resources and contacts with people of other cultures. In a computer lab with real interlocutors abroad for authentic communication, the media matched and reinforced the subject matter of the course. The direct goals in terms of content and technological skills were demonstrated and exercised on the Internet, while knowledge construction was optimized in the combination of f2f and online conversations with mentors, the instructor, and peers. The course could not have been nearly so transformative or empowering if it had been taught theoretically in a regular classroom. Conversely, affordances of the globalized classroom were what could make the experience transformative and empowering.

The course also turned out to match the aspirations of the students, which, more than anything, made it a welcome and therefore positive form of globalization. In foreign language learning, there are target languages and cultures that students wish to learn about, contact, and add to their own repertoire of language use or cultural identity. The Tsukuba graduate students' stated desires included discussions with native speakers of English, American and British in this case. It left little to be desired as English discussion practice precisely because the students were focused on the content and people rather than on the language. Characteristics of the globalized classroom provided for optimal motivation and uninhibited conditions for authentic communicative language learning.

Student comments indicating that they were empowered to *continue* exploring online education show an autonomous determination that is not often seen in Japan. Usually there are few if any complaints in Asia about instructors being the sage on the stage, nor are proverbs cited to the effect that learners are not a vessel to be filled but a flame to be lit. Since it is usually considered the role of the teacher to motivate students, positive statements of the students' own volition indicate that the learning was transformative. The ways that they went about using ICT for their education, and the expectations that they held about teaching EFL in the future, were positively transformed.

Data mostly translated from Japanese showed what students authentically thought about the experience. But the Learning Zero to III formulation as presented by Mezirow was found to be an awkward framework to describe the results. Students' learning arguably exceeded Learning II but did not upset their cultural identity. The goal of education should never be directly to change students psychologically or culturally any more than educators would want their own children to join a cult. There is a Western or American cultural attitude about progress whereby change itself or shaking up the status quo is to be desired, whereas older cultures harbor recollections that changes often go in unpredictable or dangerous directions.

Constructivism was found to contribute to positive learning outcomes as reported by the graduate students, because they readily welcomed the approach. Students also noticed and welcomed the frank atmosphere. If they could laugh and be open with the instructor, quite unlike the usual class in Japan, it provides evidence of universality in how the lowering of inhibitions fosters optimal learning. The atmosphere transformed the first day, but not into something alien to the students. Cooperative learning, value clarification, and enjoyable experiences are hallmarks of Japanese education before examination pressures mount in secondary schools. This course may have revived the ambience of such playful or informal learning rather than that of customary adult study. So a moderately constructivist approach in this case could be considered to have fostered transformative learning and empowerment across cultures.

Although this chapter has been more about learning and pedagogy than technology, applications of ICT were essential to the globalized classroom. Even virtual communication is shown to be real communication when the discussions are authentic and lead to knowledge construction. However, more work needs to be done before concluding that current technologies represent a panacea for all cultures. A scholar from Ghana (Afele, 2003) does argue throughout his book that Africans need ICT as well as food, because they urgently need knowledge to solve their own problems. That would be empowerment.

In sum, while constructivism and ICT were welcomed in the case of this course, the case of Thailand noted above is cautionary about obstacles to anticipate in less globalized societies. Depending on the learning goals, the pedagogy should be adjusted with intercultural sensitivity to prevent institutional or learner resistance. The Tsukuba case showed that a globalized classroom was possible in one non-Western situation where the level of English and general background knowledge was relatively high. It also exemplified some characteristics fleshing out the notion of a globalized classroom as an explanatory concept. Virtually every comment volunteered by students in their full report in McCarty (2005b), in other archived course data, and orally during the week of the course pointed to transformative learning and empowerment with ICT skills. Thus, characteristics of the globalized classroom were at the same time conditions for a positive form of globalization unfolding within the students, changing from unfamiliarity and skepticism toward online education to constructed knowledge and enthusiasm to use their new skills to learn more.

References

Afele, J. (2003). *Digital bridges: Developing countries in the knowledge economy.* Hershey, PA: Idea Group Publishing.

Anderson, T. (2004). Toward a theory of online learning. In T. Anderson & F. Elloumi (Eds.), *Theory and practice of online learning.* Retrieved November 3, 2005, from http://cde.athabascau.ca/online_book/ch2.html

Burn, J., & Thongprasert, N. (2005). A culture-based model for strategic implementation of virtual education delivery. *International Journal of Education and Develop-*

ment using ICT, 1(1). Retrieved November 3, 2005, from http://ijedict.dec.uwi.edu/ /viewarticle.php?id=17&layout=html

Ells, R. (2000). *Webagogy*. UW computing and communications. University of Washington. Retrieved October 27, 2005, from http://staff.washington.edu/rells/webagogy/ index.shtml

Gagnon, Jr., G. W., & Collay, M. (n.d.). *Constructivist learning design*. Retrieved October 27, 2005, from http://www.prainbow.com/cld/cldp.html

Howard, D. (2002). *Enhanced by technology, not diminished: A practical guide to effective, distance communication*. New York: McGraw-Hill.

Imel, S. (1998). Transformative learning in adulthood. *ERIC Clearinghouse on Adult Career and Vocational Education, ED423426*. Retrieved September 7, 2005, from http://ericdigests.org/1999-2/adulthood.htm

Karagiorgi, Y., & Symeou, L. (2005). Translating constructivism into instructional design: Potential and limitations (electronic version). *Journal of Educational Technology & Society, 8*(1), 17-27. Retrieved September 7, 2005, from http:// www.ifets.info/journals/8_1/5.pdf

Kearney, A. T. (2004, March/April). Measuring globalization: Economic reversals, forward momentum: 2004 A.T. Kearney/Foreign policy globalization index. *Foreign Policy*. Retrieved September 7, 2005, from http://www.foreignpolicy.com/ story/files/story2493.php

Kluver, R., & Fu, W. (2004, February). The cultural globalization index. *Foreign Policy*. Retrieved September 7, 2005, from http://www.foreignpolicy.com/story/ cms.php?story_id=2494#

Labour, M., Juwah, C., White, N., & Tolley, S. (2001). Culture and ethics: Facilitating online learning. In C. Higgison (Ed.), *Online tutoring e-book*. Retrieved September 7, 2005, from the Heriot-Watt University and The Robert Gordon University Online Tutoring Skills (OTiS) Project Web site: http://otis.scotcit.ac.uk/onlinebook/ otisT608.htm

Mason, J. (2003, March). *Perspectives on trans-cultural issues in e-learning*. Paper presented at the Symposium de Versailles, France. Retrieved September 7, 2005, from http://www.initiatives.refer.org/Initiatives-2003/_notes/_notes/mason.htm

McCarty, S. (2004, September 10). A picture of online education. *Archive of CRN Home Page Topics for Discussion*. Tokyo: Child Research Net. Retrieved September 7, 2005, from http://www.childresearch.net/cgi-bin/topics/column.pl?no=00221 &page=1

McCarty, S. (2005a). Cultural, disciplinary and temporal contexts of e-learning and English as a foreign language. *eLearn Magazine: Research Papers*. Retrieved September 7, 2005, from http://www.elearnmag.org/subpage.cfm?section= research&article=4-1

McCarty, S. (2005b). Global communications in a graduate course on online education at the University of Tsukuba. *GLOCOM Platform, Colloquium #60*. Japanese Institute of Global Communications, International University of Japan. Retrieved September 7, 2005, from http://www.glocom.org/special_topics/colloquium/20050325_mccarty_global/mccarty_global.pdf

McCarty, S., Ibrahim, B., Sedunov, B., & Sharma, R. (2006). Global online education. In J. Weiss, J. Nolan, J. Hunsinger, & P. Trifonas (Eds.), *International handbook of virtual learning environments* (pp. 723-787). Dordrecht, The Netherlands: Springer.

McVay Lynch, M. (2004). Update on mentoring project. *WEB: WAOE Electronic Bulletin, 4*(3), 4 paragraphs. Portland State University, OR: World Association for Online Education. Retrieved October 26, 2005, from http://waoe.org/communication/webframe9-fall2004.htm

Mezirow, J. (1991). *Transformative dimensions of adult education*. San Francisco: Jossey-Bass.

Stiglitz, J. (2002). *Globalization and its discontents*. London: Penguin Books.

Tuomioja, E. (2003). Globalisation—Threats and opportunities. In T. Varis, T. Utsumi, & W. Klemm (Eds.), *Global peace through the global university system* (pp. 21-24). Hameenlinna, Finland: RCVE, UNESCO Chair in Global E-Learning, University of Tampere.

United Nations Division for the Advancement of Women (2002, December 23). Information and communication technologies and their impact on and use as an instrument for the advancement and empowerment of women. *Report of the Expert Group Meeting, Seoul, Republic of Korea*. Retrieved September 7, 2005, from http://www.un.org/womenwatch/daw/egm/ict2002/reports/EGMFinalReport.pdf

Zakaria, F. (2004, February 2). The one-note superpower. *Newsweek*. Retrieved October 27, 2005, from http://msnbc.msn.com/id/4051669/

Chapter VII

Do the Philosophical Foundations of Online Learning Disadvantage Non-Western Students?

David Catterick
University of Dundee, Scotland

Abstract

A product of its historical origins, online learning is firmly rooted in the educational values that dominate post-secondary education in Britain, Australasia, and North America. With the increasing numbers of international students studying degree programs online, this chapter asks whether students from diverse educational cultures are disadvantaged in their learning by the teaching approaches implemented within online teaching environments. Active learning, reflective practice, and collaborative learning are all based on a cognitive, constructivist tradition (Fox, 2001), one which is evidently not shared by much of the rest of the world (Kim & Bonk, 2002; Wright & Lander, 2003). Employing evidence from the field of cross-cultural psychology (Allik & McCrae, 2004) and taking Chinese students as an example (Cheung, Leung, Zhang, Sun, Gan, Song, & Xie, 2001; Lin, 2004; Matthews, 2001), the author suggests that there may be some cause for concern within online instructional practices. The chapter concludes with three possible responses to the issue, two of which might go some way towards ensuring that international students find themselves on a more even playing field in their online degree program of study.

Introduction

The online delivery of degree programmes is a relatively new phenomenon in the field of higher education. Like so many technologies applied to the field of education, the arrival of the virtual learning environment (VLE) or learning management systems (LMS) seemed to precede the underlying educational philosophy needed to give it both support and credibility within the academic community. This meant there was something of a need to play catch-up, and the result was what the author terms the "Magpie Effect," a process of appropriating a variety of educational philosophies in order to justify the pedagogical value of the emerging technology. This is evidenced by the number of educational technologists who still post to discussion lists like the *Distance Education Online Symposium Listserv* (DEOS-L) asking the list for help in justifying the rationale of VLE use to university policy makers. This may seem like an overly cynical opening for a chapter on distance learning, but even if the reader views things in a slightly different way, there are two notions which would not seem so contentious:

1.   It is higher education institutions in Britain, Australasia and North America (BANA) which have been at the forefront of online degree programme development and delivery.

2.   The philosophical foundations of online distance learning have arisen out of Western (particularly BANA) educational paradigms.

In this chapter, the author argues (from a theoretical rather than an empirical perspective) that in spite of the supposed global reach of online distance learning, the Western philosophical "software" that runs on the technology might disadvantage students who do not share the same constituent values. In exploring this hypothesis, the example of ethnic Chinese international students studying within an online degree program will be used. This choice stems from a combination of the author's six years' experience of teaching in universities in the People's Republic of China, his eight years' experience of teaching Chinese students in UK higher education, and the fact that many Chinese students joining online distance learning programs in BANA countries are of ethnic Chinese origin.

Exploring the Historical Context of the Prevailing Educational Philosophy

By the time online learning became a feature of higher education in the mid-1990s, the landscape of educational philosophy had already long since been radically transformed as a consequence of the shift from behaviourist beliefs about the nature of learning to cognitivist ones (Mayer, 1996). Essentially, the change was the result of a growing conviction among educational philosophers and theorists that the mental processes which constitute learning and development are the product of symbolic activity within individual minds (Atkinson & Shiffrin, 1968). Supported by breakthroughs in the study of memory and problem-solving, cognitivism quickly became the touchstone for educational research eventually giving rise to a theory of information processing (ibid, 1968). Over the intervening decades, different branches of cognitivism have developed, but the most influential, and arguably the most controversial (Fox, 2001; Liu & Matthews, 2005), is constructivism. Grounded in the philosophical writings of Lev Vygotsky (1896-1934) and, later, Jean Piaget (1896-1980), constructivism portrays learning as a process in which the individual translates information from the people and world around them into a form that is intelligible to them at the personal level. With Vygotsky (1978) himself emphasising the role of social context on cognitive development, positing that "all the higher functions originate as actual relationships between individuals" (1978, p. 57), and Piaget emphasising the role of environmental stimuli (Piaget, 1953), constructivism fundamentally rejected the knowledge transmission model of the behaviourist era. In constructivism, knowledge was portrayed not as an objective reality transmitted from teacher to student, but rather co-constructed in the interactions between teacher and learners. This key philosophical shift placed far more emphasis on the role of the learner in the learning process, as it focused upon providing learners with the opportunity to contextualise knowledge within the framework of their own experience and schema. Words like interaction, collaboration, and facilitation seemed to take on a growing importance in the educational literature which, in turn, engendered a shift from teacher-led instructional strategies to more learner-centred ones.

But while this shift in educational philosophy was already well-established in the BANA nations by the mid-1990s, the same shift had not affected mainstream education in whole swathes of the rest of the world. As a so-called "foreign expert" working in Chinese higher education institutions during the 1990s, the author personally saw the philosophical conflicts which resulted when the usually young, well-meaning foreign teacher adopted cognitivist and constructivist approaches in the classroom. As the barriers to these approaches materialised, some foreign teachers took upon themselves a personal agenda of regime change at the philosophical level. Unfortunately, this frequently damaged the social fabric of the classroom relationship, which is a vital aspect of constructivist approaches. One of the most enlightening studies addressing this fallout is by Li (1999) who details the findings from a three-year study of student responses to and opinions of Western teaching staff in his institution in China. What Li's study points to is a world of conflict in which the students slowly withdraw from the classroom and thereby the learning process. Students cite the fact that the classroom experience did not live up to their expectations of what constitutes quality learning (Li, 1999). In this chapter, it will be argued that the cultural imperialism at the heart of the process which Li describes is also evident in online distance learning, meaning that there is a similar risk of disenfranchising the online learner.

Teaching Approaches Resulting from the Educational Philosophy

Before investigating the implications of conflicting educational philosophies, it is important to consider in more detail the connection between educational philosophy and teaching approach, and understand the key teaching approaches commonly associated with a cognitivist educational philosophy. While it would be easy simply to see the adoption of a teaching approach as an entirely bottom-up process which teachers themselves are fully able to rationalise, the reality is that the well-developed quality assurance mechanisms in BANA countries (which are themselves the product of the same philosophical foundations) add a significant top-down influence. In addition, it is important to note that decisions about teaching approach should not necessarily be seen as conscious ones. In fact, a survey of online teaching staff would likely reveal that teaching approaches can be subscribed to without the teacher being fully aware of the philosophy which underpins them. Evidence for this can be found in in-service staff development programmes (at least in UK higher education) which introduce staff to various techniques such as fostering active learning, but present them at face value rather than in their philosophical context. In his own teaching in China, the author found himself in the rather absurd situation of trying to defend his use of Western teaching strategies without having properly considered and debated the values from which they stemmed. Now, years later, it is time to consider whether something similar might be happening in online teaching contexts.

The following (non-hierarchical) list is far from comprehensive, but would probably be recognisable to many BANA teaching staff as the teaching approaches which characterise their own online teaching. In summarising each teaching approach, there has been a conscious attempt not to oversimplify the issues and to avoid critiquing what the author personally believes are (in some cases, at least) approaches that are not systematically supported by thorough, well-grounded research.

Teaching Approach #1: Promoting Active Learning

Active learning is a rather nebulous term used to describe a range of instructional approaches which seek to promote active involvement of the learner in learning process (De Vita, 2000). Even the term "active learning" invites a contrast with the notion of passivity in learning, and is used as one of the main arguments against the transmissional mode of teaching common in behaviourist approaches. Active learning acknowledges the cognitivist view that the learner is not simply an empty vessel, but someone who plays an integral role in the learning process (Vygotsky, 1978). In online learning, the active learning typically finds its expression in contributions to online discussion fora and synchronous discussion (Dalgarno, 2001).

Teaching Approach #2: Promoting Reflective Practice

Reflective practice (Kolb, 1984) has become a key teaching approach, particularly in contexts where the learners are post-experience professionals. At its simplest, reflective practice involves "thinking about one's work" (Parker, 1997, p. 2) and is the product of the positivist notion that mental processes can be observable. Reflective teaching involves a "willingness to engage in constant self-appraisal and development [which] implies flexibility, rigorous analysis and social awareness" (Parker, 1997, p. 2, quoting Pollard & Tann, 1994, p. 9). As knowledge is seen to be constructed rather than received, there is clearly a need to have a mechanism by which to monitor and evaluate one's own practice. One such tool, the learning cycle, was developed by David Kolb (1984) and is now in widespread use (see Figure 1).

The idea of the learning cycle is that the learner can begin at any point on the cycle and use the framework as an aid to reflection. In online degree programmes, this typically involves learners from a professional background reflecting on a critical incident or case in their professional life and demonstrating reflective practice before integrating it into an academic written report.

Teaching Approach #3: Promoting Collaborative Learning and Group Interaction

Collaborative learning is defined by UNESCO (United Nations Educational, Scientific, and Cultural Organization) as learners working together "in groups on the same task simultaneously, thinking together over demands and tackling complexities" (*Definitions of Open Learning*, n.d., p. 1). Collaborative learning is very much seen as "the act of shared creation and/or discovery" (*Definitions of Open Learning*, n.d., p. 2) with the interaction in small groups being seen as a trigger for metacognitive activity. In online distance learning, collaborative learning can be facilitated through the use of "break out" groups who discuss an issue without significant input from the tutor before feeding back to the larger forum.

Figure 1. Kolb's learning cycle as quoted in Smith (2001)

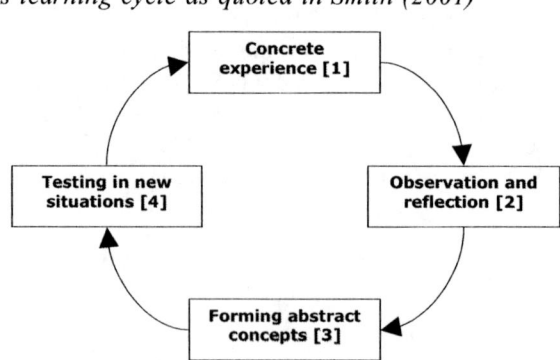

Teaching Approach #4: Promoting Autonomous Learning

Littlewood (1999, p. 74) citing Ryan (1991, p. 210) defines autonomy as a process of "self-determination" or "self-regulation," a process in which "one experiences the self to be an agent, the 'locus of causality' of one's behaviour." Autonomy sees learning as going beyond a partnership between teacher and learner with the locus of control shifting far more to the learner than in previous, more teacher-centred approaches. In online learning, learners are encouraged to use online research to promote their learning, sometimes with the intention that what the learner finds is incorporated into the content of the course. On a wider scale, autonomy is considered a key transferable skill in societies which value independent thought and also fits in with the relativistic worldview of post-modernity.

To the younger, Western learner, these teaching approaches are simply accepted as part of the educational process. To learners from educational cultures still influenced by more traditional practices, these values and teaching strategies may produce a certain cultural dissonance which frequently has a negative impact on the learning experience, at least in the short term.

Culture, Personality, and the Chinese Learner

Over the past five years, BANA countries have seen an unprecedented growth in the number of mainland Chinese international students studying degree programs abroad. This growth has been matched by the number of ethnic Chinese students studying for degrees online (International Students in Australian Universities, IDP Education, 2004). These learners are likely to encounter some, if not all, of the teaching approaches previously described. But how are these approaches different from the ones previously encountered by the students? Though learning objectives are the key determinant of student success, it is conceivable that one consequence of not conforming to the teaching approaches could possibly be the student failing the program. Space does not allow me to explore the integration of assessment into teaching approaches. Suffice it to say that if as part of an assessment a student is asked to provide evidence of reflective practice (*Teaching Approach #2*) and fails to do so, they will likely fail.

Exploring the Notion of Culture

One of the most common ways of investigating culture is by profiling national cultural characteristics. This has become increasingly common predominantly in the context of global business interaction with key work by Hofstede (1991) and more recently by Inglehart and Baker (2000). While high-context/low-context and male/female cultural dichotomies do go some way towards creating a framework for understanding cultural differences, it must be remembered that national boundaries are sometimes rather arbitrarily drawn and may well be based more upon geography and political expediency rather than shared cultural history or ethnicity. Even ethnicity may prove problematic, as it may indicate a shared heritage rather than cultural homogeneity. Holliday (1999) calls for researchers to recognise the importance of what he terms "small cultures," a paradigm which "attaches culture to small social groupings or activities wherever there is cohesive behaviour, and thus avoids culturist ethnic, national, or international difference" (1999, p. 237). It might be useful, however, to take Holliday's notion of "small cultures" one step further by suggesting that it may be more beneficial to think in terms of the "culture of the individual," a realisation that cultural features need to be examined at the lowest common denominator, which is, of course, the individual rather than the national or the ethnic.

What allows us to make this transition is the growing body of research into personality. The personality inventory is a tool widely used in this type of research and is based on the principles of psychometric testing. A number of these inventories report results in the form of a personal profile, an extended prose text which summarises individuals' main strengths and weaknesses, their communication preferences and how they best function in a team. Personality inventories have until relatively recently been designed around a universalist (etic) view of personality; that is to say, based on the theory that personality will broadly exhibit the same characteristics whatever the cultural background of the individual. Cheung et al. (2001) and her colleagues at the University of Hong Kong have, over the past decade and a half, challenged this view of personality arguing, that while many aspects of personality measured by a standardised, globally-administered instrument are indeed universal, there are a number of key elements which are missed by the etic tools. Using the *Five Factor Personality Inventory* as a starting point, Cheung et al. (2001) created a culture-specific (emic) personality inventory for ethnic Chinese learners and workers called the Chinese Personality Assessment Inventory (CPAI). Cheung's tool, though starting from the culture of the individual, focuses on certain unique elements which she claims points to the existence of what she terms a "Chinese tradition." Cheung is careful not to claim that these components are unique to Chinese culture, but she does portray them as key elements of the psyche of ethnic Chinese individuals.

The Chinese Tradition

Chinese tradition, as it is defined by Cheung et al. (2001), contains six key characteristics: *Ren Qing*; *Ah-Q mentality*; *harmony*; *face*; *thrift vs. extravagance*; and *modernization*. Of these, only the first four can be considered to be relevant to educational contexts and thus relevant to the content of this chapter. In this next part of the chapter, these four characteristics will be used as predictors of response to the cognitivist teaching approaches referred to earlier.

1.   *Ren Qing* (translated as relationship orientation)

      Ren Qing literally translates into the English language as "human emotion." *Ren Qing* "covers adherence to cultural norms of interaction based on reciprocity, exchange of social favours, and exchange of affection according to implicit rules (Cheung et al., 2001, p. 408). This complex interplay of interactions focusing on social favours and obligations is difficult (for the outsider) to grasp except perhaps at the surface level, when someone receives a favour they are expected to pay it back at some point in the future. Favours might take the form of gifts carefully chosen to match the givers' own perception of the depth of the relationship (Chan, 2002).

2.   *Ah-Q mentality* (translated as defence mechanism)

Ah-Q is a well-known, satirical Chinese character from the Chinese literary canon. His name is used to indicate the "defense mechanisms of the Chinese people, including self-protective rationalization, externalization of blame, and belittling others' achievements" (Cheung et al., 2001, p. 408).

3.   *Harmony*

Harmony is defined by Cheung as referring to one's inner peace of mind, contentment, interpersonal harmony, avoidance of conflict, and maintenance of equilibrium (2001, p. 408). Harmony, both personal and interpersonal, is seen to need protecting at all costs. On the surface, we might equate harmony with the Western concept of not rocking the boat, but this under-represents the role of maintaining equilibrium among all parties rather than simply monitoring one's own input in a situation.

4.   *Face*

Although the concept of face exists in a variety of cultures, in the Chinese tradition, face refers to something more complex involving the interplay of relationships. In the Chinese tradition, face is "the pattern of orientations in an interpersonal and hierarchical connection and social behaviours to enhance one's face and to avoid losing one's face" (Cheung et al., 2001, p. 408). One of the key differences between face in the Western sense is that in ethnic Chinese circles, face is not only lost, it is also protected (avoiding your own loss of face) and given (praising another individual in front of their superiors). The rest of the chapter will examine how these characteristics might impact on the response of ethnic Chinese students to cognitivist teaching approaches.

Comparing Teaching Approaches and Chinese Culture

While there are a number of things that ethnic Chinese learners might recognise within the value system of online education, there are certain values inherent within the teaching approaches that might seem as puzzling and as alien to them as the four Chinese tradition characteristics seem to the Westerner. It is possible to see how these may lead to feelings of cultural dissonance for some Chinese learners, not least because they may perceive there to be an essential conflict between their own educational heritage and the values inherent in online learning.

Teaching Approach #1: Promoting Active Learning

Evidence of active learning in higher education is often seen in terms of involvement in discussion or contribution to debate. In promoting active learning, the teacher would, for example, expect students to contribute to an online discussion forum, behaviour often reinforced by rewards or penalties. Despite this, some students remain "silent" or uninvolved, a phenomenon known in face-to-face contexts as communication reticence or communication apprehension and in online learning as lurking. Communication reticence, as the name suggests, results from students remaining uninvolved in what are considered normal classroom processes such as asking or answering questions. Cheng (2000) and Jones (1999) both examine communication reticence in the context of non-native speakers communicating in an English language environment. While Cheng (2000) suggests that linguistic factors play a key role, Jones (1999) cites the influence of cultural background. Whatever the cause, and personality issues aside, the anecdotal and perhaps stereotypical view of many teaching staff in higher education is that communication reticence is more typical of Chinese students than other non-native or native speakers of English. The notion implicit in many such observations is that it is only through the use of productive language and contribution to debate that learning can occur. In Confucius' writings (Book XVI, *Record on the Subject of Education*), the system of college education is described as one in which the students "listened, but they did not ask questions; and they could not transgress the order of study imposed on them" (Ulrich, 1947, p. 20). With communications reticence woven into the cultural heritage of a society, we might expect to see the behaviour justified. One cultural justification for communication reticence was heard by the author. A student said that, in their approach to learning, Western learners were like hot water bottles, hot on the outside and hot on the inside. Chinese learners, in contrast, were like thermos flasks, equally hot on the inside but cool on the outside. In the traditional Chinese classroom, the link between active participation in the class and the process of learning is one which may seem far from obvious.

Teaching Approach #2: Promoting Reflective Practice

Reflection, as we have seen, is an activity focusing on the individual's experience and their own independent evaluation of that experience. One interesting study on cross-cultural aspects of reflective practice is Stockhausen and Kawashima's (2002) study of post-experience Japanese nurses studying at an Australian university. The chapter focuses on the cultural barriers experienced by these nurses in grasping reflective practice as a key concept that would enhance their professional standing. In the opening section of the article, by way of explaining the barriers, the authors point out that,

Japanese culture is principled on interdependence, interconnectedness and interrelations ... [and] the behaviour of Japanese people is governed by social sensitivity and their extreme concern regarding social interactions and relationships and the avoidance of conflict. (Stockhausen & Kawashima, 2002, p. 119)

The authors go on to describe how in Japan, nurses are "devoted to patients while being required to function subserviently to predominantly male physicians" (2002, p. 119) which means that any reflective practice would impact upon these "interconnected" relationships and social roles in the hospital, a case perhaps of the educational value being in contradiction with social values. Though the students in this study are Japanese, and we have no data available to compare the professional working cultures of Japan and China, it would seem that Japanese learners are as concerned about harmony as Chinese learners. This can be explained by the fact that other Confucian Heritage countries share some of the characteristics which constitute Chinese tradition. It would seem, based on this evidence, therefore, that at least as far as harmony is concerned, BANA teaching approaches may conflict with deeply-held socio-cultural values. Though the credibility gap barrier may not be insurmountable (as we see in Stockhausen & Kawashima's 2002 study), it is important for Western teachers to reflect upon the impact that their teaching approaches might have in other contexts.

Teaching Approach #3: Promoting Collaborative Learning and Group Interaction

In the Confucian tradition, the teacher is portrayed as the "fount of all wisdom," or in Western parlance "the sage on the stage." This seems to contrast sharply with constructivist notions of co-construction of meaning. In the traditional Chinese class-room, teacher-centeredness has a profound influence on the role of the learner. In Book XVI, *Record on the Subject of Education*, the subservience of the learner to the teacher is emphasised by the following analogy "Those who first yoke a young horse place it behind, with the carriage going on in front of it" (Ulrich, 1947, p. 23), that is, that the learner is subservient to the teacher and needs to be carefully developed. As the source of all wisdom, the teacher is the most important person in the classroom, which influences the way the relationship with other learners is viewed. Learner input via collaborative and group interaction might therefore be seen as immediately less expert and the time spent in collaboration could well be considered as detracting from teacher input. This is, again, not to suggest that these are insurmountable barriers, but where collaborative and group interaction does occur, there could be a further problem in the nature of the group dynamic. Ren Qing (relationship orientation) suggests that the complex web of favours might have an influence on the negotiation of team roles as favours are called in. The assumption that the division of labour in a group task is an equal one may be faulty, but whether or not it is equal, cultural norms would suggest it is likely to be fair according to a non-Western code of social ethics.

Teaching Approach #4: Promoting Autonomous Learning

Autonomous learning, as evidenced by the prefix "auto," emphasises the individual's role in learning. In any collectivist society, the concept of self is primarily understood in one's relationship to the wider group, and we have already seen the complex web of interactions and obligations that make up Ren Qing. Autonomous learning in Ryan's

(1991, p. 210) sense of "self-regulation" and "self-determination" may be seen as desirable traits to be inculcated in BANA countries, but elsewhere in the world these may be seen as destabilising forces. In Chinese, the word that is used to translate the English word "individual" is one which bears the connotation of selfishness or self-centredness, concepts which seem to run counter to the sense of self as informed by the wider social context. For Chinese learners, autonomous learning may be seen as an abdication of responsibility by the teacher. Though they may agree to go along with this approach, if a problem is encountered such as failing an assessment, then there is a real possibility that the Ah-Q (defensiveness) characteristic may become evident. In this scenario, if the failed assessment leads to the possibility of the student not receiving their award, the teacher might be blamed for not having taken a more active role in assisting the student. Tied in with this is the notion of face. While the author was teaching in China 10 years ago, students would express surprise that he would be prepared to fail a student. If a student were to receive a fail grade, it might suggest that he would lose face because it would reflect badly on his teaching record. The concept of students taking responsibility for and managing their own learning should probably not be assumed given the wide diversity of students currently studying on online programs.

Responses to Cultural Dissonance

If one attributes even partial validity to the issues presented thus far in this chapter, then a response strategy needs to be considered. The fact that these teaching approaches are at the very heart of the higher education system in BANA countries and are reinforced by assessment and quality assurance mechanisms means that options for change are relatively limited. In this final section of the chapter, the author proposes three possible responses available to staff.

1.   **Non-accommodation response:** The first response is already very common in face-to-face higher education. The response is based on the notion that the teaching approaches and the educational philosophies which underpin them are part of our own higher education heritage and that these approaches have developed for sound reasons. The argument runs that BANA countries offer world-class higher education and state-of-the-art delivery of online learning and this is proving to be a great attraction to international students from across the world. In this view of Western higher education as a model of success, the learner must simply adapt to the learning context. In the strongest non-accommodation response model, no support is offered to help underpin the acculturation process. As evidence, proponents would point to the large number of students successfully completing degree programs online each year. Critics of this response, on the other hand, would point to the methodological problems associated with tracking studies (e.g., How do we measure "success?") and the fact that higher education is becoming more client-driven with a greater emphasis on the overall student experience.

Despite these criticisms, in many institutions in BANA countries this seems to be the default response.

2. **Intervention response:** The intervention response shares many of the same characteristics as the non-accommodation response, promoting the notion that teaching approaches should remain unchanged. Where it differs is in the view that differences in the educational culture need to be acknowledged and addressed by some form of intervention strategy. The intervention typically forms part of the induction program, either prior to or as the learners start the degree study online. While this response is more accommodating of learner diversity, critics might point to the resource implications in the design and delivery of an online support module. Others suggest that drawing a distinction between home and international students in the delivery of support is unnecessary.

3. **Modification response:** The modification response is without a doubt the most far-reaching of the three responses. The modification response is based on the notion that the educational philosophies which inform teaching approaches in BANA countries need to be re-evaluated and possibly modified. The argument is that given the fact that a significant and growing proportion of the online student body have been educated in educational cultures which do not share the same values, we need to consider issues of accessibility. One practical measure would be to reevaluate the emphasis placed on certain teaching approaches such as reflective practice. To what extent are these approaches simply the ones in vogue? Critics of this response point to the importance of stakeholders in the educational process, in particular the role played by employers in determining the type and range of skills they desire in graduates. A further criticism focuses on the issue of change management, the argument being that change may not be practicable via a unilateral approach given the increasing role played by quality assurance agencies in higher education, who increasingly assess programs according to what is seen as best practice in teaching approach.

Conclusion

Cross-cultural research is notoriously prone to oversimplification of issues, ethnocentrism, and stereotyping, and the author is conscious of the fact that in this chapter he has been at risk as far as these issues are concerned. This chapter has been very much a call to thought rather than a call to action, though in this chapter it is hoped that the Western reader will see their own teaching approaches reflected. If they are convinced of the possibility of cultural dissonance, then invitation is to consider which response is most appropriate in their particular context. Future research needs to test the theoretical hypotheses presented in this chapter through a large-scale empirical study of an online degree context. With the expansion in international student numbers in online degree programs set to continue in the near future at least, this is an area of research whose time very much has come.

References

Allik, J. M., & McCrae, R.R. (2004). Toward a geography of personality traits: Patterns of profiles across 36 cultures. *Journal of Cross-Cultural Psychology, 35*(1), 13-28.

Atkinson, R. C., & Shiffrin, R. M. (1968). Human memory: A proposed system and its control processes. In K. Spence & J. Spence (Eds.), *The psychology of learning and motivation: Advances in research and theory (Vol. 2)*. New York: Academic Press.

Chan, B. (2002, October). A study of the relationship between tutor's personality and teaching   effectiveness: Does culture make a difference? *International Review of Research in Open and Distance Learning, 3*(2).

Cheng, X. T. (2000). Asian students' reticence revisited. *System, 28*, 435-446.

Cheung, F. M., Leung, K., Zhang, J. X., Sun, H. F., Gan, Y. Q., Song, W. Z., & Xie, D. (2001). Indigenous Chinese personality constructs: Is the five-factor model complete? *Journal of Cross-Cultural Psychology, 32*(4), 407-433.

Dalgarno, B. (2001). Interpretations of constructivism and consequences for computer assisted learning. *British Journal of Educational Technology, 32*(2), 183-194.

Definitions of Open Learning (n.d.). Retrieved June 20, 2005, from http://www.unesco.org/ education/educprog/lwf/doc/portfolio/definitions.htm

De Vita, G. (2000). Inclusive approaches to effective communication and active participation in the multicultural classroom. *Active Learning in Higher Education, 1*(2), 168-180.

Distance Education Online Symposium Listserv (n.d.). Retrieved September 15, 2005, from http://www.ed.psu.edu/acsde/deos/deos-l/deosl.asp

Fox, R. (2001). Constructivism examined. *Oxford Review of Education, 27*(1), 23-35.

Hofstede, G. (1991). *Cultures and organizations: Software of the mind.* London: McGraw Hill

Holliday, A. (1999). Small cultures. *Applied Linguistics, 20*(2), 237-264.

IDP Education. (2004). *International students in Australian universities.* Canberra: IDP Education Australia.

Inglehart, R., & Baker, W. E. (2000). Modernization, cultural change, and the persistence of traditional values. *American Sociological Review, 65*(February), 19-51.

Jones, J. F. (1999). From silence to talk: Cross-cultural ideas on students' participation in academic group discussion. *English for Specific Purposes, 18*(3), 243-259.

Kim, K. J., & Bonk, C. J. (2002). Cross-cultural comparisons of online collaboration. *Journal of Computer-Mediated Communication, 8*(1).

Kolb, D. (1984). *Experiential learning: Experience as the source of learning and development.* NJ: Prentice-Hall

Li, M. S. (1999). Discourse and culture of learning—Communication challenges. Unpublished academic presentation. *AARE-NZARE*. Melbourne.

Lin, E. J. -L., & Church, A. T. (2004). Are indigenous Chinese personality dimensions culture-specific?: An investigation of the Chinese personality assessment inventory in Chinese American and European American samples. *Journal of Cross-Cultural Psychology, 35*(5), 586-605.

Littlewood, W. (1999). Defining and developing autonomy in East Asian contexts. *Applied Linguistics, 20*(1), 71-94.

Liu, C. H., & Matthews, R. (2005). Vygotsky's philosophy: Constructivism and its criticisms examined. *International Education Journal, 6*(3), 386-399.

Liu, L. (2005). Rhetorical education through writing instruction across cultures: A comparative analysis of select online instructional materials on argumentative writing. *Journal of Second Language Writing, 14*(1), 1-18.

Matthews, B. (2001). The relationship between values and learning. *International Education Journal, 2*(4), 223-232.

Mayer, R. E. (1996). History of instructional psychology. In E. De Corte & F. E. Weinert (Eds.), *International encyclopaedia of developmental and instructional psychology* (pp. 29-33). Oxford: Pergamon Press.

Parker, S. (1997). *Reflective teaching in the postmodern world: A manifesto for education in postmodernity.* Buckingham, UK: OUP.

Piaget, J. (1953). *The origin of intelligence in the child.* London: Routledge & Kegan.

Pollard, A., & Tann, S. (1994). *Reflective teaching in the primary school: A handbook for the classroom.* London: Cassell.

Ryan, R. M. (1991). The nature of the self in autonomy and relatedness. In J. Strauss & G. R. Goethals (Eds.), *The self: Interdisciplinary approaches.* New York: Springer.

Smith, M. K. (2001). David A. Kolb on experiential learning. *The encyclopedia of informal education.* Retrieved October 28, 2005, from http://www.infed.org/b-explrn.htm

Stockhausen, L., & Kawashima, A. (2002). The introduction of reflective practice to Japanese nurses. *Reflective Practice, 3*(1), 117-129.

Ulrich, R. (1947). *Three thousand years of educational wisdom.* London: Oxford University Press.

Vygotsky, L. (1978). *Mind in society.* London: Harvard University Press.

Wright, S., & Lander, D. (2003). Collaborative group interactions of students from two ethnic backgrounds. *Higher Education Research & Development, 22*(3), 237-252.

Chapter VIII

Theorizing a Multiple Cultures Instructional Design Model for E-Learning and E-Teaching

Lyn Henderson
James Cook University, Australia

Abstract

This chapter demonstrates the inadequacy of multicultural and internationalization instructional design models as the solution for equitable outcomes in the learning, credentialing, and employment stakes in the 21ˢᵗ century. Internationalizing learning and teaching eclipsed multiculturalism as the acclaimed strategy when Western universities entice international non-English-speaking-background students to their campuses or offer degrees to such e-learning students who reside in their own countries. Global and Western businesses establishing niches in overseas countries also use the concept of internationalizing their e-learning materials for the cultural training of staff. In their place, a theoretical model of multiple cultures provides the rationale and strategies for creating and adapting e-learning resources for local, national, and international e-learning contexts.

Introduction

The multiple cultures model (Henderson, 1996) accommodates a variety of combinations of cultures and pedagogies, and academic, industry, and government contexts. Broadly interpreted, culture is the way of life of a people. It is the manifestation of the patterns of thinking and behavior that results through a group's continuing adaptation to its changing social, historical, geographic, political, economic, technological, and ideological environment. Culture incorporates race, ethnicity, religion, class, gender, values, traditions, language, lifestyles, and nationality as well as workplace and academic cultures (Hofstede, 1996; Terpstra & Sarathy, 2000). E-learners[1] and e-teachers[2] belong and participate in more than one culture but demonstrate subsets of these in specific cultural contexts.

For better or worse, the Western model of academic research, writing protocols, and publication standards has become global academic currency. Thus the term, "global academic culture," will be used to reflect these and other common practices, such as credentialing degree programs. Likewise, regardless of the differences in managing businesses in various countries, our globalized economy with its multinational industries has been significantly boosted by international free trade rationales and practices and, in consequence, values global cultural practices. Within this economic culture resides a global culture of training and professional development of staff to work more effectively within specific national and international business cultures. The same situation applies in government so that there is, in effect, a global bureaucratic culture that offers e-training and e-professional development within each bureaucracy's own cultural context. Instructional design of e-learning and e-teaching materials based on the multiple cultures model enables instructors to empower, extend, and enrich the learner's culturally-specific knowledge and ways of thinking and doing by achieving a praxis between these and the demands of particular academic, industry, and government global cultures.

Three major issues are explored to substantiate the benefits of the multiple cultures model of instructional design, which has been utilized, especially in Australia, the United States, Canada, and Singapore. They include the limitations of multicultural or internationalization models; the parameters of the various benefits of a multiple cultures model that accounts for various ethnic, class, gender, academic, and workplace sub-cultures in the design of e-learning materials; and designing and adapting e-courses to incorporate behaviorist, constructivist, and social constructivist e-learning and e-teaching.

Limitations of Multicultural and Internationalization Models

As argued previously (Henderson, 1996), how instructional design of e-learning and e-teaching takes cognizance of multiculturalism and internationalization is exemplified by focusing on the ways it includes and excludes issues of culture. What continues to be experienced on a global scale can be identified as a culturally-blind or unintentional exclusion of issues of culture that result in exclusionary and culturally-homogeneous educational e-learning resources. The result can be, for instance, the universalization of Western or corporate knowledge and culture as natural, necessary, and, in effect, beyond criticism. This chapter challenges this stance.

"Multiculturalism," "cultural diversity," and "cultural pluralism" have not worked, either in Western societies' educational systems or, in particular, the development of e-learning materials delivered to culturally-diverse learners (Edmundson, 2003, 2004). If they had changed the status quo, there would be no need for this book. The "localization of internationalization" of e-learning resources is the new buzz concept. Such learning materials contain localized elements of international teaching and training materials. However, like multiculturalism, it has largely adopted a "soft" approach that does not challenge the status quo. One outcome is the focus on the "etiquette," "feel good," and "exotic" areas of the targeted culture.

Such e-instructional design would include some or all of the following. It is common to include relevant etiquette customs in the materials, such as using both hands when accepting a business card from East Asians and to engage in non-business conversation before commencing the meeting's agenda. Traditions, such as arranged marriages, dress, festivals, myths, and legends are interesting to learners and are usually included in curricula. Other obvious "must include" items are those involving graphics (for example, not using five-sided stars as a rating system because they have religious significance, Hutchinson, Rose, Bederson, Weeks, & Druin, 2005); preferred color schemes (e.g., "some parts of Chinese culture see people marrying in black and being buried in white," Fiesner & Hart, 2005, p. 85); language (not relying solely on the online automatic translations of English into the targeted language or vice versa as they can be too literal and therefore inaccurate, Hutchinson et al., 2005; Tractinsky, 2000); and a right-hand Web navigation menu for those whose writing system is right to left. Such inclusions are not inappropriate *per se*. Indeed, they are crucial and need to be included (Friesner & Hart, 2004; Henderson, 1996; Hutchinson et al., 2005; Voithofer, 2004). However, they are problematic if they are cosmetic, tokenistic, and/or stereotypical (Henderson, 1996).

Tokenism

Tokenism is another instructional design issue that can be found in e-learning resources. In an attempt to localize the courseware, superficial cosmetic changes, such as modifications to the coloring, hair, or eyes of graphic characters and incorporation of the targeted e-learner's music with roll-over menu items or pop-up glossaries, "risk becoming one more example of cultural arrogance—apartheid in a glitzy plastic dress" (Andrews, 1995, p. 8). In fact, Hedberg and Brown (2002) warned that "catchy homepages" using pop-ups, animation, and graphics intended to grab attention could produce the opposite result because "grammar is context specific in Chinese languages so that the student builds up a picture of the meaning of symbols as the text is being read" (Friesner & Hart, 2004, p. 84). Perhaps age and familiarity with variously designed Web sites may be confounding factors.

However in a multiple cultures model, an online Web site would not eschew examples of attention-grabbing animation or pop-ups at relevant points in the online materials, especially when a needs analysis cannot be administered due to an inability to obtain information directly from intended e-students in time for development to occur. Needless to say, the inclusion would be purposeful rather than cosmetic. Thus animation would have a cognitive function, such as tracking economic trade routes or exemplifying a concept such as a community of practice within an e-learning/e-teaching multiple cultures context. In the same vein, a pop-up window would not have a function that was trivial, nor would it cover any text content on the Web page to which it was related. For instance, if a pop-up window were used as a glossary, then it would appear in a margin left empty for that purpose. Another function of the pop-up window would be to present a researcher's point-of-view to a text-box interaction question into which the student had just typed in an answer and clicked the finished button. The researcher's answer would end with a metacognitive activity that required the student to compare and contrast their answer with that of the instructor and post their conclusion with justification to the online discussion forum. Attention to such sound pedagogic practices is integral to an effective multiple cultures model, and as it should be to multiculturalism and internationalization.

In that case, why are these examples not just instances of good pedagogic practice? Although "attention grabbing" Web elements are part of business, educational, and personal Web sites in the students' countries, researchers advised e-instructional designers that Chinese e-learners' understanding could be adversely affected if the elements were used in educational Web materials. Hence, if use of these Web elements were judged through a multicultural or internationalization lens, then they would not be programmed into the e-materials because it was an easy "soft" decision to make for reasons of equity. However, with the multiple cultures model, both conditions would be weighed and found in favor of *cognitive* attention-grabbing design and equitable learning experiences for all Chinese e-learners, those who were most likely to be adversely affected and those who would not be unfavorably influenced.

Another example of tokenistic internationalization, particularly talked about in the corridors at international conferences, is the inclusion of an article from anyone with an Asian (or Middle-Eastern or Eastern European) family name, regardless of the specific nationality of the targeted students or the quality of the article, and see such practices as adequately meeting appropriate internationalizing requirements. To take any such tokenistic practices out of this category would be an assessable critique of that token, in this example it would be the article.

Stereotyping

Even with a growing body of literature to draw upon (Faiola & Matei, 2005; Friesner & Hart, 2004; McCarty, 2005; Ng, 2002; Tjitra, 2000), the following types of cultural stereotyping in developing and teaching cross-cultural e-courses can be exposed: (a) the Asian learner is a rote learner and benefits more when a course is structured with step-by-step instructions (Tjitra, 2000); (b) students in East-Asia, ex-Soviet Eastern European, and Middle-East Islamic countries do not challenge authority, including that of an author; (c) students from such cultures are individualist competitors due to endemic credentialing; and (d) consequently they are passive and accepting of what is delivered. A reason for instances of such stereotypes can be found in any student group and therefore used to justify globalized e-teaching and e-learning practices and materials that are culturally centric.

Hence "educators should be cautious about stereotyping students based on nation of origin or a static notion of culture" (McCarty, 2005, p. 1; Tylee, 2002), including religion (as the aftermath of September 11th has demonstrated). Komiyama (in press; cited in McCarty, 2005) informed her readers that, regardless of age, Japanese peer groups are "raucous (but) reserved with those of different status" (p. 1) and their social constructivist collaborative group work was successful. Neo (2005) and Wesley-Smith (2003) replicated Komiyama's finding with Malaysian and indigenous Hawaiian higher education students, respectively. Kennedy (2002) provided a fascinating systematic overview of traditional interpretations of the Chinese learner counterbalanced by recent re-interpretations as well as when, how, and why these were confirmed or contradicted in his study of the preferences of Hong Kong adult Chinese learners. To be read in conjunction with Kennedy's work, Chan and Elliott (2000) published an exploratory study of Hong Kong Chinese teacher education students' world views with the aim of resolving conceptual and empirical issues. Epistemologic issues for Brunei Darussalam vocational students caught between tradition and modernity, and ethnic identity superceding religion for teenagers in Kosovo and Macedonia, are explored by Minnis (2000) and Babuna (2000), respectively. Such research is mandatory reading for global e-learning instructional designers as well as both e-instructors and, especially when implementing a multiple cultures model, their e-students. With respect to the latter point, Singaporean and Vietnamese Chinese e-learners would be required to compare and contrast Kennedy's findings with their own experiences.

Yet there remains a complexity when editing e-courses with respect to stereotyping. Two examples will suffice.

First, Australian educators are taught that indigenous students prefer working in groups. However, Henderson and Putt (1999) revealed that adult indigenous students elected to work alone when the content was new (for example, a critical theory examination of the relationship between class and education) and then revise together. Reasons had to do with cultural cognition, specifically, privacy, control over pacing, preventing shame if the answers were incorrect, testing their own thinking, and, as one student explained, not wanting to waste time with a peer who knew as little as she did (Henderson & Putt, 1993). In contrast, they preferred working together when the content was familiar (for example, teaching primary school math) as they would be operating from an informed knowledge base. In current-traditional learning, the learner approaches the person who possesses the relevant knowledge and who will give precise information devoid of extraneous or doubtful content (Henderson & Putt, 1999).

The second example involves a successful Master of Education e-course that is edited for each new intake of e-learners within urban, rural, and remote areas of Australia and Canada in order to acknowledge their various professional work and "in-house" learning cultures (armed forces; health; government; middle management; professional sport; and schools, colleges, and universities). Attentive avoidance of the stereotyping mentioned above occurred when editing the e-course for a blended learning context (face-to-face with online discussion forums and blogs) with Singaporean Malay and Chinese students. Part of the assessment was an oral critique of various authors' work. In a previous blended course, they had conducted paired seminars with aplomb. However, during the presentations, a visible level of anxiety was noticed. During feedback and debriefing, the students informed the instructor that this was the first time they had had to critique in public. The students had a mental model that a seminar describes, clarifies, and contrasts various authors' theses, while a critique demands positive and negative criticism of the author's work. They contended that they would have been only a little less anxious if their critique had been via the discussion forum or blog. Critique within an essay was the least threatening as it was just between student and instructor. Given this, should an oral or online critique be avoided? In line with the multiple cultures model the answer would be a resounding, "No!" Regardless of the teaching mode, acknowledging cultural cognitive styles (Faiola & Matei, 2005; Nisbett & Norenzayan, 2002; Nisbett, Peng, Choi, & Norenzayan, 2001), or as referred to in this chapter as cultural ways of thinking and doing, calls for scaffolded modeling by the instructor in ways that escalate the students' entry into this form of assessment over time. This constructivist practice advocates that the e-instructors collaborate to produce a mapped sequence of induction into assessable tasks among the e-courses. As exemplified later in the chapter, the multiple cultures model argues that all e-learners be provided with opportunities to master various academic tasks that are a valued part of a global academic culture for reasons of equitable outcomes.

Multiple Cultures Theoretical Model for E-Learning

One of the major problems with the multicultural and internationalization models is their avoidance of the cognitive, pedagogic, and epistemological aspects of the various cultural educational contexts. An alternative way to conceptualize the cultural contextualization of instructional design of e-learning is a multiple cultures model (Figure 1; also see Henderson, 1993, 1996; Wild & Henderson, 1997). Researchers (Collis, 1999; McLoughlin, 1999; Ng, 2002; Ngeow & Kong, 2002; Ziguras, 2000) confirmed the workable premise of a multiple cultures model through tweaking it for their own contexts. Indeed, Calder (2000), Yonkers (2003), and Lea (2003) delineated the inherent differences in organizational cultures, academic cultures, training cultures, and teaching and learning pedagogies between and, crucially, within each of these differing cultural groups. Both Yonkers' (2003) and Lea's (2003) work stressed that for worthwhile outcomes, a critical business strategy to achieve employee training or delivery of off-shore academic qualifications does not simply target political, religious, and national differences. Fundamentally, to achieve sustainable learning outcomes, a mix and match between the global academic or training cultures and those of the e-learners is called for in developing and implementing the multiple cultures model. Otherwise, the result could well be a

Figure 1. Multiple cultures theoretical model

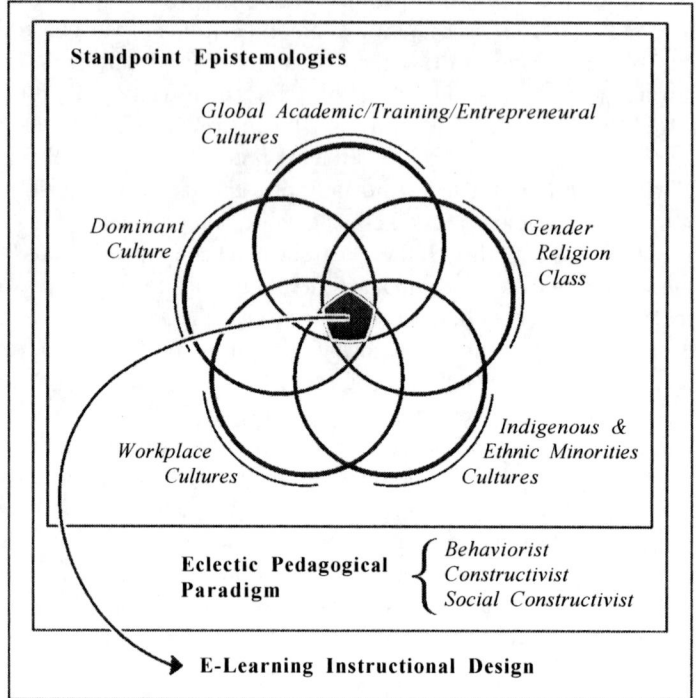

misguided "dumbed-down," rather than challenging, selection of academic content and assessment types and requirements.

The multiple cultures model of e-learning delineated in Figure 1 strives for a coherent interplay among the various cultural logics: global academia or training cultures; the majority societal epistemologies of the e-learners and those of indigenous and ethnic minorities; issues of gender, class, religion, age, kinship, politics, and various workplace cultures; and pedagogies. Instructional design aims for a coherent partnership among these in the e-learning and e-teaching context, whether it is local, national, or global.

Epistemology and Standpoint Epistemologies

In Figure 1, the inner section of the diagram contains the epistemologies or worldviews of the various cultural players in the e-learning instructional design paradigm (Henderson, 1996). Two examples will suffice to help clarify the concept.

The first example is that of Confucian dynamism (Hofstede, 1996). This epistemology is apparently shared by Chinese e-learners from differing parts of Asia and other countries and who maintain aspects of Confucian Heritage Cultures (Smith, 2001). It is perceived to include characteristics such as a "strong bias towards obedience, the importance of rank and hierarchies, the need for smooth social relations" and the importance of education (Friesner & Hart, 2004, p. 83) coupled with individual materialistic pursuits (Zhu & He, 2002). Further to this and the previous discussion of avoiding stereotyping, Cheng (2000) pointed out that the Chinese term, "knowledge," consists of two characters: "One is 'xue' (to learn) and the other is 'wen' (to ask) (p. 441). Thus the e-learning goal for students whose world view is that of Confucian Heritage Cultures would be "to cultivate oneself as an intelligent, creative, independent, autonomous being" (Lea, 1996, p. 34). This means that, because epistemologically the quest for knowledge involves both acquiring and questioning information (Cheng, 2000), then the multiple cultures e-learning materials would have this built into the tasks and assessment.

Another example is a gaping difference between Australian non-indigenous and indigenous epistemologies. The former, which is common to Western societies, encompasses the belief that knowledge (information) is "the birthright of every individual. This value is not negated by the fact that it is not followed in practice where power, privilege, and the law limit an individual's right and ability to access information" (Henderson, 1996, p. 97). One of the components of aboriginal espistemologies is the notion that all knowledge is owned. However some knowledge is owned, private, and non-negotiable while other knowledge is owned individually or jointly and is negotiable. "Knowledge belongs to or 'owns' the people without the 'owner' having to be personally responsible for the origin of that knowledge (West, 1993; referencing this information highlights the fact that, in Western epistemologies, the source has to be acknowledged)" (Henderson, 1996, p. 97). Gaining knowledge is not a right but a privilege. Currently, some youths are not initiated into certain knowledge because the elders do not believe that they would take appropriate custodial care of that knowledge. Aboriginal and Torres Strait Islander[3] artists do not have the right to use the traditional symbols, stories, dances, and songs of other indigenous Australians, even at a wedding or for a school activity, without permission to share those traditions. This is in contrast to non-indigenous artists who believe they have artistic freedom to take inspiration from anywhere and anyone (McDonald, 1993).

Consequently the multiple cultures model caters for the epistemologies of global, national, and minority cultures (Figure 1). In so doing, it privileges the standpoint epistemologies of individuals and groups in the various cultures, but ensures particular cognizance of those whose worldviews lose out in the implementation of soft multicultural and soft internationalization instructional design. For instance, depending on whether it were industry, government, or higher education, the e-resources in multiple cultures instructional design would include articles, videoed lectures or talks, and activities from the differing epistemologies of: management and lower-rung employees; right-wing and left-wing politicians; Islam, Hindu, and Christian followers; first generation immigrants' maintenance of traditional customs compared with their peers back in their homeland who have changed in step with the 21st century; and, what is sometimes lost sight of in the globalization of e-learning materials, between gender and class in various ethnic groups within and between nations (Figure 1).

As Harel and Papert (1991) pointed out, standpoint epistemology caters for "epistemological pluralism" as it does not presume that any one epistemology is incontrovertible. The various ways of constructing knowledge are acknowledged, and learners are prompted to query those epistemologies in the construction of their own knowledge (Haas & Steiner, 2001; Harding, 1986). Instructional design advocates of standpoint epistemology would challenge e-learners to consider: How is a particular epistemology socially, politically, and economically constructed and for what purposes (Koo, 2001)? Do standpoint epistemologies provide greater emancipatory, social, and educational validity than merely a range of perspectives and theories? What is the impact of Asian, Indonesian, European, Russian, Australian, Middle Eastern, African, or The Americas colonialism and post-colonialism on people's ways of knowing, their views of whom and what they are, and what they consider worthwhile to teach and to learn (Alcoff, 2003; McConachy, 1999; McLaughlin, 1999; Pizarro, 1998; Thaman, 2003)? How do various epistemologies or world views (for example, Western, indigenous, Latino, Middle Eastern, or Asian) reveal themselves, for instance in mathematical, medical, technical, or social theories and solutions? A fundamental ingredient of e-education would include activities centered on these sorts of queries. Through such an approach as exemplified here and in the next sections, the various multiple cultures delineated in Figure 1 are made visible and debatable.

Global Academic Cultures

The e-learning multiple cultures model needs overtly to incorporate the specific require-ments of academic cultures (Figure 1). These are expressed through the following culturally-specific ways of promoting cognitive development in colleges and universi-ties: the content to be taught, the types of assessment required, and the written, online, and oral genres to be mastered. Currently, world academic cultures are based on Western academic parameters, and it is therefore inescapable when delivering global e-learning courses and post-graduate degree programs. An instance of the importance is the Israeli situation where publications in their first language, Hebrew, do not count for university promotion. Another instance is the Chinese government's economic, political, and educational mandatory policy on learning English in schools and its impetus for university students to obtain Western English language higher degrees (Friesner & Hart, 2004).

Societies' Dominant Culture

The inherent cultural imperialism in this global academic culture, plus the fact that any country's academic culture is embedded within that society's dominant culture (Figure 1), means that e-learning materials need to include exploration of the systemic issues to do with power, control, and disadvantage. These aspects are usually missing from, or superficially treated in, multicultural models. For instance, a comparative examination of the information rich and information poor in global, national, and within-national contexts and the various programs targeting redress is of importance in educational situations. At a recent symposium on information and communication technologies (ICTs), a representative of the World Bank presented a fascinating talk that included funding a local university professor's (Mitra, 2005) "hole-in-the-wall" computer project in a poor rural area of India. The keynote speaker went on to describe how a self-taught illiterate orphan boy living on the street was called on by his community to fix the computer's glitches. Significantly, there was no mention of the project's provision for that boy's education or, for that matter, any of the other poorest boys and girls who now had some computer skills but nowhere to go with them as they were not attending school. The status quo was not challenged during the speaker's presentation.

Indigenous and Ethnic Minorities[4]

Drawing on the multiple cultures needs analysis survey, the answers would inform e-instructional design by incorporating the multi-racial/ethnic cultures in particular societies so that relevant parts of their culture's knowledge and preferred ways of thinking and doing are incorporated in a manner that goes beyond tokenism. A constructive practical implementation is overtly acknowledging the various e-learners' significant traditions and customs by not scheduling assignment due dates at times of special religious observances. Another would be setting an activity in economics or business e-courses that demonstrated certain principles or practices through an example involving indigenous peoples' economic exporting enterprises (e.g., Aboriginal Exporters Directory http://www.dfait-maeci.gc.ca/foreign_policy/aboriginal/business/business-en.asp). In this case, the multiple cultures model would be best served by not drawing further attention to the indigenous enterprises as the content for an activity, unless an e-learner wished to discuss or research the indigenous aspects further. If this occurred, it would naturally become an extra online forum discussion topic. The positive impact of the assessment task as originally described on the e-learners and e-instructor (if different from the content specialist) would be powerful because the instructional design presents the indigenous business example as if it were a regular part of an e-course and thereby renders it legitimate. In so doing, the example cancels any implication of tokenistic inclusion.

However, some things are academically inescapable. Various ethnic minority groups within any nation do not have a choice but to become bi- or multi-cultural to achieve equity in the education and subsequent employment stakes. For example, during an e-tutorial teleconference with Indigenous Bachelor of Education students, one e-learner was overheard saying, "Why doesn't she [the e-lecturer] ever believe us?" In Western academic contexts, students have to justify the source of their ideas and arguments through referencing. As explained previously, this is not part of the practiced epistemology of indigenous peoples. If it had not already been built into the e-course materials in the section on plagiarism, the e-student's comment provided what educators call "a teaching moment." It allowed the differing epistemologies of academic culture and indigenous (or other cultures) to be examined and the rationale for justification of what would be unsubstantiated statements if left without referencing.

Another example highlights the inadequacy of the belief that students can easily switch between the majority and their own ethnic minority cultures. When debriefing with an indigenous student in a neutral setting, over coffee in a nearby shopping center, both the lecturer and student were concerned as it was his repeat practicum. The lesson had involved reading a story book to Grade 2 students. The lecturer realized that the credit-level student had quickly read each page of the story in his mind and, without a break in the pace, he then told the story of that page to the children. In effect, he was putting into practice his culture's tradition of storytelling. It was also an example of culture switching. However, it was not until he asked, "Why do teachers have to *read* stories?" that the lecturer realized that it was not merely a matter of being able to switch language and behavior codes in the appropriate settings. The crucial lesson to both of us and, by extension, to those belonging to majority and minority cultures was that each has to recognize the value in the bi-cultural practice (Bowskill, McCarty, Luke, Kinshuk, & Hand, 2000). This is an underlying principle in the multiple cultures model.

Gender

Gender issues are important in epistemologies, pedagogies, and content of e-learning (e.g., Haslanger, 2000; Looi, 2002; also see examples previously mentioned). There are diverse sources available online: for instance, statistics of women's education, rates of pay by gender and occupation, and health by country and within a country by ethnicity (Haslanger, 2000); statistics for indigenous women's mortality rates, domestic violence, education, and imprisonment (Kauffman, 2003; Rappaport, 2004; Susskind, 2000); information concerning the neglected rights and conditions of female refugees and those in occupied countries (Susskind, 2004); and literature, such as, Arabic prison narrative written by women (Boulos, 2003). Domestic and multi-national "sweat shop" factories in China and third-world countries also impact female (and male) roles, rights, health, justice, and education (Susskind, 2000) within and across national and international economic, political, ethical, and social values.

In the multiple cultures' e-course and e-programs, these are issues that have a legitimate place in e-learning materials regardless of discipline. If e-instructors were concerned as to where to include some of this type of content, ethics would be a relevant area for any discipline. They could also be included in the same manner as suggested in the indigenous export enterprise example.

Another example of inclusion follows: If either physics, medicine, mathematics, warfare, or computer science were the discipline under study, an online search of female and male by nationality/ethnicity could add to the e-students' understanding of which women contributed to our global knowledge or were highly prized participants in a particular area of endeavor. Additionally, it would not be difficult to add commentary whether online database sources continue to maintain or have rectified the gender imbalance in these areas in online and print materials (Kramarae & Spender, 2000; Spender, 1996).

Organizing an Internet project between a mixed-gender class of teenage students in a Western school and single-gender high schools in certain Middle Eastern countries would solve any problems associated with boys and girls learning together. What is more important academically? Is it that the e-learners collaborate in mixed gender groups when this is not their norm or that the topic is interrogated by students who feel comfortable in a gender-segregated grouping? In the multiple cultures model, a relevant e-activity would be discussion of the historical, religious, educational, and economic rationales for single-sex schools, or, as is occurring in some high schools, single-sex math and science classes, in both countries. This strategy negates possibility of tokenistic characteristics and a "them versus us" mindset.

In Torres Strait Islander culture in Australia, gender and kinship are entwined. For example, nieces should not contradict their uncles, particularly in public forums. In the Bachelor of Education blended e-learning Remote Area Education Program (RATEP) at James Cook University in Australia, the students at one RATEP centre at the tip of Cape York decided that these cultural norms would not be maintained within the confines of the RATEP context. In this way, each individual became involved in lively teleconference and online critiques and debates (Henderson & Putt, 1999; York & Henderson, 2001). However, at another RATEP site, it did not take the e-instructor long to realize that the niece had asked to work with her uncle because she was cognitively lazy and allowed her uncle to do the thinking and planning; she had planned to do only the practical part of the activity.

In these myriad ways, the multiple cultures model does not merely encourage, but stipulates, the integration of various value systems if the intention is to maximize equity. Equity is not a simple matter of multiculturalism or the Asianization, Indianization, Middle Easternization, East Europeanization, Africanization, or any "...ization" of the e-learning resources of whatever groups are to be the consumers. Equity of e-learning means maximizing the learning outcomes for all the e-learners.

Eclectic Pedagogic Paradigm and E-Instructional Design

The second layer in Figure 1 contains an essential mix of pedagogic e-teaching and e-learning paradigms and practices. When theorizing the multiple cultures model back in the mid-nineties (Henderson, 1994, 1996), proposing that instructional design should candidly acknowledge the reality, and worth, of eclectic pedagogic practices was a risk. A line had been drawn in the sand between behaviorist e-learning and constructivist or social constructivist e-learning instructional design. Even a cursive look through journal articles and books published since the early 1990s weights best interactive multimedia and online pedagogic design and implementation at the constructivist/social constructivist end of the behaviorist-social constructivist pedagogic continuum. Generally ignored were the undergraduate and postgraduate realities of a standard 10-14 week e-course or intensive 10-day blended mode course. Rarely have online courses, or face-to-face teaching, been totally constructivist or social constructivist for their duration. In contrast, an eclectic blend of behaviorist, constructivist, and social constructivist pedagogies reflects reality and thus sits convincingly in an interactive multimedia, online, and/or blended curriculum, whether within an e-course or over an e-program (Ally, 2004; Edmundson, 2004; Henderson, 1996; Henderson & Putt, 1999; Henderson, York, Jose, & McGowan, 2000; York & Henderson, 2001, 2003).

This section will not elaborate the theoretical background and characteristics of these pedagogies, as this has been more than adequately covered in other chapters in this book. More importantly, the section will explore examples from the author's e-instructional design to demonstrate how the pedagogies can be utilized and how they can be programmed to be used in a behaviorist or constructivist way or how activities can be changed from only behaviorist to constructivist or social constructivist in an e-course or blended course. In addition, attention is focused on incorporation of the epistemo-logical layer's contexts (Figure 1) to maximize effective e-teaching and e-learning outcomes.

Behaviorist or instructivist pedagogy incorporates the theory that the degree of a learner's understanding can be tested by assessing the behavioral outcome after learning some set content, such as occurs in an online multiple choice quiz that presents a pre-set number of randomly chosen items from a data base. The e-student's answers are automatically marked with instant pre-programed feedback and the results submitted to the online grade book on the institution's Learning Management System. Another instantly graded item could be a comparison of the e-student's typed response to a short audio or video English-as-a-foreign-language dictation test. These tests are essentially private for e-learners whose epistemologies involve losing face (Kennedy, 2002; Tjitra, 2000) or feeling shame (Henderson, 1996) in public testing. The e-instructor can reduce the allocated time limit on repeat taking of such tests, which has motivational worth (Henderson, 1993; Malone, 1981) for e-learners.

After engaging in an interactive Web lecture on these three teaching and learning pedagogies, the e-learner would be required to complete an online multimedia click-and-drag activity by clicking on one of a list of characteristics and dragging it into the column associated with behaviorist, constructivist, or social constructivist pedagogy. If that characteristic does not belong, it is programmed to move back to its original place in the list. Such activities are seen to be of little cognitive worth as the student eventually gets it correct through trial and error. In fact, it would not even require regurgitation of learned content. Indeed, this would be irrefutable if the dragged item had one and only one correct place to which it belonged. However, if the interaction as in the example given has fuzzy boundaries in that some of the items could reside in more than one category, then a follow-up online text interaction would require the education or instructional design e-learners to explore the pedagogic value of such an activity. Their answer would probably include frustration when they thought an item should go into a particular category but it was programmed into another. For example, the fact that behaviorist problems can be authentic, in that the scenario can be found in real life, is sometimes ignored by students as authenticity is claimed as a particular facet of constructivist and social constructivist pedagogy. After clicking on the submit answer button, a further inbuilt text interaction would now require the student to engage in metacognitive explanation as to their thinking during the activity and to compare those thoughts and strategies with why the e-instructor programmed the activity in a particular way. This, too, would be submitted, and a final text activity would then ask the e-student if they wished to change their initial answer about the worth of the activity and to explain why or why not.

All these text questions and answers would then be submitted through the learning management system to the e-lecturer or, if it were a blended subject, the questions and answers would appear in a pop-up window with a date of submission automatically generated and a request that the student type in their name and student number, print the contents, and bring it to a face-to-face tutorial. The online students would be required to debate the topic in a discussion forum. A synopsis of Henderson's (1996) findings would have been distributed some time during the debate to inform further discussion. (Henderson's 1996 thesis established that indigenous Bachelor of Education students engaged in higher order thinking skills during the click-and-drag interaction as well as during the following metacognitive activities.) In ways described, the online activity turned from a behaviorist to a constructivist activity to become a social constructivist task within a distributed cognitive environment.

Research (Henderson, Patching, & Putt, 1994) found intriguing epistemological and self-empowerment outcomes from metacognitive activities built into the e-course interactive materials designed for indigenous Australian Bachelor of Education e-students. Initially, the students found it difficult to interrogate their own thinking and the strategies they subsequently took. They claimed they did not engage in such thinking because asking "why" questions of their elders when learning were not condoned or answered (Henderson, 1996) and, therefore, asking why or how of yourself as to what you were thinking was also pointless. Students reported that because they individually completed inbuilt metacognitive activities over the semester, they became more confident to query their peers publicly. Interviews were also conducted some months after graduation to see if there was transference, an important consideration for any e-instructor. One student was adamant that it was specifically these experiences that empowered her to question openly the comments and ideas of non-indigenous teachers, even in school meetings. She was delightedly amazed as this was something that was not part of their post-colonialism epistemology. This example demonstrates the integration of shared epistemological systems by the e-learners and between them and their Western e-instructor.

To take these examples further, effective e-instructional design requires the under- and post-graduate e-learners to construct individually their own multiple choice quiz on some aspect of the e-course content. They could use a Java script template provided or, if the course requires such programming skills, program their own quiz (constructivist exercise) and later in the e-course with an e-partner via e-mail (social constructivist activity). The same strategy would be used when the e-students create a reflective metacognitive activity, already modeled in the e-course, by using the provided online template (constructivist exercise). The interaction presents one or more questions, the students answer each in the left column of a three-column text-interaction box. After they click the "finished" button, the answer programmed by the e-instructor (in this case, it would be the e-student acting as instructor) appears in the middle column. The other e-student is then required to type in their reflective comparison and evaluation of the answers into the third column. In both these examples, the e-students would be required to answer and evaluate each others' quizzes and metacognitive activity in the online discussion forum (social constructivist activity). Involvement in a wiki or blog (social constructivist) would better illuminate the development of their thinking and evaluative reflection (constructivist) during these exercises. Additionally, the best of the e-students online interaction activities would be included in the next year's cohort of student's e-course. This is a worthwhile example of social constructivist distributed cognition. The pedagogic package, learning through taking another's e-quiz and e-activity, deconstructing their own responses through reflection, and then creating their own items, should provide worthwhile self- and peer-enhanced cognitive outcomes. These eclectic pedagogical activities are not "pie-in-the-sky" suggestions, but have been integral in the author's undergraduate and postgraduate blended- and e-courses, and are the subject of ongoing research (Henderson & Coombs, submitted for publication).

Eclectic pedagogy is crucial in multiple cultures e-learning resources. All e-teachers need such a repertoire of educational pedagogic or andragogic strategies to assist e-learners to achieve various personal, national, and international goals. This situation occurred in 2004 in a Master of Education subject offered to e-students in blended mode in Singapore. One of the students, recently appointed to an educational government department, utilized Singapore's focus on educating for an innovative, flexible, and economically-viable society. His solution to helping educators to see value beyond behaviorist pedagogy was to create a social constructivist WebQuest. The WebQuest forced staff who had grown up with, and were more comfortable learning and teaching with, behaviorist face-to-face strategies to thereby inservice themselves in a social constructivist manner as to how this policy would be implemented in their school and administrative contexts. This is a worthwhile e-andragocial example of productive pedagogies in which the assessment allows the postgraduate e-learner to situate their major task within their working environment. The assessed piece then adds additional value to the e-student from their employer's and, in the above case, colleagues' recognition as a knowledge worker or enterprising self of merit (Garrick & Usher, 2000; Henderson & Coombs, submitted for publication).

The following is an example of both the sharing of epistemologies and distributed cognition in a social constructivist e-learning environment with the 2005 cohorts of the Australian James Cook University's Master of Education subject mentioned previously. In the first semester, the Malay and Chinese Singaporean e-students created an *E-Learning Quest: Online Teaching and Learning* through individual activities and the normal social constructivist roles associated with Web quests. With respect to the former activities, each e-student had to present a story board of the site's layout, navigation, and common attributes (e.g., text font and sizes, color scheme, background, tables, and icons) with the best selected according to highest number of votes awarded by students and the e-instructor. The latter activities in this e-learning Quest were the normal social constructivist collaborative roles associated with WebQuests as well as a jointly decided assessment rubric. Unlike traditional WebQuests, both this and the second semester's Quest assessment had to include behaviorist, constructivist, and social constructivist online activities using the templates provided (see above) or programing other interactions. In addition, all e-students were required to include content that addressed e-learner epistemologies (with respect to sub-cultural groupings based on gender, ethnicity, and workplace).

The first semester's Quest became content for the 2005 second semester's e-students in Australia and Canada and the appointed e-instructor residing in the USA. These e-students' task was to critique the instructional design and the content of the *E-Learning Quest: Online Teaching and Learning*. Discussion of the critique would query if the students perceived the instructional design was influenced by the Singaporeans' culture, as suggested by research (Bowskill et al., 2000). The second cohort was also expected to update the former cohort's Quest with appropriate Web article links. In both cases, these links had to be annotated. There is absolutely no pedagogic value in having WebQuest links (or other e-course links) without an annotation as to, for example, its relevance to the topic in terms of, for instance, the major concepts, breadth, and depth of content, school or higher education level, and discipline focus (Henderson & Coombs, in press). The second semester 2005 cohort also constructed e-learning or e-teaching Quests in various educational contexts. For example, three technical and vocational instructors collaborated to create an *E-Instructional Design Quest* to support fellow staff in the latter's adventure into creating Web sites for their particular vocational area while an individual student (her partner withdrew from the e-course) elected to create an *E-Teaching Quest: Constructing Metacognitive Activities* for fellow university instructors. All the 2005 Quest sites will become part of learning content for the next year's cohort, who will also critique the sites in terms of its instructional design and educative value as well construct other Quests. From these examples, it is clear that the e-instructors, who are also the e-instructional designers, take seriously the adoption of the constructivist and social constructivist theory of distributed cognition during the creation of each cohort's Quest and over time between cohorts through the intrinsic and extrinsic role of assessment for e-postgraduate students.

It will have been noticed that in the various examples presented in this chapter, both the undergraduate and postgraduate e-learners were presented with assessable tasks that normally reside with the e-instructor. The Web content in the e-courses contained these types of interactions so that they acted as scaffolded models within a constructivist cognitive e-apprenticeship paradigm for the students' own construction of online interactions. Past e-students commented that this gave them a better sense of ownership and empowerment as they were inducted into not only learning online but also into teaching online (Henderson & Coombs, submitted for publication).

Additionally, advance organizer downloadable files offered linear or horizontal flow charts, Venn diagram, or concept map overviews of the menu item list and their sub-topics (which appeared on the top of each page in each of the menu item topics) in each e-course module. The instructional design justification was threefold. First, the e-students could use a hard copy for note-taking to support their mental model of where each section logically fitted into the whole. Thus, second, the advance organizers provided differing designs to demonstrate that it is important for educators to cater for learners whose way of thinking is different from their own. For example, indigenous Australians (Osborne, 1982, 1986) and South American, Middle Eastern, and Southern European are generally thought to prefer holistic big-picture approaches (Edmonds, 2004). Third, such deliberate e-instructional design allows the incorporation of various components in the layers of the multiple cultures model as depicted in Figure 1. In these ways, through the multiple cultures model, the e-students create living sites of pedagogic engagement that change during and after the completion of their particular e-course.

These rather lengthy examples provide yet a further e-global instructional design issue that the multiple cultural model helps solve. The costs of editing e-courses are usually not funded adequately, if funded at all. By having e-students create content and interactions for the next cohort of students in the ways described, the hidden costs of the e-instructor's time in editing and updating the Web e-course content and its links to online literature can be reduced. This would be particularly important in e-courses that do not use textbooks but rely on utilizing current journal articles and chapters in books as well as online resources that specifically target the areas that the e-instructor wishes to cover.

So far the chapter has not explored e-instructional design with respect to collaboration in discussion forums or blogs (Goodfellow & Lea, 2001; Housden, Forsyth, and Bateman, 2003; Salmon, 2004). It is not because the area is not as significant as others covered; it is because the area has been addressed in other chapters. Nevertheless, one area is significant to the particular themes in this chapter, and therefore this section briefly examines online discussion spaces. These are "worlds constructed with words" (Bowskill, et al., 2000, p. 5) and attached pictures or graphics. Being able to rework comments before posting them supports those who are working in a language other than their first language. However in e-global education, the concept of social presence, defined as "the degree to which an individual is perceived or experienced as a 'real' person," is understood to be a more significant factor in engagement and learning outcomes (Thompson, 2000, cited in Wentling, Waight, Gallaher, La Fleur, Wang, & Kaufer, 2000, p. 23). The e-instructor's ability to create a high level of social presence contributes significantly to instructional effectiveness and learner satisfaction (Thompson, 2000, cited in Wentling et al., 2000). Research findings by Swan and Shih (2005) indicated that the e-learner's perception of the presence of their fellow students is less important than that of the e-instructor and the design of the e-course in determining the e-learner's success and satisfaction. These views accord with the contention voiced in previous research: Effective e-instructors must necessarily be warm demanders (Henderson, 1993, 1994, 1996; Henderson, Patching, & Putt, 1994; Henderson & Putt, 1999; Henderson, York, Jose, & McGowan, 2000). As such, they allow e-learners into aspects of their personal and professional lives (Scorza, 2005) while simultaneously, (a) not negating that there remains a power differential between e-instructor/assessor and e-student and consequently, (b) demanding the highest standards from each e-student. E-instructors also acknowledge what and how the e-learners have taught them. Examples include the e-learners offering aspects of their ways of thinking and doing, further insights into content, and/or different arguments emanating from the students' different epistemologies. The human and cognitive are entwined, and through these methods the e-students and e-instructor confirm the personal and academic.

Conclusion

It would not be surprising if an initial reaction is an automatic dismissal of the multiple cultures model by e-instructors and e-instructional designers, claiming it to be an impossibility to implement. Examples of actual cases and possibilities were provided in this chapter to counter this belief. Additionally, other worthwhile exemplars have been offered and discussed in this book. Luck, Jones, McConachie, and Danaher (2004) supported Gregor, Jones, Lynch, and Plummer's (1999) warning that various stakeholders can disparagingly "magnify traditional problems of politics, management, expectations, hidden agendas, disruption to the balance of power, technical concerns, and difference in cultural values" (p. 6). Such a knee-jerk reaction would ensure the continuation of the status quo of unproblematized soft multicultural Westernized, or Asianized, or any other form of internationalized, model of e-learning.

Not technology-*driven* but technology-*enabling* e-learning sometimes means that e-instructional designers and e-instructors need to "think outside the square." Indigenous Bachelor of Education students still felt the limitations of studying in their remote small communities even though they were in e-mail contact with other students and their instructors, conducted assessable online discussion forums, and could search the Web for various educational and recreational purposes (watching "Days of our Lives" was one of the latter!). It did not take the two instructors long to brainstorm a solution: an *International E-Conference: Perspectives on Indigenous E-Learning and E-Teaching*, in which the indigenous final year students would contribute postings as well as promote participant discussion of an allocated e-paper. The result was James Cook University's first online Web-based conference. There were 680 subscribers (of which 156 were participants, with the majority of the remainder being lurkers) from Sweden through to South Africa; Great Britain through to Japan; Russia through to the Middle East and India; the Americas, South East Asia, Australia and New Zealand. This may seem an impractical e-global strategy for just one part of the assessment. Crucially, students evaluated their outcomes in terms of being offered and courageously taking empowerment and ownership of their learning in a supportive but public asynchronous world environment. The undergraduate e-students also became e-teachers of neophytes in the area of online indigenous learning (Henderson, York, Jose, & McGowan, 2000). The most telling example was how the indigenous students (Aborigines, Torres Strait Islanders, Maoris, and those from Botswana and Madagascar) wove the social with academic critique and the way this was juxtaposed with some academic participants' initial inability to value, let alone see, what had occurred. It was the multiple cultures model in action.

References

Alcoff, L. (2003). Philosophy in/and Latino and Afro-Caribbean studies: Introduction. *Nepantla: Views from South, 4*(1), 133-137.

Ally, M. (2004). Foundations of educational theory for online learning. In T. Anderson & F. Elloumi (Eds.), *Theory and practice of online learning* (pp. 7-30). Athabasca, Canada: Athabasca University and Creative Commons. Retrieved December 2, 2005, from http://cde.athabascau.ca/online_book/pdf/TPOL_chp01.pdf

Andrews, S. (1995, October). Some cultural and perceptual implications of courseware development and the use of technology within a multicultural, multilingual society (A cautionary tale). In P. Alexander (Ed.), *Proceedings of the International Conference on Computer-Assisted Education and Training in Developing Countries* (pp. 7-13). Muchleneuk, Pretoria: University of South Africa.

Babuna, A. (2000). The Albanians of Kosovo and Macedonia: Ethnic identity superceding religion. *Nationalities Papers, 28*(1), 67-93.

Boulos, T. R. (2003, November 7-9). *The manifestations of violence in Arabic prison narrative written by women.* Paper presented at Middle East Studies Association Conference, Anchorage, Alaska.

Bowskill, N., McCarty, S., Luke, R., Kinshuk, & Hand, K. (2000). Cultural sensitivity in voluntary virtual professional development communities. *Indian Journal of Open Learning, 9*(3), 361-379.

Calder, J. (2000). Beauty lies in the eye of the beholder. *International Review of Research in Open and Distance Learning, 1*(1), 1-15.

Chan, K. W., & Elliott, R. G. (2000). Exploratory study of epistemological beliefs of Hong Kong teacher education students: Resolving conceptual and empirical issues. *Asia-Pacific Journal of Teacher Education, 28*(3), 225-234.

Chen, A., Mashhadi, A., Ang, D., & Harkrider, N. (1999). Cultural issues in the design of technology enhanced learning systems. *British Journal of Educational Technology, 30*(3), 217-230.

Cheng, X. (2000) Asian students' reticence revisited. *System, 28*, 435-446.

Collis, B. (1999). Designing for differences: Cultural issues in the design of WWW-based course. *British Journal of Educational Technology, 28*(3), 201-215.

Edmonds, R. (2004). Best practices in e-learning. *Learning on Demand Program: SRI Consulting Business Intelligence.* Retrieved December 2, 2005, from http://www.sric-bi.com/LoD/reports.shtml

Edmundson, A. (2003). Decreasing cultural disparity in educational ICTs: Tools and recommendations. *Turkish Online Journal of Distance Education-TOJDE, 4*(3). Retrieved October 12, 2005, from http://tojde.anadolu.edu.tr/tojde11/articles/edmundson.htm

Edmundson, A. (2004). *Cross-cultural dimensions of globalized e-learning.* PhD thesis, Walden University.

Faiola, A., & Matei, S. A. (2005). Cultural cognitive style and Web design: Beyond a behavioral inquiry into computer-mediated communication. *Journal of Computer-Mediated Communication, 11*(1), article 18. Retrieved May 12, 2006, from http://jcmc.indiana.edu/vol11/issue1/faiola.html

Friesner, T., & Hart, M. (2004). A cultural analysis of e-learning for China. *Electronic Journal on E-Learning, 2*(1), 81-88. Retrieved October 2, 2005, from http://www.ejel.org/volume-2/vol2-issue1/issue1-art24-friesner-hart.pdf

Garrick, J., & Usher, R. (2000). Flexible learning, contemporary work, and enterprising selves. *Electronic Journal of Sociology, 5*(1). Retrieved December 2, 2005, from http://www.sociology.org/content/vol005.001/garrick-usher.html

Goodfellow, P., & Lea, M. (2001). Opportunity and e-quality: Intercultural and linguistic issues in global online learning. *Distance Education, 22*(5), 65-84.

Gregor, S., Jones, D., Lynch, T., & Plummer, A. A. (1999). *Web information systems development: Some neglected aspects.* Paper presented at the International Business Association Conference, Cancun, Mexico.

Haas, T., & Steiner, L. (2001). Public journalism as a journalism of publics: Implications of the Habermas-Fraser debate for public journalism. *Journalism, 2*(2), 123-147.

Harding, S. (1986). *The science question in feminism.* Ithaca, NY: Cornell University Press.

Harel, I., & Papert, S. (1991). *Constructionism.* Norwood, NJ: Ablex Publishing.

Haslanger, S. (2000). Gender and race: (What) are they? (What) do we want them to be?" *Nous, 34*(1), 31-55.

Hedberg, J., & Brown, I. (2002). Understanding cross-cultural meaning through visual media. *Educational Media International, 39*(1), 23-30.

Henderson, L. (1993). Interactive multimedia and culturally appropriate ways of learning. In C. Latchem, J. Williamson, & L. Henderson-Lancett (Eds.), *Interactive multimedia: Practice and promise* (pp. 165-183). London: Kogan Page.

Henderson, L. (1994). Reeves' pedagogic model of interactive learning systems and cultural contextuality. In C. McBeath & R. Atkinson (Eds.), *Proceedings of the International Interactive Multimedia Symposium* (pp. 189-198). Perth: Promalco.

Henderson, L. (1996). Instructional design of interactive multimedia: A cultural critique. *Educational Technology Research and Development, 44*(4), 85-104.

Henderson, L., & Coombs, G. (submitted for publication). *Designing and teaching postgraduate distance education: Knowledge production, intellectual capital, and enterprising selves.*

Henderson, L., Patching, W., & Putt, I. (1994). The impact of metacognitive interactive strategies and prompts embedded in interactive multimedia in a cross-cultural context: An exploratory investigation. In A. Gooley (Ed.), *Open Learning '94: Proceedings of the 1ˢᵗ International Conference on Open Learning* (pp.181-186). Brisbane: Queensland Open Learning Network and The University of Queensland.

Henderson, L., & Putt, I. (1993). The Remote Area Teacher Education Program (RATEP): Cultural contextualization of distance education through interactive multimedia. *Distance Education, 14*(2), 213-231.

Henderson, L., & Putt, I. (1999). Theorizing audioconferencing: An eclectic paradigm. *Canadian Journal of Educational Communication, 27*(1), 21-37.

Henderson, L., York, F., Jose, G., & McGowan, A. (2000, April 24-28). Learning with the Internet: Empowerment in cross cultural open learning contexts. Paper presented at *Creating Knowledge in the 21ˢᵗ Century: American Education Research Association (AERA) Annual Meeting,* New Orleans.

Henderson, M. (1996). *Multimedia interactivity: An investigation into learners' mediating processes during click-drag activities.* BEd Hons. James Cook University, Townsville.

Hofstede, G. (1996). *Cultures and organizations: Software of the mind (rev. ed.).* New York: McGraw-Hill Professional.

Housden, L., Forsyth, F., & Bateman, C. (2003). Online adventures in the global world of e-learning — The musings of 3 armchair cultural explorers. *Knowledge Tree: An E-Journal of Flexible Learning in VET, 4.* Retrieved October 19, 2005, from http://www.flexiblelearning.net.au/knowledgetree/edition04/pdf/Online_elearning.pdf

Hutchinson, H. B., Rose, A., Bederson, B. B., Weeks, A. C., & Druin, A. (2005). The international children's digital library: A case study in designing for a multilingual, multicultural, multigenerational audience. *Information Technology and Libraries, 24*(1), 4-9.

Kauffman, P. (2003). Diversity and indigenous policy outcomes: Comparisons between four nations. *Proceedings of 3ʳᵈ International Conference on Diversity in*

Organisations, Communities, and Nations, February. Retrieved December 5, 2005, from http://www.dfait-maeci.gc.ca/aboriginalplanet/750/resource/canada/documents/diversityindigpolicy-en.asp#t6

Kennedy, P. (2002). Learning cultures and learning styles: Myth-understandings about adult (Hong Kong) Chinese learners. *International Journal of Lifelong Education, 21*(5), 430-445.

Komiyama, Y. (submitted). Japanese learning styles in the online learning environment. In J.B. Son (Ed.), *Internet-based language instruction: Pedagogies and technologies*. Toowoomba, Australia: Asia-Pacific Association for Computer-Assisted Language Learning. Retrieved December 5, 2005, from http://www.elearnmag.org/subpage.cfm?section=research&article=4-1

Koo, H. (2001). *Korean workers: The culture and politics of class formation.* Ithaca, NY: Cornell University Press.

Kramarae, C., & Spender, D. (Eds.). (2000). *Routledge international encyclopedia of women: Global women's issues and knowledge.* New York: Routledge.

Lea, P. (2003). Understanding the culture of e-learning. *Industrial and Commercial Training, 35*(4/5), 217-219.

Looi, C. K. (2002). Cultural issues and the design of e-learning. *Information and Systems in Education, 1*(1), 32-37.

Luck, J., Jones, D., McConachie, J., & Danaher, P. (2004). Challenging enterprises and subcultures: Interrogating best practice in Central Queensland University's course management systems. *Studies in Learning, Evaluation Innovation and Development, 1*(2), 19-31.

Malone, T. (1981). Towards a theory of intrinsically motivating instruction. *Cognitive Science, 4*, 333-369.

McCarty, S. (2005). Cultural, disciplinary and temporal contexts of e-learning and English as a foreign language. *eLearn,* (4). Retrieved May 12, 2006, from http://www.elearningmag.org/subpage.cfm?section=research&article=4-1

McConaghy, C. (1999). *Indigenous learning on-line: Is it empowering?* Keynote address to the James Cook University Learning On-Line Conference. Retrieved from http://www.soe.jcu.edu.au/learnit/

McDonald, H. (1992, September). *Aboriginal and Torres Strait Island expressive arts in the socially critical curriculum.* Paper presented at Aboriginal Studies: A National Priority: Conference of the Aboriginal Studies Association, Sydney, Australia.

McLoughlin, C. (1999). Culturally responsive technology use: Developing an on-line community of learners. *British Journal of Educational Technology, 30*(3), 231-243.

Minnis, J. R. (2000). Caught between tradition and modernity: Technical-vocational education in Brunei Darussalam. *International Journal of Educational Development, 20*(3), 247-59.

Mitra, S. (2005). *The "hole in the wall" experiments: Self-organizing systems for gender parity in primary education* (commissioned paper). Washington: The World Bank Group.

Neo, M. (2005). Engaging students in group-based co-operative learning: A Malaysian perspective. *Educational Technology & Society, 8*(4), 220-232.

Ng, E. (2002). Critical features for enhancing the design of Web-based learning materials. *Proceedings of International Conference of Computers in Education* (pp. 528-534). Retrieved May 22, 2006, from http://doi.ieeecomputersociety.org/10.1109/CIE.2002.1185997

Ngeow, K., & Kong, K. (2002). Designing culturally sensitive learning environments. *ASCILITE 2002* (pp. 873-876). Retrieved May 22, 2006, from https://secure.ascilite.org.au/conferences/auckland02/proceedings/papers/055.pdf

Nisbett, R. E., & Norenzayan, A. (2002). Culture and cognition. In H. Pashler & D. L. Medin (Eds.), *Stevens' handbook of experimental psychology: Vol. 2: Cognition* (3rd ed.) (pp. 561-597). New York: John Wiley & Sons.

Nisbett, R. E., Peng, K., Choi, I., & Norenzayan, A. (2001). Culture and systems of thought: Holistic vs. analytic cognition. *Psychological Review, 8*, 291-310.

Osborne, A. (1982). Field dependence/independence of Torres Strait Islander and aboriginal pupils. *Journal of Intercultural Studies, 3*(3), 5-18.

Osborne, A. (1986). *Torres Strait Islander styles of communication and learning* (Torres Strait Working Papers 1). Townsville: James Cook University of North Queensland.

Pizarro, M. (1998). Chicana/o Power! Epistemology and methodology for social justice and empowerment in Chicana/o communities. *Qualitative Studies in Education, 11*(1), 57-80.

Rappaport, E. (2004). *Indigenous peoples: A backgrounder*. Retrieved November 29, 2005, from http://www.madre.org/articles/int/indigenous.html

Salmon, G. (2004). *E-moderating: The key to teaching and learning online* (2nd ed.). London: Taylor & Francis.

Scorza, J. (2005). Do online students dream of electric teachers? *Journal of Asynchronous Learning Networks, 9*(2), 41-46.

Smith, S. (2001). Approaches to study of three Chinese national groups. *British Journal of Psychological Society, 71*, 429-441.

Spender, D. (1996). *Nattering on the net: Women, power, and cyberspace*. North Melbourne: Spinifex.

Susskind, Y. (2000). Violence against women in Latin America. *MADRE*. Retrieved May 22, 2006, from http://www.madre.org/articles/lac/violence.html

Susskind, Y. (2004). Confronting the Bush agenda: Reasserting women's human rights. *MADRE*. Retrieved May 22, 2006, from http://www.madre.org/articles/int/confrontingthebushagenda.html

Swan, K., & Shih, L. F. (2005). On the nature and development of social presence in online course discussions. *Journal of Asynchronous Learning Networks, 9*(3), 55-62.

Terpstra, V., & Sarathy, R. (2000). *International marketing* (8ᵗʰ ed.). New York: Dryden Press.

Thaman, K. H. (2003). Decolonizing Pacific studies: Indigenous perspectives, knowledge, and wisdom in higher education. *The Contemporary Pacific, 15*(1), 1-18.

Tjitra, H. W. (2000). Culture specific communication and problem solving styles: The strength and problem areas of German-Indonesian work groups. In S. Stumpf & A. Thomas (Eds.), *Diversity and group effectiveness* (pp. 368-384). Lengerich, Germany: Pabst.

Tractinsky, N. (2000). A theoretical framework and empirical examination of the effects of foreign and translated interface language. *Behavior & Information Technology, 19*(1), 1-13.

Tylee, J. (2001). *Cultural issues relating to access perceptions and learning styles in the online environment.* Retrieved May 22, 2006, from http://www.appknow.com/jenny/culture.htm

Voithofer, R. (2004). Teaching computers to tell learning stories: Using critical narrative theory to frame design and evaluation strategies for online educational experiences. *Journal of Educational Multimedia and Hypermedia, 13*(1), 47-66.

Wentling, T., Waight, C., Gallaher, J., La Fleur, J., Wang, C., & Kaufer, A. (2000). *E-learning: A review of the literature.* Urbana-Champaign, IL: Knowledge and Learning Systems Group, NCS.

Wesley-Smith, T. (2003). Net gains? Pacific studies in cyberspace. *The Contemporary Pacific, 15*(1), 117-138.

West, E. (1993). *A discussion of the significant issues relating to the transmigration and ownership of oral history and cultural knowledge.* Unpublished manuscript, James Cook University of North Queensland, Center for Research, Development, and Support of Aborigines and Torres Strait Islanders, Townsville.

Wild, M., & Henderson, L. (1997a). Contextualizing learning in the World Wide Web: Accounting for the impact of culture. *Education and Information Technology, 2*(3), 179-192.

Wild, M., & Henderson, L. (1997b). Cultural contextualization of learning with the World Wide Web: A research methodology. In F. Verdejo & G. Davies (Eds.), *Virtual Campus: Trends for Higher Education and Training, IFIP 3.3 and 3.6 Joint Working Group Conference* (pp. 105-119). Madrid, Spain: Chapman & Hall.

Yonkers, V. (2003). *Replicating business education in emerging countries.* Paper presented at the Business Education and Emerging Market Economies: Trends and Prospects Conference, Atlanta, Georgia, November 7.

York, F., & Henderson, L. (2001). Giving control over destinies: Students' perspectives of an innovative cross-cultural education program. *International Journal of Instructional Media, 28*(2), 137-146.

York, F., & Henderson, L. (2003). Making it possible: The evolution of RATEP: A community-based teacher education program for indigenous peoples. *Australian Journal of Indigenous Education, 32*(3ʳᵈ Anniversary Issue), 77-88.

Zhu, J. H., & He, Z. (2002). Information accessibility, user sophistication, and source credibility: The impact of the Internet on value orientations in mainland China. *The Journal of Computer-Mediated Communication, 7*(2). Retrieved October 25, 2005, from http://www.ascusc.org/jcmc/vol7/issue2/china.html

Ziguras, C. (1999). Cultural diversity and transnational flexible delivery. In J. Winn (Ed.), *Proceedings of Australian Society for Computers in Learning in Tertiary Education (ASCILITE) Conference* (pp. 410-407). Brisbane: Queensland University of Technology. Retrieved May 22, 2006, from http://www.ascilite.org.au/conferences/brisbane99/papers/ziguras.pdf

Ziguras, C. (2000). *New frontiers, new technologies, new pedagogies: Educational technology and the internationalisation of higher education in South East Asia.* Melbourne: Monash Centre for Research in International Education, Clayton. Retrieved September 29, 2005, from http://cunningham.acer.edu.au/dbtw-wpd/textbase/ndrie/ndrie132050.pdf

Endnotes

[1]   "E-learners" is used here as a generic term for those who are learning in a formal online educational context, be it in schools, higher education, the work place, government, or the armed services.

[2]   "E-teachers" incorporates e-instructors, e-lecturers, and e-trainers. They will be used interchangeably and individually when more appropriate.

[3]   Torres Strait Islanders are Australia's second indigenous group; their traditional country are the islands between Cape York, North Eastern Australia, and Papua New Guinea.

[4]   This division of two groups, indigenous and ethnic minorities, is one of expediency for the sake of instant clarity. All cultural groups, including people who belong to a country's majority culture, for example Anglo-Australians, belong to an ethnic group. By definition, everyone has an ethnicity.

Section III

Language
and Semiotics

Chapter IX

How to Globalize Online Course Content

Martin Schell
New York University, USA

Abstract

Considering that 347 languages have over 1 million speakers each and account for 94% of the world's population, localization is unsustainable as a strategy for making online courses globally accessible. Writing Web content in Global English is the best way to ensure that people from all linguistic backgrounds have a reasonable chance of comprehending course materials. This chapter shows how to transform native English text into Global English (simpler syntax, less jargon, fewer idioms, no slang). It also discusses e-learning design issues such as cultural perspective and Internet logistics (speed and cost of connection). Finally, it addresses the future of English as a global language, particularly in reference to its supposed "rivalry" with Mandarin.

Introduction

Consider the following two approaches to discussing the use of English online.

During the occasion of preparing for the production of teaching materials to be used for e-learning, one should not neglect giving serious thought to reflecting upon the choice of language to be used for writing the e-learning content. Since English has not unequivocally become a global language, it is difficult, if not impossible, to deny its suitability as the source language for such a project. The evidence for it will be presented during the course of this chapter as follows.

Get with the program, dude! Keep it simple, stupid. Word: English is the language of choice. It's what works, but be cool about it.

Clearly, neither of the preceding paragraphs is an example of using English as a global language. The first is too stilted. Its opening sentence torments the reader with a series of phrases that hesitate to state the point: *during the occasion, preparing for, production of, to be used.* The first paragraph also has double negatives (*not neglect* and *not unequivocally*), an ordinary word that is ambiguous regarding its part of speech (*since*), and a useless phrase that repeats an obvious point (*as follows*). On the other hand, the second paragraph is too sketchy and overloaded with slang.

Let's start again:

Before producing e-learning materials for a global audience, consider the language in which the content will be written. Among the major languages of the world, English is the closest to being a *global language.* Writing your text in clear English is the best way to reach a worldwide audience, as I will explain in this chapter.

This situation naturally is an advantage for any e-learning provider who is a native speaker of English, or at least can employ native speakers to write the home page and other key parts of the Web site. However, the English normally spoken by Americans, Canadians, British, Australians, New Zealanders, Singaporeans, Indians, Jamaicans, and others is not itself a global language. Each of these countries speaks and writes its own dialect, full of local idioms and slang: American English, Queen's English, and so forth.

In order to serve a worldwide audience (as in *World Wide Web*), it is necessary to use *Global English*—English which is written in such a way that it can easily be understood by non-native speakers, as well as native speakers from diverse parts of the planet. This chapter teaches you how to recognize and write Global English.

The Case for Global English

Nowadays, most Web sites that aim for multinational markets will *localize* their content by translating it into languages spoken by major groups of Internet users: Spanish, Chinese, Russian, and so on. In August 2003, the software developer, Jordi Mas i Hernàndez (2003) tallied the presence of various languages on the Web by inputting keywords specific to each language. He found that English was the dominant language of the text on 1,280 million pages, followed by German (182 million), French (100 million), and then a cluster of four languages in the 65-70 million range: Japanese, Spanish, Chinese, and Korean.

Some people interpret his results as a call for increasing the localization of Web pages into languages other than English. Unfortunately, localization can never succeed in reaching a worldwide audience because, by definition, its purpose is to serve specific groups of users. Adding up a handful of local or regional groups does not equal a global audience.

There are presently 6,912 living languages, including 347 that have over 1 million speakers each (Gordon, 2005). Nobody will localize a Web site into all of them. How often do you see sites that offer the option of viewing pages in Bengali, Gujarati, Marathi, Punjabi, Telugu, Thai, Turkish, or Wu, each of which has over 40 million speakers?

The usual explanation for excluding these languages is that they are spoken in countries which currently have low Internet penetration. This justification reveals that localization is a short-term strategy, one which will become increasingly difficult to implement as time goes on. The number of Internet users more than doubled worldwide from 361 million in 2000 to 958 million in 2005, with doubling or tripling on every continent and in nearly all countries that began the 21st century with low percentages of users (Internet World Stats, 2005).

In poor countries, many people (especially youths) who lack a computer at home access the Internet via cyber cafes. This sharing of hardware is analogous to the pass-around readership of a newspaper, or people reading a book in a library instead of buying it. Statistics about total Internet users in such countries are often based on multiplying the number of Internet service provider (ISP) accounts by a sharing factor.[1] Because the multiplier is a rough estimate, one should view these statistics (as well as most other statistics related to the Internet) with some skepticism.

Nevertheless, the shortage of Web pages in many languages is quite obvious to people who are native speakers of those languages. If a Web site does not consider their language important enough to merit localization, these users are likely to access the English version of the site. At cyber cafes in Indonesia, for example, a few people will gather around a single user whose English is fluent enough to provide impromptu translation while they surf as a group.

There is also evidence that people who know English as a second language sometimes choose the English Web pages even when a site offers pages in their native language. A survey conducted by Research & Research found that only 8% of Hispanic American Internet users prefer Spanish-language Web sites and 41% prefer English-language Web sites. The remaining 51% said they were bilingual and would visit and purchase from sites in either English or Spanish. In other words, 92% of Hispanic American Internet users feel comfortable with English-language Web sites, despite the fact that 63% of this market segment were born outside the United States (Romney, 2000).

The high percentage who use English on the Web is supported by a comScore survey of language preferences in Hispanic American households: 21% of this ethnic group prefer to speak Spanish at home, 51% prefer English there, and 27% speak both languages (Greenspan, 2003); thus, 78% use English conversationally in the home. Similarly, 57% of Hispanic American students in kindergarten through 12th grade spoke mostly English at home in 1999, 25% spoke mostly Spanish, and 17% spoke English and Spanish equally (National Center for Education Statistics, 2003), resulting in a total of 74% who felt comfortable speaking English at home.

Transcending One's Native English

Broadening our outlook means more than becoming aware of prospective students whose native language is not English; it means thinking globally. The global language is often used between two people who are both non-native speakers. For example, a Japanese person might use English to write to a Russian or Brazilian person, who would probably be less skillful with idioms than a native speaker of English.

If your e-learning course has an online facility for students to discuss what they are learning, it is essential to establish a chat environment that discourages idioms and slang. This may seem counterintuitive because chatting is a way to open up and express oneself with few restrictions. Instant messaging can be so fast and fluid that it seems like speech instead of writing, but it lacks the nonverbal clues of face-to-face chatting (or even phone conversations). Consequently, online chat content is prone to misinterpretation, especially when participants are from diverse cultural backgrounds.

The instructor or moderator should strive to remind discussion group members that clarity is important. Pointing out incomplete sentences and gently discouraging the use of the latest slang may slow the action, but it will surely make the class discussion more inclusive. Casual Internet English is great for communicating with friends, but it is too parochial for a Web site that aims to be worldwide in outlook.

Slang should also be minimized in online course content that is intended for a global audience. A report by Stanford University's Persuasive Technology Lab (Fogg, Soohoo, Danielson, Marable, Stanford, & Tauber, 2002) listed "writing tone" among the top 10 factors that users mentioned when describing the trustworthiness of a Web site. "People generally said that sensationalism or slang hurt a site's credibility, while a straightforward, friendly writing style boosted credibility" (p. 43).

In addition to the absence of slang, Global English is characterized by smoother sentence structure, fewer idioms, and less jargon. In "Standards for Online Content Authors," Rachel McAlpine (2005) emphasizes conciseness as a key to clarity. She recommends that writers aim to limit sentences to a maximum of 21 words and paragraphs to 65 words. Indeed, it is usually less tiring to read sentences that have fewer words, and paragraphs that have fewer sentences, because reader comprehension improves when the "bites" of information are smaller. These types of streamlining will not restrict your writing style much, but they will greatly expand your potential audience by making your online content easier to understand.

Writing in Global English

Consider the following sentence that ends a paragraph promoting an online clothing store:

Which is just the right feature for users who want what works.

This type of colloquial usage is easy for a domestic audience to understand. However, the incomplete sentence can confuse non-native speakers of English, many of whom would expect the sentence to end in a question mark.

Changing the initial *which* to *this* might decrease the sentence's trendiness in the American market, but it would greatly increase the number of people who could understand the sentence in the global market. In addition, the word *just* and the idiom *what works* should be modified, resulting in

This is exactly the right feature for users who want efficient online shopping.

The "coolness" of Web content in American eyes often depends on using the latest buzzwords and slang. However, many people in other countries became fluent in English while studying or working in the United States 20 or more years ago. After they returned to their native countries, they retained their fluency but their slang eventually became outdated. For example, they might not know that an expression like "it sucks" is now inoffensive enough to appear in mainstream print media and TV ads.

Slang and idioms are not the only tendencies that hinder successful global communication. Many of the words that we consider ordinary in Standard English have multiple meanings (and even different parts of speech) that can create ambiguity in the reader's mind, particularly if he or she is less than fully fluent in English. Ambiguity also makes a translator's work harder, slower, and less accurate (N. Hoft, personal communication, September 6, 2005; G. Fletcher, personal communication, September 9, 2005). Therefore, writing your original text in Global English will bring the added benefit of saving time and money when your course content is translated from English to another language, which is a likely scenario if it attracts a lot of students.

Here are two examples of ambiguity that most native speakers of English would read without hesitation. However, a non-native speaker might become confused. And even a good translator might render the word into a phrase that is ambiguous or incorrect in the target language.

The word *once* can be confusing as a conjunction, because some readers might misinterpret it as an adverb meaning "one time." For example:

Once the prompt appears, enter the course title.

Some people might think the prompt appears only once, regardless of the number of course titles. It would be better to write:

After the prompt appears, enter the course title.

A similar type of confusion can occur if you use *since* as a conjunction, because it can be misinterpreted as an adverb or preposition meaning "after."

Keep a log, since the use of this device produces momentary fluctuations in the supply of power to other electrical equipment in the room.

Someone might think that the log does not need to be started until a fluctuation occurs. To remove the ambiguity, use *because* as the conjunction:

Keep a log, because the use of this device produces momentary fluctuations in the supply of power to other electrical equipment in the room.

After you finish your final draft, read through your text again and look for points of ambiguity. If you find any words or phrases that could hinder comprehension or translation, try to replace them. However, you cannot anticipate everything that might seem unclear to a reader or translator.

A more comprehensive approach to removing ambiguity is to put some redundancy into your writing. This does not mean reiterating each sentence with a subsequent one that starts with "In other words...." You do not need to be that blunt. Simply write in a way that provides some overlap between your sentences, so they support each other and create a clear context for all of the paragraph's ideas.

For example:

We recommend the purchase of this factory because it is a good medium-term investment. If our company buys the manufacturing facility this year, we will be able to upgrade it by the middle of next year. After we modernize the equipment, the factory will provide additional production capacity to help us meet the increase in demand for our products that is expected two years from now.

Note the redundancy of key concepts in this example: *purchase...buy, factory...facility, upgrade...modernize*. In addition, the references to time are in chronological order and support the use of *medium-term*.

To appreciate the effectiveness of Global English, remember that the Web is still primarily a written medium despite the use of animation and music. People who are not completely fluent in English usually can read our language more easily than they can speak it. They can go over written words several times at their own pace with a dictionary, a process that is awkward during a conversation or a performance.

Globalizing One's Perspective

Globalization of our thinking involves broadening our minds to accommodate other worldviews. I recall editing a speech by a Japanese businessman who asked, "Why is it that the term *classical* always refers to Europe? If we want to refer to the traditional arts and culture of other regions, we must insert another adjective: classical *Japanese* music, classical *Indian* dance, classical *Chinese* calligraphy."

In this global era, it is respectful as well as strategically important to avoid alienating entire cultures (i.e., markets). You can never anticipate all of the possible types of touchiness that might exist, but you can do a little research, particularly if your course material focuses on a specific region or culture.

People often say, "History is written by the victors," but there are exceptions to this cliché; Genghis Khan, for example, never lost a battle. If a country wins a war of independence, its people generally date their sovereignty from the year of declaration, not the year of the subsequent peace treaty; for the United States, it is 1776 rather than 1783. However, most Western history books ignore the August 17, 1945 declaration of independence in Indonesia and refer to The Hague Conference late in 1949 instead.

The national languages of Indonesia and Malaysia are often combined into *Malay* in discussions of the number of native speakers of various languages. For example, the online marketing company Global Reach (2004) states, "Malay is the same language that is spoken in Indonesia" (footnote 26) when tallying the number of speakers online, but indicates that most of them live in Indonesia. So, an Indonesian might wonder why the combined language is not called Indonesian instead of Malay. The confusion is primarily due to the conflation of modern Bahasa Malaysia with the older language that gave birth to it and its sister Bahasa Indonesia (Labor Law Talk, 2005), a situation analogous to combining Romanian and French into *Romance language speakers* and then saying, "Romance is the same language that is spoken in France."

Other cultural assumptions are unrelated to political favoritism. They merely lead to embarrassment or confusion, without arousing national pride. One example is shown by Jakob Nielsen (1999) in his seminal book *Designing Web Usability*. A banner ad for Apple Computer asked users to turn on a virtual light switch by clicking it. However, the switch was in the down position, which *is* the "on" position in many countries. Nielsen says this type of variation among countries is rarely mentioned in guidebooks that tell how to internationalize software or Web sites, but it can be discovered by testing the image on a sample of users overseas before uploading to the World Wide Web (p. 315).

Logistical Considerations

Although digital subscriber line (DSL), cable, satellite, and other fast connections are now well established in industrialized economies, a significant fraction[2] of users rely on older ways to access the Internet. Many of your prospective students are likely to use an integrated digital services network (ISDN), or even 56 kilobits-per-second (Kbps) modems. Connection rates and speeds can be low, particularly during business hours when Internet traffic is heavy in their countries, overloading the local ISPs. Therefore, it would be a mistake to design a Web site that only works smoothly if it is accessed via a broadband connection.

In addition, it is important to consider that Internet time is often charged by the minute, as is telephone time. Thus, your students might be paying their ISP and telecom company a dollar or more per hour to access your course's Web site. These additional costs can severely impact online course enrollment.

Therefore, streamlining your content is a key to retaining students. It is wise to reduce the loading time of every page on your site, in order to make each student's participation smoother and cheaper. Also, talk to your Webmaster about how to make pages easy to re-access if a student's connection unexpectedly fails.

Citing a presentation by Robert Miller at a computer conference in 1968, Jakob Nielsen (1999) summarizes three thresholds of attention span (pp. 42-44):

1. A delay equal to 0.1 second is the limit for most users to feel that the system is reacting "instantly."

2. A delay of 1 second is the limit for feeling that one's flow of thought is uninterrupted (for example, after clicking on a link to read another page of text).

3. A delay of 10 seconds is the maximum for keeping a user's attention on the site.

Allowing for a half-second of latency in system responsiveness, Nielsen (1999) cautions that the 10-second limit for maintaining a person's attention on the task is reached with only 34 kilobytes (KB) for modem connections and 150 KB for ISDN connections (p. 48). Any Web page over these limits is likely to seem slow when loading, thereby provoking impatience.

Connection speed does not matter much for text-rich Web pages because they rarely exceed 10 KB. However, be careful about delays in loading time due to the inclusion of photos, music, or animation on your Web site. A digital photo in .jpg format is likely to exceed 34 KB, and a .wav file of instrumental or vocal music is typically 5-10 KB per second of playing time.

When you plan a Web page, check the size of every multimedia file that will be part of it. Minimize or eliminate the use of moving images and carefully consider the visual quality of each photo in relation to its file size. Even with an ISDN connection, a page that totals 500 KB is likely to take more than half a minute to appear on screen.

Try to make explanatory text as independent of the images as possible. Work with your Webmaster and include the ALT attribute in the HyperText Markup Language (HTML) code for each page. This attribute lets you insert descriptive text that displays in the box which outlines the photo while its image is loading on a user's screen.

Plan your tables and graphs to accommodate translation of the text into other languages. German, for example, typically expands the length of the equivalent English text by about 30% (Nielsen, 1999, p. 318). This can lead to problems in a table if your Web designer does not make the column widths flexible enough.

The Future of Global English

Is another language likely to replace English as the global language? After the British Council published *The Future of English?* by David Graddol in 1997, the mass media began sounding an alarm that English was being surpassed by "Chinese" (Lovgren, 2004). The excitement arose because Graddol (2000) divided English speakers into three categories (p. 10): those who speak it as a first language (native speakers, or L1), those who speak it fluently as a second language that has some official status in their country (L2), and those who are learning English as a foreign language (EFL).

Graddol (2000) estimated that there are 375 million L1, 375 million L2, and 750 million EFL speakers of English (p. 10, Figure 4). Although the L1 figure is well above those for Hindi and Spanish, it is far below the 1,100 million that he estimated for "Chinese" (p. 8, Table 1). The popular press echoed his estimates without asking him why his three-way analysis of L1, L2, and "foreign language" applies to English but not to "Chinese."

Most linguists do not recognize a monolithic language called "Chinese" that is spoken as a first language by nearly everyone in the People's Republic of China (PRC). "Chinese" consists of several large languages that are unified by a common system of writing but are mutually unintelligible when spoken (Columbia University, 2001).

Mandarin is the official language of the PRC and the standard language of instruction in its public schools. This situation is analogous to the use of national languages to unify diverse populations in Indonesia (Bahasa Indonesia) and the Philippines (Filipino). In its *Ethnologue* encyclopedia of world languages, SIL International (formerly the Summer Institute of Linguistics) claims that two thirds of the 1,300 million people in China speak Mandarin as their native language, yielding an L1 of 867 million (Gordon, 2005).

However, in May 2005, the PRC's Xinhua news agency reported a survey by the National Language Commission which found that only 53% of the population can speak Mandarin, and many of them "are not frequent Mandarin users, preferring their local dialect" ("Half of all Chinese people can't speak Mandarin," 2005). This yields a combined L1+L2 of 689 million; and if all of the L1+L2 Mandarin speakers among the 23 million Taiwanese and "51 million overseas Chinese" (Graddol, 2000, p. 37) are included, Mandarin *might* exceed the estimated 750 million L1+L2 total for English.

Regardless of the numbers, there are two solid reasons why Mandarin is not a strong candidate to be a global language: It is hard to speak and hard to write. Tones in speech and ideograms in writing make it virtually inaccessible as a second language to the majority of the world's people. Adults whose native language is a tonal one such as Thai or Vietnamese sometimes learn Mandarin by overhearing conversations or watching movies, but speakers of non-tonal languages have a lot more difficulty doing so and need twice as much time in an immersion setting such as Automatic Language Growth (J. M. Brown, personal communication, 1990). Learning enough ideograms to read a newspaper requires a long-term diligent effort.

Graddol's (2000) report contains much more than a tally of speakers at various levels of fluency. He predicts that English will remain globally dominant but it will be influenced by non-native speakers. "New hybrid language varieties" (p. 36) will arise as millions of people "migrate" from EFL to L2 (e.g., using English to speak to fellow countrymen when no foreigners are present); for example, an "Asian standard English" might emerge in that region (p. 56).

It is widely recognized that the globalization of American movies, music, and fast food make English trendy among millions, even billions, of people who are not fluent in it. This cultural "wave" is supported by a socioeconomic "wave" in many developing countries, where governments have decreed in recent years that English should be taught as a foreign language in elementary schools. It is unclear, however, whether these two waves will be sufficient to create a critical mass of L2 speakers in dozens of countries, each of which will develop its own form of English.

Consider the case of Singapore, which has four official languages: English, Mandarin, Malay, and Tamil. English is the default language when two Singaporeans from different ethnic groups make each other's acquaintance, earning it an L2 in the typology of Graddol (2000, p. 11, Table 5). This L2 "Singlish" is flavored with words and structures from other languages (including non-Mandarin forms of Chinese) and thus appears to be a harbinger of the hybridization that he predicts will occur during the next few decades. However, few if any "Singlish" words have entered the vocabulary of L2 English speakers in Thailand or the Philippines, let alone more distant areas.

A Japanese acquaintance of mine recounted an incident that occurred when she was teaching her native language to Indonesians in North Sumatra. One day, her students invited her to go hiking, pronouncing the word in Japanese fashion (*haikingu*) as part of a Japanese sentence. Etsuko was confused when they told her everyone would gather in the evening—she understood *haikingu* to be a day trip on level ground or in low hills. Instead, the students trekked up a small mountain, arriving at the peak in time for sunrise. In Indonesian, the borrowed word *hiking* refers to an activity that Japanese consider to be mountain climbing.

It therefore seems to me that the proliferation of "hybrid languages" predicted by Graddol will make Global English even more essential in the future, as a way for speakers of diverse forms of English to communicate with each other. To be truly effective, information and communication technology (ICT) must be accompanied by the development of human infrastructure, specifically the ability to express ourselves clearly to audiences who do not share our cultural background. In addition to transcending our native English when we produce online courses, we should promote the use of Global English in physical schools and other organizations.

Graddol (2000) presents a pyramid diagram (p. 12, Figure 6) to explain how the expansion of viewpoint beyond a person's village is accompanied by changes in the choice of language in India. At the base of the pyramid are local languages used within families and learned by infants as L1. A step higher are languages of wider geographical scope, which are used in media broadcasts and primary schools. Another step higher are state languages (e.g., Malayalam in Kerala), which are used in government offices and secondary schools. At the top are Hindi and Indian English, which are used nationally and in universities. I propose that Global English is a step beyond the top of his pyramid, serving as a lingua franca for international communication and e-learning.

Conclusion

Localization is essential in marketing, but it is incomplete as a global strategy for online course design because it can never accommodate everyone. The limits of localization are becoming more apparent in the 21st century, with Internet access increasing dramatically in virtually every country. It is likely that the total number of Internet users will surpass

1 billion in early 2006, but it is very unlikely that any Web site will localize its content into all of the 347 languages that each claim at least 1 million speakers.

To make the Web truly a worldwide medium, it is essential to write English text in a way that can be easily understood by non-native speakers: simpler syntax, less jargon, fewer idioms, no slang. Writing online course materials in Global English is the best way to ensure that people from all linguistic backgrounds have a reasonable chance of comprehending your content. Global English will become more important in the near future as e-learning expands its scope and market. It will also become essential for maintaining English as a lingua franca if the expansion of L2 speakers leads to a proliferation of new varieties of the language in diverse cultures throughout our world.

Suggested URLs

http://www.algworld.com/history.htm (Automatic Language Growth and the work of Dr. J. Marvin Brown at AUA Language Center in Bangkok)

http://www.anglistik.tu-bs.de/global-english/GE_Was_ist_GE.html (A list of links to online articles that use the term Global English)

http://www.davidcrystal.com (The work of Prof. David Crystal, editor of *The Cambridge Encyclopedia of the English Language*)

http://www.globalenglish.info/globallyspeaking/index.htm (Tips on intercultural communication in the Internet age)

http://www.globelanguage.com (Translation company co-owned by George Fletcher)

http://hotwired.wired.com/hardwired/wiredstyle/index.html (Wired Style: a trendy set of guidelines that are basically *not* Global English)

http://www.netratings.com (Nielsen-Net Ratings)

http://www.oecd.org/document/60/0,2340,en_2649_34225_2496764_1_1_1_1,00.html (OECD broadband statistics, based on ITU data)

http://www.research-research.com (Research & Research)

http://www.world-ready.com/academic.htm (A list of links offered by Nancy Hoft, a consultant in "world-readiness")

References

Columbia University. (2001). *Chinese language*. In *The Columbia Electronic Encyclopedia* (6th ed.) New York: Columbia University Press. Retrieved December 6, 2005, from http://www.bartleby.com/65/ch/Chinese.html

Federal Communications Commission (2005, June 10). *Frequently asked questions (FAQs) about FCC Form 477 (local telephone competition and broadband reporting)*. Retrieved October 2, 2005, from http://www.fcc.gov/broadband/broadband_data_faq.html

Fogg, B. J., Soohoo, C., Danielson, D., Marable, L., Stanford, J., & Tauber, E. R. (2002, November 11). *How do people evaluate a Web site's credibility?* Stanford, CA: Persuasive Technology Lab, Stanford University.

Global Reach. (2004, September 30). *Global Internet statistics (by language).* Retrieved May 24, 2005, from http://global-reach.biz/globstats/index.php3 (the table's footnotes appear in full at http://www.global-reach.biz/globstats/refs.php3)

Gordon, R. G., Jr. (Ed.). (2005, May). Statistical summaries. In *Ethnologue* (15th ed.). Retrieved May 23, 2005, from http://www.ethnologue.com/ethno_docs/distribution.asp?by=size

Graddol, D. (2000). *The future of English?* (2nd ed.). London: British Council.

Greenspan, R. (2003, April 9). *Hispanics driven to auto sites.* ClickZ Network. Retrieved May 23, 2005, from http://www.clickz.com/news/article.php/2178711

Half of all Chinese people can't speak Mandarin: Report. (2005, May 23). *Taipei Times,* 5. AFP Beijing. Retrieved May 24, 2005, from http://www.taipeitimes.com

International Telecommunication Union (2003). *Technical notes.* Retrieved May 24, 2005, from http://www.itu.int/ITU-D/ict/statistics/WTI_2003.pdf

International Telecommunication Union. (2005, April 26). *Economies by broadband penetration, 2004.* Retrieved May 24, 2005, from http://www.itu.int/ITU-D/ict/statistics/at_glance/top20_broad_2004.html

Internet World Stats. (2005, September 30). *World Internet users and population statistics.* Retrieved October 2, 2005, from http://www.internetworldstats.com/stats.htm

Ipsos. (2005, March 2). *The majority of global Internet users using a high-speed connection.* Retrieved May 26, 2005, from http://www.ipsos-na.com/news/pressrelease.cfm?id=2583

Labor Law Talk. (2005). *Indonesian language.* Retrieved November 6, 2005, from http://encyclopedia.laborlawtalk.com/Indonesian_language

Lovgren, S. (2004, February 26). *English in decline as a first language, study says.* National Geographic News. Retrieved May 23, 2005, from http://news.nationalgeographic.com/news/2004/02/0226_040226_language.html

Mas i Hernàndez, J. (2003, September 2). *La salut del català a Internet.* Retrieved May 25, 2005, from http://www.softcatala.org/articles/article26.htm

McAlpine, R. (2005). *Standards for online content authors.* Quality Web Content. Retrieved September 5, 2005, from http://www.webpagecontent.com/arc_archive/177/5/

National Center for Education Statistics (2003). *Status and trends in the education of Hispanics: Language spoken at home.* Retrieved November 4, 2005, from http://nces.ed.gov/pubs2003/hispanics/Section11.asp

Nielsen, J. (1999). *Designing Web usability: The practice of simplicity.* Indianapolis, IN: New Riders.

NUA (2001). *Methodology.* Retrieved May 24, 2005, from http://www.nua.ie/surveys/how_many_online/methodology.html

Romney, L. (2000, January 6). The cutting edge: Survey looks at online habits of U.S. Latinos. *Los Angeles Times*. Retrieved May 29, 2005, from http://www.latimes.com

Web Site Optimization (2005, January). *January 2005 bandwidth report*. Retrieved May 26, 2005, from http://www.websiteoptimization.com/bw/0501/

Endnotes

[1]   According to NUA (2001), "An Internet User represents a person with access to the Internet and is not specific to Internet Account holders. When the figure for Internet Account holders is the only information available, this figure is multiplied by a factor of 3 to give the number of Internet users" (para. 2).

However, in its Technical Notes for "Internet indicators," the International Telecommunication Union (ITU) implies that the factor can vary from country to country: "Countries that do not have surveys generally base their estimates on derivations from reported Internet Service Provider subscriber counts, calculated by multiplying the number of subscribers by a multiplier" (2003, p. 4).

[2]   For most of this century, South Korea has had the world's highest proportion of Internet users who subscribe to broadband. According to ITU figures for the country, 11.9 million of 31.6 million Internet users subscribed, resulting in a penetration of less than 38% at the end of 2004 (W. Yasandikusuma, personal communication, May 27, 2005).

However, "broadband penetration" figures are calculated in different ways, showing perhaps the greatest variance of all Internet statistics. The term *broadband* is sometimes applied to speeds less than the ITU minimum of 256 Kbps (V. Gray, personal communication, May 26, 2005). For example, the Federal Communications Commission (FCC) of the United States defines *broadband* as a connection that "enables the end user to receive information from and/or send information to the Internet at information transfer rates exceeding 200 kilobits per second (kbps) in at least one direction" (2005, question 5).

In addition, the term *penetration* is defined in several ways. Some surveys divide a country's total number of broadband subscribers by the total number of inhabitants. Although the U.S. had the most broadband subscribers as of December 2004, the ITU (2005) ranked it only 16th globally on the basis of 11.4% penetration of its general population, compared to 24.9% for South Korea.

Other surveys divide the total number of households or users who have broadband capability installed (but might not actually subscribe) by the total number of "active Internet users." For example, over 69 million U.S. households had the capability as of December, 2004, yielding a penetration of 54.7% for home users according to Web Site Optimization (2005). This figure is bloated even more in the "Face of the Web 2004" study by Ipsos-Insight, which claims that 62% of the entire world "accessed" the Internet via broadband in October, 2004 (Ipsos, 2005).

Chapter X

E-Learning Localized:
The Case of the OOPS Project

Meng-Fen (Grace) Lin
University of Houston, USA

Mimi Miyoung Lee
University of Houston, USA

Abstract

The power of Internet provides unprecedented opportunities for learners to obtain diverse content and for educators to quickly distribute resources. In the increasing globalized learning environment, OpenCourseWare (OCW) is one of the recent movements to utilize the Internet in making educational materials freely available to the world. However, the fact that these materials are offered mainly in English poses challenges to the non-English speaking population in many parts of the world. In response to such concern in the Great China Region, a localization project called the Opensource OpenCourseWare Prototype System (OOPS) was born in Taiwan in February, 2004 (Lin & Chu, 2005). OOPS aims to break the language barrier and deliver the openly-accessible English educational materials to the Chinese-speaking audience in their native language. This chapter presents the detailed background and history of this project, and highlights three challenges that OOPS has faced in its early stage of development. They are: (1) access to materials, (2) issues about translation, and (3) complexity of intra-cultural communication. Based on the first author's direct experience with the project, suggestions and implications for future research are also offered.

Introduction

One of the modern marvels is the invention of the Internet. The Internet is believed to have provided the vehicle for information exchanges beyond geographical boundaries. The widespread availability and use of the Internet and the growing number of its users worldwide have brought our offline behaviors and routines into the online dimension. The demographics of Internet users shifted over the years from the middle-class male white dominance of the early years to greater numbers of minority population, including females and people with modest income in America (Pew, 2005). Others countries such as Taiwan also have experienced similar changes. According to a 2004 Taiwanese Internet user survey, there were more female users (59%) than males (41%) online. The same survey also showed a small increase of users in the age group between 35 and 44-year-olds, compared to the previous year (Yam.com, 2005). A similar survey in China indicated that the male to female user ratio was 60.6% to 39.4%, with almost 60% of the users under the age of 30 (China Internet Network Information Center, 2005). Nevertheless, both surveys pointed out that the majority of Internet users in Taiwan and China had the educational level beyond the post-secondary degree.

Consistent with the American Internet usage pattern, the two surveys in Taiwan and China indicated that checking email and browsing the Internet were the two major activities for going online. Blurring the boundaries between work and leisure, formal and informal learning, the advancement of the Internet has made it possible for many of us to obtain information from remote sources and experience it more flexibly. It appears, however, that language still poses as one of the more significant barriers for knowledge sharing in this age of globalized e-learning. Even though the Internet has been regarded as the vehicle bringing the world to our fingertips, surveys on the users in China reveal otherwise. For example, only 9.3% of China's Internet users visit English language Web sites (China Internet Network Information Center, 2005). In a different survey, when asked what language-based Web sites they most frequently visit in addition to those in Chinese, 33% of Taiwan's Internet users indicated that they did not visit any other language-based Web sites (Yam.com, 2005). Considering the fact that English is the most widely-used language in the cyberworld, the above statistics shows that language still "remains a significant barrier discouraging users from venturing out farther into the cyberworld" (Liu, Day, Sun, & Wang, 2002) for the non-English population. In response to such concerns, the Opensource OpenCourseWare Prototype System (OOPS) establishes a bottom-up movement to help learners break the language barrier and bring more openly-shared knowledge sources to the Great China Region. OOPS was set up with the goal of translating an array of online education materials made available to the public through the OpenCourseWare (OCW) initiative into Chinese.

Before introducing OOPS in more detail, the authors will explain the background of the OpenCourseWare movement in the next section.

Background of the OpenCourseWare Collection

The OpenCourseWare (OCW) movement, initiated by MIT[1], is a free and open collection of educational materials for faculty, students, and self-learners around the world provided via the Internet. MIT OCW provides visitors with course syllabi, lecture notes, and course calendars for over 1,000 courses. In addition, most courses include supplement materials such as multimedia simulations, problem sets and their solutions, past exams, reading lists, sample student projects, and a selection of video lectures. First announced in April, 2001, the MIT OCW pilot site opened to the public in September 2002, with initial offerings of 32 courses. The site was officially launched in September 2003, with 500 courses online. Clearly a global initiative, the site has received almost 120 million hits from visitors in more than 210 countries, territories, and city-states around the globe in 2004. Materials have already been translated into at least 10 different languages (MIT, 2005).

The apparent success of the MIT site has inspired other OCW initiatives. Utah State University (USU) launched its OCW in March 2005[2], followed by Johns Hopkins Bloomberg School of Public Health (JHSPH) in April 2005[3]. These two institutions added additional courses to MIT's offerings, making the current OCW collection very unique. Six of Japan's top universities also announced their OCW in May 20054. A notable fact about this group of OCW is that only the materials meeting the following criteria were included: the course materials that (1) the professors felt comfortable sharing, (2) could be easily digitized, and (3) most importantly, are free of copyright and intellectual property restriction. Different users would find this OCW collection useful in different ways. For example, educators are interested in utilizing the materials for curriculum development while self-learners and students may draw upon the materials for self-study or supplementary use. Course materials contained in this collection may be copied, distributed, translated, and modified by anyone as long as the users observe the following rules: (1) the adapted material is for non-commercial use, (2) the original faculty authors receive proper credit, and (3) the adapters openly share the materials in the same manner as done by OpenCourseWare[5]. Following the same principles, OOPS aims to bring the openly- shared knowledge to the Chinese/Taiwanese population in their own language.

OOPS Model

OOPS is an independent grass roots project, headquartered in Taiwan, designed to translate and adopt OCW for the Great China Region, commonly referred to as China, Taiwan, and Hong Kong. The most distinguishing characteristic of OOPS is that volunteers in various disciplines, recruited from all over the world, mainly run the project. These volunteers choose courses from OCW sites and translate them. In February 2004, the entire MIT OCW site was copied to a local server hosted in Taiwan, marking the beginning of OOPS. Through media coverage, Bulletin Board System (BBS) postings, and forwarded emails, OOPS quickly attracted volunteer translators in cyberspace. According to an online OOPS volunteers survey, the top three reasons for volunteering are self learning, knowledge sharing, and helping others. OOPS currently includes courses from the entire OCW collection from MIT, JHSPH, and USU.

Volunteers

As of June, 2005, OOPS has over 700 registered volunteers, translating more than 800 courses. Thirty-five courses are completed so far. OOPS volunteers live all over the world, with the largest participants being from Taiwan (342), followed by those from China (148), and the United States (33). In regards to volunteers' highest degrees earned, the master's degree ranks the first with 48%, followed by bachelor's degree with 37%. Volunteers' occupations vary widely, but the students group clearly constitutes the majority with almost 50% of the total volunteers (OOPS, 2004).

The Process

OOPS uses an "adoption" approach, where volunteers can choose the courses they want to "adopt." On the Web site, OOPS displays an icon, immediately next to each course title, specifying the course's adoption status in four levels: (1) waiting to be adopted, (2) already adopted, (3) nearly finished, or (4) completed. Volunteers browse through the project Web site and look for courses in which they are interested. They adopt the courses they want to translate via an online submission form.

OOPS divides all course contents into two levels. The level-one contents include standard components most courses share. They consist of a course home, syllabus, calendar, and list of readings and assignments. Some courses might have additional items such as study materials, exams, simulations, or video. In short, the level-one contents are all HTML pages within each course. Level-two contents mostly PDF files that include actual PowerPoint slides of lecture notes, class handouts, or exams.

Volunteer translators are required to translate the entire level-one contents first. The translated work will then be seen by an editor before volunteers proceed to the level-two contents. This process provides the editor with an early opportunity to catch possible errors and edit for styles. Once the translator accepts the editor's suggestions, the level-one content is sent to a reviewer (when available) before they are posted online. The reviewers consist of content experts from different fields, and they perform the final review for accuracy in technical terminology before the material is published online. The volunteers are encouraged to submit the level-two contents in small portions, as they are usually very lengthy. This cyclical process is performed for each portion of the level-two work: editing, maybe reviewing, and publishing online. In other words, OOPS publishes level-one content online in its entirety while the level-two contents are posted in small portions. Figure 1 illustrates the process.

Figure 1. OOPS publishing workflow

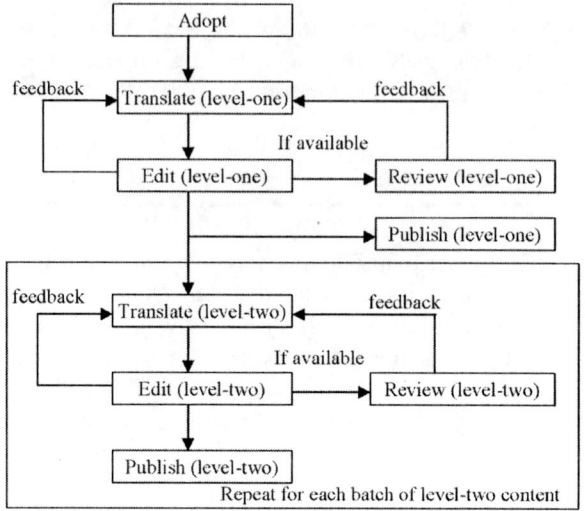

Quality Control

Each language has its unique rhythms and structures. In this sense, the process of translation from English, an alphabet-based language, into Chinese, a pictographic-based language, is not an easy task. The meaning of a sentence also depends on its context and the particular culture "of which the sentence's language is the linguistic expression" (Gordon & Alexander, 2005, p. 141). In addition to the considerable differences in usage, grammar, and sentence structures between English and Chinese, it is particularly challenging for the translators to convey the subtle meanings and nuances from one to another. How can a volunteer-based project such as OOPS strive for better quality? OOPS employs a "signal" system, an icon at the top of every translated page, to indicate the quality of translation (see Figure 2). Each color light bulb represents a different task in the workflow. The icon is OOPS' way of informing the readers the progression of the translation. Together with the icon, on top of each translated page displays the name and brief bio of the translator, editor, and reviewer. Based on the icon and the bio, readers can then form their own judgment about quality.

In addition to the icon system, OOPS offers a discussion forum for the translators to post their questions and share possible solutions as another way of improving the overall quality of translation. The next section details the appearance and functionality of the discussion forum.

Figure 2. OOPS quality icon displayed on each translated page

The Discussion Forum

An online discussion forum was set up where volunteers and visitors could interact. The appearance and functionalities of this forum is very similar to any other Web-based asynchronous discussion forum. All postings remain online since the project's inception. Participation in this forum does not require registration. Volunteers seeking help from their fellow translators actively use the forum. In addition, the forum serves as the place to post news, announcements, and other project-related information. Figure 3 shows a screen shot of the online forum. The first column is the subject of the discussion thread, followed by the number of replies, the person who initiated the thread, number of times this thread has been viewed, and the time and last person who responded to this thread. All discussion threads are organized in reverse chronological order; the ones with the last replies appear at the top.

Figure 3. OOPS online forum

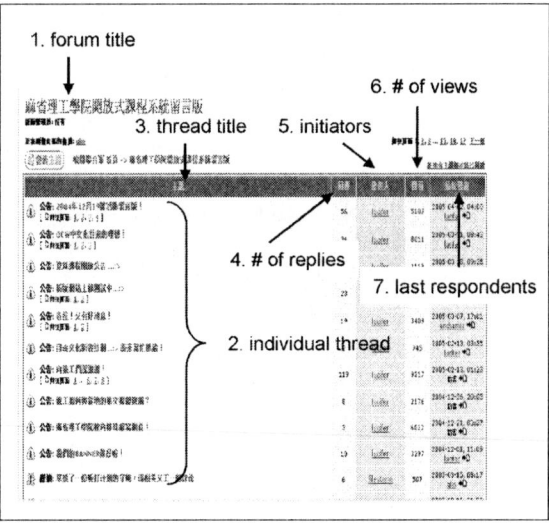

The forum serves several functions in this online community: It is a place for help seeking for volunteers who encounter difficulties in translation, a place for voicing opinions and making suggestions, and a place for making announcement and soliciting inputs from the community. More importantly, this forum provides a mountain of textual evidence of some of the promises and challenges OOPS has faced. Three major themes surfaced during our investigation: access, translation, and intra-cultural differences. The authors will address each theme in the next section.

Issues and Challenges

As an organic community, OOPS continues to grow and change. Investigating this early stage of the OOPS project, the authors came to recognize some challenges identified by the OOPS participants. As indicated in the previous section, the issues can be divided into three interrelated dimensions: (1) access, (2) translation, and (3) intra-cultural concerns.

Access

The observation of the online forum revealed that the two main complaints of site visitors are: (1) "lack of depth" in course contents, resulting mainly from (2) the limited access to referenced materials such as books or journal articles. According to Lin's (2005b) Story Thread Analysis study, 10.35% of postings on the OOPS online forum were in the category of "I cannot find materials." The following posting, signed by "a disappointed passerby" illustrates the point well.

Almost 99.99% of the courses have only course outlines and syllabus. It is like browsing through a CD category, knowing what songs are available yet unable to hear them. (thread #636)

Two independent factors seem to contribute to the first problem. As mentioned earlier, what could be made available in the OCW collection is limited to three factors: what the professors are willing to share, what could be digitized, and what could be shared without violation of copyright. As a result, the OCW collection in some cases might lack the "actual" course contents, in spite of the wide range of disciplines covered by the collection.

Compounded with this given problem, OOPS' translation workflow adds another challenge to this issue. As described earlier, OOPS posts level-one contents when they are ready, even though level-two contents are still under translation. Furthermore, OOPS allows translators to turn in level-two contents in small chunks. Imagine among over 1,000 courses in English, with only thirty-five of them completely translated and with the remaining ones mostly with level-one translation only, it is understandable that users could initially feel disappointed.

Table 1. Courses published online by month and by level

Month	Level-one	Level-two	Completed
Apr-04	5	2	6
May-04	4		1
Jun-04	16	5	4
Jul-04	9	11	1
Aug-04	15		
Sep-04	11	4	
Oct-04	13	3	2
Nov-04	23		1
Dec-04	24	1	
Jan-05	26	3	
Feb-05	22	2	1
Mar-05	30	5	2
Apr-05	41	11	4
May-05	27	4	9
Total	266	43	31
Average	19	4.6	3.1

To better illustrate the point, the authors have examined the daily announcement for online courses on the project Web site. The announcements reveals that fifteen courses were completely translated in OOPS' first year. Further examination of these courses indicates that all of them had only limited contents. It is common for the volunteer translators to finish the courses with fewer contents first as the courses with heavy contents require more time for translation: Interested learners who visit the site are likely to click on courses labeled "finished" but could have easily been disappointed by these earlier products. Table 1 shows the number of level-one and level-two courses which are published, as well as completed courses online by month, indicating that level-one translations have grown at a somewhat steady pace, averaging 19 courses every month, while level-two and completed courses are in small decline, averaging about 4.5 and 3 courses each month. These numbers illustrate that the difficulties in the translation are at level-two.

The issue concerning "lack of depth" seems to be related to the availability of the materials used in the original (U.S.) site and the way OOPS' publishing process works. The second access issue, on the other hand, centers on the accessibility to referenced materials. While OCW has compiled a carefully-selected list of required readings[6], the collection in many cases cannot provide access to the actual materials due to the copyright issues. Learners from non-English speaking countries are likely to face obstacles in obtaining the materials. It is likely that the libraries in those countries have neither the resources nor the access to the books and journals required in the OCW courses. These copyrighted materials may not be so easily accessed from the libraries in some countries.

The two access issues are mostly brought up by OCW users. Observing the forum also revealed one challenge which the volunteer translators face the most—translation.

Translation

In the following section, the authors provide several examples to illustrate some of the challenges in bringing educational materials from one language to another.

Puns and Idioms

Puns and idioms are always very difficult to translate without jeopardizing the original nuance. One of our favorite examples comes from a course in physiology and uncon-sciousness: "Oh no, I have an exam tomorrow, and it is very *impotent* for my grades!" (thread # 376, Lin's italics). How does one translate this in Chinese? Idioms are not any easier. With an example like "[T]he sketch is only as good as the witness" (thread #522), the translators have to first comprehend the meaning within the context of the course as well as the American culture, before they can produce a translation that would be easily understood by Chinese/Taiwanese audience.

As seen from these examples, the issues of the content translation are closely related to the translators' familiarity with daily lives of American students on which the course content is based.

Everyday Lives

Understanding the cultural context of the course contents proved to be a crucial aspect of the translation process. Jianhua, a college instructor teaching marketing and business English in China posted many questions about different food items that he had encountered in the course materials. During the month of June, 2004, he posted several questions to the online forum seeking help with translations for terms such as Strawberry Daiquiri (thread #232), chocolate-frosted Wheaties (thread #252), Fruit Roll-ups and Burrito Bandit (thread #253). These were examples used in the course to demonstrate how different products distinguish themselves by anchoring different consumer population and therefore positioning themselves in terms of marketing and pricing. In some discussions, other translators were able to provide the descriptions of the food items. Cases are not limited to food items. For example, Jianhua also asked the following question in June, 2004, "What is *Tivo* service?" (thread #290). Some volunteers described *Tivo* as a digital TV program recorder that allows instant playback and storage. After reading the descriptions and suggestions for the translation, Jianhua concluded that "[I]t seems China does not have such an item" and decided to leave the term in English, following the suggestion offered by many others. It is not intuitive for translators to quickly guess that the initial B.H. refers to a professor named William (thread # 409). These examples show just a tip of the iceberg of the difficulties that the translators face during the translation process. It appears that in many cases, the confusion arises due to the fact that these "everyday" American consumer goods simply did not exist in everyday lives of the translators.

School Context

In a class survey in one of the MIT courses, a student's response reads "TA (teaching assistant) should pick better candies with the class money" (thread #238). Jianhua asked on the forum what TA and candy have to do with the class. Several people quickly pointed out that this is an American humor, showing perhaps a more relaxed atmosphere of the American classrooms and rather an informal nature of student-TA interaction in many cases. Jianhua, however, expressed doubts about such interpretation. He could not imagine someone replying with such "rude" humor in the "formal" class survey. The teacher-student relationship in many Asian cultures, even though it has become more casual in recent years, is still considered quite hierarchical. When Lin asked Jianhua about this discussion several months after, he was still convinced for an additional meaning to the posting. He thought the question seemed "not serious enough" to be discussed in a classroom. For Jianhua, "graduate students complaining about candy" just sounded "too childish." Jianhua continued on by pointing out: "In my school, a class survey usually asks questions about teacher's teaching method, textbook selections. Such an item on the survey sounds too childish to me" Jianhua's reaction might help illustrate the fact how some translators felt foreign and detached from common practices of U.S. classrooms. In addition to the differences in classroom atmosphere in higher education, some common terminologies in the U.S. were also unfamiliar to the Chinese/Taiwanese ears. Examples such as "a course reader" (thread #351) and "Stellar reading" (thread #551) were not readily recognized by many OOPS translators, as the practice of using course readers was rather rare in the Chinese/Taiwanese educational environments.

Another example concerned take-home exams. While take-home exams are a rather common practice in the U.S. college classrooms under the goal of fostering in-depth thinking and creative ideas, such strategy is rarely used in the Great China region, where the competition for a good high school and college is more than fierce. In Chinese/Taiwanese culture where the students are driven to be more concerned about the immediate scores than the long-term learning outcome, the concept of a take-home exam, understandably, is considered as less than a fair form of evaluation for some (thread #553, #363).

There was a similar case when Lin translated a general course about conducting research. The professor devoted a session on addressing the topic of Human Subjects Form, giving detailed accounts of its history, rationale, proper procedures, and the researcher ethic. As a scholar educated in the U.S., she was very familiar with the concept and understood the importance of it. However, when translating this section, she had a hard time not only in coming up with a proper Chinese terminology, but also in conveying the concept. In Chinese/Taiwanese cultures where collective benefits have been traditionally valued more than individual rights (Hofstede, 2001), the notion of protecting research participants has yet to be regarded as a top priority in the research community. For this reason, Lin was concerned that the concept of human subject process might not be readily communicated to the users. She searched on the Internet and did find some academic documents from that region addressing this issue. However, it appeared that these documents were written for the Western readers in English. It seemed safe to say that the concept of human subject in research has just begun to surface in Taiwan. She could not locate any information confirming or disconfirming the same movement in Hong Kong or China. In this case, she took the liberty and added an expanded translator's note in her own words containing additional information around this concept.

Furthermore, there has been a long debate about the issue of whether OOPS should translate the titles of reference materials such as books and journal articles into Chinese (for example, thread #328). This is a tricky issue. The proponents emphasize the fact that the entire Web site does keep the original English side by side with the translated Chinese in the first place. The opponents believe leaving the original English could better facilitate readers' ability to find the materials. In addition to the issues discussed above, the different usages of Chinese language among the Great China regions also have posed challenges, and it is discussed in the following section.

Intra-Cultural Issues

In 2000, Sina Net, one of the biggest Chinese Web sites, and The Common Wealth Magazine conducted the first-ever survey on *International Chinese Internet Usage* (Sina.com, 2000). This survey targeted the Chinese/Taiwanese populations in four major regions—China, Hong Kong, Taiwan, and North America. In this effort, they had to create six different versions of the survey in order to accommodate the differences in terminology usage and Chinese character encoding.

It is true that the residents of China, Taiwan, and Hong Kong share one official spoken language—Mandarin. In case of the written language, however, the situation is not as simple. Since the Cultural Revolution, the people in China use the simplified version of the Chinese written characters, while residents of Hong Kong and Taiwan continue using the traditional characters. In addition to this difference, the two forms of Chinese characters use different encoding systems for information storage and display. Only very recently did the majority of Internet browsers come to accommodate the differences by allowing users to easily switch from one encoding to another. In the above mentioned survey effort, the organizers even created a version of the survey that was entirely graphic in order to work around the encoding issue. The differences in encoding may no longer be a major issue in today's Internet environment; however, the differences in the language usage can easily cause confusions among users from different regions. In preparing for the survey, Sina Net and Chinese World Magazine organized local experts to modify the survey according to their local usage and culture. Furthermore, these local experts helped with the data analysis. Their help was crucial to understanding and interpreting the survey: commonly-used terms such as "computer," "printer" and "Internet" are translated differently, just to name a few. For example, the word "computer" is translated into " 電腦 " in Taiwan but " 电算机 " in China. "Printer" is called " 印表機 " in Taiwan and " 打印机 " in China, and "Internet" is regarded differently as " 網路 " and " 网络 " in Taiwan and China respectively.

While it is possible for users from one region to understand the different terminologies in the examples given above, one should not assume that in general. Generally speaking, a translator first adopts a course and translates it according to the usage with which he or she is familiar. Then, an editor comes in and edits the translation, possibly in his/ her regional terminologies. Regardless, once the translation goes through editing and reviewing, the next step is to create two separate online versions—one with the traditional Chinese characters and another with the simplified Chinese characters. Microsoft Word® has a built-in function that would convert a simplified-encoded file into a traditional-encoded one and vice versa. Nevertheless, this seemingly simple-step with a click of the mouse has shown occasional glitches. For example, the system has made a consistent mistake of converting the English word "project" in traditional Chinese as "計畫" to simplified Chinese as "计画" when the correct characters for it should be "计划". Only when both the translator and the editor happen to be from the same region, discrepancies in terminology usage would be minimal.

The point raised here is that even among the Great China regions, who share the common language of Mandarin, there are differences associated with local languages that significantly affect the translation process. These differences might include terminology usage, computer encoding, and even Internet usage pattern. Because OOPS targets all Chinese users, these differences surface during translation process. Even though an individual volunteer translates according to his or her local context, OOPS as a whole faces the challenge of creating documents that will be comprehensible for different regional audiences.

Discussion

In its early stage as an e-learning localization model, the OOPS project has seen a number of issues and challenges as mentioned earlier. While there is no easy solution to these issues whose ramification goes well beyond the local scene, some suggestions can be made at this point to better facilitate the current OOPS project. The authors will address each of the issues raised above and discuss suggestions with possible implications for a larger context of globalized e-learning.

Access

The two access issues, what materials are made available and what materials are practically accessible, are difficult to resolve. In many cases, the Copyright and Intellectual Property restrictions dictate the accessibility of the materials. One possible solution to this problem is Open Access (OA) (Brody, 2001). Research[7] has shown that articles which are made available online free of charge receive more citations than the copyrighted ones. This means the OA not only benefits the readers but also the authors of the materials by increasing their accessibility. If more referenced materials in the OCW collection are openly accessible, self-learners can then have access to them online. Nevertheless, the authors understand that it would be unreasonable to request OCW producers such as MIT professors to use only OA materials in their courses. MIT professors foremost have responsibilities to serve their students, who can easily gain access to the course materials. Furthermore, until OA is widely accepted in academia and in more journals in the Institute for Scientific Information (ISI) index, people seeking tenure promotions may not choose OA as a publication outlet, resulting in limited content in OA.

Another possible solution is to make more video lectures available. For example, currently MIT has about ten courses with complete video and/or audio and several others with supplemental video and/or audio. According to MIT OCW's 2005 evaluation report, 21% of users cited lecture videos as most valuable in achieving their goals for site access (MIT, 2005). The authors are aware of the many reasons why video and audio cannot be the key elements of OCW. Viewing video lectures demands high bandwidth, which limits the accessibility of the materials. Such limitation can hinder the OCW's aim to make materials as accessible as possible. In addition, video production and storage can be costly. Even with these concerns, the authors cautiously suggest that video lectures can provide a sensible solution to the issue related to accessing materials. As technology further develops, the issue of bandwidth and cost might be gradually reduced. Given the current copyright restriction, producing more video lectures seems to be a solution.

Translation

According to Lin's observation, questions regarding content-specific translations were few. Most translators are competent enough to understand the subject per se, making possible the translations on a very technical level. The issues had more to do with contextualizing the information fit for the local culture and learning environment so the translation would make a better sense. Interestingly enough, however, the translators did not seem to be quite aware of the fact that cultural difference is the source of the difficulty for their translation process. On one occasion, Lin posted a question on the forum asking translators to share any examples they had encountered that are related to cultural and language differences. She was surprised to receive no response regarding this issue. This can mean that while many postings clearly showed questions regarding adapted meanings of some terms, the volunteers did not problematize the cultural differences.

Table 2. An example of how OOPS put Chinese and English side by side

Week	Unit	Date
1	｢ 究技巧介紹 Introduction to Research Skills	
2	｢ 究設計的專業道德和成見 Professional Ethics and Bias in Research Design; Lab Animals in Research	
3	｢ 究設計與以人｢ 對象的｢ 究 Study Design and Human Subjects in Research	
4	資料收集、管理與分享 Data Acquisition, Management, and Sharing	｢ 交作業一 Assignment 1 Due

They might not have paid much attention to such issues even though they did encounter them. The authors speculate that it might need someone who has had an experience with both cultures to have the sensibility to recognize the "differences." Most of these volunteer translators do not have much experiences of the actual U.S. culture in which many of the terms are contextualized. As a consequence, the translators with a lack of experience at U.S. school contexts end up spending much more time on minor issues as seen in the case with Jianhua's examples earlier.

Our suggestions for the apparent translation challenges are as follows:

1. **Reference authoritative data source for technical terminologies:** OOPS compiles a list of government-sponsored database such as National Institute for Compilation and Translation[8] for technical terminologies and the Central News Agency[9] for a unified translation of people, place, and events. Volunteers are also encouraged to refer to peer-reviewed journals for terminologies in the field when translating.

2. **Publish translated Chinese and original English side by side:** One thing OOPS insists from the beginning is to put the translated Chinese and original English next to each other. By doing so, OOPS encourages all readers to be the eyes for translation mistakes, a notion of promoting collective knowledge similar to that of the Wikipedia[10]. Take the course offered in Health, Science, and Technology (HST.502) which Lin translated as an example. The first four weeks of the course calendar looks like Table 2.

3. **Add "translator notes":** Translators are encouraged to add "translator notes" for further clarification. The notes can be used to add supplemental materials or explanation about the materials from the translator's perspective. They can also be used to communicate to the learners some of the challenges experienced during the translation process. Also, other translators can use the notes to learn the processes by which certain terminologies have come to be chosen for different translations.

Quality Support

One of the ways that OOPS attempts to sustain high quality translation is through fostering a sense of community among its volunteers. OOPS online forum is designed for such a function. As mentioned earlier, the volunteers visit the forum to share and discuss the translation challenges and possible solutions. While the format of current online discussion forum serves as a good starting point, improvements can be made to the current design.

1. **Divide the online forum into sub-groups by discipline and by geographic areas:** Having discipline-specific sub-groups can help volunteers (1) to meet others in similar content areas, and (2) to seek and provide help from others with specific content questions. By forming sub-groups in geographic areas, volunteers can create local offline connections/networks which in turn can facilitate efforts such as regional promotion for the OOPS projects.

2. **Cultivate moderators for active discussions:** Research indicates the importance of a moderator in online learning. As mentioned by Salmon (1998), effective online moderation can help students move from simply gaining access to materials, to socializing with others, sharing information, and eventually achieving knowledge construction collaboratively. Gray (2004) further emphasizes the important role of a moderator in informal learning context of an online community as critical in sustaining the community over an extended period and enhancing the learning function. Just like volunteer translators adopt a course and take ownership in seeing its translation to completion, OOPS can empower capable volunteers to be the moderator for each discussion subgroup. These moderators will then take ownership of the forum support members through active participation and constant encouragement.

3. **Create volunteer mentors:** Additionally, OOPS can create a special taskforce composed of experienced volunteers. These volunteers can act as mentors to newcomers by "adopting" them and by helping them with early questions. This taskforce can benefit OOPS in two ways. First, by channeling experienced volunteers to mentor newcomers, this taskforce allows experienced volunteers to share with newcomers what they have learned. The taskforce can solve what Lin (2005a) called the tension between newcomers and old timers where the two groups represent different and, at times, competing needs within the community. Secondly, the taskforce not only provides a means for bringing the two groups closer, such a taskforce has the potential to create a community of practice (Lave & Wenger, 1991; Wenger, 1998; Wenger, McDermott, & Snyder, 2002) where value creation is one of the key factors. The taskforce offers an opportunity for experienced volunteers to remain and give back to the community what they have learned. Such value creation and proliferation is the key to community sustainability.

Intra-Cultural Issues

The issues pertaining to the differences within the Greater China do not have easy solutions. At this point, the authors make the following two suggestions to minimize the identified challenges.

1. **Create a database of commonly-used terms juxtaposing the Chinese and Taiwanese translations:** Many international organizations such as Microsoft have created their own database with different translations or terminologies used in China, Hong Kong, and Taiwan. Unfortunately, these databases are not openly available to the general public. OOPS has started to create a table on a wiki platform, a Web-based publishing and collaborating mechanism that allows everyone access and permission to the writing of the content. In OOPS' case, a wiki-based database could encourage everyone to contribute to the compilation of the different terms, a daunting task, yet possible through collective knowledge. If this database can be further developed with a search function, then it can help solve some of the confusion of different terminology used in different regions.

2.   **Edit for local usage:** Human eyes are still the best and final defense for the finished translation. Always have an editor check on these different usages and change them according to the local custom. This step is time-consuming, yet important in assuring that all materials are adapted and tailored to best fit for the regional users.

Conclusion

OOPS is still in its early stage, but has already received much attention from many educators. The fact that OOPS is operated completely by volunteers is highly significant in itself. One explanation for this early success of OOPS can be found in the regional factors: Volunteer/learners are highly educated, and technology-savvy as well as having access to broadband Internet connections (Lin & Chu, 2005). In the current OCW movement where many institutions such as MIT, JHSPH, and USU play the role of OCW producers, OOPS is unique as the largest OCW consumer. OOPS provides an important model that aims to empower knowledge consumers beyond language barriers, to take a lead in localizing open knowledge by reproducing these valuable resources in a culturally-appropriate manner.

In this chapter, we briefly mentioned Open Access as a possible means to broaden available resources. The current Creative Commons (Garlick, 2005) movement also advocates the shift of paradigm from "all rights reserved" to "some rights reserved." Open Access is compatible with peer review and can be academically rigorous. For example, *International Journal of Instructional Technology & Distance Learning* salutes not only open access, it also embraces the creative commons license, granting article authors the right to reproduce and reuse any of their published articles. When more academia embraces open access as equally rigorous and significantly more valuable to the research and learning community, we can predict that more educational materials will be accessible via the open Web. Nevertheless, in the globalized e-learning context, learners from other parts of the world still face the language barriers. Even if learners could obtain reading materials through international inter-library loan, those materials might still be printed in English. What role will open access play in globalized e-learning remains an exciting trend to watch.

The world has much to learn from OOPS' experience and we need to continue observing its development. When OOPS has more translated courses online, we need to start understanding about the users. Who are they, and how has translation helped them? We will have to continue to watch this development.

OOPS has been extremely successful in drawing a large number of volunteer translators who are highly educated. There are two significances in this observation. First, highly educated volunteers probably reflect the value of education in the Chinese/Taiwanese population in general. The regional high level of education provides an already existing pool of talents. On the other hand, however, such a well-educated group might also exemplify a necessity prerequisite of such a translation project. This could certainly be a challenge to regions with lower education levels, on average, which might be the very ones who could benefit from such open knowledge the most (Lin & Chu, 2005).

It can be assumed that MIT as a brand name was a significant part of the OOPS attraction. The need for more localized version of the educational materials was also a driving force behind the OOPS project. Nevertheless, such a brand-name effect could also result in the homogenization of "the cultural traditions of the non-western world through the process of Western cultural domination" (Bunt-Kokhuis, 2005, p. 269). The authors recognize this as an important concern, and plan to direct our future research in this regard as OOPS matures continuously.

In this chapter, the authors have attempted to address the challenges of OOPS in the current stage. The biggest hope OOPS brings is its apparent success as a volunteer-based model of e-learning localization project. In this unique grassroots effort, the issues and suggestions discussed above will provide a helpful guideline for OOPS and other similar e-learning projects. Continuous observation of OOPS will shed light to the future implementation of more localization projects like OOPS that will help open doors for global learners to the educational resources only available in other languages (in many cases, English).

References

Brody, T. (2001). *Mining the social life of an eprint archive.* Open Citation Project Web site. Retrieved November 10, 2005, from http://opcit.eprints.org/tdb198/opcit/

Bunt-Kokhuis, S. V. D. (2005). Globalization and the freedom of knowledge. *Higher Education in Europe, 29*(2), 269-284.

China Internet Network Information Center. (2005). *Bi-Annual China Internet Developing Report.* Retrieved June 10, 2005, from http://news.xinhuanet.com/it/2005-01/19/content_2481448.htm

Garlick, M. (2005). A review of Creative Commons and Science Commons. *EDUCAUSE Review, 40*(5), 78-79.

Gordon, D., & Alexander, G. (2005). The education of story lovers: Do computers undermine narrative sensibility? *Curriculum Inquiry, 35*(2), 133-159.

Gray, B. (2004). Informal learning in an online community of practice. *Journal of Distance Education, 19*(1), 20-35.

Hofstede, G. H. (2001). Individualism and collectivism. In *Culture's consequences: Comparing values, behaviors, institutions and organizations across nations* (pp. 209-278). Thousand Oaks, CA: Sage Publications.

Lave, J., & Wenger, E. (1991). *Situated learning : Legitimate peripheral participation.* Boston: Cambridge University Press.

Lin, M. -F. (2005a). *Boundary learning in an online community of practice.* Paper presented at the World Conference on Educational Multimedia, Hypermedia, & Telecommunications, Montreal, Canada.

Lin, M. -F. (2005b). Story thread analysis: Storied lives in an online community of practice. *International Journal of Instructional Technology and Distance Learning, 2*(9), 61-82.

Lin, M. -F., & Chu, L. (2005, July). *Experiencing open knowledge the OOPS way.* Paper presented at the 5th IEEE International Conference on Advanced Learning Technologies, Kaohsiung, Taiwan.

Liu, C.-c., Day, W.-w., Sun, S.-w., & Wang, G. (2002). User behavior and the "globalness" of Internet: From a Taiwan users' perspective. *Journal of Computer Medicated Communication, 7*(2). Retrieved September 10, 2005 from http://www.ascusc.org/jcmc/vol7/issue2/taiwan.html

MIT. (2005). *2004 program evaluation findings report.* Retrieved July 15, 2005, from http://ocw.mit.edu/OcwWeb/Global/AboutOCW/evaluation.htm

OOPS. (2004). *OOPS December Status Report.* Retrieved June, 10, 2005, from http://www.twocw.net/Global/oops/20041219.xls

Salmon, G. (1998). Developing learning through effective online moderation. *Active Learning, 9,* 3-8.

Sina.com. (2000). *International Chinese Internet Usage Survey.* Retrieved June, 10, 2005, from http://www.sina.com.tw/service/about/news/news_00_0216.html

Wenger, E. (1998). *Communities of practice: Learning, meaning, and identity*: Cambridge University Press.

Wenger, E., McDermott, R., & Snyder, W. M. (2002). *A guide to managing knowledge: Cultivating communities of practice.* Boston, MA: Harvard Business School Press.

Yam.com. (2005). *2004 Taiwan Internet User Survey.* Retrieved June 10, 2005, from http://survey.yam.com/survey200/chart/result.html

Endnotes

[1]   See MIT OCW at http://ocw.mit.edu

[2]   See Utah State University's OCW at http://ocw.usu.edu

[3]   See Johns Hopkins Bloomberg School of Public Health's OCW at http://ocw.jhsph.edu

[4]   See Japan's OCW at http://www.jocw.jp/

[5]   See Creative Commons at http://creativecommons.org/

[6]   OCW usually provides a list of reading materials drawing from book chapters and journal articles. When these materials are copyright-free, they are included in OCW in full text.

[7]   For example, see the Open Citation Project http://opcit.eprints.org/

[8]   http://www.nict.gov.tw/

[9]   http://client.cna.com.tw/name/

[10]   http://www.wikipedia.org/

Chapter XI

What Can Cave Walls Teach Us?

Ruth Gannon Cook
DePaul University, USA

Caroline M. Crawford
University of Houston - Clear Lake, USA

Abstract

The question raised in this chapter, "What can cave walls teach us?" is essential because education is increasingly taught within a ubiquitous global electronic venue. Since much of the current electronic learning (e-learning) education environment has been produced in the United States of America, Canada, and Western Europe, many other countries, such as China, Japan, India, and Africa are currently left out of e-learning designs. So the question of how to provide e-learning that accommodates the diverse learning needs of multicultural and multinational learners is becoming critical. This chapter discusses some of the ways instructional designers and educators can utilize lessons learned from the past to facilitate a renaissance of learning across cultures and nations and incorporate prior learning legacies into facilitative, 21st century e-learning. Positive by-products will include more equitable learning opportunities for targeted learners through e-learning and, optimally, more well-rounded learners.

In the Beginning:
An Introduction to Semiotics

Over 20,000 years ago, our human ancestors painted beautiful pictures on cave walls. While those paintings might not have been viewed as educational in nature, they probably were used for more than decorating the living area. The cave wall paintings depicted animals and scenes which the ancient cave dwellers used to tell stories, and those stories were the antecedents of education. The question raised in this chapter is, "What can cave walls teach us?" This question could become increasingly important in a world wherein education is taught within a global electronic venue.

Increasingly, education is accessible through electronic venues (e-learning), and is currently produced predominantly in the United States of America (examples, such as Massachusetts Institute of Technology (MIT), New Horizons® Computer Learning Centers, Inc., Nova Southeastern University, Pennsylvania State University, University of Phoenix); Canada (examples, such as Carleton University, ELearn Corporation®, Elluminate, Inc.®, Madonna University) and Western Europe (examples in the United Kingdom, such as Conation Technologies, University of Leeds; and, in the Netherlands, such as Europe/MiddleEast/Africa (EMEA) Corporation®, and University of Twente (Konrad, 2003)). Other countries, such as China, Japan, India, Indonesia, Brazil, Argentina, Peru, Mexico, and countries of Africa, are often left out of e-learning designs. So the questions related to providing e-learning to accommodate the diverse learning needs of multicultural, multinational learners become even more critical. The answers, at least in part, may be "written on the walls" of human ancestors. If e-learning can be designed to consciously utilize semiotics, then it can better meet the growing multicultural and multinational needs of non-Western cultural groups and can improve the literacy and socio-economic opportunities in developing nations. Semiotic tools, the old-fashioned "crayons" of the mind, such as metaphors, pictures, and other symbolic representations, can have a profound effect on electronic learners, if we choose to utilize them, in a careful design for e-learning. If these meditative tools are incorporated into online learning, the legacies passed down through millennia of human education can be extended to future generations of learners.

This chapter will not include technology issues, like bandwidth and new technological enhancements, but will discuss ways that instructional designers and educators can include lessons learned from the past to facilitate a renaissance of e-learning across cultures and nations. This chapter will include how to incorporate semiotics into electronic interactive activities, self-regulation strategies, and collaborative community goals. Positive by-products of the conscious inclusion of semiotics in instructional design include more equitable learning opportunities for targeted learners through e-learning and, optimally, more well-rounded learners.

Definition of Terms

For the purpose of this chapter, the following operational definitions were used:

- **E-learner:** Any student enrolled in an electronic (online or distance education-delivered) course.

- **Semiotics:** The definition of semiotics utilized in this chapter is the "study of patterned human communication behavior, including auditory/vocabulary, facial expressions, body talk, touch (proxemics), signs, and symbols" (Webster, 1989, p. 1324). As such, semiotic research focuses on symbolic interpretation and understanding, and is integral to the question raised in this chapter.

- **Sign:** A sign is a representation of anything that stands for something else, such as the word dog or a drawing of a dog that represents the animal recognized in most cultures as a dog (Driscoll, 2000).

- **Student:** Any person enrolled in a course of study or person taking an educational or training course. For the purposes of this chapter, the words student and learner will be used interchangeably.

- **Tool:** The traditional dictionary meaning assigned to the word "tool" is "anything, which, held in the hand, assists a person to do manual or non-manual work. (Webster, 1989, p. 1535)

Some Lessons from History

Ancient educators used available tools to convey meaning with signs, symbols, inscriptions, and stories. Ancient cave dwellers painted pictures on cave walls all over the world over ten thousand years ago. Five thousand years ago, Phoenician merchants told stories of lurking dragons at the end of the world, and two thousand years ago a group of men spread stories of one man who would rule the world. Gutenberg's press five hundred years ago, electricity one hundred years ago, along with the telephone and media, and computers fifty years ago, all have served as vehicles of communication that have influenced national and family cultures. All have utilized some form of semiotics, signs, or stories, to convey meaning.

As sociocultural tools, signs, and symbols take on enriched meaning, affecting the functions of human consciousness as well as their environment (Vygotsky, 1935, 1962, 1978, 1981). Ultimately, everyday language and discourse come under the scrutiny of this discipline, since it becomes a metalinguistic descriptor of ordinary communication (Dant, 1991). Ordinary language identifies and uses written material and verbiage to communicate and express meaning. Language also incorporates these "tools" to construct meaning. In some psychological schools of thought, such as the structuralist school of thought, tools are analyzed in order to study the social context of language in a meaningful way (Vygotsky, 1981; Wertsch, 1985a, 1985b).

Verbal transmissions of words and phrases also convey culture (Hayes, 1996). The "knower's" access to the world is attained through this particular form of expression, but the symbolic process can never be fully commanded by the knower because it is too dependent upon other aspects of the symbol than exclusively sound (Verene, 1993). The knower is dominated by and dependent upon the symbol. Already the icons and metaphors, for example, on the World Wide Web, are dependent upon the symbolic representations conveyed by webs of meaning transferred to the virtual realm from the written word. So it is important to be aware of other factors that influence verbal transmissions, such as metaphors and narratives, and include these in course designs that will be used by a wide array of learners, including hearing-impaired learners of all nationalities and cultures.

Contributors to the Literature on Semiotics

A review of literature is important in order to focus on why semiotics could be an important key to successful retention and assimilation of knowledge in online courses. "A substantive…literature review is a precondition for doing substantive…research" (Boote & Beile, 2005, p. 3). "The literature review should set the broad context of the study, clearly demarcate what is and what is not within the scope of the investigation, and justify those decisions…(it) allows the author not only to summarize the existing literature but synthesize it in a way that permits a new perspective" (p. 4). There are countless global donors through millennia who have contributed to semiotics and the language and communications systems that have shaped human knowledge. But there are several authors who have contributed seminal work to the field of semiotics and their reference needs to be included in this chapter.

Giambattista Vico (1668-1744), an Italian professor of rhetoric, was perhaps one of the earlier contributors to the field of semiotics. He created terms for how humans make intelligible and chronicle history, which he called the "trues" or "intelligibilities" of history (Danesi, 2005). Vico believed that, because humans make history, the historical life of nations follows a common pattern in each nation, so humans can also demonstrate the ways in which these "trues" or "intelligibilities" are achieved and reinforced in acts of making history. He also pointed to the metaphor as the crucial factor in the development of language. He purported that all the things depend upon human choice, and those choices influence the languages, customs, and deeds of peoples. Those choices also reflect values and influence war and peace. He held that

The greatest drawback of our educational methods is that we pay an excessive amount of attention to the natural sciences and not enough to ethics…. Our young men, because of their training, which is focused on these (scientific) studies, are unable to engage in the life of the community, to conduct themselves with sufficient wisdom and prudence; nor can they infuse into their speech a familiarity with human psychology or permeate their utterances with passion…. As a consequence, those whose only concern is abstract truth experience great difficulty in achieving their means, and great difficulty in attaining their ends. (Robbins, 1999)

Charles Sanders Peirce has been called one of the pioneering founders of the field of semiotics (and also of the theory of pragmatism) and one of America's important philosophers (The Johns Hopkins University Press, 1997). His contributions included research on probability theory, symbolic logic, and semiotics. He posed that the crucial question rests with the character and function of representability, not on actual existence. Reality, to Peirce, is already conceived as a process that can (and must) be indefinitely extended. Peirce's semiotics is not "based on the *word* as 'sign' but on the *proposition* as that which unifies consciousness and creates intelligibility or comprehension. Peirce's theory of semiotics was not a theory of language, but a theory of the production of meaning" (San Juan, 2006, online). He assigned levels to signs as representations, first as perhaps an "icon," based on resemblance; a second as an "index," based on correspondence to fact; and a third may be a general sign or "symbol" (Searles, 2005).

The Swiss linguist, Ferdinand de Saussure, has been viewed as the founder of European semiotics in the late nineteenth century (Turner, 1993). He believed that language was more than definitions and pronunciation; rather it was a language system that carried the culture's system of priorities, values, and views of the world. Saussure pointed out that humans cannot think or communicate without some form of language. In fact, humans must incorporate new ideas and concepts through existing language, whether through verbal conveyances or visual representations (Turner, 1993). Saussure also pointed out that the relation between "signifier" and "signified" is arbitrary, since there is nothing in the word to attach it to the object. Saussure's view of linguistics posited that the state of language elements (synchronic linguistics) needed to be studied as well as the language's social history (diachronics)..

In the 1920s, Lev Semenovich Vygotsky suggested that functions and semiotic tools of activities comprised elements of culture and cultural-historical development that explicated the process of internalization (Wertsch, 1985a). This was an innovative approach in psychology since psychologists had, up to that point, attempted to explain consciousness from an internal, spiritual standpoint. Vygotsky offered an alternative explanation for mental functions. He suggested that the primary tools of activities, represented in signs and symbols, acted as agents for, and subsequently provided definition for, culture, and served as intervening links to consciousness. Mediation of these tools, which Vygotsky called "tool mediation" (1985b), was the structural and genetic central feature of mental functioning, which, in turn, became a necessary liaison to consciousness (1985b). Vygotsky assigned the word "tool" to the activity of work, but his definition included not only physical tools, such as hammers, but also mental tools, such as metaphors, symbols, and narratives. He also included as tools, auditory/vocal and visual expressions; body talk (kinesthetics); touch (proxemics); prostheses (extensions of limbs), and proxemics. His seminal research transformed psychology with his introduction of an intermediate link of action/object which he called the "unit of analysis", a building block in the explanatory principles of psychology. He believed the historical study of behavior was not auxiliary, but formed its very base (Lee, 1985). Vygotsky's research offered a basis for a culturally-grounded theory of cognition, with the concept of "mediated tools" linking culture to the functions of consciousness. Vygotsky's translated works also shed light on the need for the expansion of sociocultural studies so that social and cultural influences could be viewed across national boundaries as well as professional disciplines.

Of particular interest to this chapter are Vygotsky's experiments with children which inspired his theory of proximal development (Wertsch, 1985b). These experiments provide examples of how the planned use of semiotics can enhance learning. For example, one study of children uses task factors that involve pencils. The children ask themselves where they need to go to find a pencil and talk to themselves during the discovery process. Vygotsky felt these egocentric utterances constitute a turning point in their development and indicate their first conscious reflections of situations. If a child breaks a pencil or has to hunt for one, she or he uses the capacity to reflect and reorganize thoughts and behavior. In doing so, that child internalizes and searches for what she or he learned at home about what to do, or what to look for, and refers back to prior experiences and associations. Today, e-learning instructional designers can still encourage analytical skills in designing exercises that enlist prior experiences in e-learning activities.

B. F. Skinner (1993), like Vico, pursued research on semiotic tools, such as metaphors, because they seemed to have a strong impact on society (Verene, 1993). Studies conducted in the 1950s and 1960s by Skinner and contemporaries suggested that metaphors were not just alternatives to literal language, but were already embedded in iconic thought (Danesi, 1993; Dant, 1991; Turbayne, 1962; Verene, 1993). They posited that responses to metaphors and image schemata facilitated communication and learning and seemed to inspire iconic thinking, to fill conceptual gaps, and to take on a literal quality as descriptors of culture (Danesi, 1993).

Increasingly, through the last several decades, semiotics has been utilized as a tool to help provide universal conceptualizations of basic human tendencies (Verene, 1993). But making sense of semiotic tools, such as metaphors, can vary, even within the same social group, depending upon the culture of both the narrator and the listeners (Gee, 1990). In the extension of learning into the electronic realm, the evolving group of global metaphors that assign electronic terms to metaphors, such as, "virtual" Webs, "virtual" navigation systems, "virtual" galleries, and assign new meanings to ship navigations, market places, and art museums, can inspire new communication medium icons, such as "trash cans," "lighthouses," "open doors," and conjure almost-universal responses from a global group of cyber-learners.

Sociocultural Tools for E-Learning

While novel techno-terms and icons are invented on a daily basis to create a new global language, this language and text is still mediated by the readers with the same human brain functions and cultural lenses of the learners they possessed prior to the new language encounter. The learners use their personal cultural lens and knowledge bases to attempt to interpret the signs and symbols of this new language.

In the haste of such rapidly changing learning environments, such as that of e-learning, the creation of the new medium of knowledge often bypasses old successful methods of communication (McLuhan, 1976). But since the history of human learning is not solely based on the achievements of individual minds; it is also based "on the recognized forms of representation that enabled ancestors to make their ideas and feelings public through culture forms" (p. 349). Also, since reading does not consist of simply words and letters, the other, less identifiable aspects of reading may have even greater effect upon the making of meaning" (Gannon Cook & Crawford, 2004, p. 448; Zaltman, 1997). Literacy includes the forms of representation that convey anthropological, historical, artistic, and inherently recognizable meaning on multiple levels of cognition. Further, cultural signs are integrated into daily communicative environments, and are absorbed into subconscious communications (Turbayne, 1962; Wertsch, 1985). While these signs, symbols, and representational language are seldom prioritized in the planned design of electronic courseware (Connell, 1997; Crawford, 2001; Fernlund, 1995; Hayes, 1996), these semiotic tools serve as proxemics; learners mediate their culturally-influenced knowledge with these recognized signs and the new content material, then assimilate both into the stored knowledge to facilitate a more thorough assimilation of the new language or text (Chandler, 1998, 2001). Current iconic representations and metaphors used in technology are rapidly taking on grass-roots recognition among peoples of many cultures and languages. So, to assure this new evolving "technoculture" is thoroughly integrated into online courseware design, the "old" knowledge needs to converge with the new. Maboudian (2000) explains:

Awareness of semiotics when selecting a visual in a web site can help the web designer understand the variations in (student) interpretations. According to Berger (1998) semiotic 'Codes are highly complex patterns of associations that all members of a society learn. These codes or 'secret structures' in people's minds, affect the ways hat individuals interpret the signs and symbols they find in the media and the ways they live' (p. 26). Berger reminds us that codes can be so commonplace that they seem to be natural. The codes are not only the elements we see, but are the meanings we learn to give them. (Maboudian, 2000, p. 278)

As such, semiotics creates a sustainable social component within an e-learning environment, so as to enhance the learner's conceptual understanding and cognitive integration of the subject matter, as well as level of comfort within a potentially awkward, cumbersome, and isolative learning environment.

Recognizable symbols can embed cultural information that provides a subconscious inclination towards new information (Danesi, 1993; Eisner, 1997). An example of a metaphor that has been utilized in the electric realm uses mosaic tiles to describe the individual nature of learning and resistance to change: "The tiles in a person's mosaic are limited by language and experience ... as the mosaic forms, a cognitive framework occurs...there is an emotional commitment to that way of understanding the world ... the patterns built into an individual's cognitive mosaic reduce confusion and enhance that person's framework" (Danesi, 1993, p. 106).

Another example of a metaphor used in an e-learning context defines education as a "landscape" that requires a map to learn one's location and direction, and may even require an entirely new map during the journey. "What comes across over and over again in studying these ideas is that metaphorically, the map-makers are part of the landscape being mapped" (Danesi, 1993, p. 152). The second metaphor example is particularly relevant to e-learning. Teachers of e-learning may well require "new maps" just to learn the terrain, and they have to learn how to draw those maps by learning the new instructional technology. They know, in doing so, they are still a part of that educational landscape being mapped, but they still need to learn the terrain in order to navigate across it and arrive at their destination.

If new forms of media communication absorb old forms (McLuhan, 1968, 1976), then some of the semiotic aspects of those forms are still embedded in the new technology forms. Print (text) communication draws upon technologies of photographic reproduction, graphic design, and printing. Radio, by contrast, uses an oral channel and spoken language and relies on technologies of sound recording and broadcasting, whilst television combines technologies of sound- and image-recording and broadcasting... "These differences in channel and technology have significant wider implications in terms of the meaning potential of the different media" (Fairclough, 1995, p. 38-39; http://www.aber.ac.uk/media/Documents/S4B/sem13.html" \l "Fairclough_1995). Real time clips of events on a computer accomplish the same effect of making this information more personal, but almost instantly, and these are available at the learner's fingertips. So, if there is conscious planning of which icons, pictures, and video clips to embed, and why to add these components (beyond just style), then learners' sociocultural knowledge can mediate with these tools to facilitate more integrated content knowledge.

Two Case Studies Assess Many Customers and Nationalities in Two Major Urban Universities

Two researchers conducted several research studies that compared e-learning courses designed with embedded semiotics and courses without embedded semiotics. The findings of those two studies, while not generalizable, suggest the e-learning courseware designed with embedded semiotics can be more successful at conveying meaning than courseware without the semiotic representations (Gannon, Cook, & Crawford, 2004). Other studies conducted over the last 10 years, since the rapid growth of e-learning, have supported these findings (Connell, 1997; Eisner, 1997; Gallini, Seaman, & Terry, 1995; Green, 1997, Greeno & Hall, 1997; Hayes, 1996; Salomon, 1997).

The first study was conducted at a large urban public university with a diverse cultural and national student population in the southwestern United States. Students who participated in traditional, electronic, and hybrid (a combination of both) courses were given a survey of 10 questions (in a Likert-type of format, ranging from 1 [least] to 5 [most]), that asked about which courses they thought they learned from the most and why they thought they learned more from these courses. Of the 160 students who participated in the study, 128 preferred online course content delivered with graphics, signs, symbols, and stories to those that were delivered without graphics, metaphors, or graphics (see samples as follows). The remaining 20% of the students did not care whether they were provided with pure text online or with the semiotic components (Gannon Cook, 1999).

Figures 1 and 2 are screen captures of the two courses the students were asked to review. Figure 1 was a course with online text and an asynchronous Web discussion board. Figure 2 was a course with graphics, embedded metaphors, graphics, and an asynchronous Web discussion board.

The second study was conducted at an urban private university in the Midwestern United States. This study was designed for students that were part of an online degree program, and the survey was conducted with adult learner students (N = 80) (Gannon-Cook & Crawford, 2004). One course contained only an asynchronous Web discussion board with a colored background (see Figure 3), and the second contained graphics, metaphors, *PowerPoints*, narratives, and an asynchronous Web discussion board (see Figure 4). Using the same survey instrument, this study reported similar findings, with 78% of students preferring course content delivery that included graphics, signs, symbols, and stories. The majority of the students preferred the course that was supplemented with semiotic-enhancements.

Figure 1. Screen capture of online text and an asynchronous Web discussion board

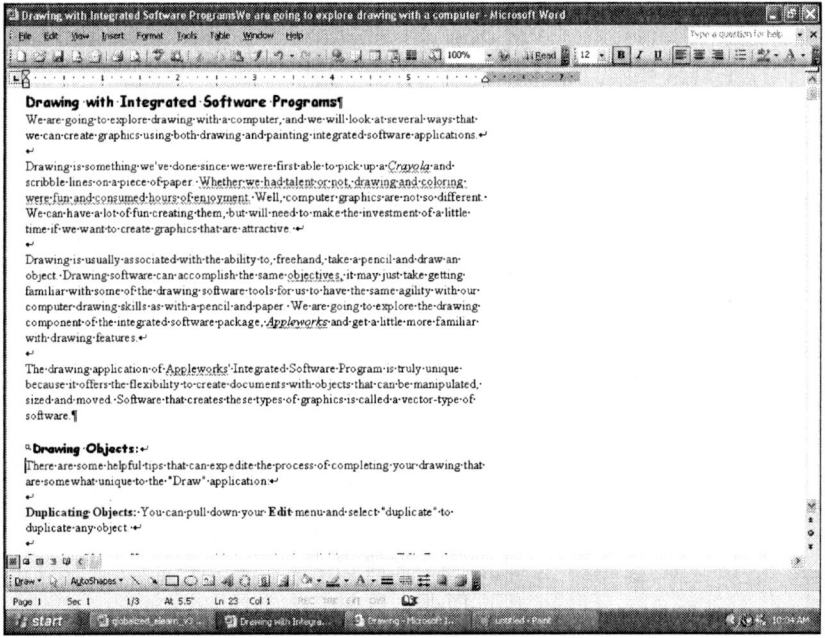

Figure 2. Screen capture, with embedded metaphors, graphics and asynchronous Web discussion board

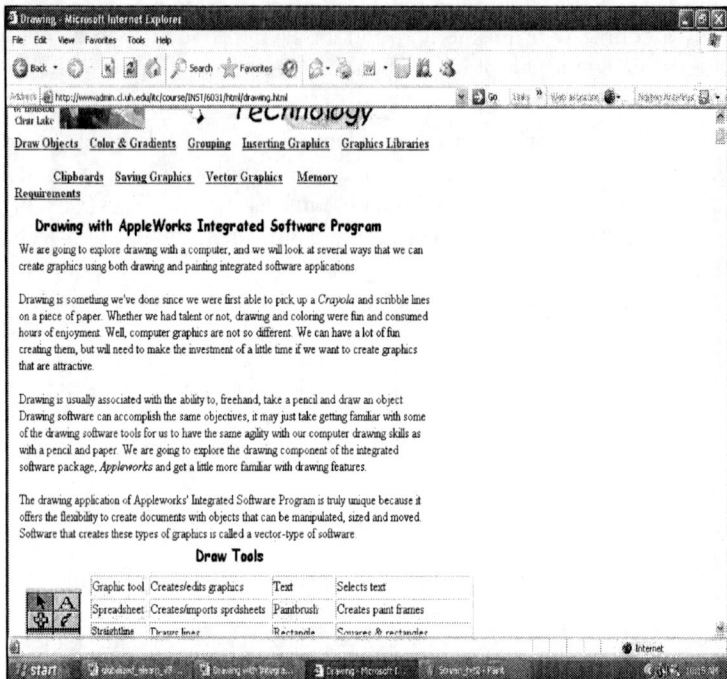

Analyzing the Signs and Writings on the Virtual "Walls" of Web Boards

The researchers looked at the findings of the two quantitative studies, but also looked at the qualitative data included in the comments and suggestions of the students. The metaphors used in one of the courses were repeatedly mentioned. One student remarked that "I liked the idea of the ship setting course on the ocean," "ships hit rough seas too." Another student liked the metaphor of a regular classroom with chalkboard Web boards and a "nice smiling" teacher. Several in the course with the classroom metaphor remarked that they liked the ideas that reinforced their ideas of what they used when they were very young, like the virtual use of crayons, and virtual playgrounds. While these metaphors might need some adjusting to make their use universal, chances are good that, even without a language translator, there would be a number of countries that would have students who would recognize crayons or a playground. Throughout the courses that embedded semiotics, thematic metaphors, narratives, inscriptions, and icons were utilized to enhance and subconsciously reinforce the content being introduced to the students.

Figure 3. No graphics or metaphors, just text

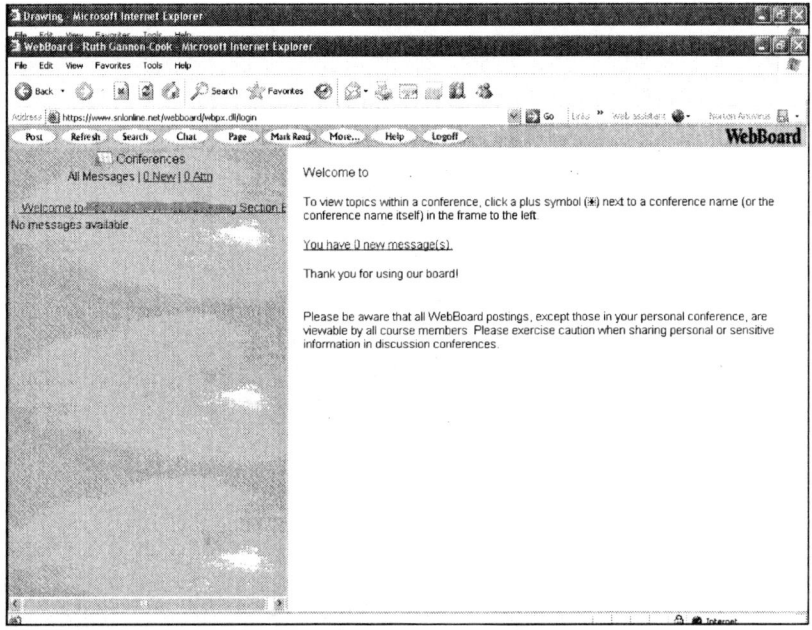

Figure 4. Inclusion of graphics and metaphors

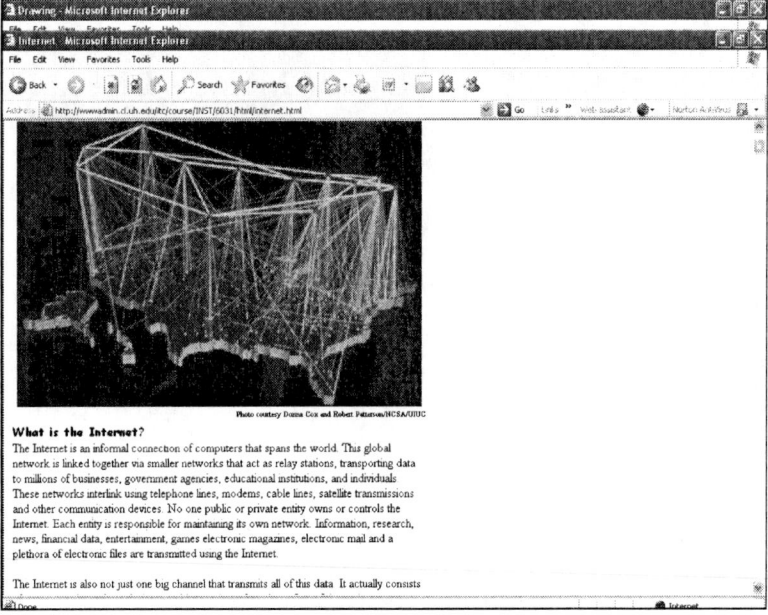

Figure 5. Examples of non-cultural specific icons (Courtesy Microsoft Works® 2002); (Note: Several icons are more Eurocentric, such as the lighthouse or the Eiffel Tower).

While it would take more research for instructional designers to utilize semiotic tools that are not offensive to the cultures of the students in the courses, there are sufficient enough representations depicted by icons to assure that there would be a number of culturally-acceptable representations located to create culturally-acceptable e-learning courses in most countries. Signs and symbols, as far back in time as the petroglyphs on the walls of Lascaux Caves (Ministry of Culture and Communication, 2005), conveyed meanings and traditions that were understood on a subliminal level and today still convey traditions and meanings that are recognized in the 21st century (see Figure 5).

Ways Instructional Designers can Include Lessons Learned from the Past

This section will include how to incorporate semiotics into electronic interactive activities, self-regulation strategies, and collaborative community goals.

Electronic Interactivities that Facilitate E-Learning Through the Use of Semiotics

Electronic interactive activities that focus upon encouraging student mediation by enhancing the e-learning environment include Internet research, electronic Web boards and chatrooms, list-servs and Weblogs (BLOGs), instant messaging, See You See Me (CU See Me) technology, and other interactivities. All of these interactive tools are intended to enlist and engage the student, both with the instructor, and with other students. To incorporate one, several, or all of the above-listed technologies is the choice of the instructional designer and the institution. It is important to remember, however, that the electronic vehicle of conveyance is not, by itself, the desired end result. The knowledge content, infused with the semiotic, metaphorical representations, is the key consideration in making decisions that include technology, for without this content, there is only a technology vehicle that familiarizes the learner with that technology or, perhaps, provides a few tidbits of information to the reader.

While there must be care taken when selecting an international metaphor that crosses both national and cultural boundaries, a few examples of the kinds of semiotic representations that can be included in instructional design to facilitate better mediation with and integration of knowledge content include: navigation metaphors, icons, inscriptions, and narratives (Gannon Cook & Crawford, 2001).

Navigation metaphors. Some of the most elementary navigation metaphors include courses with the following themes:

- A ship navigating the ocean, river, or sea, compared to the student navigating the course
- A swimmer succeeding in learning how to swim in the ocean, river, or sea
- A runner running to win a race or running to cross a country or state
- An explorer searching for new discoveries and lands
- A survivor searching for rescue and learning how to survive
- A traveler exploring the world
- An artist honing her or his craft
- Children learning how to play games
- Parents teaching children how to be safe, and how to learn
- Shepherds learning how to apprentice to take care of the flock of sheep, goats, or cattle
- People sitting around a campfire at night telling stories

Further, navigation metaphors suggested for integration within a more "sophisticated", or advanced, learning environment include courses with the following themes:

- Teachers learning how to teach their students
- An astronaut exploring the galaxies
- A train engineer operating a train through various types of country sides and terrains
- A race car driver preparing for a big race
- An architect designing buildings, or planning cities
- A doctor exploring ways to diagnose problems
- Interior designers or landscape architects exploring ways to save space and design a comfortable environment
- A chef teaching how to cook recipes

Navigation metaphors enhance the learning environment. "According to psychologists, people develop cognitive 'maps' or more abstract 'schemas' to help them find their way around their environment (Tolman, 1948, p. 201)" (Tolman, 1948, as stated by Marion Walton, 2005, para. 1). Further, navigation metaphors, according to Presson and Montello (1988), are influenced by emotions and value-judgements, which are, in turn, influenced by individual and environmental experiences. As such, the introduction of navigation metaphors into the learning environment support the learner's integration of the information within the learning environment into the learner's cognitive schemas of understanding, also referred to as conceptual framework of understanding (Vygotsky, 1935, 1962, 1978, 1981).

Icons, Inscriptions, and Narratives

The old expression, "a picture is worth a thousand words" (author unknown) seems to have merit when it comes to e-learning. As the authors of this chapter discovered in their research (Gannon Cook & Crawford, 2004), icons strategically placed in their course designs seemed to reinforce the related subject matter to the learner (Blair & Caine, 1995). Case in point, in the instruction of graphic design, students were introduced to virtual artist studios using the *Microsoft Office, Accessories Paint Program* with artist easels, palettes, and electronic paintings (see Figures 6, 7).

Inscriptions were more difficult to include in global e-Learning classes, particularly since quotations and texts were unique for each culture. The authors opted to recommend these be reviewed and unique for each culture. So the authors opted to recommend these be reviewed and unique inscriptions for each culture inserted if inscriptions were used. The authors also opted, for this research, to review icons and narratives for their research. The use of inscriptions might be more useful in the design and presentation of courses that could segment specifically-targeted student groups, for example, a group of

Figure 6. Artistic metaphor

Figure 7. Winter metaphor

Bangkok, Brazilian, or Nigerian students would each have expressions or quotations that could be incorporated into the e-course templates, depending on the student group enrolled in that section of the e-learning course.

As instructional designers begin working with semiotics, simple narratives work best for beginning students. A "fail-safe" narrative in most languages that works very effectively with students is the narrator that stands in front of a campfire and tells stories to the persons sitting around the campfire. Most cultures have storytellers, and indigenous tribes around the world have used campfires as a way of gathering the novices to share their teachings in narratives. But other generic narratives could include stories of wayfarers and their journeys to find home, or searchers who venture to distant shores to search for family members. Many myths have similar stories in a number of cultures, so the choice of mythic narratives can also prove to be fairly culturally-neutral choices.

Self Regulation

Self-regulation is viewed as a process of initiating and sustaining thoughts and actions to attain goals and outcomes (Schunk & Zimmerman, 1997). Some researchers support the supposition that self-regulation is the merger of cognition and motivation (Bandura, 1991; Garcia, 1995; Pintrich, 1989; Pintrich & De Groot, 1990; Schunk, 1994; Zimmerman, 1989, 1990); however, McManus (1995) most clearly defines self-regulation as, "Given the broadest definition, self-regulated learning (SRL) is an amalgam of numerous cognitive, metacognitive, motivational, and social factors which effect how a learner approaches learning (McManus, 1995, para. 3). When looking at activities that assist e-learning, self-regulation activities cannot be overlooked. It is important to include the topic of self regulation since little learning can actually take place without the consent and willingness of the learner to exert self-regulation necessary for learning in both traditional and e-learning environments.

While the learner within any learning environment initially focuses her or his efforts towards defining and controlling the learning environment and content material so as to successfully venture through the units of instruction, in the instance of e-learning, the learner also needs to maintain the focused role of central agent within the e-learning milieu. Holmberg suggests that "a basic general assumption is that real learning is primarily an individual activity and is attained only through an internalizing process" (1995, p. 47). The learner's ability to control her or his learning environment, as well as the learner controlling how she or he learns, still remains central to the learning process. Accordingly, because this aspect of learning is so crucial to success, much research attention has been focused upon self-regulation and activities to enhance the learner's success within learning environments, including e-learning environments (Bandura, 1991; Corno & Mandinach, 1983; Schunk, 1994; Zimmerman, 1989, 1990, 1994).

There is a large body of research available on the effects of sociocultural factors on learning (Connell, 1997; Driscoll, 2000; Eisner, 1997; Maboudian, 2000; Salomon, 1978; Vygotsky, 1935, 1962, 1978, 1981; Wertsch, 1985). Few research studies, however, have focused on the sociocultural aspects of self-regulation. Since most learners come to the learning environment with preconceived ideas about learning because of their cultural and previous educational experiences, and since there is a body of research that supports the concept of scaffolding new learning on these prior cultural experiences, it could be worthwhile to include semiotic tools to mediate prior learning experiences with new content and self-regulation materials.

Research on adult learners suggests they come into learning experiences with a "rich store of experiences" (Taylor, Marineau, & Fiddler, 2000, p.e), they don't always "connect the dots" of their work experiences with childhood or familial cultural protocols (Gallini, Seaman, & Terry, 1995; Gannon Cook & Crawford, 2005). So, some reminders that help students "revert to some strategies that worked for them at an earlier stage of their lives" (Taylor, Marineau, & Fiddler, 2000, p. 3) may help jar old memories that resonate with learning performance expectations so they can relate to and resonate with both the course and, in the case of e-learning, the online team dynamic.

Self Regulation Tools. Tools, such as narratives, could provide examples that access positive learning experiences. For example, one technique to facilitate self-regulation is associated with "calling upon the ancestors." This technique uses childhood examples of how parents and elders nurture each learning event, such as tasting new foods, planting seeds, searching for monsters under the bed, or going to visit grandparents, to help students get in touch with their internal locus of control. Ancestors and present day, families of many different nationalities and cultures, "call upon the ancestors" to remind family members that the family circle passes on their wisdoms to future generations (Gannon Cook, 1998). These associations can still be evoked through mediation tools, such as narratives and analogies, to remind students of the legacies of family and facilitate the learner's self-responsibility for learning.

E-Learning and Self Regulation. Semiotic enhancements to the e-learning environment can encourage self-regulation and support the learners' focus upon the learning objects and assessment systems. Most learners desire support structures within e-learning environments because online learning can be lonely and leave learners feeling isolated. Encouragement to e-learners to embrace self-regulation by presenting e-learning tools, such as frequently-asked questions (FAQs) and step-by-step graphically-enhanced examples, can offer unprecedented opportunities for instructional levels of e-learner content scaffolding. But for the desired outcome of successful e-learning, a structured e-learning environment with clear and articulated objectives, assessments, and self-regulation guidelines are imperative. The focus of self-regulation and control of the e-learning environment is to scaffold and reinforce learning. Once the learner feels more comfortable and secure in her/his zone of learning, she/he can venture to the next level of exploration through the units of instruction, and interact more effectively with the instructor and class colleagues. Self-regulation thus allows the learner to establish her/his own informal time management system that is integral to the success of the learner within the e-learning environment.

Time Management

Most online courses are self-paced, but require a regular time commitment each week. Online courses are no less time-consuming than "face to face" courses, but this can be misleading to students who sign up for their first online courses believing the courses will take less time commitment than traditional classes. It is always best for the student to set up some type of calendar that includes due dates for her/his course assignments and exams, but also includes dates on the same calendar for other deadlines, such as work deadlines and personal commitments, such as holidays or important family events. In this way there is a continuity that is inclusive of all of the aspects of the student's life that allows her/him to schedule enough time to meet responsibilities and deadlines.

E-Learning Time Management. The Golden Rule inscription, "do unto others as you would have them do unto you" is an expression that sometimes seems forgotten in the bombardment of everyday adult responsibilities and information overload, particularly in online environments. Sometimes there seems to be electronic "road rage" and lapses of everyday civil courtesies in online courses. So observance of the Golden Rule should be stressed to assure that every student makes a diligent effort to observe courtesies to each other and the instructor. At the beginning of each online course session, restating the school mission, explaining the learning environment, and reminding students of their responsibilities, can be important time-saving devices because, through these initial disclosures, many unnecessary and redundant questions are avoided

The next time-saving device is the posting of the electronic calendar of events and due dates so the students have an icon, a clear picture, of expected timelines for the course. Then the instructor can also post rubrics for assignments that allow the student some "flexible boundaries" and clarify expectations of course requirements. In addition, reasonable response times for both students' and instructor emails and course postings can also help reinforce students' time management skills.

Discussion: The Far-Reaching Lessons of Cave Drawings

If the research on online student attrition is accurate, and approximately 40% of students taking e-learning courses drop out without completing them (United States Distance Learning Association, 2001), then a closer look is needed to find remedies that can help students complete these courses. The primary reasons that have been cited for this attrition thus far have been that the students either have not taken online courses before, or have been ill-prepared because of self-regulatory or time-management skills (2001). More research could shed light on additional reasons for this attrition and provide insights into how to increase completion rates for e-learning courses. Few research studies have focused on the sociocultural aspects of self-regulation in student retention, particularly with respect to e-learning, and more are needed.

This chapter has discussed how the tools of semiotics can excavate sociocultural knowledge of learners and mediate with that knowledge to integrate it with new contents introduced in e-learning courses. Semiotic tools can scaffold on that primal knowledge and mediate the new materials to reinforce their confidence, their self-regulatory skills, and increase their chances of succeeding in e-learning.

Students choose e-learning for many reasons, but convenience and accessibility are often at the top of the list (United States Distance Learning Association, 2001). But once in the courses, they often feel isolated and uncomfortable, so instructional designers and educators can include semiotic tools as "comfort" items, familiar and recognizable symbols, to help them along the virtual path of their lessons. Using past experiences and representational tools to mediate and reinforce learning could reinforce the student's chances of crossing the finish line and completing e-learning courses.

In viewing best practices for e-learning, students' existent knowledge can be bridged with what they need to know by using a variety of the semiotic tools discussed in this chapter. While technological tools require in-depth preparation to be sure the tools fit with the sponsoring institutions' technological architecture and delivery systems, so too should the psychological tools of semiotics require in-depth planning to maximize the success of e-learning courses. If some of the semiotic tools mentioned in this chapter could be included in e-learning instructional designs, such as the example of the Lascaux Caves archeology lesson (Ministry of Culture and Communication, 2005), then, indeed, the writing would be "on the walls." The content matter would have a better chance of being understood, and once again the ancient wisdoms of our human ancestors could speak virtually to the e-learners.

References

Bandura, A. (1991). Social cognitive theory of self-regulation. *Organizational Behavior and Human Decision Processes, 50,* 248-287.

Berger, A. A. (1998). *Media analysis techniques.* Thousand Oaks, CA: Sage Publications.

Boote, D. N., & Beile, P. (2005). Scholars before researchers: On the centrality of the dissertation literature review in research preparation. *Educational Researcher, 34*(6), 3-15.

Carleton University. (2005). Retrieved October 10, 2005, from http://www.carleton.ca/

Chandler, D. (1998). *Semiotics for beginners D.I.Y. semiotic analysis: Advice to my own students.* Retrieved December 29, 1998, from http://www.aber.ac.uk/~dgc/sem 12.html

Chandler, D. (2001). *Semiotics for beginners.* Retrieved January 11, 2005, from http://www.aber.ac.uk/media/Documents/S4B/sem01.html

Conation Technologies. (2005). Retrieved from www.ea09.dial.pipex.com

Connell, M. (1997, Summer). AI or IA: The choice is yours! *Educational Technology Review, 7,* 27-29.

Corno, L., & Mandinach, E. B. (1983). The role of cognitive engagement in classroom learning and motivation. *Educational Psychologist, 18,* 88-108

Crawford, C. M. (2001). Developing webs of significance through communications: Appropriate interactive activities for distributed learning environments. *Campus-Wide Information Systems Journal (CWIS), 18*(2), 68-72.

Danesi, M. (1993). *Vico, metaphor, and the origin of language.* Bloomington: Indiana University Press.

Danesi, M. (2005). *Giambatista Vico*. Retrieved June 20, 2005, from http://www.press.jhu.edu/books/hopkins_guide_to_literary_theory/ferdinand_de_saussure.html

Dant, T. (1991). *Knowledge, ideology, and discourse: A sociological perspective*. London: Routledge.

Driscoll, M. (2000). *Psychology of learning for instruction*. Boston: Allyn and Bacon.

Eisner, E. W. (1997). Cognition and representation. *Phi Delta Kappan, 78*(5), 349-353.

ELearn Corporation®. (2005). Retrieved October 13, 2005, from http://elearncampus.com/index.aspx

Elluminate, Inc®. (2005). Retrieved October 13, 2005, from https://www.elluminate.com/

Fairclough, N. (1995): *Media discourse*. London: Edward Arnold.

Fernlund, P. (1995). Teaching for conceptual change. In B. Blair & R. Caine (Eds.), *Integrative learning as the pathway to teaching holism, complexity, and interconnectedness*. Lewiston, UK: EMText.

Gallini, J., Seaman, M., & Terry, S. (1995). Metaphors and learning new text. *Journal of Reading Behavior, 27*(2), 187-191.

Gannon Cook, R. (1998, September). Technoculture and semiotics: Legacies for on-line instructional design. *Bulletin of Science and Technology*, 105-115.

Gannon Cook, R. (1999). *The use of symbolic representation and inscriptions in on-line course design*. A study conducted at the University of Houston-Clear Lake, Houston, Texas.

Gannon Cook, R. (2004). *The use of symbolic representation and inscriptions in on-line course design*. A study conducted at DePaul University, School for New Learning, Chicago, IL. Submitted for publication.

Gannon Cook, R., & Crawford, C. (2004). From silos to communities: Addressing electronic isolation through interactivities. *Society for Information Technology and Teacher Education International Conference 2004*(1), 445-452). Retrieved October 20, 2004, from http://dl.aace.org/14315

Gannon Cook, R., & Crawford, C. (2005). *The interstices of interactive activities in e-learning environments*. Proposal for presentation accepted for the American Educational Computing and Technology Conference, Orlando, FL.

Gannon Cook, R., & Crawford, C. M. (2001). Metaphorical representation within a distributed learning environment. In J. D. Price, D. A. Willis, N. Davis, & J. Willis (Eds.), *SITE 2001 Annual—Society for Information Technology and Teacher Education* (pp. 1086-1088). Charlottesville, VA: Association for the Advancement of Computing in Education (AACE).

Garcia, T. (1995). The role of motivational strategies in self-regulated learning. In P. R. Pintrich (Ed.), *New directions for college teaching and learning: Self-regulated learning in the college classroom* (pp. 29-42). San Francisco: Jossey-Bass.

Gee, J. (1990). *Social linguistics and literacies: Ideology in discourses*. London: The Falmer Press.

Greene, M. (1997). Metaphors and multiples: Representations and history. *Phi Delta Kappan, 78*(5), 387-394.

Greeno, J. G., & Hall, R. P. (1997). Practicing representation. *Phi Delta Kappan, 78*(5), 361-366.

Hayes, B. (1996). Speaking of mathematics. *American Scientist, 84*(2-3), 110-113.

Holmberg, B. (1995). *Theory and practice of distance education.* London: Routledge.

Johns Hopkins University Press, The. (1997). *Semiotics.* Retrieved October 25, 2005, from http://www.press.jhu.edu/books/hopkins_guide_to_literary_theory/semiotics.html

Konrad, J. (2003, September 17-20). *Review of educational research on virtual learning environments [VLE]* – Implications for the improvement of teaching and learning and access to formal *education in Europe.* Paper presented at the European Conference on Educational Research, University of Hamburg. Retrieved October 14, 2005, from http://www.leeds.ac.uk/educol/documents/00003192.htm

Lee, B. (1985). Intellectual origins of Vygotsky's semiotic analysis. In J. W. Wertsch (Ed.), *Culture, communication, and cognition.* Cambridge, UK: Cambridge University Press.

Maboudian, W. (2000). Gender representation in visuals on school Web pages course for in-service teachers. *Society for Information Technology and Teacher Education International Conference 2000*(1), 276-281. Retrieved May 12, 2003, from http://dl.aace.org/489

Madonna University (2005). Retrieved October 13, 2005, from http://www.madonna.edu/

Massachusetts Institute of Technology (2005). Retrieved October 13, 2005 from http://ocw.mit.edu/OcwWeb/Global/all-courses.htm

McLuhan, M. (1968). *War and peace in the global village.* New York: Bantam.

McLuhan, M. (1976). *The medium is the messenger.* New York: McGraw-Hill.

McManus, T. F. (1995). *Testing learner self-regulation in a Web based learning environment.* Retrieved January 1, 2003, from http://www.edb.utexas.edu/mmresearch/Students96/

McManus/srltest.html Microsoft Office. (2003). *Accessories Paint Program.* Redwood, WA: Microsoft Corporation.

New Horizons Computer Learning Centers, Inc.®. (2005). Retrieved October 13, 2005, from http://www.newhorizons.com

Nova Southeastern University. (2005). Retrieved October 13, 2005, from http://www.nova.edu/

Pennsylvania State University. (2005). Retrieved October 13, 2005, from http://www.worldcampus.psu.edu/

Paloff, R., & Pratt, K. (1999). Building learning communities in cyberspace: Effective strategies for the online classroom. San Francisco: Jossey-Bass Publishers.

Paloff, R., & Pratt, K. (1999). *Building learning communities in cyberspace*. San Francisco: Jossey-Bass.

Pintrich, P. R. (1989). The dynamic interplay of student motivation and cognition in the college classroom. In C. Ames & M. Maehr (Eds.), *Advances in motivation and achievement: Motivation-enhancing environments* (Vol. 6, pp. 117-160). Greenwich, CT: JAI Press.

Pintrich, P. R., & De Groot, E. (1990) Motivational and self-regulated components of classroom academic performance. *Journal of Educational Psychology, 82,* 33-40.

Presson, C. C., & Montello, D. R. (1988). Points of reference in spatial cognition: Stalking the elusive landmark. *British Journal of Developmental Psychology, 6,* 378-381.

Robbins, B. (1999). *Giambattista Vico*. Retrieved June 20, 2005, from http://www.mythosandlogos.com/Vico.html

Salomon, G. (1997). Of mind and media: How cultures' symbolic forms affect learning and thinking. *Phi Delta Kappan, 78*(5), 375-380.

San Juan, E. Jr. (2006). *Knowledge, representation, truth: Learning from Charles Sanders Peirce's Semiotic*. Retrieved May 6, 2006, from http://facpub.stjohns.edu/~ganterg/sjureview/vol2-2/06Juan-Knowledge.htm

Schunk, D. H. (1994). Self-regulation of self-efficacy and attributions in academic settings. In D. H. Schunk & B. J. Zimmerman (Eds.), *Self-regulation of learning and performance: Issues and educational implications* (pp. 75-99). Hillsdale, NJ: Erlbaum.

Schunk, D. H., & Zimmerman, B. (1997). *Self regulated learning*. Retrieved June 25, 2005, from http://education.calumet.purdue.edu/vockell/EdPsyBook/Edpsy7/edpsy7_self.htm

Taylor, K., Marineau, C., & Fiddler, M. (2000). *Developing adult learners: Strategies for teachers and trainers*. San Francisco: Jossey-Bass

Tolman, E. C. (1948). Cognitive maps in rats and men. *Psychological Review, 55,* 189-208.

Turbayne, C. (1962). *The myth of metaphor*. New Haven, CT: Yale University Press.

Turner, G. (1993). Film languages: Culture and language. In D. Graddol & O. Boyd-Barrett (Eds.), Media texts: Authors and readers. London: Multilingual Matters.

United States Distance Learning Association. (2001). *Research Information and Statistics*. Retrieved from http://ww.usdla.org/04_research_info.htm

University of Leeds. (2005). Retrieved October 14, 2004 from http://www.leeds.ac.uk

University of Phoenix. (2005). Retrieved October 10, 2005, from http://university.phoenix.edu/

University of Twente. (2005). Retrieved October 14, 2004, from www.utwente.nl/en

Verene, D. (1993). Metaphysical narration, science, and symbolic form. *Review of Metaphysics, 47,* 115-132.

Vygotsky, L. S. (1935). *Mental development of children during education*. Moscow-Leningrad: Uchpedzig.

Vygotsky, L. S. (1962). *Thought and language*. Cambridge, MA: MIT Press.

Vygotsky, L. S. (1978). *Mind in society*. Cambridge, MA: Harvard University Press.

Vygotsky, L. S. (1981). The genesis of higher mental functions. In J. V. Wertsch (Ed.), *The concept of activity in Soviet Psychology*. Armonk, NY: Sharpe.

Walton, M. (2005). *What is Web navigation?: Navigating the world and 'navigating' a Web site: What is the difference?* Retrieved October 25, 2005, from http://www.writing.uct.ac.za/what/nav3.htm

Webster's new lexicon dictionary of the English language. (1989). New York: Lexicon Publications, Inc., p.638.

Wertsch, J. V. (1985a). *Cultural, communication, and cognition: Vygotskian perspectives*. Cambridge, UK: Cambridge University Press.

Wertsch, J. (1985b). *Vygotsky and the social formation of mind*. Cambridge, MA: Harvard University Press.

Zaltman, M. (1997). Lieber, R. (Ed.). Storytelling: A new way to get close to your customers. *Fortune, 2*(1), 102-110.

Zimmerman, B. J. (1989). A social cognitive view of self-regulated academic learning. *Journal of Educational Psychology, 80*, 329-339.

Zimmerman, B. J. (1990). Self-regulated learning and academic achievement: An overview. *Educational Psychologist, 25*, 3-17.

Zimmerman, B. J. (1994). Dimensions of academic self-regulation: A conceptual framework for education. In D. H. Schunk & B. J. Zimmerman (Eds.), *Self-regulation of learning and performance: Issues and educational implications* (pp. 3-21). Hillsdale, NJ: Erlbaum.

Chapter XII

Electronic Paralanguage:
Interfacing with the International

Katherine Watson
Coast Community College District, USA

Abstract

Psychologists and linguists agree that communicative elements other than words alone transmit more than 65% of the meaning of any linguistic message. New messages in new languages can be learned quickly and in their cultural context if instructional materials are sheathed in the L2 ("foreign") "electronic paralanguage" rather than in the students' native "L1" language. That is, L2 acquisition can take place at an extraordinarily rapid pace if the Netiquette and interfaces, page layouts, buttons, and alternative correspondence styles of the L2 mode of expression are employed. Exemplary adult students of French as a Second Language have demonstrated achievement of unusually high-level reading, writing, and cultural competence skills quickly in an online environment that immerses them in their new L2. Indeed, these students' success demonstrates at least two things: First, learning a new language may be at least as effective, and is clearly more complete, in an online environment than it is in a traditional classroom, and second, that educators online should attend to all features of the electronic environment, rather than simply to the subject matter that it transmits.

Introduction

Psychologists and linguists agree that communicative elements other than words alone transmit more than 65% of the meaning of any linguistic message (Birdwhistell, 1952; Collier & DiCarlo, 1985). And it is not just kinesics, our "body language," which affects the way in which our words are understood. Intonation and pitch, loudness, and the use of hesitations or pauses all comprise "paralanguage," the influential vocal but non-verbal noise that sheathes every human utterance.

In cyberspace, it is page layout, background color, graphics-to-text ratio, arrangement of words and pictures on a page, and even typeface which act as a kind of "electronic paralanguage," enveloping the electronic texts and offering cyberspatial "suprasegmentals" that augment or detract from meaning. Web designers have begun to attend to page layout, line length, font, and page color, as these features affect cognition (Hudson et al., 2005), and non-English language users of the Internet have noticed how variations in these features affect understanding (Hudson et al., 2005, Vasquez, 2000). These "beyond-words" features of electronic data delivery can affect comprehensibility, if not comprehension, and they transmit ineffable cultural information.

Learning new subject matter online, with the aid of data delivered in the parlance that characterizes that subject matter and that envelopes it in the most pertinent electronic paralanguage, is different from learning in conversational contexts or in the traditional classroom. That is, just as the harmony of figure and ground can augment the message transmitted by a work of art, so can the concord of language and electronic paralanguage expedite understanding online.

Language Learning and
Linguistic Competencies

Favored with a complicated cerebrum with which he can coordinate, communicate, and comprehend data transmitted aurally, visually, tactilely, or in writing, the human adult exploits his experience each time he takes on a new learning task, profiting from techniques honed throughout his life (Dobrovolny, 2003). If his task is to learn a new language, the human adult will automatically try to compare/contrast/discern patterns in the new mode of expression that might relate to those of the language(s) he already knows (Singhal, 1998). Because babies learn their mother tongues while they are expanding their understanding of color, texture, sound, sight, and movement, the flowering of their first language, their "L1," happens in parallel to development of cognition. Moreover, L1 acquisition flows smoothly in a sea of L1 paralanguage.

But the learning of secondary languages, "L2s," does not occur in like manner (Cook, 2005). Rather, it is self-analysis, self-criticism, and self-correction, all resulting from interaction with native speakers, that influence this process. Interaction is key, especially for the comprehension of the non-verbal, and yet novelty is a defining feature of all human expression. Indeed, it is the development of at least three sorts of competencies, explained below, that underlies human linguistic understanding (Thanasoulas, 2000).

Three Competencies Necessary to Understanding

Each sentence that each human being produces in any language is novel, never having being uttered before in exactly the same way or in exactly the same context, but people understand one another if they share basic *linguistic competence* in the same language. And perhaps even more interestingly, people know how to react to one another's utterances, based upon their shared *communicative competence*, their ability not necessarily to create grammatically-perfect structures, but rather to say things that are contextually fitting in an appropriate way. Thus, if we humans understand one another's grammatical structures, if we generally recognize that linguistic interaction is an amicable social act, then we are on the way to communicative competence.

As James (1969) has said, in defining this second sort of competence, "(we) can tell whether our interlocutor is speaking seriously or in jest, we can use information we have about the interlocutor to interpret his utterances (e.g., the political party he belongs to and whether he had a domineering mother) and our knowledge of whether the interlocutor is a stranger, a friend, or a professional foe (will) undoubtedly affect the inferences drawn about what his sentences imply."

And finally, the person who would learn a new mode of expression should also attend to the need to attain a tertiary *cultural competence*, defined as an ensemble of congruent behaviors, attitudes, and strategies comprising a system designed to facilitate the integration of human behavioral patterns. Cultural competence embraces an understanding of thoughts, communications, actions, customs, beliefs, values, and institutions of alternative racial, ethnic, religious, or social groups, as Kalyampur and Harry have noted (1999). He who is culturally competent has moved beyond the "cultural destructiveness" characterizing those who would mock or denigrate another point of view, he has passed beyond the ignorance of "cultural blindness," and he has attained a degree of masterful proficiency in his interactions with others.

A Novel Exploration in Second Language Learning Online

At Coastline Community College, in Fountain Valley, California (http://coastline.edu), students in an online French course have been able to attain high levels of competence in their new language quickly and extraordinarily well because their course materials have taught them to place language in a cultural context. This has been possible because the Internet provides them French language materials swathed in an electronic paralanguage incorporating French Netiquette and interfaces, layouts, design/array, colors, and buttons that augment and expedite the learning of words, grammar, and meaning. Rather than feeling their eyes float toward "home page" or "next" or "back," and rather than being directed to the typically "low-context" (Hall, 1976) or quick and straightforward systems typical of American Web-delivered data, these learners are immersed immediately into a "high-context" (Hall, 1976), unhurried, frequently elliptical and text-heavy set of materials; moreover, with "page d'accueil," "suivant," and "précédent" replacing the aforementioned Anglophone buttons, the eyes have no escape from the French context. Indeed, francophone patterns of communicative behavior are quickly integrated online.

Online learners of French at Coastline begin within weeks, often without realizing it, to accept that the francophone world prefers the implicit, the highly contextual, the nuanced, the creative; French Web materials tend to harmonious colors and shades (e.g., http://www.academie-francaise.fr/), often with images sliding gently or dancing rhythmically (cf. http://www.louvre.fr http://www.cite-sciences.fr/); sites tend to be text-heavy as well (cf. http://www.herodote.net/). Thus, online language learners find right away that skill in writing, often imbued with a poetic style (even the prime minister is lauded as a poet: http://www.abidjan.net/qui/profil.asp?id=541), is not only valued, but required as a precursor to understanding.

Coastline Community College, in Orange County, California (http://coastline.edu), offers a linguistic/paralinguistic portal to students of French language and culture in the form of four semester-length courses bristling with links to authentic, francophone-produced data. Course homepages retain as little of the College's boilerplate template as possible, so that the aforementioned French-named buttons demand to be clicked upon for clarification, and the course *matière,* or content, is made up of Web resources from throughout the French-speaking world, sites brought together in the interest of a few general topics. For instance, the question of language and society brings together sites about the nature of Breton, the history of the French language, the essence of dialect versus language, the imposition of American-language films in French movie theatres, and the artistic need for dubbing as opposed to sub-titling in film. Students' question topics comprise small Web portals, lists of lists, amassing French-sourced information in a single place concerning a general topic area. Likewise, course *ressources* pages facilitate improvement in grammar and vocabulary acquisition and in media awareness, with each *resources* page offering URLs from everywhere in the interest of news or language.

Hyperlinks and links from around the world, combined with free-of-charge and easily translatable interfaces, have become the heart of this novel educational experience. And these have been demonstrated to promote steady, enduring progress in writing improvement and critical thinking, as well as in international cultural awareness. Coastline student writers begin their work in French as most second-language learners do, seeking a correct answer to each question and, in the American tradition, reasoning in a linear way from thesis to conclusion. They produce short, direct, present-tense utterances. Gradually, however, sentences become longer and more complex, graced with metaphors and linguistic nuance (e.g., long student papers responding to short questions at http://www.classebranchee.com/classe/motpasse.asp?noclasse=10975653, mot de passe : etudiant).

Because Coastline has been offering completely-online French courses for more than thirteen years, the institution has been able to remain in the marketing eye of international promoters of linguistic/cultural materials based in the francophone Net; these promoters have used the college to beta-test tools and software, communications curricula and services, stylistics improvement programs, and vocabulary data bases. Free applets and interfaces have borne a fruitful array of international connections and resources for Coastliners' use, along with electronic pen pals and news-rich communiqués from Asia, Southeast Asia, Africa, Haiti, Australia, and India, not to mention Europe and the Americas. Students enrolled in Coastline's "French Topics Online" have been able to improve language and cultural fluency as well as international knowledge while learning to précis-write in alternative styles and to synthesize alternative perspectives without recourse to any textbooks or written materials in a completely virtual, freely-accessible space.

During the 13-plus years that Coastline has offered French language and culture courses online, most enrollees have ranged in age from 18 to 85. Unlike children, these post-pubescents arrive at their French course competently able to form and discern all the significant sounds (*phonemes*) of their native languages as well as the basic structures (word formation units, or *morphemes*), and meaning units (*sememes*) thereof. Anyone older than twelve or thirteen has attained all three of the aforementioned types of language competence defining fluency, a comfortable use of these *emic* elements, in his native language. This fact, along with the obvious actuality that adults are capable of making decisions on their own, is important for secondary language learning. That is, after having spent years honing communication strategies, adults have developed a high degree of competence in their native language's cognitive style. They are also good at blocking out what they find to be irrelevancies, they can discern and obey pattern restrictions, and they can analyze; in essence, fluent adult speakers of any L1 language have learned how to learn.

At Coastline, many enrollees arrive with the complaint that they have already studied some subject matter without success and are giving it a not-entirely optimistic new effort. Online French language students often report that they have studied the language "for years," but "don't know how to talk." Many of them suffer from the fact that, although they have become excellent analytical thinkers, largely due to Western educational practices, "Analytical thinkers… sometimes never acquire communicative fluency in a second language because their left-brain, sequential processing slows them down" (SIL International, 1998).

But it seems that in international, transnational, non-national cyberspace, adult analytical thinkers, especially those who have been trained in the American system of searching for a single right answer in a linear way, find themselves having to use all their skills in a new manner. Online-delivered course materials comprise text and images, colors, and movement; Coastline's online French courses offer francophone country-sourced materials that necessarily demand a view of the world that is different from the American one. Just as it has been reported that cultural differences in thought processes may be related to variations in what people focus on as they view images (Nisbett, 2005), so Coastline's students of French online have reported orally and in writing that they "feel the eyes moving in a different way" and "notice different stuff" when surfing the Web *à la française*. The Coastline French onliners' experience in "French Topics" may have yielded such high success (their native francophone pen pals report being impressed at their fluency, and their reading and writing skills rank them well beyond the "intermediate" level of American Council on the Teaching of Foreign Languages (ACTFL) proficiency) because they have been able to alter their learning patterns so as to harmonize with the French mentality.

Alternative Modes of Thinking, Viewing, and Analyzing the World

The Coastline online French students have come to find that many non-American cultures' worldviews are suffusing the Americanocentric Internet through a distinctively "field-sensitive" or "field-dependent" presence. That is, as has been noted by Nisbett (2005), among others, Web-based materials generated outside the USA tend to incorporate background into foreground, field into ground, so that the entire mass of material can be considered as a whole; by contrast, American-sourced materials place the figure against the ground, emphasizing the foreground as it is superimposed against a background in a "field-independent" way (Watanabe, 2003).

Thus, particular, ethnic, or even national cultural identities are seen in many non-American countries as being parts of a global, integrated whole (Griggs & Dunn, 1996); people of those countries consider themselves to be part of an international, or as modern American businesspeople say, "transnational," field. For instance, French children's textbooks generally contain timelines of international discoveries and events, artistic products, and political progress, reminding youths that human advancement is an intellectual, worldwide thing, that humans make progress thanks to one another's creativity, all in the interest of each.

Many European and Asian classrooms emphasize the overarching, the deductive, with the general rule presented, the overall picture revealed, before each detail of it is analyzed; this sort of "field sensitivity" differs from the American inductive approach, in which particular instances of a phenomenon are laid out so that students may arrive at generalizations about them on their own (Baudry, 2003; Watanabe, 2003) In American science classes, numerous experiments are carried out that are meant to lead students to generalizations; many other countries' scientific education begins with theories that are subsequently clarified through demonstration or experimentation.

The distinctive nature of field sensitivity/field dependence has led business psychologist Pascal Baudry (2003) to note that communication for the French in particular is situated in a context of abstract relationships and of relativism more than it is in a context of concrete content. The French make decisions of almost every kind on an ethno-relative, rather than an ethnocentric basis; this perspective holds that each ethnic group develops only in relation to others, since we all live in the same "field," on the same Earth. A "worldview," to this way of thinking, is literally just that, a truly global perspective. The complexity and beauty of life are viewed as they are exhibited in every production of every living being; even online productions are ultimately the fruits of beautiful human minds. Web sites are, therefore, to be designed as syntheses, representations of our artistic side, our "right brain," rather than simply as mechanical, "left brain" miscellany; as Fischer (2002) notes, the French categorization of *le Webdesign* as an art like painting or drama or sculpture must entail a "transversality of thought," a cross-pollination of mathematics/engineering with literature and the visual arts. And as Tice-Deering (2002) has pointed out, with respect to the sort of intercultural integration resulting from the necessary mental interchange that has emerged among the *Weltanschauungen* of the francophone world as they have mingled with those of Coastline's online language learners, an underlying anthropological assumption is being revealed here: As our experiences with cultural difference become more complex, our potential competence in intercultural interaction increases.

Melding Modes of Thinking into Long-Term Learning Online

It appears that the most successful Coastline Community College online learners of French have achieved what Vasquez (2000) has called a *bicognitive* or "field-mixed" manner of thinking. That is, these onliners are no longer oriented solely toward the independent, inductive thought process encouraged in American society; rather, their learning styles have come to share certain features of the dependent, the deductive. For example, Coastline's French onliners express in their essays generalizations that are inclusive, incorporating geology and geography, economics, demographics, and language as bases for political actions, rather than hoping to pinpoint a single cause for what nations do. They look for the science in art and the art in science, the physics in football and the chemistry in athletic performance, executing the kind of transversality that Fischer (2002) would have thinkers of the future exploit. Coastline's French learners seek out student colleagues with whom to do joint, interdisciplinary research projects; group work and frequent discussion like this characterize the field-dependent thinker, while individual efforts are the product of the field-independent mind. Coastline's onliners thus end up delivering Web-based research with multi-faceted subject matter examined from multifarious perspectives.

High levels of intercultural awareness and consequent linguistic competence have developed through interactivity with the non-American Net unconstrained by temporal or physical boundaries. Indeed, although Coastline's Internet-delivered courses, like traditional ones, have been scheduled to extend for a single 16-week semester each time they are offered, a dozen students have remained continuously enrolled in online French activities with the college for more than thirteen years, whether school is in session or not. Coastline's adult French language learners have reported during year-round electronic live chat sessions and in e-mail and spoken conversations that their modes of thinking, reasoning, and writing have taken on a new cultural context awareness, a field sensitivity, through participation in French language and cultural fluency courses, requiring them to read, communicate, and interact exclusively in French online. For example, a woman interested in French feminism has discovered through the francophone 'Net that much of Simone de Beauvoir's strength emanated from aspects of the existentialist philosophy that she shared and discussed with her partner Jean-Paul Sartre, a young physicist has found that the University of Geneva is performing experiments of a kind he had imagined impossible, and a dog-lover has discovered veterinary advice at http://www.chiensderace.com, where Swiss, Belgian, Canadian, and Luxembourgeois reports accompany those of French DVMs.

Indeed, online learning offers excellent, if not unparalleled, opportunities to enhance erudition through cultural, linguistic, argumentative exchanges across time and space (Stevens, 2002), and Coastline College's online French language students have thus been able to enrich their understanding of a new mode of idea exchange without ever reading hard-copy texts or meeting one another or their professor face-to-face in a physical classroom. In addition, their course materials have remained dynamic, authentic, and tailored to each student's goals at his level of competence; they select their own topics of research and progress at their own pace, working and re-working with one another for feedback, for editing, and for advice.

Altered modes of self-expression and unsolicited remarks provide evidence that the French onliners are learning in a new way. For example, instead of producing sentences with an average of seven words, in the Anglophone style (Watanabe, 2003), they have begun to generate regular sequences of ten-to-fifteen-word constructions in the francophone mode. Instead of writing short essays with more than 50% simple sentence structures, typical of American students in traditional second-language classrooms, these onliners are producing work abounding in complex and compound utterances, often using subjunctives and pluperfects, abstract adjectives, and adverbs. And instead of presenting arguments in the standard American, single-thesis, single-antithesis, single-conclusion manner (Watanabe, 2003), they are entertaining ancillary commentaries, exploring possible rebuttals to their claims, and even researching supportive documentation, in the manner of the European learner (Watanabe, 2003; Baudry, 2003). As Hall (1976) has remarked, proof of acculturation is often apparent in language use; mimicking a pattern typical among native French speakers, Coastline's French language learners begin after less than 25% of their first semester online to write in a francophone-style high-context mode (Baudry, 2003), referring explicitly to the question they are answering and embedding responses to any queries in complete sentences expressing the who, the why, and the how, rather than using two-to-five word e-mail notes in the low-context manner typifying American communication (Hall, 1976).

Since the first semester of online course offerings in French at Coastline, more than 50% of the students in each single-semester class have attained "advanced" or "advanced plus" reading and writing skills in French online, as these proficiency levels are defined by the American Council on the Teaching of Foreign Languages (ACTFL) (1986); more than 25% have attained "superior" writing skills, making themselves understood by native speakers and arguing in a francophone field-mixed style (Vasquez, 2000). But even more notably, the onliners report spending more "time on task" than ordinary classroom students do overall; that is, with 8-10 hours of live chat per week, nearly daily e-mail, and asynchronous messaging to accompany their four expository-essay-based, ordinary assignments, these learners are putting themselves in a pool of French on a far more frequent basis than they would do traditionally. In foreign language learning, perhaps more than in other areas of study, total immersion (in online learning of a new tongue, this implies interactivity and idea interchange) is necessary at least once daily if progress is to continue and frustration is to be reduced (Magny, 2002).

Serendipitously Creative Course Development to Incite Learning

All this linguistic and cultural development among Coastline's onliners has occurred rather serendipitously. The College's Distance Learning Department has saved money by avoiding "courses in a box"; neither Blackboard nor Web CT, for instance, is promoted as a template, and each instructor is encouraged to work with departmental Web experts to set up sites. French students are therefore able to immerse themselves instantly upon arriving at their course *page d'accueil*, designed for them with a French ambiance by their instructor, and aimed to pique the interest of the analytical thinker while tantalizing the intuitive one with immediate entrée into the francophone 'Net. The *ressources* link clickable from the course homepage is an example of one that depends on English-French cognates, at http://dl.ccc.cccd.edu/classes/internet/french198/ressourcessensass.htm. Rather than exhibiting a course-in-a-box Anglophone layout, pages are conceived with materials made freely available by such organizations as the francophone http://thot.cursus.edu and http://www.classebranchee.com with the former evaluating software and services and the latter providing course-building tools under the auspices of the Canadian *Office de la langue française*. Netscape Composer and Microsoft Front Page have permitted additional page creation tools; hyperlinks are simply listed/incorporated from freely-available sources, along with *gratuiciel*, that Coastline's French instructor has found, and often translated, on the international 'Net. New assignment variations, comments, and so forth, are sent to students via e-mail using AOL France and France Telecom's free Voilà service. These mail interfaces' use of *expéditeur, destinataire, daté le…, connexion* and *déconnexion* helps to keep learners' eyes from wandering to English-language words while using their new mode of expression. Indeed, on the rare occasions when College-based Outlook Express e-mail has been sent, students have remarked that the English is "obvious" and "makes me look at it." Anglophone chat interfaces with Anglophone advertising attract the eyes of learners who should be attending to things French; this is avoided as much as possible.

With very little recourse to English available, Coastline French language students are offered general, topical areas of study/Websurfing as their course content (e.g., *l'éthique* (ethics, either in business, medicine, the workplace, or elsewhere), *le voyage* (travel), etc.). *Travaux pratiques*, or course content questions, depend upon "surf reports" submitted in French via e-mail; these comprise pieces somewhat like film or book reviews enhanced by expository writing. Carnegie Mellon University's free Lycos Course Builder, which has permitted translation into French, houses many of the course's content questions in an external area safe from occasional local power outages or glitches: Even short quizzes, also written by the instructor and posted at the course home page for instant interactivity, are embedded with francophone links.

International experts in distance education (CRPUQ, 2002; Magny, 2000) have cited freedom from constraints and a desire to take advantage of opportunities of all kinds whenever they arise as features uniting effective learning objects to successful learners. Coastline's online French course material is always "up," permitting students to work whenever they wish, at their own pace, and at the intensity they wish, free from ordinary institutional limitations. The aforementioned dozen students who have continued to enroll in online French courses or to have kept in touch with synchronous chat and/or asynchronous bulletin boards throughout the thirteen years that the College has offered online French study say they have become "addicted" to their virtual *francophonie*. Their course materials, freely produced and freely accessible from anywhere, remain ready for access all the time. If a student's "learnable moment" does not come until late in the semester, he may wait until then to begin his work; no "due dates" exist.

Although projects without due dates require self-discipline to complete, it seems that Coastline online French students have been able to raise their "engagement rate" in schedule-free francophone cyberspace. That is, Coastline students' online French course activity demonstrates something that researchers have observed elsewhere: The number of minutes of active participation in coursework is frequently higher online than it is in traditional classes (Han, 1999). Coastline French onliners frequently report that they spend "way more time on this class than I do on my other ones" or "get lost in those Web sites and end up spending hours surfing around and reading stuff" with French online. These students' intrinsic motivation, their engagement in their subject matter simply because of curiosity, interest, or enjoyment, seems to be greater online than it is in other contexts. And as a result of this, their learning is more efficient and broader-based than it might be otherwise. As Brewster and Fager (2000) have noted, the intrinsically-motivated learner exploits strategies that demand greater effort and which facilitate fast information processing. This sort of learner is also more likely than his peers to feel confident about his ability to learn new material, and he is more likely to retain information and concepts longer. It is clear that retention arising from something other than external prodding is an essential feature of learning language in cyberspace. Ultimately, as a result of increased motivation to learn, it is perhaps useful to note that the aforementioned traits of the intrinsically- interested individual tend to grant him a higher likelihood of being a lifelong learner, continuing to educate himself beyond the formal institutional classroom.

An Electronic Interface Promoting Deeper Learning at a Faster Pace

It has become clear in the thirteen years during which Coastline Community College has been offering current-events French courses online that an extraordinary quality of learning has been taking place. Evidently, as the University of Quebec's Estelle Magny (2002), professor of Distance Learning, has said, the pedagogical possibilities of online learning have only just begun to be probed and the quality of their results analyzed. Cyberspace can and will permit learners to redefine their relationship with information, Magny claims, enabling them to profit from a new nexus of knowledge that will enable them to teach themselves new things however and whenever they desire, often without realizing it. Coastline's online learners of French have profited from linguistic contextual freedom in online chat and from the dynamic realism of electronically-delivered news arriving to their computers from everywhere; this has enabled them to broaden their vocabulary and their sophistication in understanding the francophone worldview while they are immersed in authentic linguistic realia in all social stylistic registers. Live chat sessions and asynchronous bulletin board postings include subjects ranging from new films and books of interest to the political difficulties of France's prime minister and the comparison of immigration concerns in France and California. Students report that they appreciate francophone page layout and content, calling it "classy" and "neatly organized, almost like a French garden," they have begun to notice how the affective domain penetrates the interactive. They have altered their field-independent cognitive style to have accommodated field dependence, resulting in a useful, bicognitive field mix.

It seems that continuously-available contact with language in all its contexts, in all its authenticity, in all its social, stylistic registers, can be realized online in a way that can force language learners to "sharpen the intellect," as Crystal (2004) has said. Indeed, as Crystal (2004), Baudry (2003), and Magny (2002), and Caron (1999) have all noted, human interaction and modes of communication are changing as a result of synchronous and asynchronous electronic systems. Happily enough for Coastline's students, the French government has embraced Internet communication. Indeed, the fact that their course materials are authentic and dynamic is a fortunate result of Prime Minister Lionel Jospin's 1997 initiative in favor of electronic connectivity: All schools and government-associated institutions were to receive high-speed connections and *soutien informatique* before 2002; government-sponsored news services, schools for children and adults, and all information sources were to be housed in cyberspace; Web development was to be granted university departmental status. Fortunately for Coastline's French onliners, their course development was to benefit. Free materials easy to download were available, usually without the busy *frénésie* characterizing Anglophone 'Net materials, and this ended up being one reason cited by Coastline students for their interest in the course. And fortunately for the Coastline students, it may be the case that the pictorial, subtly-colored, artistic nature of many francophone Web sites strengthens the message-learning process, a process that, as Crystal (2004) remarks, demands deeper study for its uniqueness. It is perhaps true that, since pictorial data are generally stored in, and decoded by, the brain's right hemisphere, while linguistic data are decoded by the left (Nisbett, 2005), written text overlying or accompanying static images may offer increased opportunities for the brain to apprehend.

Conclusion

For Coastline's non-traditional online learners of French, who have comprised a range of age from post-adolescence to octogenarian, and who never have to see any college buildings or parking lots, electronic media have enhanced their learning of a new language in multifarious contexts, permitting them to travel well beyond the bounds of any classroom and across time zones, from the American "monochronic" state of assuming that everything is tangible, happening in measurable seconds or minutes or days or years (Hall, 1976), into the polychronic francophone one (Baudry, 2003) where a multiplicity of tasks, ideas, or actions may occur simultaneously, just as they do in international, pluricultural cyberspace.

References

American Council on the Teaching of Foreign Languages. (1986). *ACTFL proficiency guidelines* (Rev. ed.). Hastings-on-Hudson, New York: ACTFL Materials Center.

Baudry, P. (2003). *Français et Américains: L'autre rive*. Paris: Village Mondial.

Birdwhistell, R. (1952). *Introduction to kinesics*. Louisville, KY: University of Louisville Press.

Brewster, C., & Fager, J. (2000). *Increasing student engagement and motivation: From time-on-task to homework*. Portland, OR: Northwest Regional Educational Laboratory.

Caron, F. (1999). *Les deux révolutions industrielles du XXe siècle*. Paris: Pocket.

Collier, G., & DiCarlo, D. (1985). *Emotional expression*. Hillsdale, NJ: Lawrence Erlbaum Associates.

Conférence des recteurs et des principaux des universités du Québec (CRPUQ). (2002, September). Les normes et standards de la formation en ligne. *Profetic, revue internationale des technologies*. Rubrique ressources, normes et standards. Retrieved August 31, 2005, from http://profetic.org/file/norm-0210-d-RAPPORT.pdf

Cook, V. J. (2005). First and second language learning. In G. E. Perren (Ed.), *The mother tongue and other languages in education, CILTR* (pp. 7-22). London: Center for Information on Language Teaching and Research.

Crystal, D. (2004). *Language revolution (Themes for the 21st century)*. London: Polity.

Dobrovolny, J. (2003, October). Learning strategies. *Learning Circuits*, *4*(10), 27. Retrieved May 5, from http://www.learningcircuits.org/2003/oct2003/dobrovolny.htm

Fischer, H. (2002). Technologies – en attendant le huitième art, le rêve de l'œuvre totale. *Le Devoir.com*, edition of Monday, 18 November, 2002, Rubrique Technologies. Retrieved September 12, 2005, from http://www.ledevoir.com/2002/11/18/13590.html

Griggs, S., & Dunn, R. (1996). Hispanic-American students and learning style. *Clearinghouse on Early Childhood and Parenting* (393607). Urbana-Champaign, Illinois: College of Education, Early Childhood and Parenting Collaborative, University of Illinois.

Hall, E. (1976). *Beyond culture*. New York: Anchor Press.

Han, X. (1999, November 15). Exploring an effective and efficient online course management model. *Teaching with Technology Today, 5*(2), 3. Retrieved May 7, 2006, from http://www.uwsa.edu/ttt/han.htm

Hudson, R., Firminger, P., & Weakly, R. (2005). Developing sites for users with cognitive disabilities and learning difficulties. Retrieved October 5, 2005, from http://juicystudio.com/article/cognitive-impairment.php

James, L. (1969). Prolegomena to a theory of communicative competence. *Extreme Psychology, Extreme Research*, Fall 1998 (p.499). Retrieved September 10, 2005, from http://www.soc.hawaii.edu/leonj/499f98/libed/competence/titlepage.html

Kalyampur, M., & Harry, B. (1999). *Culture in special education.* New York: Paul H. Brooks.

Magny, E. (2002). *Les représentations reliées à la langue seconde et à son enseignement/ apprentissage chez les formateurs universitaires et scolaires.* University of Québec papers.

Nisbett, R. (2005, September). Culture and point of view: Eye movements may betray your culture. In *Proceedings of the National Academy of Sciences, 100*(19), 11163-11170.

SIL International. (1998, September). Your brain dominance and language. *Ethnologue.com, LinguaLinks* library resources, SIL International Linguistics Center, Dallas, TX. Retrieved September 13, 2005, from http://www.sil.org/ LinguaLinks/LanguageLearn ing/OtherResources/YorLrnngStylAndLnggLrnng/ YourBrainDominanceAnd LanguageL.htm

Singhal, M. (1998, October). A comparison of L1 and L2 reading: Cultural differences and schema. *TESL Journal, 4*(10). Retrieved May 7, 2006, from http: //iteslj.org/Articles /Singhal-ReadingL1L2.html

Stevens, V. (2002). Rationale for chat in language learning. *WWW.Study.com,* Writing for Webheads, V. Stevens files. Retrieved September 14, 2005, from http:// www.homestead.com/prosites-vstevens/files/efi/why_chat.htm

Thanasoulas, D. (2000). Language and culture: A thesis. *Developing Teachers.com.* Teacher Training/Culture. Retrieved September 16, 2005, from http://www. developingteachers.com/articles_tchtraining/culture1_dimitrios.htm

Tice-Deering, B. (2002). Inquiry and research. *Ontario Library Association Database of Expertise.* Retrieved March 7, 2005, from http://www.accessola.org/action/posi- tions/info_studies/html/research.html

Vasquez, J. (2000, June). Difference is not deficiency. *IN CONTEXT: A quarterly of humane sustainable culture, 4*(27), 30.

Watanabe, M. (2003). *Comparisons of cooperative learning in the U.S., Japan, and France.* Paper presented at the Japan Society of Educational Sociology Annual Meeting, Meiji Gakuin University, Tokyo, Japan.

Section IV

Addressing Issues of Cross-Cultural Instructional Design

Chapter XIII

Adapting E-Learning Across Cultural Boundaries:
A Framework for Quality Learning, Pedagogy, and Interaction

Catherine McLoughlin
Australian Catholic University, Australia

Abstract

The chapter will, first of all, consider the challenges for educational designers of the need to maximise the opportunities of e-learning by enabling learners to participate in learning experiences, activities, and forms of communication that are congruent with their values, belief systems, and styles of learning. Second, by building on extant research and frameworks, the chapter will propose an integrated framework and set of guidelines for the development of quality learning resources for a global community of learners. The chapter makes a case for the internationalisation of learning resources informed by a flexible and pluralistic approach to design, based on the concept of constructive alignment.

Introduction: Challenges and Concerns

In higher education, the expansion of cross-border initiatives, a greater push towards internationalisation of services, and a focus on global outreach in terms of curriculum and access have resulted in the adoption of learning technologies to reach diverse learners. Along with these changes, there has been a growing imperative to integrate an international/intercultural dimension into teaching, research, and community service. When universities advertise their intention to internationalise their programs, it most often signals an intent to extend their reach, to create programs of study for a global audience of learners, and to use Web-based learning to enable diverse students to access their offerings online.

The scope and complexity of internationalisation and cross-border educational delivery have brought with them a number of concerns and issues. Global learning opportunities and connectivity provide the impetus to use ICTs to provide a raft of e-learning experiences, improved access, and democratisation. The commoditisation of e-learning, the rapid expansion of interoperability and standardisation of electronic resources and learning objects are combined with calls to ensure quality in content and process (Anderson & Eloumni, 2004; Barbera, 2004). Along with the need to facilitate mobility among students and to ensure international perspectives, collaborative learning efforts, and teamwork, there is also the pressure to preserve cultural diversity and to ensure that educational systems provide appropriate culturally-contextualised and relevant learning experiences.

E-learning opportunities and transnational delivery of education have meant that there is a transnational culturally-diverse student body communicating, interacting, and learning together. There is abundant literature attesting to the influence of culture on learning, attitudes, and styles of learning and thinking (Burbules, 2000; Burbules & Torres, 2000). Some of the challenges that arise for course developers are as follows:

- **Global vs. local perspectives:** Is learning material developed internationally-appropriate for local contexts, pedagogies, and value systems?

- **Adaptation vs. generalised approaches:** Is it possible to produce internationally-useable learning resources that can be used in any context, as opposed to generic materials that are later adapted and customised for local delivery? Which is the best approach?

- **Pedagogical uniformity vs. accommodating cultural diversity**: How do designers avoid the imposition of dominant worldviews or mainstream value systems and culturally- dissonant paradigms of learning, and instead enable learners to access learning resources that are congruent with their values, belief systems, and styles of learning? (McLoughlin, 2000, 2001)

This chapter makes a case for the internationisation of learning resources informed by a flexible and pluralistic approach to design, as opposed to the localisation of resources, which has now become something of a mantra, often a superficial solution to accommodating social and cultural diversity. Localisation tends to focus on linguistic translation, changing icons, colours, and emblems, without full appreciation of local semiotics and contextual details (Henning, 2004). However, global inclusivity and accommodation of diverse learner needs means that we must ensure cultural pluralism in instructional design, pedagogy, and all aspects of the educational experience. This can be achieved by: (1) adopting learning theories and models of cognition that accommodate inclusivity, (2) recognising the cultural pluralism and diversity in learning environments and among learners, and (3) designing learning tasks and assessment activities that are aligned with culturally-inclusive learning outcomes and pedagogies. Each of these strategies is described in this chapter.

Culture, Constructivist Learning, and Pedagogy

Increasingly, technologies are being described as "cognitive tools," which transform, augment, and support cognitive engagement among peers, school-age children, and adult learners (Reeves & Reeves, 1997). Cole (1985) describes technology as a "cultural amplifier" signifying that it transforms the nature of human productivity and can also change the processes of cognition and amplify the cultural dimensions of communication, task analysis, and problem solving. Similarly, Brown, Collins, and Duguid (1989) analyse learning as a situated achievement, incorporating authentic cultural activity in a range of settings (De Bry, 2001; Herrington, Oliver, & Reeves, 2003). These pedagogies spring from a common source, constructivist learning theory (Duffy & Cunningham, 1996). Constructivism is characterised by a set of principles relating to how knowledge is created and how individuals develop understanding. Socio-cultural theory, originating with the writings of Vygotsky (1978) emphasises that learning is a form of enculturation, in which the individual is socialised through gradual participation in tasks, scaffolded or assisted by adults until full competence is attained. One interpretation of constructivism is situated cognition, based on the work of Lave (1988) who maintains that learning is best achieved when learning tasks are encountered, practiced, and applied in real-world contexts. Situated cognition can be summarised as follows:

- Learning is situated and contextualised in action and everyday situations.
- Knowledge is acquired through active participation.
- Learning is a process of social action and engagement involving ways of thinking, doing, and communicating.
- Learning can be assisted by experts or supportive others and through apprenticeship.
- Learning is a form of participation in social environments.

The community of inquiry approach (Lipman, 1991) is based on the same principles of cognitive apprenticeship, common goals, shared inquiry, and peer learning, and offers a robust theoretical basis for the design of culturally-specific environments. Culture pervades learning, and in designing instructional environments and current theories,

Table 1. Culturally-responsive vs. traditional perspectives on learning

CULTURALLY RESPONSIVE VIEW	⟷	TRADITIONAL VIEW
Learning is a community	⟷	Individualised learning
Online distributed community	⟷	Pedagogic community
Authentic assessment	⟷	Objective assessment
Focus on process	⟷	Focus on product
Content flexible	⟷	Content fixed
Social orientation	⟷	Behavioural orientation
Teacher as a mentor	⟷	Teacher as a sage on stage
Learner as active person in the world	⟷	Passive learner

addresses issues surrounding the social and cultural dimensions of task design, communication channels, and structuring of information (McLoughlin, 1999). Cultural variations in interpreting and communicating information impinge on pedagogical and instructional design decisions, and the cultural dimensions of learning must be constantly problematised and foregrounded (Sleeter & Grant, 2003). Table 1 shows the characteristics of culturally-responsive theories of cognition, prevalent in authentic and constructivist perspectives (Herrington, Oliver, & Reeves, 2003):

In addition to adopting an appropriate pedagogical foundation for inclusion of diverse cultural needs and approaches to learning, issues of cultural inclusivity in instructional design must also be considered. In the next section, an overview of extant research on the impact of cross cultural investigations will be used as the basis for suggesting instructional design guidelines for quality e-learning.

Overview of Research on Designing for Cross-Cultural Audiences

Within the last five years, there has been an abundance of studies relevant to the design of learning environments for diverse cultural needs. Table 2 provides a summary of relevant investigations, though this is not a comprehensive list.

What can be learned from these studies? First, many studies have found that engagement, interactivity, and learning support are important aspects of pedagogy in catering for diverse learner needs online. Second, the establishment of community online and the clear articulation of expectations and cultural understandings are paramount. Third, diversity in learning approaches, style, and cultural patterns are universal. We may

Table 2. Research studies relevant to multi-cultural audiences using ICT applications

Study	Summary	Applications
Chen, Mashhadi, Ang, & Harkrider, 1999	Case study of three environments used in Singapore: two for student teachers and one for collaboration.	Even when the best instructional design is employed, these authors contend the quality of the learning is determined by the individual's experience of cultures. Social and cultural understandings need to be explicit and up-front before participants are able to build the on-line networks of trust upon which effective communication and learning is based.
Harris, Pehrson, Jin, & Jonsson, 2000	Report of an online global seminar which took place between Stanford University in the U.S. and Royal Institute of Technology (KTH) in Stockholm Sweden during the school year 1998-1999. Individuals involved came from Asia, Africa, Europe, and North America.	Relevant educational topics addressed were "How to cross the barriers of culture difference," and "How to overcome the obstacle of the language barrier." Since the program was free, some just joined for the novelty and quickly dropped out. Benefits were real-time discussions with experts after studying their contributions; barriers included expertise in the English language, Internet connections, and engagement in the learning exercises.
Lankbeck & Mugler, 2000	Interviews conducted with 54 distance learners from the University of South Pacific, which examined learning strategies, environment, and conceptions.	Two types of learners were found: Pragmatic: do what needs to be done to pass and forget the rest and; Sequential: step-by-step, following all instructions. Recommendations needed for deeper critical thinking.
LeBaron, Pulkkinen, & Scollin, 2000	A course offered to graduate students from Finland and Massachusetts was analysed. Students were given a Likert-scale questionnaire of pedagogical aspects of the course.	A collaborative approach was used. The skill and sensitivity of instructor were demonstrated to be vital to success. Collaboration across nations was not as well implemented as would have been preferred.
Smith & Smith, 2000	A study of 192 on-campus Chinese students from Malaysia, Singapore, and Hong Kong were drawn from two universities in Australia during their first semester of study in Australia. The Approaches to Studying Inventory was administered in class.	Although all students were Chinese, differences were found. Malaysian-Chinese and the Singaporeans were more dependent, and preferred clear, highly organized, and well-structured learning programs and were inclined to confine their learning to the prescribed readings and to teachers' instructions and directions. Language was noted as a barrier for the Malaysian Chinese. Differences can occur among individual national groups.
Gunawardena et al., 2001	Questionnaires and focus groups were employed with 50 graduate students with previous online experience in a study of the perceptions of online group processes.	Country difference rather than age and gender accounted for differences in perception of the group process and development. Mexicans tended to show greater agreement with the collectivist group values. Each group varied in views of power distance, aggressive-nurture, and context of communication.
Ng, 2001	Case study of an e-mail system used to promote collaboration at the Open University of Hong Kong.	Demonstrated the need to teach online learning skills and explicitly state interaction requirements; and the importance of establishing community.

Table 2. continued

Study	Summary	Applications
Odendaal, 2001	Case study of the development of an online course in South Africa. Thirty participants enrolled in the pilot online course.	Interactive online learning is relatively new in South Africa. Costs and availability of technology are the major limiting factors. The advantages of flexibility and interactivity are valued. A FAQ section was found to be extremely helpful.
Tu, 2001	Ethnographic case-study approach of six Chinese students (four female, two male) attending college in U.S. in an online environment. Participant observation was used to study privacy, social relationships, task orientation, and social interaction.	Community of social presence is extremely important to Chinese students for the following reasons: social context, online communication and interactivity. Chinese tended to observe, needed encouragement to interact. Face-saving techniques came across in online environment. Expression of emotion was important to Chinese students.
Williams et al., 2001	Action research study of five facilitators trying to address audiences from the U.S., England, and Australia.	Challenges included (1) framing, asking questions and reframing information; (2) online group participation; (3) absence of face-to-face meetings; (4) learning the interpersonal and group dynamics of online work; (5) expectations of students; (6) facilitator expectations; and (7) facilitator anxiety.
Feinberg & Vinaja, 2002	Survey of instructors in U.S. colleges and universities delivering distance education to learners in Mexico. Six hundred and twenty four questionnaires were distributed, 120 returned. Likert scale rating various incentives and perceptions of the course was used.	Intrinsic motivators to participate in online education were enjoyment and ability to keep up with technology. Extrinsic motivators were extra income and ability to obtain grants. Highest ranking benefits were the abilities to help students overcome travel restraints and flexibility in scheduling.
Kekkonen-Moneta & Moneta, 2002	Report of an instructor's experience teaching a computer course at Hong Kong University of Science and Technology by lecture to 105 students, and online to 180 and then to 129 students the next semester. Students completed a questionnaire on their experience. Scores were statistically compared.	Scores from the online students were comparable to those of the f2f students. Online students performed higher in applied-conceptual learning, suggesting that carefully designed e-learning modules facilitate engaging interactions with the content materials and, in turn, foster higher-order learning skills.
Kim & Bonk, 2002	Transcripts of two conferences, one of two Finnish universities, and one of one in the U.S. Students from Korea were in these classes. In addition, pre- and post-collaboration questionnaires were administered and interviews and a videoconference were conducted. Korean students were very anxious about communicating in English. Finnish instructors were more collegial and US instructors were more authoritarian in their communication.	American and Korean students completed assignments individually, and Finnish students worked in pairs or small teams. Korean students showed the highest level of interaction. Finnish students evidenced deeper thought and more reflection. Finnish students also included more culturally sensitive explanatory information for the reader than did the others. Encourage social interaction where anxiety is addressed early. Explicit instruction in set-up of experience helps reduce stress by increasing understanding of requirements. Online help and tips on communication differences between cultures could help.

Table 2. continued

Study	Summary	Applications
Neo & Neo, 2002	A case study of a problem-solving approach that was used to help Malaysian students learn authoring tools was conducted.	Active engagement and the constructivist problem-solving approach were appreciated by the Malaysian students.
Rattanapian, 2002	A range of qualitative approaches were used to determine what barriers to online learning existed, and what online instructional methods are best.	Barriers to online learning were similar in Thai environment as in other parts of the world: more support needed for learners, better instruction for teachers in online moderation. Active, engaging exercises were most beneficial. The authors concluded that there were no apparent culturally unique limitations to online learning.
Toyoda & Harrison, 2002	Discourse analysis of learners and native Japanese speakers were conducted of chat conversation logs.	Some parts of instruction were overlooked and would not have been apparent unless interacting with native Japanese speakers.
Alfred, 2003	Two interviews of 15 participants with interviews lasting from 1-3 hours. Individual learning biographies were developed and analysed for aspects relevant to sociocultural theories of learning.	The length of time spent in a new culture, the level of social support inherent in the culture, and the characteristics of the sociocultural environment greatly affect learning outcomes. Being knowledgeable about one's own cultural sensitivities is helpful.
Bolloju & Davison, 2003	Work described with 161 business students enrolled in a 14 week f2f class, supplemented by Web-based discussions. Four general topics were created, 12 specific to lecture, and 7 for lab work. The most popular was the general FAQ section.	Communication of standards of expectation for participation in discussion board is important. Facilitator must monitor and control discussion threads, sending out praise publicly and warning privately. A facilitator should summarize the threads.
Walsh, Gregory, Lake, & Gunawardena, 2003	An exploratory study using interviews of participants from six cultural groups. Groups identified were Anglo-American, Eastern Asia, India subcontinent, Hispanic American, Middle Eastern, and Native American. All groups except Anglo-Americans are identified as collectivist cultures by Hofstede.	Most groups wanted to present a positive face and a positive image, in addition to projecting an independent self-construal. Since most participants had lived in the U.S. for several years, they had probably adopted many Western values and attitudes, so this study did not significantly support cultural differences.
Yuen, 2003	Case study of students and teachers using CMC at the primary level in six schools in Hong Kong.	Active engagement through community learning was important. Teachers should spend time building community.

Table 2. continued

Study	Summary	Applications
Zhao, Massey, Murphy, & Fang, 2003	Study examining the Web design of 50 of the most popular Web sites in U.S. and in China that were also geographically located there (yahoo was popular in China, but since based in US, not included in China).	American sites were more personalized, and Chinese sites more historically oriented. Although the Web-based tools are culturally neutral, the individuals using them are not. "Communication—whether it is mass mediated, interpersonal, or nonverbal—is inseparable from culture, each shapes and is shaped by the other" (p. 81). "Web-based communication is not neutral to culture" (p. 82).
Hofstede & McCrae, 2004	Statistics from cross-cultural studies and personality studies were analysed & results correlated. "All 5 personality factors were significantly associated with at least 1 dimension of culture, all 4 culture dimensions were related to 1 personality factor" (p. 48).	Hofstede's (2003) cultural dimensions were validated. Correlation with the 5-Factor Model of personality "give[s] a useful overview of how personality relates to culture" (p. 62). Although this study did not relate personality to learning, other personality studies have made recommendations for best learning approaches.
Petegem, Loght, & Shortridge, 2004	Online courses from universities in Belgium and the U.S. were examined using a case study approach. Using Moore's theory of transactional distance and at least 9 of Laurillard's 12 conversational framework guidelines, levels of interactivity were assessed.	Using a highly interactive environment produced better pedagogical results. Students reported that animations, questions, and other components helped to clarify and emphasize the content and that the concept mapping exercises forced them to articulate and re-evaluate their knowledge.
Chang, 2004	Evaluation of a training program developed and implemented in the U.S. and implemented in Taiwan among Americans (n=6) and Taiwanese (n=14). A questionnaire, observations, interviews, and document reviews were administered.	Flexibility and context were important in design of training. It is important to include what local learners consider personally significant e.g., questions, stories, peers as resources; cultural characteristics can be used to identify the cultural environment. Case scenarios and narratives allow inclusion of cultural background.

conclude therefore that "no single current theory satisfactorily accounts for or predicts what happens as learning and communications technologies are taken up in diverse cultural contexts" (Ess, 2001, p. 4). Also, no one particular cultural pattern can be generalised to a specific individual (Sleeter & Grant, 2003, p. 51), and personalities of individuals vary greatly (Hofstede, 2003).

Culturally-Appropriate Pedagogy and Practice: A Framework for Designers

The need to respect and design resources for diverse cultural styles and values has been referred to in the literature, and there is acknowledgment that the development of a culturally- sensitive environment should be a shared responsibility and involve all stakeholders, that is, designers, teachers, and students. The chapter proposes a model that takes into consideration research on pedagogical practices and cultural influences on teaching and learning, and seeks to provide guidelines for development of collaborative e-learning environments appropriate to culturally-diverse students.

Recent developments in networked learning have demonstrated the potential for innovative approaches to developing communication and collaborative skills online. For example, group-based project work has been advocated for its capacity to foster professional skills and experiential learning (McLoughlin & Oliver, 2000). By enabling culturally-diverse online groups to work on complex tasks in a problem-based learning format, opportunities are provided to develop independent and interdependent skills such as teamwork and communication in global settings (McAteer, Tolmie, Duffy, & Corbett, 1997; McConnell, 2000). Collis and Moonen (2001) also propose a number of strategic design issues relating to internationalisation of ICT-facilitated education.

Designers and educators need to draw together current work on constructivism and generative learning, and on the notion that e-learning supports a global education community, enabling communication, collaboration, and interaction across cultural and geographic boundaries (Burbules, 2000). According to Wilson (1996), learning environments are places where "learners work together and support each other as they use a variety of tools and information resources in their guided pursuit of learning goals" (p. 4).

Both perspectives are consistent with the elements of the culturally-inclusive instructional design framework presented in the chapter. By integrating constructivist and culturally-sensitive design principles, a holistic framework that links activity design, learner needs, and pedagogy is elaborated with reference to a "cross cultural teaching ladder."

Figure 1. Cross cultural teaching ladder (Adapted from Biggs, 1999)

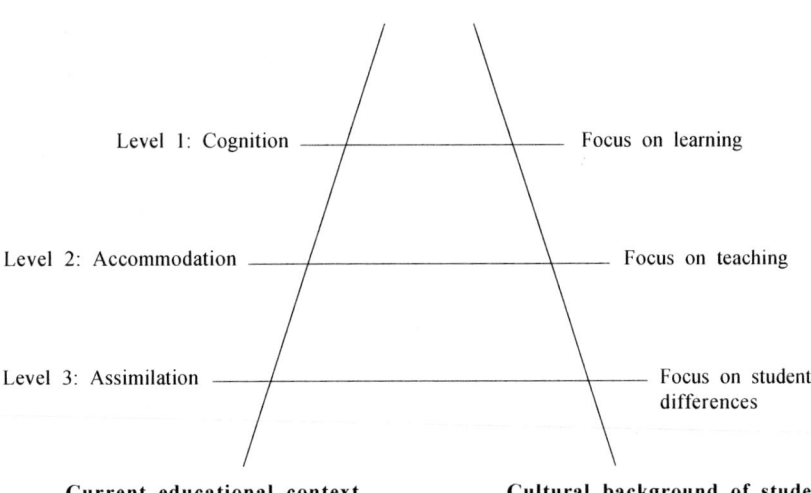

Appropriate Pedagogy: The Cross Cultural Teaching Ladder

From the perspective of the student learning experience, Biggs (1999) notes that international students may experience three kinds of problems: socio-cultural adjustment, language issues and teaching/learning issues relating to different expectations, and perspectives on learning. Among the last, a number of important findings have emerged in the literature surrounding the stereotyping of international students' capacity for learning and academic achievement (Volet, 2004). International students are often perceived to be too teacher-dependent, lacking in independent study skills, tending to adopt rote learning strategies, but the research indicates that international students often outperform their peers academically and that such conceptions are misguided (Weisenberg & Stacey, 2005).

In addressing teaching and assessment for cultural diversity, the metaphor of a "cross cultural teaching ladder," as shown in Figure 1, is a useful conceptual metaphor that avoids stereotyping and deficit-driven teaching. Adapted from Biggs (1999), the cross cultural ladder starts at the bottom rung, with a focus on student difference, which is not necessarily good practice. In a cross cultural teaching context, we might start from the position of teaching students by noticing differences objectively and by attempting processes that might be termed "assimilation," that is, we attempt to assist students to blend in with the majority rather than capitalise on cultural differences. At the second stage, teaching moves into accommodation, wherein the teacher has recognised and adjusted to student differences and tries to adopt strategies to suit. At level two, the focus is on teaching rather than on student learning, and on accommodating to student differences. At the top rung, the focus is on extending students' cognitive abilities, with the focus on learning. The ladder narrows toward the top, where the educational context meets the cultural needs of students, and it converges with good teaching.

The benefits of the model are that it conceptualises good teaching in the context of cultural differences, and it can be applied to both face-to-face and distance teaching

Table 3. Constructivist pedagogy and culturally inclusive through Web-based course tools

Teaching learning activities	Curriculum objectives	Assessment tasks
• Active learning • Authentic • Collaborative • Self-regulated • Scaffolded	• Process-based • Use of performance verbs (explain, solve, analyse, compare, evaluate) • Indicate levels of desired student performance	• Active, inquiry-based • Ensure real world authenticity • Ensure multiple perspectives • Self-directed • Include peer and self-assessment

Table 4. Continuum of inclusive pedagogies in Web-based teaching

Degree of inclusivity	Examples of program delivery
Low degree of cultural inclusivity	**Type 1 – Low level of inclusivity in teaching and learning (assimilation)** Online resources which recognise student differences without recognising differences in strategies approaches and learning differences. Offers no social interaction of dialogue. Learning is information transmission or "shovelware". Assessment is summative and focuses on products, not processes. Low level of constructive alignment. **Type 2 – Medium level of inclusivity in teaching and learning (accommodation)** Recognises that learners have different strategies and offers choice in learning tasks and adaptation of methods to accommodate students who are different. Does not include culturally-inclusive assessment practices and focuses excessively on teaching approaches rather than learning. Moderate level of constructive alignment. **Type 3 – High level of cultural inclusivity (high level of constructive alignment)**
High degree of cultural inclusivity	Recognises that while there are differences among students, their learning needs are best served by a focus on designing constructivist learning activities that recognise that: • students may adopt different learning approaches and have different levels of prior knowledge • the cultural differences and perspectives that student bring to learning are assets, not liability • setting high expectations and challenges for all students thus creating a motivating climate • assessment should be authentic, and include diagnostic assessment and outcome assessment

contexts. In Web-based environments, the ladder suggests that the educational context must meet student needs and acknowledge their cultural backgrounds.

Aligning Teaching, Assessment, and Curriculum Design

In terms of the holistic process of curriculum, task, and assessment design, how can teachers ensure that they apply culturally-inclusive principles across a course of study? Often there is a mismatch between what students see as the main focus of learning and what teachers see as their roles. For this reason, students may not always see the connection between learning objectives, assessment, and outcomes, and may develop surface approaches to learning. Students will define learning outcomes according to the types of assessment tasks they compete. If there is a match between assessment tasks and objectives, the student will learn what is intended, and "constructive alignment" is the result.

To meet the needs of multiple cultures, it is essential to achieve constructive alignment by matching the intended curriculum goals, learning activities, and assessment tasks. Table 3 provides an example of how this might be applied in design of culturally-appropriate online learning. In designing and planning for cultural inclusivity, the three dimensions of teaching are depicted as learning activities, curriculum objectives, and assessment. All three must be planned for in order to achieve consistency, balance, and compatibility. Curriculum objectives are the starting point and are depicted as in the central column in Table 3. Teaching activities are planned to support curriculum objectives and are constructivist in nature, and initiated by individual students, peers, or the teacher. In designing assessment tasks, the constructive alignment approach ensures that both processes and products of learning are assessed, and that authentic tasks where students have the opportunity to create effective performances and products are offered. In addition, authentic assessment for diversity and inclusivity would include the need for multiple indicators of learning and utilization of prior knowledge (Laurillard, 2002).

The use of an aligned design processes ensures that consistency between objectives, learning activities, and assessment. In applying the constructivist alignment model, teachers can apply social-cultural theories of learning and the notion of a learning community in developing tasks for cultural inclusivity, exemplars of which are given in Table 4. Thus, the framework for design ensures compatibility between all aspects of the learning process.

Conclusion: Implications for Cross-Cultural Design

The primary intent of this chapter has been to provide a holistic perspective on pedagogy, task, and interaction design for culturally-inclusive learning with information and communications technologies. Three significant areas of research have become important for the design of culturally-appropriate Web sites, and all derive from a constructivist view of learning. The first of these addresses the need for theoretical perspectives that are not deficit-driven, but that acknowledges and values cultural differences and gives scope for diversity and expression of multiple perspectives. The second set of factors relate to the adoption of appropriate pedagogies, and a movement up the "cross-cultural teaching ladder" to focus on learning and cognition rather than on student deficits and differences. For Web-based environments, this means creating teaching roles where teachers coach and scaffold, providing feedback to learners, as opposed to transmitting content. The third element relates to the adoption of systematic approaches to designing for cross-cultural learning on the Web by applying the principle of constructive alignment, thereby marrying constructive principles with task and assessment design. Table 4 shows how different levels of program delivery on the Web may display different degrees of cultural inclusivity with varying levels of constructive alignment.

The constructive alignment approach enables designers to evaluate the consistency between objectives, learning tasks, and assessment. Often, design parameters for culturally responsive teaching are treated superficially, and only design issues that relate to content organisation, interface design, graphics, and interactivity are considered in the creation of culturally-responsive learning experiences. This article has presented a case for consideration of the totality of the learning experience and the adoption of alignment as a starting point for planning culturally-inclusive learning environments on the World Wide Web.

References

Alfred, M. V. (2003). Sociocultural contexts and learning: Anglophone Caribbean immigrant women in U.S. postsecondary education. *Adult Education Quarterly, 53*(4), 242-260.

Anderson, T., & Elloumni, F. (Eds.). (2004). *Theory and practice of online learning.* Athabasca, Canada: Athabasca University Press.

Barbera, E. (2004). Quality in virtual education environments. *British Journal of Educational Technology, 35(1), 13-20.*

Biggs, J. (1999). *Teaching for quality learning at university.* Buckingham, UK: SRHE and Open University Press.

Bolloju, N., & Davison, R. (2003). Learning through asynchronous discussions: Experiences from using a discussion board in a large undergraduate class in Hong Kong. *eLearn Magazine,* 2003(6). Retrieved May 10, 2006, from http://www.elearnmag.org/subpage/subpage.cfm?section=tutorials&article=12-1

Brown, J. S., Collins, A., & Duguid, P. (1989). Situated cognition and the culture of learning. *Educational Researcher, 18*, 32-42.

Burbules, N. C. (2000). Does the Internet constitute a global educational community? In N. C. Burbules & C. Torres (Eds.), *Globalization and education: Critical perspectives* (pp. 323-355). New York: Routledge

Burbules, N. C., & Torres, C. (Eds.). (2000). *Globalization and education. Critical perspectives.* New York: Routledge

Chang, W. -W. (2004). A cross-cultural case study of a multinational training program in the United States and Taiwan. *Adult Education Quarterly, 54*(3), 174-192.

Chen, A., Mashhadi, A., Ang, D., & Harkrider, N. (1999). Cultural issues in the design of technology-enhanced learning systems. *British Journal of Educational Technology, 30*(3), 217-230.

Cole, M. (1985). The zone of proximal development: Where culture and cognition create each other. In J. V. Wertsch (Ed.), *Culture and cognition: Vygotskyan perspectives* (pp. 146-161). Cambridge: Cambridge University Press.

Collis, B., & Moonen, J. (2001). *Flexible learning in a digital world.* London: Kogan Page.

Crook, C. (1995). On resourcing a concern for collaboration within peer interactions. *Cognition and Instruction, 13*(4), 541-547.

DeBry, D. P. (2001). Globalizing instructional materials: Guidelines for higher education. *Tech Trends, 45*(6), 41-45.

Duffy, T. M., & Cunningham, D. J. (1996). Constructivism: Implications for the design and delivery of instruction. In D. H. Jonasssen (Ed.), *Handbook of research for educational communications and technology* (pp. 170-198). London: Prentice Hall International.

Ess, C. (2001). Introduction: What's culture got to do with it? Cultural collisions in electronic global villages, creative interferences, and the rise of culturally-mediated computing? In C. Ess (Ed.), *Culture, technology, communication: Towards an intercultural global village* (pp. 1-50). Albany: State University of New York Press.

Feinberg, M., & Vinaja, R. (2002). Faculty perceptions of bi-national distance education between the U.S and Mexico: An empirical analysis. *USDLA Journal, 16*(9). Retrieved May 15, 2006, from http://www.usdla.org/html/journal/SEP02_Issue/article06.html

Gunawardena, C. N., Nolla, A. C., Wilson, P. L., Lopez-Islas, J. R., Ramires-Angel, N., & Megchun-Alpizar, R. M. (2001). A cross-cultural study of group process and development in online conferences. *Distance Education, 22*(1), 85-121.

Harris, D. A., Pehrson, B., Jin, Y., & Jonsson, A. (2000). Distributed learning on a global scale. *USDLA Journal, 14*(6). Retrieved May 10, 2006, from http://www.usdla.org/html/journal/FEB00_Issue/distributed%20learningnew.htm

Henning, E. (2004). Crossing the digital divide safely and trustingly: How ecologies of learning scaffold the journey. *Computers and Education, 42*(4), 333-352.

Herrington, J., Oliver, R., & Reeves, T. C. (2003). Patterns of engagement in authentic online learning environments. *Australian Journal of Educational Technology, 19*(1), 59-71. Retrieved May 10, 2006, from http://www.ascilite.org.au/ajet/ajet19/herrington.html

Hofstede, G. (2003). *Culture's consequences: Comparing values, behaviors, institutions, and organizations across nations* (2nd ed.). Thousand Oaks, CA: Sage Publications.

Hofstede, G., & McCrae, R. R. (2004). Personality and culture revisited: Linking traits and dimensions of culture [electronic version]. *Cross-Cultural Research, 38*(1).

Kekkonen-Moneta, S., & Moneta, G. B. (2002). E-learning in Hong Kong: Comparing learning outcomes in online multimedia and lecture versions of an introductory computing course *British Journal of Educational Technology, 33*(4), 423-433.

Kim, K. -J., & Bonk, C. J. (2002). Cross-cultural comparisons of online collaboration. *Journal of Computer Mediated Communication, 8*(1). Retrieved May 10, 2006, from http://jcmc.indiana.edu/vol8/issue1/kimandbonk.html

Lankbeck, R., & Mugler, F. (2000). Distance learners of the South Pacific: Study strategies, learning conditions, and consequences for course design. *Journal of Distance Education, 15*(1). Retrieved May 10, 2006, from http://cade.icaap.org/vol15.1/landbeck.html

Laurillard, D. (2002). *Rethinking university education.* London: Kogan Page.

Lave, J. (1988). *Cognition in practice: Mind, mathematics, and culture in everyday life.* Cambridge, UK: Cambridge University Press

LeBaron, J., Pulkkinen, J, & Scollin, P. (2000). Promoting cross-border communication in an international Web-based graduate course. *Interactive Multimedia Electronic Journal of Computer-Enhanced Learning, 2*(1). Retrieved May 10, 2006, from http://www.imej.wfu.edu/articles/2000/2/1/index.asp

Lipman, M. (1991). *Thinking in education.* Cambridge, UK: Cambridge University Press.

McAteer, E., Tolmie, A., Duffy, C., & Corbett, J. (1997). Computer-mediated communication as a learning resource. *Journal of Computer Assisted Learning, 13*(4), 219-227.

McConnell, D. (2000). *Implementing computer supported cooperative learning.* London: Kogan Page.

McLoughlin, C. (1999). Culturally responsive technology use: Developing an online community of learners. *British Journal of Educational Technology, 30*(3), 231-244.

McLoughlin, C. (2000). Cultural maintenance, ownership, and multiple perspectives: Features of Web-based delivery to promote equity. *Journal of Educational Media, 25*(3), 229-241.

McLoughlin, C. (2001). Inclusivity and alignment: Principles of pedagogy, task, and assessment design for effective cross-cultural online learning. *Distance Education, 22*(1), 7-29.

McLoughlin, C., & Oliver, R. (1998). Maximising the language and learning link in computer learning environments. *British Journal of Educational Technology, 29*(2), 125-136.

Neo, K. T. K., & Neo, M. (2002). Problem-solving on the Internet using Web-based authoring tools: A Malaysian experience. *e-JIST, 5*(2). Retrieved May 10, 2006, from http://www.usq.edu.au/electpub/e-jist/docs/Vol5_No2/Vol5_No2_full_papers.html

Ng, K. (2001). Using e-mail to foster collaboration in distance education. Using e-mail to foster collaboration. *Distance Education, 16*(2), 191-200.

Odendaal, A. (2001). *The development of interactive online learning for distance education: A South African case study.* Paper presented at the 3rd Annual Conference on World Wide Web Applications. Retrieved May 15, 2004, from http://general.rau.ac.za/infosci/www2001/abstracts/odendaal.htm

Petegem, P. V., Loght, T. D., & Shortridge, A. M. (2004). Powerful learning is interactive: A cross-cultural perspective. *E-Journal of Instructional Science and Technology,*

7(1). Retrieved May 10, 2006, from http://www.usq.edu.au/electpub/e-jist/docs/Vol7_No1/content.htm

Rattanapian, V. (2002). Cross-cultural comparison of online learning delivery approaches used in Western and Thai online learning programs. *International Journal of Educational Technology*, 3(1). Retrieved May 10, 2006, from http://www.ao.uiuc.edu/ijet/v3n1/rattanapian/index.html

Reeves, T., & Reeves, P. (1997). Effective dimensions of interactive learning on the World Wide Web. In B. H. Khan (Ed.), *Web-based instruction* (pp. 59-66). Englewood Ciffs, NJ: Educational Technology.

Sleeter, C. E., & Grant, C. A. (2003). Making choices for multicultural education: Five approaches to race, class, and gender (4th ed.). Hoboken, NJ: John Wiley & Sons.

Toyoda, E., & Harrison, R. (2002). Categorization of text chat communication between learners and native speakers of Japanese. *Language Learning & Technology*, 6(1), 82-99.

Tu, C. -H. (2001). How Chinese perceive social presence: An examination of interaction in online learning environment. *Education Media International*, 38(1), 45-60.

Volet, S. (2004). Social affordances and students' engagement in cross-national online learning. *Journal of Research in International Education, 3*(1), 5-29.

Vygotsky, L. (1978). *Mind in society: The development of higher psychological processes.* Cambridge, MA: Harvard University Press. (Original material published in 1930, 1933, and 1935)

Walsh, S. I., Gregory, E., Lake, Y., & Gunawardena, C. N. (2003). Self-construal, facework, and conflict styles among cultures in online learning environments. *Educational Technology, Research, and Development, 51*(4), 113-112.

Wiesenberg, F., & Stacey, E. (2005). Reflections on teaching and learning online: Quality program design, delivery, and support mechanisms. *Distance Education, 26*(3), 385-404.

Williams, S. W., Watkins, K., Daley, B., Courtenay, B., Davis, M., & Dymock, D. (2001). Facilitating cross-cultural online discussion groups: Implications for practice. *Distance Education, 22*(1), 151-156.

Wilson, B. G. (1996). Introduction: What is a constructivist learning environment? In B. G. Wilson (Ed), *Constructivist learning environments: Case studies in instructional design* (pp. 3-8). Englewood Cliffs, NJ: Educational Technology Publications.

Yuen, A. (2003). Fostering learning communities in classrooms: A case study of Hong Kong schools. *Education Media International*, 40(1/2), 153-162.

Zhao, W., Massey, B. L., Murphy, J., & Fang, L. (2003). Cultural dimensions of Website design and content. *Prometheus, 21*(1), 75-84.

Chapter XIV

Universal Design for Culturally-Diverse Online Learning

Jane H. Eberle
Emporia State University, USA

Marcus D. Childress
Emporia State University, USA

Abstract

This chapter outlines a framework for designing online learning using the principles of universal design. The authors define and give practical examples of instructional design models and universal design for learning as adapted for culturally-diverse populations and global learning. Online learning in a global society presents a variety of teaching issues that must be addressed if learning is to be universal, consistent, and culturally-sensitive. Adapting principles that the Center for Assistive Special Technology has developed for learners with special needs and combining those with practical instructional design techniques and instructional strategies can ensure that diverse learners will have equal access to the learning that will take place in their online courses.

Introduction

Information technology has created new opportunities and challenges for both corporations and educational institutions. Businesses must compete in a global market. They can now enter foreign markets virtually overnight and deploy operations and resources

Figure 1. Universal design for online learning framework

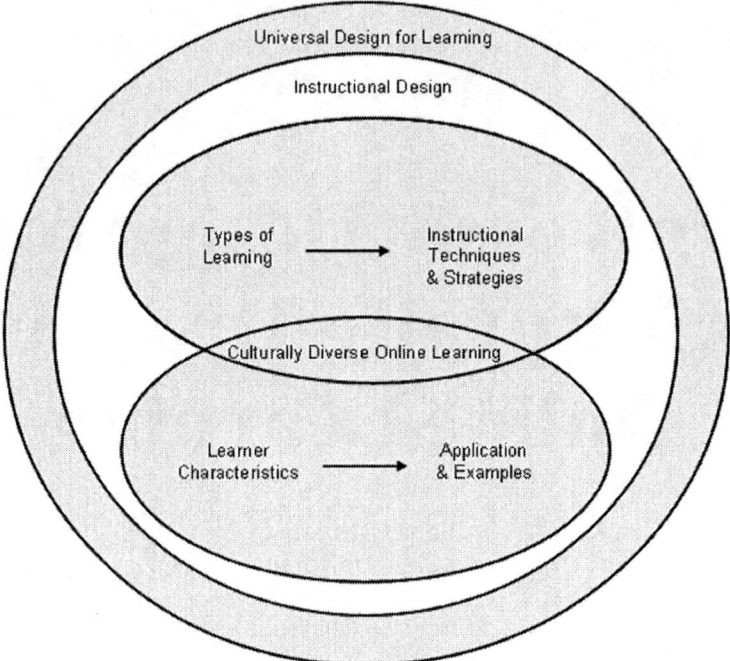

across the globe to support these new markets. A tremendous amount of information must be disseminated among employees, including sales and inventory figures, and customer service as well as other employee training. Indeed, corporations have found that with online training they can reduce training costs and keep staff knowledge and skills current at a worldwide level. This global employee-centered training must be both multicultural and multilingual.

Educational institutions such as colleges and universities have also adopted online learning in order to reach a broader/larger segment of the worldwide population and to better meet the needs of today's non-traditional and more mobile students. "Reaching the goal of global training requires solid knowledge of the differences among learners throughout the world—and careful design for these differences" (Horton, 2000, p. 439). While addressing cultural differences in a face-to-face class presents a variety of concerns, distance learning provides similar concerns as well as others. Similarly, whether global business markets or global educational markets, the challenge is the same: equity to learning access.

This chapter will focus on the use of universal design for learning (UDL) as a means to address cultural diversity and access to online learning. Figure 1 provides an advance organizer for the arrangement of this chapter's contents, showing the hierarchical relationship among UDL, instructional design, instructional techniques, and teaching strategies. It is hoped that this universal design for online learning framework will guide readers through the process of designing and delivering UDL-based online learning for culturally-diverse learners.

Universal Design for Learning: History, Definition, and Key Concepts

Universal design for learning is a research-based set of principles that together form a practical framework for using technology to maximize learning opportunities for every student (Rose & Meyer, 2000). Developing global communities that promote successful learning will benefit from these principles that, by their very nature, address the diversity of students.

As defined by the Partnership Grant at the Ohio State University (2004, para. 1):

Universal design is an approach to designing course instruction, materials, and content to benefit people of all learning styles without adaptation or retrofitting. Universal design provides equal access to learning, not simply equal access to information, Universal design allows the student to control the method of accessing information while the teacher monitors the learning process and initiates any beneficial methods.

UDL is a concept that incorporates many of the fundamental ideas of universal design, an architectural concept defined as "the design of products and environment to be usable by all people, to the greatest extent possible, without the need for adaptation or specialized design" (North Carolina State University, 1997, para. 1). The main thrust of universal design is that products are designed from the beginning, not retrofitted, to accommodate as many people as possible. With universal design for learning, curriculum is designed in the same manner. The needs of all students are considered before the teaching begins, and materials and lessons that reflect the awareness of these needs are incorporated into the curriculum so that everyone in the class has the greatest potential for learning.

Using UDL to Address Culturally-Diverse Online Learning Environments

While UDL has been used primarily to teach learners with special needs, certainly it can be adapted for online learners, and they can benefit from the UDL approach. Relying on the three main components of UDL: (1) multiple representations of information, (2) alternative means of expression, and (3) varied options for engagement, UDL assures that culturally-diverse online students will not only be able to have greater access to learning, but will be less intimidated by misconceptions or discriminated against because of lack of respect for or knowledge of differences (Meyer, 1998). Striving to accommodate differences in language, social values, and accustomed learning styles can oftentimes mean the difference between access to information and access to learning, the former being attainable by almost everyone, whereas impediments to the latter can diminish greatly the success of the educational experience. UDL promotes greater interaction among students, alternate delivery methods, and effective feedback. Developing rapport and a sense of community can enhance the distance learning experience. Palloff and Pratt (2003) emphasize the necessity for community building in online courses. They note that learning will be much more valuable if students feel a sense of ownership of the experience through the camaraderie that takes place through online discussions, sharing of information, and partnerships. This falls in line with overcoming barriers such as isolation and inhibitions, as described by Knowles (1984). Making certain that all students feel comfortable participating in the class leads to greater success for all.

Instructional Design

Applying UDL to the Dynamic Instructional Design (DID) Model

The dynamic instructional design (DID) model is intended to be a flexible and dynamic systematic way to design instruction. Built from the foundation provided by classic systems models, such as those by Robert Gagne, the model is sequential like its predecessors. However, the DID model's strength lies in the flexibility that it provides the user to respond, adjust, and change to ongoing feedback provided by the learner (Lever-Duffy, McDonald, & Mizell, 2005). The DID model's steps are: (1) Know the learners, (2) State your objectives, (3) Establish the learning environment, (4) Identify teaching and learning strategies, (5) Identify and select technologies, and (6) Make a summative evaluation. Developing a successful online course requires planning and good instructional design. Course design should take into consideration universal design and the components that will best serve the culturally-diverse student. UDL concepts can easily fit into the DID instructional design model. For more detail on integrating UDL into the DID instructional design model, see this chapter's appendix. With the basics of instructional design covered, the instructor can now focus on the specifics of applying UDL in learning (both face-to-face and online).

Figure 2. Dynamic instructional design model (Adapted from Lever-Duffy, McDonald, & Mizell, 2005, p. 39)

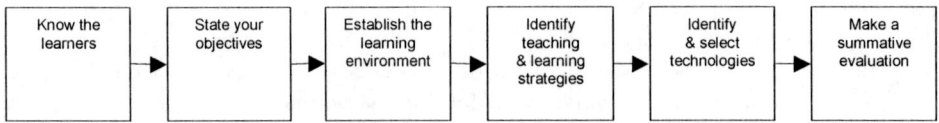

Table 1. Learning types and instructional techniques/strategies (Rose & Meyer, 2002, p. 109)

Recognition Learning	Provide multiple examples
	Highlight critical features
	Provide multiple media and formats
	Support background context
Strategic Learning	Provide flexible models of skilled performance
	Provide opportunities to practice with supports
	Provide ongoing, relevant feedback
	Offer flexible opportunities for demonstrating skill
Affective Learning	Offer choices of content and tools
	Offer adjustable levels of challenge
	Offer choices of rewards
	Offer choices of learning context

Types of Learning and Instructional Techniques/Strategies

Rose and Meyer (2002) recommend various instructional techniques and teaching strategies that can be used to support learners. These techniques and strategies are molded by learning theory, research, and advances in technology and media. Based upon brain networking theory, these network-appropriate teaching methods accommodate three types of learning: (1) recognition learning, (2) strategic learning, and (3) affective learning.

Recognition Learning

Recognition learning involves the recognition of patterns. Diverse learners mean diverse abilities to recognize patterns, whether they are symbols on a map or formatting of a term paper. Teachers can design differentiated instruction that addresses the recognition of patterns. Rose and Meyer (2002) suggest four teaching methods, which might be useful in addressing pattern recognition: (1) provide multiple examples, (2) highlight critical features, (3) provide multiple media and formats, and (4) support background knowledge.

Provide multiple examples. By providing multiple examples, instructional designers can illustrate key characteristics that define a pattern (Rose & Meyer, 2002). Exposure to more examples means more opportunities for the learner to recognize patterns (and differences in patterns).

Highlight critical features. Highlighting critical features is another method of focusing the learner's attention on the elements of a pattern that are most important. In an online learning environment, this can be achieved through graphics, animation, narration, highlighting in color, text labels on images, and video.

Provide multiple representations. Providing multiple representations of patterns through various media and in different formats can also help the learner in understanding patterns. Dual-coding theory (Paivio, 1986) and other research support the use of multiple representations through different media. In other words, providing information in both verbal and visual channels in an online learning environment provides redundancy, which in turn helps the learner understand patterns.

Support background knowledge. The last instructional support for pattern learning, supporting background knowledge, allows the learner to integrate new information into previously-learned neural networks. By creating relationships between new material and previously-learned material, instructional designers can build a scaffold on which new information (and patterns) can be placed. In an online learning environment, this background knowledge can be covered through the use of Web-based information resources such as informational Web pages, tutorials, and online dictionaries/glossaries. These resources may be explored by the learner, prior to instruction, or while online learning is occurring.

Strategic Learning

Strategic learning is a type of learning that must be accommodated. Although different learners have the same goals and objectives, they oftentimes have numerous and different ways (steps) to achieve those goals and objectives (Rose & Meyer, 2002). Strategic learning involves providing various teaching methods and media to empower learners to select their own "optimal pathways for learning strategic skills" (p. 119). Rose and Meyer (2002) suggest four teaching methods that might be useful while designing instruction to support strategic learning: (1) provide flexible models of skilled performance, (2) provide opportunities to practice with supports, (3) provide multiple media and formats, and (4) offer flexible opportunities for demonstrating skills.

Provide flexible models of skilled performance. By experiencing multiple and flexible models of skilled performance, learners can internalize effective ways of doing processes and procedures, as well as identify important features of processes and procedures (Rose & Meyer, 2002). In an online learning environment, the instructional designer may present processes and procedures through the use of digital media such as graphics, animation, audio, and video. Diagrams may also prove to be useful when explaining processes. Many of these models and examples can be found on the Web and linked to the online instruction, eliminating the need to develop new media materials.

Provide opportunities to practice with supports. Providing opportunities to practice with supports is another method that can be designed into instruction. As the old Carnegie Hall joke goes, Question: "How do I get to Carnegie Hall?", Answer: "Practice, practice, practice" (Carnegie Hall, 2005). In order to achieve complex strategic goals and objectives, learners must automatize (overlearn) the many steps necessary to complete a process or procedure (Rose & Mayer, 2002). Once this automaticity is achieved, the learner can focus on finer details and strategies. Because procedures commonly include numerous steps, many procedures must be broken-down and practiced as sub-procedures. This can be illustrated by the musician who practices only one or two notes, repeatedly, then moves to a musical measure of more notes that are practiced repeatedly; those measures are ultimately combined to create an entire musical passage. Such scaffolding can be provided in an online learning environment by the use of Web-based learning aids (job aids) such as online calculators, translators, spell checkers, thesauri, and numerous JAVA Web-based utilities.

Provide ongoing, relevant feedback. Providing ongoing, relevant feedback also supports strategic learning. When acquiring new skills, learners must be involved in a constant of flow of practice and feedback. The most important aspect of feedback for practice is that it needs to be ongoing. This ongoing feedback can be in the form of input from the instructor or through self-monitoring by the learner. In an online environment, such feedback can be achieved through tools such as a spell check in a word processing application or through applications specifically designed to improve skills and fluency through constant feedback such as those often encountered in drill and practice programs. Another solution for ongoing feedback can be found through the use of peer mentoring and expert mentoring which can be made available through email, chat/instant messaging, and most recently Internet-based audio/video teleconferencing.

Offer flexible opportunities for demonstrating skill. Offering flexible opportunities for demonstrating skill is the final teaching method recommended for addressing strategic learning. Once skills are mastered, a forum for exhibiting those newly-acquired skills should be provided. Just as students in a marching band must exhibit their musical and choreographic skills during the half-time of a football game, learners in an online environment must have a way to share their creations with others. Learning management systems, such as Blackboard and WebCT, provide quite extensive group areas in which learners can exhibit their work and receive feedback from others in the class. Presentation tools such as PowerPoint and publishing tools such as Publisher also serve as appropriate vehicles for sharing information and new skills. Perhaps, the best method for learners to demonstrate and share skills lies in the creation of Web pages. Web pages provide exposure to the entire world, a World Wide Web audience that is ready to provide critical and supportive feedback.

Affective Learning

Affective learning addresses a learner's feelings and emotions toward learning experiences (Bloom, 1956). Feelings and emotions may be exhibited simply as positive feelings toward learning or may be exhibited as interest, motivation, and persistence in a learning experience. The instructional designer should develop experiences that foster positive feelings and motivate learning. Rose and Mayer (2002) suggest four teaching methods that support affective learning: (1) offer choices of content and tools, (2) provide adjustable levels of challenge, (3) offer a choice of rewards, and (4) offer choices of learning context.

Offer choices of content and tools. Having a choice of content and tools empowers the learner to take responsibility for his/her learning and how it is approached. Once again, providing Web-based resources which include audio, video, text, and images gives the learner the opportunity to choose the most appealing format for content. In addition to streaming audio/video content, new technologies such as blogs, Wikis, RSS feeds, and podcasting provide even more opportunities for learners to select timely, up-to-the-minute content from a plethora of sources.

Provide adjustable levels of challenge. Providing adjustable levels of challenge is yet another method that can be employed by instructional designers to support affective learning.   Instructors can adjust the level of difficulty for learners, based upon their language skills or comfort level, frustration level, and other affective factors. In an online learning environment, this might be achieved by designing some assignments as games or activities with different levels.

Offer a choice of rewards. Offering a choice of rewards is a method that can be closely related to the adjustable levels of challenge method. By designing instruction such as games and other scenario-based activities, instructional designers can motivate learners and build their meta-awareness. With engaging activities containing immediate feedback and results, an intrinsic desire to achieve can be sparked.

Offer choices of learning context. Offering choices of learning context is the fourth and final teaching method recommended by Rose and Meyer (2002) to address affective learning. Learning context is perhaps one of the most critical factors encountered when addressing the needs of all learners. Should all activities be designed as independent or as cooperative/collaborative assignments? Obviously, the answer is "no." Some learners thrive in cooperative learning activities, while others detest them. For example, learners from some cultures are more comfortable with individual activities, while others are more comfortable with cooperative/collaborative activities (Kirkbride, Tang, & Westwood, 1991; Tse, Francis, & Walls, 1994). By providing learners with a choice of context, at times an instructor can build a level of comfort and perhaps even foster a desire in the learner to attempt a new and different learning context.

Because they are built upon the basic tenets of UDL, the previously-mentioned instructional techniques and teaching strategies are truly universal. They recognize that individual learners have different background knowledge, levels of skills/readiness, cultures, and languages, and strive to assist learners with attaining their maximum level of success. Because these techniques and strategies are grounded in basic UDL principles, they may be applied not only in an online environment, but in any learning environment.

Learner Characteristics and Application/Examples

When designing culturally-diverse online learning, there are a variety of learner characteristics and factors to be considered. These characteristics and factors include clientele identification, abilities/disabilities, language, culture, gender, time barriers, and technology. Table 2 illustrates these characteristics and factors, with examples for implementation into an online learning environment.

Table 2. Learner characteristics and application/examples

Clientele Identification	Students post brief biographies of themselves with pictures, if appropriate
	Use KWL (What you Know; What you Want to Learn; What you Learned) survey
	Have students post information about the region where they live
	Provide private communication to discuss any special needs students may have
Abilities/Disabilities	Provide information for self-help
	Provide statement for accommodating students with disabilities
	Provide online access for writing labs, and so forth
	Monitor writing samples
	Use a variety of navigational styles and media
Language	Determine need for translations
	Use simplified writing
	Use international English
	Avoid too much text; use graphics to explain points.
	Allow time for absorption and reflection
	Avoid idioms or local expressions
	Use universally-understood graphics; avoid symbols that may be confusing
	Use international telephone numbers and addresses
	Avoid using videos
Culture	Develop cultural awareness and sensitivity
	Respect other cultures' religions and spirituality
	Encourage students to discuss their cultural similarities and differences
	Develop awareness of place of education in specific cultures
	Avoid national chauvinism
	Avoid using pictures of people from specific cultures
Gender	Avoid stereotyping gender roles
	Avoid judging cultures for whom gender roles are specific
	Encourage collaboration between genders
	Use gender-appropriate language
Time Barriers	Format dates clearly
	Identify time zones
	Use asynchronous communication
Technology	Use lowest tech possible to deliver message
	Avoid media that may promote confusion

Clientele Identification

Just as "knowing the student" is the initial process in the DID model, identifying clientele is an important first step for designing global learning using UDL. Client identification can aid the instructor in adapting materials for various cultural, language, abilities, and technological differences. Posting a short biography of oneself will serve as a model for similar student postings. These can be invaluable in getting to know clients/learners and their needs, and can encourage further communication and collaboration of ideas among class members.

Although the K-W-L-H Technique developed by Donna Ogle is a graphic organizer intended to help actively engage students during reading, it can be used effectively with online students to determine their academic needs and support their self-directed learning (Pedroni, 2004). Using K-W-L-H, the student lists: (1) what is *Known* about the subject; (2) what one *Wants* to know; (3) what one *Learns* during the course; and (4) *How* one can learn more. This technique can help the student focus on the path that he/she needs to take to make the class more meaningful, and can aid the instructor in developing and adapting course materials.

Students' information concerning their geographic locations can help answer the following questions posed by Horton (2002):

- Where are your learners located?
- How does this locale affect how they learn best?
- What aspects of their work and daily life contribute to their willingness and ability to participate in your course? (p. 442)

This information can aid not only the instructor's flexibility in keeping the course meaningful, but it can greatly increase the students' affective domain by allowing them to participate at their comfort level.

Abilities and Disabilities

Special needs including learning disabilities, visual, hearing, and motor challenges should be discussed privately with individual students. Providing opportunities and encouragement to do so should begin immediately, and a statement for accommodating students with disabilities should be a part of the online syllabus. Along with this, instructors should make available information for self-help, such as online access to writing labs and tutorials. Writing samples can be an indication of the students' abilities and should be used periodically. Students with special needs may need to be encouraged "to compose discussion postings off-line to allow for spell checking and grammar checking before posting" (Palloff & Pratt, 2003, p. 50). Whether the students have special needs or varied learning styles, they can be accommodated by giving them "navigational choices necessary to take the course in their preferred style" (Horton, p. 446) or to adapt to their needs. Horton goes on to state that "We must provide multiple pathways. Link facts to details, details to theory, theory to facts, and so on. We can suggest a path through the material—perhaps in a table of contents or syllabus—but we should not force everyone to follow that path" (p. 50).

Language

There are many issues that should be of concern regarding language barriers in online learning. To use a universal design approach, one must remember that every student's needs should be addressed before the work of the class begins. Determining what translations will be necessary and how these are to be achieved will make the course flow more smoothly if accomplished before assignments begin. Using simplified writing structures, international English, and avoiding idioms and local expressions can enhance communication for all. Communication, after all, is about sharing ideas, and students should not have to guess what the instructor means. There should be adequate time allowed for students to read, internalize, and reflect on course material. The asynchronous nature of online learning can actually be a positive factor because it allows time for students to process their thoughts before replies are made.

Simple graphics that can be easily understood by everyone and that are free from bias, cultural, and emotional meanings will guarantee that meanings do not reflect other than what the instructor intends. According to Horton, "every hand gesture is obscene or rude somewhere in the world" (p. 458), so simply avoiding hand graphics is common sense. For example, forming a circle with one's fingers to indicate "O.K." simply means "O.K." in the U.S.; however, there are some exceptions in other countries. In Japan, the gesture means "money." In Brazil and Germany, the gesture may be considered obscene (Haynes, 2005). A picture may be worth a thousand words, but instructors should be certain the meanings of those 1,000 words are not distorted. Images that are internationally recognized will assure that sensitivities to all learners are maintained. Because videos contain so much detail that may distract the viewer from the main idea, videos should be avoided if there is a chance that they may cause more confusion than help. Using international calling codes for telephone numbers, including the country in an address, and using both metric and standard U.S. measurements are examples of simple ways to make a course more inclusive. These examples may seem like small details; however, they can make a big difference to students who use these resources. Minor inconveniences such as confusion between the use of inches and centimeters can add up to lots of frustration when not addressed.

Culture

Learning about other cultures can be exciting and rewarding, and instructors who model this attitude can help their students learn to be respectful of the diversity of the course population. Developing sensitivity to the cultural differences among students in an online course is a key to building community, trust, and collaboration. Instructors who support UDL in the classroom will need to devise activities, discussions, and other appropriate venues for students to celebrate their diversity. The UDL online class should encourage students to discuss their cultural similarities and differences and, by the same token, an awareness of the place of education in specific cultures should be clear. According to Hancock, Barnhart, Cox, and Faldasz (2005), "The facilitator must remember that many countries do not support the Western beliefs of feminism, individualism, and secularism" (p. 67). This should be considered, as it affects the learners' reactions to activities and collaboration. Further, Hancock et al. (2005) state that it is important to consider what is expected from the educational endeavor.

- Some developing countries see online learning as a way to increase literacy.
- Some governments see online learning as an access to education for those that have lacked access because of location or gender.
- Some students see online learning as a way to improve their own lives.
- Online learning can be a threat to governments that have attempted to control a country's power. (p. 67)

Surely these factors can affect the way international students view themselves as learners, and the understanding of this can enrich the instructor's and the other students' experiences just by their acknowledgment that education has different meanings for different peoples. Horton (2000) mentions the need for avoiding covert national chauvinism:

National chauvinism can creep into your work in a number of ways. Most of the time it is innocent and unintended. It consists of acting as if your culture and your country is the only one that matters. To avoid national chauvinism, adapt your designs so everybody can understand and participate. (p. 452)

This certainly can be construed as an example of UDL.

Gender

While gender roles may be specific in some cultures, it is incumbent upon the course facilitator to avoid stereotyping gender roles. For example, flippant remarks concerning the stereotypical housewife/student may seem cute to some, but are totally inappropriate. Rather, collaboration between genders and gender-appropriate language should be the norm. Again, the main principle of UDL is to encourage equal access to learning, and inhibiting any learner by inappropriate comments does not fulfill this goal.

Time Barriers

Global e-learning, by its very nature, will span time zones. To accommodate this and make learning more viable, learners' time zones should be identified; dates for assignments should be stated in a clear format, and asynchronous communication should be used. Assigning a synchronous open chat may be counter-productive for students living in different time zones. Imagine how unfair it would be to discuss pertinent issues with students who are experiencing the middle of the night, the middle of the day, and/or anything in-between.

Technology

Hancock et al. (2005) state, "Distance education courses need to be designed with the target country's technology and audience in mind" (p. 70). In other words, use the technology that will accommodate everyone even if it means slowing down the speed or using less attractive technology to convey the information. Horton (2000) puts it this way, "Never use a big file to do what a small one does better" (p. 444). It is equally important to refrain from using any technology that confuses the learners. As stated previously, videos, with their attention to detail, may be less effective than a simple line drawing. Piloting different media before the course begins can save many headaches later.

While the original intent of universal design for learning may not have been conceived with online learning in mind, the concept is readily adapted for such use. Planning ahead for all students' needs rather than retrofitting the course to accommodate diverse needs can save time and frustration for instructors and students alike. It is time for online learning to embrace UDL. The results can only be rewarding for all.

The Future of UDL in Online Learning

The demands of diverse and global learners, world markets, and policies on accessibility will most certainly influence the future of online learning and will emphasize the need for UDL. All online learning will soon be expected to meet the needs of all learners, regardless of cultural background. With the application of alternative formats and activities, UDL will be the key to addressing these objectives (Center for Applied Special Technology - CAST, 2000).

Curriculum of the future will be universally designed to achieve effective and successful instructional practices and meet the needs of diverse learners and learning contexts. It will comprise a distributed "network" of learning resources (materials, experiences, and people) presented in different media from many locations. (CAST, 2000, para. 3)

The Center for Applied Special Technology (CAST) outlines the three approaches to implementing their vision for a curriculum of the future, which may be applied to online learning (CAST, 2000):

1.   Content will be provided through multiple representations with multiple strategies for acting upon it. Strategies include providing alternative routes and increased engagement for learners. Various Web-based media such as streaming audio and video will most likely play an important role in the universally-designed online curriculum.

2.   Curriculum will be constructed as modules and accessed via networks. Strategies include customization for the learner, providing alternate versions of modules adapted to different cultures and locations, and continuously updating the selection of timely learning resources. The modularity of Web pages and learning management systems will facilitate the universally-designed online curriculum.

3.   Materials, experiences, and supports will be drawn from a wide range of sources and integrated into the core structure of the curriculum. Strategies include taking advantage of Internet resources, providing relevant, real-world experiences, and providing a forum for the sharing of information and expertise. Along with standard e-mail, mailing lists, and discussion boards, new Web-based communication tools such as Wikis, blogs, RSS feeds, and podcasts will undoubtedly provide learners with opportunities to share information in meaningful and relevant learning experiences.

It appears as though the future holds a never-ending supply of exciting and innovative tools which may enable learners to thrive in a universally-designed online classroom. Designers and instructors should strive to use these tools, when appropriate. By combining sound universal design principles and new Web-based tools, online designers and instructors can "pave the way for educational materials with sufficient breadth, depth, and flexibility to reach all learners and learning contexts effectively" (CAST, 2000, parag. 5).

Conclusion

Educational institutions and corporations are faced with the legal and ethical challenges of meeting the learning needs of all of their constituents. Universal design combined with effective instructional design will undoubtedly play a key role in assuring that all learners in the corporate and educational sectors are provided with quality online materials and resources that address their individual learning preferences. New technologies, especially those that are Internet-based, will most assuredly become important components of UDL-driven learning. By using UDL-based instructional design and learning strategies described in this chapter, online learning environments will become more inclusive for diverse populations, regardless of language, culture, abilities, and gender.

References

Blackboard, Inc. (2005). *The Blackboard learning system.* Retrieved November 14, 2005, from http://www.blackboard.com/products/as/learningsys/

Bloom, B. (1956). *Taxonomy of educational objectives, the classification of educational goals—Handbook I: Cognitive domain.* New York: McKay.

Burgstahler, S. (2002). Distance learning universal design, universal access. *Educational Technology Review, 10*(1). Retrieved January 4, 2005, from http://www.aace.org/pubs/etr/issue2/burgstahler.cfm

Carnegie Hall. (2005, June 28). *Wikipedia: The free encyclopedia.* Retrieved June 28, 2005, from http://en.wikipedia.org/wiki/Carnegie_Hall

Center for Applied Special Technology. (2000). *Envisioning future curriculum.* Retrieved September 14, 2005, from http://udl.cast.org/udl/index.cfm?i=189

Hancock, J. Barnhart, S., Cox, P., & Faldasz, D. (2005). The global needs assessment: Instructional design considerations for a global community. *AACE Journal, 13*(1), 65-72.

Haynes, J. (2005). *Communicating with gestures.* Retrieved September 14, 2005, from http://www.everythingesl.net/inservices/body_language.php

Horton, W. (2000). *Designing Web-based training.* New York: John Wiley & Sons.

Kirkbride, P. S., Tang, S. F., & Westwood, R. I. (1991). Chinese conflict preferences and negotiating behaviour: Cultural and psychological influences. *Organizational Studies, 12,* 365-386.

Knowles, M. (1984). *The adult learner: A neglected species* (3rd ed.). Houston, TX: Gulf Publishing.

Lever-Duffy, J., McDonald, J. B., & Mizell, A. P. (2005). *Teaching and learning with technology.* Boston: Allyn and Bacon.

Meyer, A. (1998). Universal design in the classroom. Excerpt from *Smart uses of the smart machine: Computers and your child's learning.* Retrieved October 22, 2004, from http://www.edutopia.org/php/article.php?id=Art_496&key=137

North Carolina State University. (1997). *What is universal design?* Retrieved November 5, 2004, from http://www.design.ncsu.edu/cud/univ_design/ud.htm

Paivio, A. (1986). *Mental representations: A dual coding approach.* New York: Oxford University Press.

Palloff, R., & Pratt, K. (2003). *The virtual student.* San Francisco: Jossey-Bass.

Pedroni, L. (2004). KWLH. *My eCoach® eLibrary.* Retrieved June 29, 2005, from http://www.my-ecoach.com/online/resourcepub.php?resourceid=1598

Rose, D. H., & Meyer, A. (2000). Universal design for learning: Associate editor column. *Journal of Special Education Technology, 15*(1). Retrieved February 15, 2005, from http://jset.unlv.edu/15.1/asseds/rose.html

Rose, D. H., & Meyer, A. (2002). *Teaching every student in the digital age.* Alexandria, VA: Association for Supervision and Curriculum Development.

The Ohio State University. (2004). *Universal design for learning: Elements of good teaching*. Retrieved February 16, 2005, from http://telr.osu.edu/dpg/fastfact/undesign.html

Tse, D. K., Francis, J., & Walls, J. (1994). Cultural differences in conducting intra- and inter-cultural negotiations: A Sino-Canadian comparison. *Journal of International Business Studies, 24*, 537-555.

WebCT, Inc. (2005). *WebCT Campus Edition*. Retrieved November 14, 2005, from http://www.webct.com/software/viewpage?name=software_campus_edition

Appendix

- **DID step one:** Knowing the learners is arguably one of the most important steps when designing instruction that is appropriate for all learners. Through both formal user analysis and informal assessments, a snapshot of the learners' current knowledge, skills, and dispositions can be attained. In addition, factors such as the learners' physical and cognitive developmental stages, learning styles, and cultural/language backgrounds can be considered. With such information, the designer can begin to develop appropriate goals and objectives for the instruction.

- **DID step two:** Stating your objectives gives the designer the opportunity to precisely state what the learner should be expected to do, once the instruction is complete. These measurable and observable performance objectives typically use action verbs to describe the desired performance. One advantage of using clearly-written performance objectives is that they are understood, regardless of language and cultural background, leaving little room for misinterpretation.

- **DID step three:** Establishing the learning environment provides an opportunity to develop instruction that fosters a comfortable context for the learners, an environment that supports learning and promotes positive interactions between the learners and the instructor.

- **DID step four:** Identifying teaching and learning strategies gives the instructional designer the chance to select teaching strategies that will be appropriate for each of the learners.

- **DID step five:** Identifying and selecting technologies presents an opportunity to choose which technologies and tools will support and enhance the chosen teaching/learning strategies. Such technologies and tools are especially important in an online environment that is used to address diverse cultures and languages.

- **DID step six:** Making a summative evaluation is perhaps (and unfortunately) the most neglected step of any instructional design model. A plan to evaluate the effectiveness of instruction is a must. First, it lets the instructor know how well the learners achieved the objectives stated in step two of the DID model. Second, it helps the instructor in determining what revisions need to be made in the instruction to improve learning in the future.

Chapter XV

Beyond Localization:
Effective Learning
Strategies for
Cross-Cultural E-Learning

Patrick Dunn
Networked Learning Design, Ltd., UK

Alessandra Marinetti
The Global Fund to Fight AIDS, Tuberculosis & Malaria, Switzerland

Instructional design cannot, and does not, exist outside of considerations of culture.

~ Henderson, 1996, p. 85

Abstract

Instructional systems are products of the cultures in which they are developed. Culture, which we define here as "the collective programming of the mind which distinguishes the members of one group or category of people from another" (Hofstede, 2001), has a pervasive influence on instructional systems, regardless of whether these systems involve self-paced e-learning, synchronous or asynchronous computer-based learning activities, or online communities of learners. The issue of culture's impact on instructional systems becomes most relevant and challenging where such systems are transferred across cultural boundaries or developed for multiple cultures. This is currently happening in many large, globally-dispersed organizations that use e-learning technologies to support the learning of their staff around the world. Theories of learning and of cultural dimensions suggest that the effectiveness of certain types of learning systems will be affected where they are used in culturally-diverse environments. The aim of this chapter is to highlight the issues that designers of a wide range of e-learning experiences face when designing e-learning for culturally-diverse learner groups. We provide some models to support learning practitioners, focusing in particular on the importance of a conscious, culturally-informed selection of instructional strategies as the most critical part of the design and development process.

Introduction

It is clear to anyone who has taken on the task of designing learning products or services for different national or regional cultures, that such products or services (we will call them "instructional systems[1]") are to some extent shaped by the cultures in which, and for which, they are developed. Culture, which for the purposes of this chapter, is defined as "the collective programming of the mind which distinguishes the members of one group or category of people from another" (Hofstede, 2001, p. 9), appears to have a pervasive influence on instructional systems, whether these systems involve classrooms, teachers, computers, videos, hand-held computers, cell-phones, or informal communities of learners.

While the issue of cultural influences on instructional systems has for some time been of interest to academics and a relatively small cohort of globe-trotting trainers from large organizations, it is gradually becoming one of the more important challenges faced by developers of e-learning products. Theories of learning and of cultural difference suggest that the effectiveness of instructional systems may be reduced where such systems are transferred into cultures for which they were not designed, or into culturally-diverse environments. Yet much of the rationale for e-learning, particularly in large organizations, rests on its ability to provide effective learning experiences, cost-effectively, to large, widely-distributed audiences. As an increasing number of large, globally- dispersed organizations use e-learning programs to support the learning of their people around the world, there is a growing need to support the designers of these programs in considering cultural factors.

Our particular interest is in forms of e-learning "…in which information and communications technology is used to promote connections: between one learner and other learners, between learners and tutors; between a learning community and its learning resources" (Goodyear, 2001, p. 9). This is a view of e-learning in which a learning network is regarded as a means of connecting people, as much as a means of distributing learning resources. Indeed, we believe that cultural diversity is just one of the pressures that will erode the use of less connected e-learning approaches where learners interact solely with content.

Our aim in this chapter is to highlight the issues that designers of instructional systems are likely to face when designing e-learning for a culturally-diverse learning environment, and to go some way in providing the basis for supporting them. In particular, our focus is on the importance of a conscious, culturally-informed selection of learning strategy as the most critical part of the design process. It is our contention that selection of learning strategy is most likely to be effective if it is:

A conscious decision in the design process; "gut feel" decisions, based on "common sense" may lead to problems in a cross-cultural environment, as they will be based on the designer's own culturally-induced worldview;

Informed by an understanding of the specific cultures involved;

Based on appropriate, researched models of cultural values;

Founded on the principle that networked learning technologies should aim to connect people, rather than merely distribute information.

A theme running through this chapter is our view that what is currently called "localization" generally involves too shallow a process, as it does not usually include consideration of learning strategy.

The perspective of the authors of this chapter is primarily one that arises from the context of training and staff development in large organizations whose primary purpose is not educational, such as governmental and internal agencies and corporations.

Learning with Technology: Culture's Effects

One problem facing learning designers is that the effects of culture are experienced at various levels. Both Trompenaars (1997) and Hofstede (2001) use the metaphor of an onion to show how the various layers of a culture relate to each other, and are experienced differently. Hofstede's view is that the outer layers of a culture are more visible, superficial, and potentially changeable, whereas inner layers involve elements that are less visible and change more slowly. Hofstede's model is shown in Figure 1.

In the context of interactions within a culturally-diverse environment, it is of course important to consider the outer layers of the onion. So, for example, when giving corrective feedback to learners in some East-Asian cultures, use of red highlights would be inappropriate, because this is the color of good luck, unlike in the West, where red tends to denote problems or errors. Similarly, where designing a relaxing entry page to a Japanese online module on effective employee relationships, it would be unwise to use shades of white, because in Japan white is the color of mourning. Care also needs to be taken where using a language shared between many cultures, such as English or Spanish. For example, in American English, "tabling a motion" means the exact opposite of what it means in UK English.

Figure 1. Hofstede's "onion" model

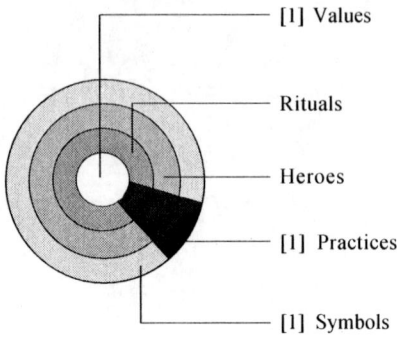

[1] Values

Rituals

Heroes

[1] Practices

[1] Symbols

However, an implication of Hofstede's model is that in attempting to understand the influences that a culture exerts or in analyzing a culture's response to a changing situation (such as the introduction of new learning technologies), it is important to consider all levels of culture, not just the more obvious, superficial ones. All software systems, of which instructional systems using technology are a subset, are visible embodiments of underlying cultural values that may be invisible, or at best undeclared. So understanding detailed but superficial variations at the level of symbols is a necessary condition, but is not sufficient. Henderson (1996) states: "When instructional design translates the topic into a tangible object, such as IMM software, it becomes an artifact of the culture in which it is embedded" (p. 1). Watson, Ho, and Raman (1994, cited in Collis, 1999, p. 12) note that the customs of the culture that develops a particular piece of collaborative software are often reflected in it, resulting in modifications of both technical and social aspects, when it is used outside the original cultural context.

Hofstede's (2001) widely-used model of value preferences is helpful in providing a basis for learning designers who need to understand how values vary in different cultures. The model is summarized in Table 1, with the LTO dimension adjusted slightly to reflect Trompenaars' similar dimension[2].

There is an increasing number of studies that appear to show how cultural values influence the nature of instructional systems, and it is noteworthy that these cases are generally consistent with existing models of culture.

For example, Morse (2003) evaluated an undergraduate distance learning program delivered to two groups of learners from cultures described by Hall (1977) as "high and low context"[3]. He found that the high context cultures, which included students from China, Singapore, Sri Lanka, and Pakistan, used the online resources in different ways from the low context group, which included students from the U.S., UK, New Zealand, and Australia. The high context group had different reasons for using the technology, emphasizing "the ability to say what is appropriate," in contrast to the low context group,

Table 1. Hofstede's five dimensions of cultural difference

In **High Power Distance (High PDI)** cultures, the less powerful members of society accept that power is not equally distributed.	In **Low Power Distance (Low PDI)** cultures, there is a general acceptance that power should be equally distributed.
High Individualism (High IDV) cultures show few ties beyond those of the nuclear family.	In **High Collectivism (Low IDV)** cultures, people belong to strong, cohesive in-groups.
In **Masculine societies (High MAS)**, men are assertive, tough, and concerned with winning material success, whereas women are more modest and interested in quality of life.	In **Feminine societies (Low MAS)**, both men and women are equally concerned with quality of life.
In **High Uncertainty Avoidance cultures (High UAI)**, people feel more threatened by uncertain or unknown situations, leading to a need for formality and clear rules.	**Low Uncertainty Avoidance cultures (Low UAI)** are more comfortable in managing uncertainty, and are generally informal.
Long-term Orientation (High LTO) cultures value perseverance and thrift, and generally regard time as overlapping (synchronous).	**Short-term Orientation (Low LTO)** cultures think more short-term and generally regard time as linear and sequential.

which valued "personal convenience and the ability to study anytime, anywhere." Their values were reflected in their priorities as learners.

Selinger (2003) undertook a formative evaluation of the Cisco Networking Academy, a program involving more than 300,000 students in 149 countries. She discovered widely-differing uses of the same online materials in differing cultures. For example, students in Denmark and Sweden were encouraged to take greater responsibility for their own learning than those in France. The Scandinavians had greater autonomy, collaborated more, and relied less on the tutor than those in France, where there was little use of group work or peer support. These findings are broadly consistent with Hofstede's model, the Scandinavians being, in Hofstede's terms, more feminine (low MAS), lower power distance (low PDI), and lower in uncertainty avoidance (low UAI) than the French.

In one of the very few quantitative studies in this area, Edmundson (2004) showed that learners in the Indian office of a global organization had significantly different preferences and perceptions in a specific educational context (a simple technical e-learning course), particularly in relation to forms of motivation, degree of support for cooperative learning, learner control, teacher roles, and value of errors. Other studies, such as those by Zakaria and Gould (2001) and Haulmark (2002) also indicate that learners in different cultures use learning technologies in significantly different ways, and imply that instructional systems that ignore cultural values may be less effective in producing the required learning outcomes.

But at what stage in a design process should a learning designer consider cultural values? In the next section we will argue that the most critical part of the design process is the point at which the learning designer makes decisions about what we call the "learning strategy."

Learning Strategy and Values

Because not every instructional approach is effective in every learning context, it is necessary to determine *when* a particular approach is the best possible match for the learner's needs, the instructor's teaching style, the learning environment, and the instructional goals. It is also important to determine *how* an instructional approach should be used in a given context (Nelson, 1999).

The way that learning experiences are designed varies greatly in different situations. A school teacher, a corporate trainer, and a personal development coach might not recognize each others' learning design processes. But at some point in any process, a decision is made, implicitly or explicitly, about what may be called a "Learning Strategy." And it is our contention that, for learning experiences to be effective in multi-cultural environments, this decision must take into account the cultural values of the learning designer and of the learners.

The term "strategy" in the context of learning design is, to use used Goodyear's (1999) description, "a broad-brush depiction of plans - of what should be done to achieve certain objectives" (p. 3). It is what film producers might call a "treatment," or an "approach"; what architects (such as Lawson, 1997, p. 91) might call "the integrative idea." Traditional writers on instructional design, such as Gagne, Briggs, and Wager (1992, p. 28), explain the purpose of a strategy (they call it "instructional strategy") as to outline "...how instructional activities will relate to the accomplishment of the objectives." So, for example, a leadership learning program for senior school teachers may be based on a strategy of offering personally-challenging experiential learning in a face-to-face setting, preceded by scheduled online discussions and supported by complex networked online simulations. Using current terminology, this is a form of "blended" strategy.

According to traditional instructional systems design (ISD) methodologies, selection of strategy should be the output of a sequence of planned stages such as needs analysis, objective setting, and so on. Thus strategy selection is both planned and explicit. Certainly, such an approach is likely to avoid situations such as where a teacher walks into their classroom and asks, "What shall I do today?" or the e-learning designer who strings together a loose sequence of multiple-choice quizzes or drag and drop exercises with no larger picture of the learning challenge in mind. But there is also a case for arguing that a highly-experienced learning designer will be able to make strategy decisions intuitively and implicitly and still be successful. They can rely on their experience — their "common sense." Yet it is precisely by relying on common sense approaches that many problems arise in multi-cultural situations. Much of our "common sense" relies on our deeper values, which are an underpinning of our cultural conditioning, and are largely invisible to us. Don Norman (1996), in discussing product design, makes this point strongly: "Cultural issues are perhaps the hardest to identify and deal with. Once people are acculturated, their thoughts, beliefs, and actions are biased, without their conscious awareness. Of all the problems...cultural issues are probably the most insidious" (p. 236).

Various authors, such as Reigeluth (1999), emphasize the importance of values as the foundations of particular learning strategies, and this appears to lie at the heart of the problem facing the learning designer. In a multi-cultural situation, the learning designer

Table 2. Cultural implications of Nelson's theory

Values from Collaborative Problem Solving—Nelson	Cultural Implications of These Values
Learning to use naturally effective collaborative processes	Different cultures value and use collaboration differently. The methods used to introduce and support collaborative learning will differ between cultures.
Learning environments that are learner-centered	Learner-centered environments will tend to challenge the authority of tutors/teachers in high power-distance cultures. These environments will have to be introduced very carefully.
Cultivating supportive, respectful relationships among learners, as well as between learners and the instructor	Supportive relationships between learners may suit more feminine and more communitarian cultures. The nature of "respect" in high power-distance cultures will be quite different from that shown in low power-distance cultures, with instructors in the former preferring a clear delineation of status. Methods and strategies to support this will have to vary between cultures.
Developing a desire for life-long learning	Cultures with long-term orientation have always tended to regard life-long learning as normal (for example, through apprenticeship, guild, and mentoring approaches), unlike those with shorter-term orientation. Introducing and supporting life-long learning in short-term oriented cultures will be more challenging.

will have to bring to the surface not only their own values and those of the learners, but also those of the particular learning strategies they may be considering.

Let us say, for example, that a designer working in a multi-cultural environment is considering, as a basis for their learning strategy, a collaborative problem-solving approach. In order to provide a robust basis for this approach, they are reviewing Nelson's theory of collaborative problem solving (Reigeluth, 1999, p. 242). Helpfully, Reigeluth's notes introducing Nelson's theory provide an explanation of the values on which it is based. Table 2 shows how some of the values underlying the theory suit some cultures more than others.

Given the example above, it appears that culturally-determined values may influence both the selection of learning strategy, and the methods used within that strategy. Our experience suggests that this can be disturbing for learning designers who are accustomed (one might even say acculturated) to tackling learning problems in environments that are generally culturally homogenous, and of which they themselves are a part. Although there has been much written (such as in Hofstede's original source on the subject—2001) about the general characteristics of how people from different cultures may learn differently, there are few established tools to support a learning designer in grappling with selection of specific learning strategies based on an understanding of cultural values.

Figure 2. Mapping Reigeluth and Moore's framework against models of culture

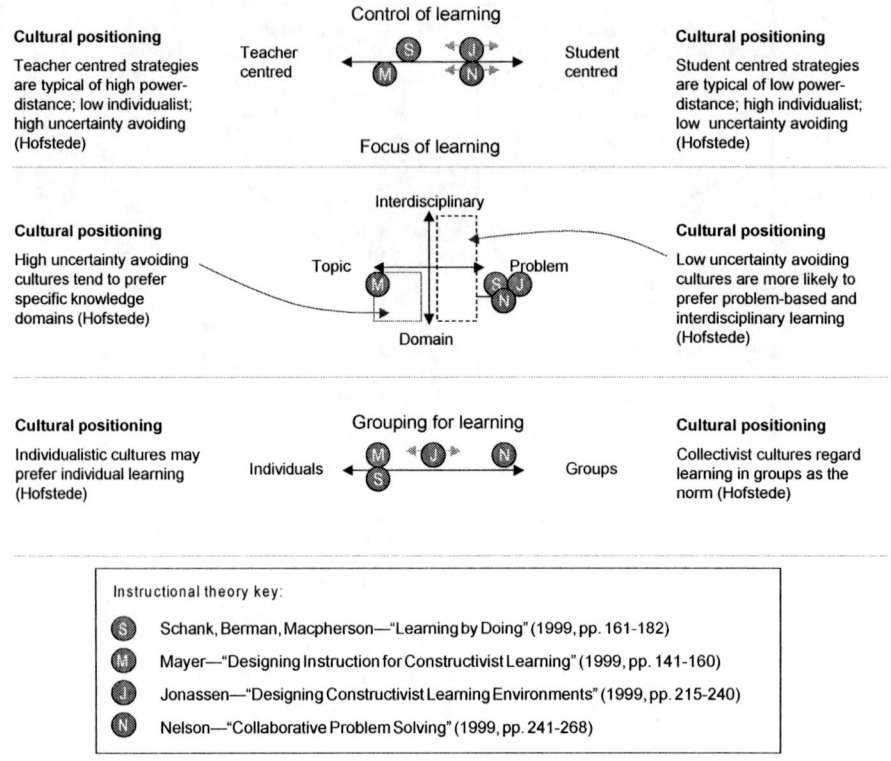

One basis for a decision support tool would be a structure, such as Reigeluth and Moore's framework for comparing instructional strategies (1999, p. 56), which categorizes learning strategies or theories. If a chosen model of culture identified the learning-related norms and preferences of specific cultures within the components of the framework, then mapped these against the positions of specific learning strategies and theories on the same components, such a framework might support decision-making as to which approaches (theories) are most appropriate for a culture.

Figure 2 illustrates how this approach might work, using four of the instructional theories from Reigeluth (1999): Mayer, Jonassen, Nelson and Schank, and Berman and Macpherson. Although there may be debate about the exact location of the theories on the particular components of the framework, that is not the main point of the exercise. We are attempting to show that a structure of this type may be useful in mapping theories in a way that is useful in highlighting cultural issues.

Figure 2 positions four example instructional theories on Reigeluth and Moore's framework, and provides example notes relating to how models of cultures may map onto the framework. The cultural positioning notes are samples only and are not intended to be comprehensive.

Human Mediation and
Learning Strategy

The authors suggested in the introduction to this chapter that the networked learning technologies are regarded as a means of connecting people, as much as a means of distributing learning resources. However, in a multi-cultural networked environment, strategies that connect people together can present particular problems, and opportunities, to learning designers, and the role of human mediation needs to be carefully considered.

The nature and degree of human mediation in a networked learning environment varies somewhat. An increasingly common model is one in which a facilitator, moderator, or tutor acts as a means of adapting learning resources to the local needs of culturally-diverse learners. Perhaps this could be termed "human localization." For example, the Cisco Networking Academy (Selinger, 2003) uses networks to distribute learning materials to a large number of countries, while allowing tutors in those countries to customize the learning experience for learners. Local adaptation of materials by tutors means that culturally-based expectations on the part of learners are more likely to be met. The Cisco Networking Academy illustrates the point that, in many cases, the ability of an appropriately-experienced person to identify particular requirements and respond sensitively to them will be greater than any current technology provides. Various models are available to assist tutors in adapting learning resources. For example, Henderson (1996, pp. 95-96) proposes a set of 14 "pedagogic dimensions of interactive learning," that provide a basis for considering the various ways in which a system may have to respond to varying cultural needs.

A different, more sophisticated form of human mediation is required where the strategy adopted is based on the principles of a community of practice (Wenger, 1999). Such communities are most often associated with forms of learning that involve the cultivation of understanding in learners, or "meaningful learning," what various authors (such as Kember, 2000, p. 104) refer to as "deep" learning. In the context of a community of practice, according to Wenger's account, learners "negotiate" meaning through discussion, and over time develop a sense of trust and mutual respect. As these conditions develop, so does a safe, supportive learning environment where learners are free to express themselves. Community members develop a sense of identity through their mutual engagement with one another, progressively making sense of their domain. Understanding develops through this process of negotiation of meaning.

Where a learner participates in a community that draws from a range of values that are very different from their own, as is often the case in multi-cultural environments, the negotiation process towards meaning-making may take a different shape, and make particular demands on community members. A sense of trust and mutual respect is only likely to develop where individuals initially heighten their awareness of their own cultural preferences and conditions, and then gradually integrate the various cultural perspectives into their own. In a process similar to what Bennett (1993) describes as the three stages of ethnorelativism (acceptance, adaptation, integration), they are likely to have to take a mental journey towards a point where the differences within the community become part of their own identity. The skilled and sensitive facilitator can play a key role in progressing this journey by helping to surface cultural differences, using tools such as Hofstede's dimensions. These can provide a framework for interpretation and understanding of the behavior of diverse community members.

Conclusion: Beyond Localization

"The term 'localization' is an impossibly light rendering of the real task. A truer model of knowledge transfer would be less like moving a piece of stuff and maybe sculpting it a bit to local needs, and much more like a local construction of knowledge at the source of need" (Patrick Lambe, 2002 p. 16).

So far in this chapter we have largely avoided using the term "localization." So why introduce it now, apart from because it is in the title? We do so to highlight two key assumptions about how e-learning should be developed for multi-cultural environments that we believe are incorrect, so as to summarize our position.

Firstly, localization, as currently applied to e-learning products and services, assumes that a piece of e-learning originates in one culture, is based on that culture's values, and is then exported to, and adapted for, other cultures. Our research suggests that unless the values of the various cultures for which the learning is intended are taken into account to start with, the quality of the learning experience may be compromised. Secondly, current e-learning localization practice assumes "content" as a starting point. The surface features of this content are then modified somewhat to accommodate the surface feature preferences of other cultures. The authors' view is that e-learning's starting point should be an effective learning strategy, developed with cultural diversity in mind, and one intended to use learning networks to put people in contact with people.

References

Bennett, M. J. Towards ethnorelativism: A developmental model of intercultural sensitivity. In R. M. Paige (Ed.), *Cross-cultural orientation: New conceptualizations and applications* (pp. 27-70). New York: University Press of America.

Collis, B. (1999). Designing for differences: Cultural issues in the design of WWW-based course-support sites. *BJET.*

De Jong, T., & Ferguson-Hessler, M. (1996). Types and qualities of knowledge. *Educational Psychologist, 31*(2).

Edmundson, A. (2004). *The cross-cultural dimensions of e-learning.* PhD dissertation, Walden University

Gagne, R., Briggs, L., & Wager, W. (1992). *Designing instructional systems.* In *Principles of instructional design,* Wadsworth.

Goodyear, P. (1999). Pedagogical frameworks and action research in open and distance learning. *European Journal of Open and Distance Learning.*

Hall, E. (1977). *Beyond culture.* Anchor Press/Doubleday.

Hannafin, M. J., & Land, S. M. (1997). The foundations and assumptions of technology-enhanced learning environments. *Internation al Journal of Learning and Cognition, 25*(3).

Haulmark, M. (2002). *Accommodating cultural differences in a web-based distance education course: A case study.* Presented at the 9th Annual International Distance Education Conference, Texas A&M University.

Henderson, L. (1996). Instructional design of interactive multimedia: A cultural critique. *Educational Technology Research & Development.*

Hofstede, G. (2001). *Culture's consequences. Comparing values, behaviors, institutions and organizations across nations* (2nd ed). Sage.

Kember, D. (2000). *Misconceptions about the learning approaches, motivation, and study practices of Asian students.* Higher Education. Kluwer Academic Publishers.

Lambe, P. (2002). *The autism of knowledge management.* Retrieved from www.straitsknowledge.com

Lawson, B. (2002). *How designers think—The design process demystified.* Architectural Press.

Morse, K. (2003). Does one size fit all? Exploring asynchronous learning in a multicultural environment. *JALN.*

Nelson, L. (1999). Collaborative problem solving. In *Instructional design theories and models.*

Norman, D. (1996). Design as practiced. In *Winograd—Bringing design to software.* Addison Wesley.

Reigeluth, C. (1999). What is instructional-design theory and how is it changing? In *Instructional - Design Theories and Models.*

Reigeluth, C., & Moore, J. (1999). Cognitive education and the cognitive domain. In *Instructional-design theories and models.*

Selinger, M. (2004). Cultural and pedagogical implications of a global e-learning programme. *Cambridge Journal of Education.*

Trompenaars, F. (1997). *Riding the waves of culture: Understanding cultural diversity in business.* Nicholas Brealey Publishing.

Wenger, E. (1999). *Communities of practice: Learning, meaning, and identity.* CUP.

Zakaria, N., & Gould, E. (2001). *Applying cross-cultural theory to instructional design.* Geneseo.

Endnotes

[1]   The term "instructional system" is the first of many used in this chapter that are, themselves steeped in cultural assumptions. It is a broadly North American term, and one that other English-speaking cultures, such as the UK, may find unfamiliar or imprecise. Based on Hannafin and Land's model of instructional systems (1997), it encompasses the technological, psychological, pedagogical, cultural, and pragmatic components of systems.

[2]   We have found that Trompenaars' views on time-orientation are generally more readily understood by learning designers, so tend to work a blend of Hofstede's and Trompenaars' versions.

[3]   Which tends to correlate highly with Hofstede's IDV dimension (individualist/communitarian)

Chapter XVI

The Cultural Adaptation Process (CAP) Model:
Designing E-Learning for Another Culture

Andrea Edmundson
eWorld Learning, USA

Abstract

At the conclusion of the study, The Cross-Cultural Dimensions of Globalized E-Learning *(Edmundson, 2004), the cultural adaptation process (CAP) model was introduced as a proposed guideline for evaluating existing e-learning courses and for matching them to the cultural profiles of targeted learners. In theory, the model could facilitate the development of culturally-adapted and accessible e-learning courses, which in turn provide opportunities for all learners to achieve equitable learning outcomes. In this chapter, the author illustrates, with a hypothetical example, how to use the CAP model. As a result of this mock exercise, modifications to the model are recommended. However, the CAP model would benefit from further exploration, use, and development by researchers and practitioners in the field.*

Introduction

Research is an iterative process, whereby concepts from one study are applied and tested, then validated, modified, or discarded. In the study, *The Cross-Cultural Dimensions of Globalized E-Learning* (Edmundson, 2004), the researcher was interested in determining if and how cultural differences might affect learning outcomes when members of a non-Western culture were given an online training course designed in a Western culture. *Learning outcomes* were defined by Henderson (1996) as any results that reflect the acquisition of skills and knowledge, such as the effectiveness of instructional techniques and students' perceptions or attitudes. The purpose of the study was to ascertain if learners from both cultures could achieve equitable learning outcomes, under the premise that e-learning should be designed to meet the needs of learners from different cultures. The CAP model is based on a synthesis of findings from that study integrated with findings about culture and cultural dimensions from studies in education and industrial anthropology. However, the practicality of the model has yet to be tested, validated, or modified. Therefore, in this chapter, the author first explains the concepts behind the CAP model and then guides readers through a detailed mock example of how to use it. In conclusion, as a result of completing this practical example, improvements to the CAP model are recommended. This chapter is not meant to be a reiteration of the original study (Edmundson, 2004) but, instead, is an attempt to put a proposed "e-learning adaptation" tool into practical use.

The Cultural Adaptation Process (CAP) Model

How the CAP Model Was Created

In simple terms, the model (Figure 1) is intended to guide the user through two analyses: identifying certain characteristics of an existing e-learning course, and determining if those characteristics matched the cultural profiles of the targeted learners. If not, what might need to be done, if anything, in order to adapt the course to the needs of those learners? The model provides a matrix in which, from left to right, the course complexity is considered, and from top to bottom, in which the potential steps to adapting an e-learning course for a targeted culture are progressively presented. In addition, the attributes from Level 1 to Level 4 range over a continuum, in a manner similar to the cultural dimensions described in the literature. Industrial anthropologists have defined cultural dimensions and categories of characteristics across which cultures can be compared and contrasted such as how members of a culture communicate, perceive times, accord social status, or perceive themselves in relation to the environment.

Figure 1. The cultural adaptation process (CAP) model – version 1 (Edmundson, 2004)

	Level 1	Level 2	Level 3	Level 4
Step 1: Evaluate content type and examples	Simple information, core knowledge, news, or updates, such as product knowledge, company procedures	Low-level, cognitive hard skills; simple knowledge and concepts, such as those used in application software; most computer-related skills	Some soft skills; complex knowledge, such as project management, presentation skills, marketing strategy	Mostly soft skills; attitudes and beliefs, such as negotiation skills, motivation, teamwork, conflict resolution
Step 2: Identify pedagogical paradigm, include instructional methods, activities, and so forth	Instructivist-objectivist, with behavioral objectives and sharply-focused goals; low-context communication; Mimetic	More closely related to instructivist-objectivist than constructivist-cognitive paradigm	More closely related to constructivist-cognitive than instructivist-objectivist paradigm	Constructivist-cognitive with cognitive objectives, unfocused goals; High context communication; Transformative
Step 3: Identify media	Lecture, handouts, simple demonstrations	Satellite broadcasts, audio-conferencing, recordings, television	Threaded discussions, list servers, online chat, e-mail	Videoconferencing, Web-based training, streaming with media and Web conferencing

Step 3: Identify national level cultural dimensions of learners and *critical* cross-cultural dimensions (associated features and characteristics) of the course.

The following dimensions of e-learning appear to be *closely related* to cultural dimensions found at the national level. Research indicated that a user's cultural profile (e.g., see the works of Hofstede) will dictate what learners are likely to prefer with respect to these dimensions.

Critical cross-cultural dimensions	Unsupported	◄ Cooperative learning* ►		Integral
	Extrinsic	◄ Origin of motivation* ►		Intrinsic
	Non-existent	◄ Learner control ►		Unrestricted
	Didactic	◄ Teacher role ►		Facilitative
	Errorless learning	◄ Value of errors ►		Learning from experience

Step 4: Identify national level cultural dimensions of learners and *assistive* cross-cultural dimensions (associated features and characteristics) of the course.

The following dimensions of e-learning are related to the potential *preferences* of groups of e-learners. Assess their preferences before modifying or developing any e-learning course because these are known to change based on variables other than cultural dimensions at the national level.

Assistive cross-cultural dimensions	Mathemagenic	◄ User activity ►		Generative
	Abstract	◄ Experiential value ►		Concrete
	Non-existent	◄ Accommodation of individual differences ►		Multifaceted
Step 5: Adaptation strategies	Translation	Localization	Modularization	Origination

Course Characteristics

In *Cultural Adaptation: A Necessity for E-Learning*, Marinetti and Dunn (2002) provided guidelines for adapting courses of differing levels of complexity to meet the needs and expectations of learners in different cultures. This matrix provides the foundational framework of the CAP model and helps categorize course complexity based on the type of content, instructional methods, and the types of media used. For the purpose of discussion, levels of complexity were labeled as Level 1 through Level 4 when incorporated into the CAP model.

E-learning courses are cultural artifacts, meaning that each course is somehow affected by the cultural environment of the people that designed it. Marinetti and Dunn posited that Level 1 courses (i.e., simple content, sharply focused, and presented via simple media, such as a lecture) are relatively unaffected by cultural influences, and thus little or no adaptation other than translation might be necessary. Translation could be as simple as practicing "globalized English" (i.e., by rewriting the content without idioms or dialects) or by changing spelling and phrases to British English, for example. Level 2 and Level 3 courses contain increasingly stronger manifestations of cultural differences and require *localization*, such as including images that are familiar to the targeted culture, addressing the etiquette of the targeted culture, avoiding taboos, making adjustments for gender issues, and so forth, to make them acceptable to another culture. When a Level 2 course requires localization, it also requires the lower level of adaptation, translation. When a course is characterized as Level 3, it requires not only translation and localization, but probably the use of reusable learning objects (RLOs), as well. RLOs are sections, or chunks, of a course that could be changed, or "plugged in," depending on the different cultural characteristics of the targeted learners. Using RLOs, or cultural learning objects (CLOs) in this case, assumes that some components of the course would still be acceptable to the targeted learners. When a course is categorized as Level 4, it is assumed that its characteristics are so different from those of the targeted culture, are so embedded with cultural influences, or both, that it would need to be written "from scratch," a process labeled as *origination* by Marinetti and Dunn. Thus, in Step 1 through Step 3 of the CAP model, the course is analyzed for degree of cultural influence and complexity.

In addition to cultural complexity, the CAP model includes the concepts of *critical* and *assistive* dimensions in Steps 4 and 5. These concepts provide even more specific information about the characteristics of the course under consideration. They were derived from Henderson's (1996) multiple cultural model (MCM), in which she described 14 sets of characteristics, or features, of e-learning courses, represented as continua with polar extremes that could vary based on the preferences or characteristics of different cultural groups. In the MCM, the course features and characteristics represented on the left side reflect an objectivist-instructivist pedagogical paradigm, while those on the right are characteristic of a constructivist-cognitive paradigm. In Edmundson's (2004) study, these 14 dimensions were combined into 9, creating the simplified multiple cultural model (SMCM) used in that study:

1. **Pedagogical paradigm:** *Instructivist/objectivist—constructivist/cognitive.* Four closely related dimensions (i.e., *epistemology, pedagogical philosophy, underlying psychology,* and *goal orientation*) were combined to create a singular dimension, pedagogical paradigm.

2. **Experiential value:** *Abstract—concrete.* When instruction has abstract experiential value, learning is removed from reality. Instruction with concrete experiential value integrates the learning process with the learner's world.

3. **Teacher role:** *Didactic—facilitative.* A didactic exposition of knowledge (e.g., a lecture) contrasts with facilitative pedagogical techniques that enable exploratory learning without controlling outcomes.

4. **Value of errors:** *Errorless learning—learning from experience.* Under an errorless learning paradigm, students learn until they generate no mistakes or until the instructional method does not allow for errors. In contrast, the learning from an experiential approach to instruction uses errors in the educational process.

5. **Motivation:** *Extrinsic—intrinsic.* Extrinsic motivation originates from factors outside the learner (e.g., the need for high grades or the presence of engaging materials). Intrinsic motivation comes from an internal desire to learn.

6. **Accommodation of individual differences:** *Non-existent—multifaceted.* In some contexts, learning and knowledge are structured so that there is no need for accommodation of individual differences. When accommodation of individual

differences is existent, on the other hand, knowledge and learning are presented in a variety of ways so learners can utilize the tools that best suit their preferences.

7. **Learner control:** *Non-existent—unrestricted.* In this dimension, the student either learns along a predetermined path or by independent discovery.

8. **User activity:** *Mathemagenic—generative.* A mathemagenic approach permits learners to access the same content in different ways, while a generative approach encourages learners to engage in the process of creating and elaborating content.

9. **Cooperative learning:** *Unsupported—integral.* In this dimension, learners work independently or learning is encouraged through cooperative activities.

In Edmundson's (2004) study of 250 learners from Eastern and Western cultures using the SMCM, the dimension of cooperativism vs. individualism, and the origin of motivation had strong effects on e-learning preferences (alpha = .05), and were characterized in the CAP model as *critical cultural dimensions*. Three dimensions (i.e., teacher role, learner control, and value of errors) had an indeterminate impact statistically, but appeared likely to matter (noticeable differences in raw responses, but not significantly different at alpha = .05) and, until further research indicates otherwise, should be treated as critical dimensions. The remaining dimensions (i.e., user activity, experiential value, and accommodation of individual differences) were categorized as *assistive cultural dimensions* because their potential importance cannot be discounted by the results of one study. Neither group had a strong preference for either "opposing" pedagogical paradigm (i.e., instructivist or constructivist). Because the pedagogical paradigm actually serves as an underlying description of the two polar extremes of the remaining eight dimensions, the concept is integrated into the model, instead of being listed as a separate dimension.

In summary, Steps 1 through 3 of the CAP model help the user identify course characteristics and cultural complexity, as put forth by Marinetti and Dunn (2002), and Steps 4 and 5 help the user identify specific course characteristics that may be related to culture, as described by Henderson's (1996) MCM and Edmundson's (2005) critical and assistive dimensions. Step 6 recommends possible adaptation strategies based on course complexity.

Learner Characteristics

In Step 4 and Step 5, the model also refers to the need to identify the characteristics of the targeted learners with respect to cultural dimensions, comparing them to course characteristics. The assumption that the user would be familiar with seminal research studies about cultural dimensions (e.g., work by Hofstede, Trompenaars and Hampden-Turner, Hall) has proven erroneous, and thus more guidance needs to be provided in future versions of the model. For clarity, a brief overview of that research is provided here. A common theme in all of these theories is that they reflect a tendency from simplicity to complexity on each continuum, as described in the matrix designed by Marinetti and Dunn (2002), and the cultural dimensions of e-learning described by Henderson (1996) and tested by Edmundson (2004). Hofstede (1984, 1997, 2001), Trompenaars and Hampden-

Turner (1998), and Hall (1953, 1981) identified and characterized cultural dimensions, primarily with respect to business communications; however, they posited the probable effects of many of these dimensions on education.

Hofstede's (1984, 1997) studies identified five cultural dimensions and calculated numerical indices for each national culture to provide a basis of comparison. In nations with a low-power distance index (PDI), teachers and students tend to be perceived as equals. Teachers are not authoritative subject matter experts, but rather are facilitators of student-centered education. In high-PDI nations, teachers are authorities, and students do not question their knowledge (Hofstede, 1997). Students in nations with a high-individualism index (IDV) expect to be treated as equals among peers and faculty, preferring to work as individuals and expecting recognition for individual merit. In contrast, members of collectivist societies depend on social relationships and may expect differential treatment based upon their social class. Globally, collectivist societies are predominant (Hofstede, 1997). In cultures with a high-masculinity index (MAS), students compete openly, are achievement-conscious, and are disappointed by failure, whereas, in a low-MAS culture, teachers and students hold more relaxed expectations. In a nation with a high uncertainty avoidance index (UAI), the teacher is regarded as an expert—an unquestionable authority. Students prefer a structured learning environment, which is manifested through precise objectives, strict timetables, precise answers, and rewards for accuracy. In contrast, in low-UAI cultures, teachers act as facilitators of learning; students are comfortable with vague objectives, loose timetables, and multiple solutions to problems, and prefer to be rewarded for originality. Hofstede's fifth cultural dimension, long-term orientation (LTO), was theorized after his original 1984 study; he did not propose specific ramifications of this dimension in education.

Trompenaars and Hampden-Turner (1998) also described eight cultural dimensions at the national level. Each of their dimensions, like Hofstede's, was described as a continuum bounded by two extreme, opposing characteristics. Unlike Hofstede, they rarely speculated about the implications of cross-cultural dimensions in education. However, those implications could be important, and thus are mentioned briefly here. In their first category, "relationships and rules," Trompenaars and Hampden-Turner (1998) identified five dimensions. *Universalism vs. particularism* relates to the balance between rules and relationships. Universalists tend to adhere to rules, whereas particularists regard rules as flexible guidelines over which relationships typically take precedence. The *individualism vs. communitarianism* dimension, similar to Hofstede's IDV, refers to the tendency to perceive oneself primarily either as an individual or as a member of a group. Members of *affective vs. neutral* cultures may be, respectively, emotionally expressive or emotionally detached and objective, in verbal or non-verbal communication. The *specific vs. diffuse* dimension accounts for the degree and level of interaction between people. Members of specific cultures tend to use direct and purposeful communication, while diffuse cultures tend to be less direct, often to the point of appearing evasive. The *achieved status vs. ascribed status* dimension relates to whether a culture accords status based on accomplishments or according to markers of group membership. This dimension shares characteristics with Hofstede's PDI. Trompenaars and Hampden-Turner also described two dimensions in the category "attitude toward time." *Orientation to past, present, and future* reflects how members of a culture perceive the importance of each of these periods. The dimension *sequential vs. synchronic* is related to whether time is perceived as linear and composed of discrete events or as circular and composed of integrated, overlapping events. Lastly, they categorized "attitudes towards the environment." Members of *inner-directed* cultures believe they have significant control over the outcome of events and aggressively try to manage situations, whereas members of *outer-directed* cultures believe they are subject to an external locus of control, and thus are more comfortable and flexible when confronted with change.

Hall (1981) envisioned cultural differences as poles on opposite ends of continua that resemble the indices and characteristics, respectively, of Hofstede (1984, 1997) and Trompenaars & Hampden-Turner (1998). According to Hall, members of monochronic (*M-time*) cultures tend to emphasize schedules, promptness, and segmentation of activities. Their communication tends to be low context, depending more on direct language than on subtle signals or context. In contrast, members of polychronic (*P-time*) cultures engage in multiple activities simultaneously and tend to focus on relationships and the completion of transactions, rather than on scheduled events. Their communication is high context because it is dependent upon what they already know about their culture. In the mock example below, how many of the cultural dimensions and characteristics of learners fit into the model will become clearer.

The Practical Application of the Model

The purpose of the CAP model is not to create "cultural experts" or to create culturally-perfect e-learning courses. With multiple formats and platforms for e-learning, multiple types and levels of content, and a multitude of cultures (and subcultures within them), no one can truly be an expert about all cultures. However, one can master a process. Thus, the primary purpose of the CAP model is to generate a consistent process by which producers and consumers of e-learning consistently address the existing characteristics of an e-learning course and initiate research into the culture of the targeted learners in order to adapt or redesign e-learning to fit their needs, if necessary. The model was designed so that its users (i.e., instructional designers or consumers of e-learning) can come from a position of relative ignorance about the culture of the targeted culture and adapt an e-learning course designed for learners of another culture. Consumers of e-learning might be faculty of international online universities, corporations with outsourced personnel, or even development workers providing e-learning opportunities for under-developed nations.

A secondary goal of the model is to make this analytical process easy. The idea is not to denude an existing e-learning course of all of its cultural manifestations, but instead to confirm or increase its acceptability by the targeted culture and to avoid offending targeted learners in any way that could deter them from learning or achieving equitable outcomes. From this perspective, it is not necessary to spend time identifying characteristics of the culture that created the e-learning course; instead, the process of analyzing the acceptability of the e-learning course is accelerated by focusing on the attempt to meet the primary needs of the targeted learners from another culture.

In this chapter, the author illustrates how to use the model from a Western perspective (American) to evaluate a course for an Eastern culture (India); however, the process should work for anyone and for any culture.

A Framework for the CAP Model

It is important to realize that the CAP model was proposed as a tool to be used within the framework of an overall needs assessment, which would typically be conducted when selecting or developing any e-learning course for targeted learners of any culture:

1.   Know or research at a high level the educational characteristics of the targeted culture, especially with respect to the effects of the culture on education.

2.   Differentiate the characteristics of the targeted learners from the general population.

3.   Use the CAP model to compare characteristics of the targeted learners in relation to the associated features or characteristics of the proposed e-learning course and, subsequently, identify potential adaptations to the e-learning course.

   The model is constructed to give instructional designers an idea about what might influence the achievement of equitable outcomes before they actually make changes to a course. The information gathered from this process allows the designer and consumer to ask the right questions and to identify an appropriate focus group. As noted by Edmundson (2004):

   A group's profile did not have to match the profile of the e-learning course in order for its members to achieve learning outcomes that were equitable to those of the other (originating) group. Moreover, learners indicated that they were willing to try new approaches to learning that did not match their profiles. (p. 182)

4.   Present the proposed e-learning course to a focus group of representative learners.

5.   Pilot test the resulting course with a statistically-valid sample of the targeted learners.

6.   Measure (pre-selected) learning outcomes.

7.   Gather feedback from targeted learners with respect to various factors (e.g., attitudes, preferences, motivations). This provides qualitative information that complements quantitative data gathered in the previous step.

8.   Redesign the e-learning course, based upon achievement of measurable outcomes and feedback from targeted learners.

9.   Publish results for other educational designers and consumers of e-learning.

10.   Monitor results of changes and, if necessary, repeat steps 1 through 9.

The Mock Example

In order to simultaneously investigate the usefulness of this model and to propose ways in which to improve it, a plausible example of its application will be given, using the two cultural groups explored in the original study (Edmundson, 2005): technology workers from the United States and India working for the same American software development corporation. To facilitate understanding of this example, a course that is available to readers on the Internet was used in this analysis.

The Corporate Education Department of the American company wanted to teach "logical thinking" to both groups of employees. In training and educational vernacular, logical thinking skills would be considered soft skills (i.e., defined as skills that involve emotions, attitudes, and behavioral changes). According to Marinetti and Dunn (2002), such a course would be very culturally affected. The pertinent questions are as follows: Can the Corporate Education Department anticipate that learners from the Indian culture would achieve the same learning outcomes as their American colleagues if they participate in this course designed by the American culture? If not, what would need to be changed, and how?

Needs Assessment

Following the framework of the aforementioned needs assessment, one would first identify the characteristics of the general population of the Indian educational system. In addition, one must investigate the characteristics of the targeted learners as a subset of the general population because these two groups may be significantly different. For example, the characteristics of learners in the technology industry may be notably different from those of the general population of Indian learners.

General Characteristics of Indian Education

According to a country profile of India (Economist Intelligence Unit, 2004), India has a moderate literacy rate of 65.2%, with male literacy somewhat higher than that of women. In addition, a large pool of highly-educated, vocationally-qualified technology workers exists. Many students attend a wide range of universities and colleges; their attendance is often based on religion or caste instead of ability, and educational systems often exist for the promotion of propagation of Hindi. The system tends to be based on rote learning (Cameron, 2002; Wu, Kaul, & Sankar, 2005). The country is very culturally heterogeneous, as evidenced by a large variety of ethnic groups, languages, and religions. The official language is Hindi, although at least 16 official languages are spoken, one of which is English (Country Watch, n.d., People section; Economist Intelligence Unit, 2004).

Characteristics of Specific Targeted Learners

The targeted learners are Indian technology workers employed by an American software development company with an office in India. They are fluent in English, computer savvy, and highly educated. The majority range in age from 18 to 35 (Edmundson, 2004).

Steps 1–3: Characterizing the E-Learning Course

To use the CAP model, the steps must be followed from left to right, as well as top to bottom. Analysis will begin from left to right to establish the minimum level of course complexity and then proceed from top to bottom to establish more specificity. The model shows the analysis of the e-learning course being completed before characterizing the targeted learners, but the process can begin in either order, because the information from one action complements the other.

Left to Right on the Model

The course selected for this application of the model was "Forging Breakthroughs" (Ninth House Publishing, n.d.). On their Web site, www.ninthhouse.com, the Ninth House publishers have made available one module (entitled "Logical Thinking") of the six-module course. This course is based on the book, The Fifth Discipline: The Art and Practice of the Learning Organization, by Peter Senge (1990). This online demonstration module was selected so that readers of this chapter can examine the course while following the logic of the example. Thus, the next direction to pursue would be to identify the obvious cultural characteristics of the e-learning course under consideration. In other words, what items or characteristics are so unique to the American culture that they might not be known in another culture? In contrast, what characteristics are so well known that they would not interfere with learning? As the course is examined for its level of complexity, the proposed adaptation strategy is considered in order to generate ideas about what might need to be tested, adapted for the learners, or both.

Level 1: Translation

The course is conducted in American English. Because the targeted learners are educated technology workers, translation to English would be unnecessary. However, attention to idioms and the difference between American and British English, used in Indian educational institutions (Wikipedia, n.d.), might need to be addressed. In this particular module, the course presenters talk about such issues as computer hackers, credit card theft, and firewalls. This vocabulary is not so much particular to the American culture as it is to the field of information technology, and thus should not be summarily eliminated. For the Indian learners, who are educated technology workers with exposure to the American culture, these concepts would likely pose few challenges to understanding. In addition, they have probably had exposure to the media and American culture, and thus probably can recognize vocabulary such as "war games" and Harley-Davidson (motorcycles). Again, depending on the targeted audience, these references would not necessarily interfere with the learning process. However, the model forces the uninitiated or unaware designer to identify potential issues without making assumptions.

Level 2: Localization

In the module *Logical Thinking* (Ninthhouse Publishing, n.d.), men and women from a variety of ethnic groups are visually presented in all of the scenarios, which take place in sophisticated corporate offices in metropolitan areas. Both men and women hold management positions. Women wear modest business attire, such as business suits with skirts. Men in management positions are wearing suits and ties, although the men in technology positions are dressed more casually (e.g., shirts, slacks, no jacket or tie).

Certain characteristics of the module can be explored further within the context of the learners' education level and sophistication (worldliness). For example, the roles of men and women in business might be different, as well as what is considered appropriate clothing for the environment and for different positions within the environment. Note also that the roles of men and women in business, and the power associated with their positions, are not necessarily a reflection of the roles of men and women in the overall society.

The learners' levels of education and exposure to other American businesses indicate that minimal localization is necessary. According to Country Watch (n.d., People section), men and women in larger metropolitan areas are more likely than people in rural areas to be familiar with Western habits, which may include shaking hands with persons of the opposite gender, a custom that may not be accepted by the general population. Public displays of affection are not appreciated in India, and modest clothing is expected, whether of Western or Indian style. Indians respect titles, and formality in their use is expected. Although touching does not occur in e-learning, visual representations of someone's head being touched may be offensive to Indian learners. In addition, body language, such as pointing, winking, and standing with hands on hips (Country Watch, n.d., Etiquette section) might offend learners. As an example, the American gesture signaling "okay" (thumb and finger forming a circle) has a different, crude connotation in India.

Localization also may require sensitivity to one of the many religions in India (Country Watch, n.d., Etiquette section; Economist Intelligence Unit, 2004). In addition, colors such as black and white are considered unlucky. Religiously observant Hindus do not eat beef, and Muslims do not eat pork, so representations of cattle or pigs as food should be eliminated or avoided. Certain habits of minimal consequence in the American culture may be offensive in India, such as eating from another person's plate, touching the feet, wearing shoes in a temple or home, or not covering one's head in a holy place. All of these surface-level characteristics, according to Country Watch (n.d., Etiquette section), should be considered and placed on a list to be explored during pilot testing or with focus groups.

Levels 3 and 4: RLOs and Origination

To better determine if the course is more complex than Level 1 and Level 2, it is necessary to move down the model (Steps 1–3) and closely examine the course content, instructional paradigm and related methodologies, and media used. Armed with this information, the user can better design pilot testing, focus groups, and questionnaires to determine whether RLOs are the best option, or if origination is necessary. In addition, other potential solutions for adaptation may arise, especially because RLOs or origination may not be options, as in this example.

Top to Bottom on the Model

Step 1: Content Type and Examples

This is the first module in a series of six in the e-learning course, "Forging Breakthroughs" (Ninthhouse Publishing, n.d.). The module "Logical Thinking" has three major topics, with several subtopics. The first topic is "How People Think," under which author Peter Senge presents in video his model called "the ladder of inference." With this model, he illustrates how people take the data available to them (e.g., observations, television, and experiences), select some of that data, add meaning to it based on their unique experiences, and subsequently draw conclusions. In the second section, "Mental Models," he discusses how individuals' mental models influence their thoughts, whether consciously or subconsciously. In the third module, "Essential Dynamics of Thought," Senge describes different levels of abstraction and how they affect each individual's thought process. The majority of the content is considered "soft skills," indicating that the course is at least a Level 3 and probably a Level 4.

Step 2: Pedagogical Paradigm, Instructional Methods, and Activities

This e-learning program takes advantage of a multitude of instructional techniques that are highly interactive. First, users have the option of taking a brief tutorial about how to use the e-learning program. In addition, a movie featuring a business professional gives an overview of the entire course. Learners are then presented with choices. They can view a conversational lecture by Peter Senge via streaming video. Before getting into the gist of the content, viewers watch a streaming video scenario of an office crisis in which the characters apparently lack the skills in logical thinking that will be taught in the e-learning course. These characters will presumably, through the course of the module, benefit from the skills learned. At the conclusion of any movie or lecture, users are given the option of reviewing the materials presented up to that point. In addition, they have the option of reviewing alternative scenarios that also illustrate the points made in the lecture.

After learners have elected to move forward, feeling they have adequately learned the skills, they are presented with a challenging quiz. The subtle differences between the responses in the multiple-choice questions test the learner's ability to discern important points made in the module. This particular module has two quizzes, one after each section. Each quiz consists of four multiple-choice questions. If users select an incorrect response, they receive immediate feedback about why the response was wrong and which response would be correct. Users are allowed to make two errors, and then the correct response is given automatically. Each section of the module builds on information learned in a previous one, a characteristic of constructivist learning. Whenever information or a new video is being loaded into the program, other information is simultaneously presented through streaming audio (for which text is also available). Thus, programs never have downtime, unless the user elects to pause.

Lastly, after all lectures and quizzes have been completed, users are asked to complete a workbook exercise that forces them to reflect upon how to apply what they learned into their own situations or environments. The workbook can be completed online or it can be printed. Users are first asked to remember one of their own experiences. They are then led through a series of five questions that illustrate to learners that they have indeed understood the concepts presented in the module. Users also have a choice of two additional scenarios in which to practice what they have learned. All workbook responses are recorded in the program and can be printed, as well. This tendency to use constructivist and interactive approaches to teaching indicates, at the least, a Level 3 course.

Step 3: Media (Technology)

This is a well-developed, interactive e-learning program requiring the use of sophisticated media, such as streaming video, streaming audio, Flash (Macromedia, 1995-2005), and other resource-intensive information and communication technologies (ICTs). Thus, targeted learners can only benefit thoroughly from this e-learning course if they have access to broadband connectivity, sophisticated computers, administrative rights to their computers in order to download plug-ins, and the peripheral equipment (e.g., microphones and headsets) needed to support interactive media. Alternative media are always available to the user (e.g., an audio presentation of the quiz instead of having to read the quiz, the ability to print a workbook instead of completing it online) so the technology does not prohibit participation, but so interactivity is maximized. This sopisticated use of media indicates a Level 4 course.

Thus, in summary, with respect to content type, pedagogical paradigm and instructional methods, and complexity of media, this course was designated as a Level 4 course:

1. **Content type:** The course promotes the acquisition of soft skills—those that express attitudes and beliefs known and documented to be characteristic of the originating culture (e.g., Americans are fond of logical thinking and believe possession of this mental ability leads to better work).

2. **Pedagogical paradigm:** The course exemplifies constructivist-cognitive approaches to teaching that involve cognitive activities, unfocused or undirected goals, and a transformative philosophy or approach built around problem solving and critical thinking.

3.   **Media:** Course activities and methodologies, especially simulations, are highly interactive and Web-based, and are supported by sophisticated media (even though simpler alternative media are often provided).

Completion of this first analysis of the course generated the beginnings of a list of potential items to explore through pilot testing. These items may require eventual modification in order to meet the needs of the targeted learners.

Characterizing the Targeted Learners Within the Context of Critical and Assistive Dimensions

As mentioned previously, in designing the original model, it was assumed that the users would be familiar with seminal research studies on cultural dimensions, such as those of Hofstede (1997), Trompenaars and Hampden-Turner (1998), and Hall (1981). However, experience has shown that users need more guidance. For now, each of the critical and assistive dimensions will be related to one or two dimensions of culture from these studies as examples, but not discussed in detail. A future version of the model will include more precise guidance for identifying the cultural characteristics and dimensions of the learners.

In the model, the critical and assistive dimensions will be considered in order, from top to bottom. The characteristics of each dimension within the course will place it along the continuum between Level 1 to Level 4. The characteristics of each dimension are then compared to the characteristics of the targeted learners to determine where the course may need to be adapted.

Step 4: Identify Critical Cultural Dimensions (in Context of Target Culture)

Cooperative Learning

This dimension, taken from a multiple cultural model (Henderson, 1996), describes whether learners work independently in the course or if learning is encouraged with cooperative activities. Edmundson's (2004) study showed that this dimension was very important to learners.

What exists in the course: According to the model, in a Level 1 course, cooperative learning is completely unsupported. In contrast, in a Level 4 course, cooperative learning is integral. In the online course selected for this example, a form of cooperative learning is manifested in the learner's interactions with the fictional characters in the module. (Note: If students were enrolled to complete all six of the modules of this course, they would also be given an opportunity to interact with each other and with specialists in the field via the Internet, including with the author of the course.)

Indian learner characteristics: Because the Indian culture is more collectivist and communitarian than American culture (Hofstede, 1997) and is focused on group goals and responsibility (Trompenaars & Hampden-Turner, 1998), one would anticipate that the targeted learners would prefer a course in which learning was generated through cooperative activities.

Potential adaptations to consider: When evaluating this course for use within the Indian culture, it would make sense to determine if a lack of active cooperative or collectivist activities would deter learners from learning or decrease their motivation to learn. If, however, the targeted learners participated in all six modules, they would have opportunities to share their experiences with each other, the author, and other users.

Origin of Motivation

According to Henderson's (1996) model, extrinsic motivation originates from factors outside of the learner (e.g., the need for high grades or the presence of engaging materials). Intrinsic motivation comes from an internal desire to learn.

What exists in the course. According to the model, in a Level 1 course, the level of motivation is extrinsic. In contrast, the origin of motivation in a Level 4 course is intrinsic. In this example, at least initially, the motivation was extrinsic because the course was required. However, the learners' motivation to complete the course may be positively affected by the presence of engaging course features, the desire to improve one's self, or to contribute to the success of the group. Edmundson's (2004) study indicated that the source of motivation was important to learners, and favored intrinsic motivating factors.

Indian learner characteristics. With respect to Hofstede's (1997) dimensions, learners from low-IDV countries (e.g., India) may choose to participate in order to become "better members of society." Trompenaars and Hampden-Turner (1998) speculated that communitarians consider the success of an individual to be tied to the success of the group.

Potential adaptations to consider. Because both the Indian and American technology workers were required to take this course, the origin of motivation was external, at least initially. It should be noted, of course, that a poorly-designed course can be demotivating for learners. In general, and also in this case, the source of intrinsic motivation is unknown. (Note: Origin of motivation is more frequently external, in the form of an effect of the environment or a characteristic of the learners, rather than an internal characteristic of a course. It may be an item best considered in the process of needs assessment or used in marketing techniques.)

Learner Control

According to Henderson (1996), nonexistent learner control exists if the student must follow a predetermined path, in contrast with being allowed to learn by discovery. In the study by Edmundson (2005), both American and Indian learners expressed a strong desire to control how they interacted with the course.

What exists in the course. In a Level 1 course, learner control is nonexistent. The instructional designer or the person conducting the course designs the path of learning, and the student is expected to follow it faithfully. In contrast, in a Level 4 course, such as the one used for this example, learner control is unrestricted, and learners have the option of choosing a linear path or of learning topics in any order of interest or preference to them.

Indian learner characteristics. Based on Hofstede's (1997) work, learners from a high-PDI country (e.g., India) might not question control mechanisms or authority within an e-learning course, such as a deadline, timed activities, or required activities, and might rely on the excellence of the instructor. However, according to Hofstede, their moderate UAI indicated little fear of trying new activities. Edmundson (2005) found that Indian learners were amenable to trying course features and activities that represented pedagogical paradigms different from their own, and preferred to control how they interacted with the course.

Potential adaptations to consider. At this point, adaptations seem to be unnecessary because learners can select their own paths to learning or follow one selected by the e-learning course.

Teacher Role

In a Level 1 course, the instructional designers or instructors take on a didactic role; in other words, they present knowledge to the learners, and the learners are expected to absorb that knowledge. In contrast, in a Level 4 course, the instructional designers or instructors take on a facilitative role, whereby learners are expected to learn on their own or among themselves by interacting with the course with limited guidance.

What exists in the course. In this course, the teacher role is distinctly facilitative. Learners can request guidance at any time, but it is not required.

Indian learner characteristics. In high-PDI countries (e.g., India), learners are expected to confer authority to the instructor or course designer and to be willing to follow predetermined paths to learning (Hofstede, 1997). In addition, such learners are expected to rely on instructor excellence as their source of knowledge. With respect to this course, Peter Senge is a well-known, respected author in the United States. However, in the study conducted by Edmundson (2005), both the American and Indian participants indicated they preferred to be guided by a facilitator, rather than instructed by an expert. Thus, lack of an actual instructor may have meant little to the targeted learners in this example. In addition, they preferred to control how they interacted with the course. (Note: This is an example of how the CAP model also obliges users to test their assumptions about targeted learners and to be willing to challenge the prescribed cultural dimensions.)

Potential adaptations to consider. For this e-learning course, the instructor (Senge) is a noted Western authority on the topic; thus, the Indian learners are expected to accept the authority of this expert. If he were found to be unfamiliar to them, it might be beneficial to promote the course to Indian learners based on the reputation of the author. However, with respect to the course itself, no adaptation is anticipated. During the focus group and pilot testing, learners should be asked about their impressions of the author's credibility and the validity of the information presented by him.

Value of Errors

In a Level 1 course, learners are expected to perform without errors before they are judged to be "taught" or "educated." In contrast, in a Level 4 course, learners learn from their facilitated experiences, as well as from their errors.

What exists in the course. For the course used in this example, learning from experience is preeminent. Learners are given positive and informative feedback when they make errors and, although they are allowed to reenact their choices or preferences that caused errors, they are not obliged to do so, which would be the case with errorless learning activities.

Indian learner characteristics. In general, the Indian educational system promotes errorless learning in the form of rote learning (Cameron, 2002; Wu et al., 2005). However, their low UAI (Hofstede, 1997) indicated that learners may be willing to try a different, less structured path to learning. Study results (Edmundson, 2005) also indicated that Indian learners were amenable to trying course features representing contrasting pedagogical paradigms.

Potential adaptations to consider. No adaptations are anticipated because the learners will probably accept this approach and perhaps be motivated by it. However, during the focus group and pilot testing process, learners should be questioned about their preferences for or perceptions of this experiential "learning from your mistakes" approach.

Step 5: Identify Assistive Cross-Cultural Dimensions (in Context of Target Culture)

User Activity

In a Level 1 course, user activity is mathemagenic. In other words, content is repeated in different activities until students learn the concepts presented. In contrast, in a Level 4 course, information is presented in a generative matter, in which learners build their own learning, usually upon the foundation of previous concepts learned.

What exists in the course. In the course used for this example, generative activities are the norm. Information is presented in a variety of formats, but in segments that build upon the understanding of previous concepts.

Indian learner characteristics. As mentioned above, Indian learners have expressed a preference for controlling how they interact with the course (Edmundson, 2004). In addition, a low UAI (Hofstede, 1997) indicated a willingness to try different approaches.

Potential adaptations to consider. No adaptations are anticipated because user activity supports user preferences. However, a post-course or post-pilot test survey might reveal participants' attitudes toward a heavily-generative format. Given that Indian educational models tend to rely on rote memorization, it would be useful to see how Indian learners accept an approach that requires more work on the part of the learner.

Experiential Value

In a Level 1 course, little or no experience is provided for learners. Instead, they learn information in an abstract manner, separate from the reality in which it might be used. In contrast, in a Level 4 course, learners are given concrete, realistic experiences.

What exists in the course. In the course used in this example, the learners are given concrete experiences through the fictional characters presented via sophisticated, interactive media in the module.

Indian learner characteristics. Although rote memorization is common in India, a low UAI (Hofstede, 1997) indicated a willingness to try different approaches, as did the study of Indian learners by Edmundson (2004).

Potential adaptations to consider. No adaptations are anticipated because learners can choose their level of experiences. However, a post-course or post-pilot test survey would reveal participants' attitudes toward a heavily experiential format, especially because this course relies heavily on problem solving and critical thinking skills.

Accommodation of Individual Differences

In a Level 1 course, accommodation of individual differences is nonexistent, whereas, in a Level 4 course, learners' preferences can be accommodated in many ways.

What exists in this course. In this Level 4 course, the tendency is toward multifaceted instructional techniques and technologies, providing a wide range of learning options, from text-based formats to simulations.

Indian learner characteristics. Although Indian learners are members of a communitarian culture (Hofstede, 1997; Trompenaars & Hampden-Turner, 1998), this characteristic does not preclude their ability to function as individuals.

Potential adaptations to consider. No adaptations are anticipated. However, a post-course or post-pilot test survey would reveal participants' attitudes toward such an accommodating format in relation to the options they selected or preferred among those available.

Utilizing Current Research

Steps 4 and 5 in the model draw on seminal research about culture and cultural dimensions. However, cross-cultural research is constantly being conducted, especially with respect to the relationships between culture, national culture, learning, and e-learning. Thus, the results of recent studies should also be reviewed for other characteristics that may affect the achievement of equitable learning outcomes, a step that was not part of the current version of the CAP model. For example, in a recent study, *The Relationship Between National Cultures and the Usability of an E-Learning System* (Downey, Cordova-Wentling, Wentling, & Wadsworth, 2004), learners from high-PDI cultures tended to make more navigational errors in e-learning systems. The study defined *usability* as "the ease-of-use and operational suitability of the interactive displays and controls that serve as the user interface to a computing system" (para. 4).

Learners in this example worked for a software development company, so the results of this study would probably be moot, although they might be important in another situation with different learners. The study also showed that learners in high-PDI countries might be less willing than learners in low-PDI countries to take a leadership role in e-learning, and would instead prefer group collaboration and group work.

Another study (Jaju, Kwak, & Zinkhan, 2002) about experiential learning and learning styles, as described by Kolb (Smith, Doyle, & Jeffs, 2005), and cultural dimensions, as described by Hofstede (1997), it was found that students from India preferred more active experimentation and abstract conceptualization ("convergers"), whereas American students preferred reflective observation and concrete experience ("divergers"). In other words, Indian learners are "strong in the practical application of ideas" and "can focus on hypo-deductive reasoning on specific problems," whereas American learners are "strong in imaginative ability" and "good at generating ideas and seeing things from different perspectives" (Chalofsky, 2005). These studies supported the concept that learning styles are affected by culture, and thus should be considered in the process of instructional design.

Information from studies such as these and that of Edmundson (2005) should be used in conjunction with the CAP model to identify as many potential adaptations and determining elements as possible to be addressed in focus groups and pilot studies.

Figure 2. A sampling of potential adaptations to consider based on the mock example

Course characteristics	Learner characteristics	Potential adaptations to consider	How to measure or evaluate impact/preferences
Use of American English	Taught in schools with British English	• Change words, idioms, colloquialisms • Provide learners with a glossary • Do nothing	Determine learner familiarity with American English and idioms, and other colloquialisms used in the course.
Use of American icons and brand names, such as Harley Davidson motorcycles	Highly educated, work for Americans and are frequently exposed to American culture through mass media, work, colleagues	• Replace with those known to Indian learners • Explain differences • Do nothing	Determine learner familiarity with American icons, pop culture, and other colloquialisms used in the course via focus group
Lacks cooperative activities and group work except through simulations and post-course communications	Prefer cooperative activities and group work	• Create RLOs to replace individualistic activities with more cooperative ones • Create and present a supplemental cooperative activity just for the Indian learners • Do nothing; learners may accept and/or adapt to individualistic activities	Pilot test the course for equitable learning outcomes; survey participants about reaction to activities provided
Embodies cognitive-constructivist educational paradigm	More accustomed to instructivist-didactic approach to teaching	• Create a course based on paradigm to which the learners are accustomed • Do nothing; learners accept and/or adapt to different paradigm	Pilot test the course for equitable learning outcomes; survey participants about reaction to activities provided

Generating an Action Plan

Using the information from Steps 1 through 5, users of the CAP model now have a list of course characteristics and potential preferences of targeted learners (based on their educational system, education, employment, cultural dimensions, and so forth). Known issues and ideas about possible changes to be made have also been generated. Compiling these items helps visualize what needs to be explored in pilot testing, focus groups, and questionnaires for learner feedback, as shown in Figure 2.

Step 6: Determine Best Adaptation Technique

For this example, creating RLOs or a new course is not an option. Instead, the model is applied to determine if and where the course may be acceptable or unacceptable for a group of targeted learners from a different culture. The action plan is a way to compile the information gathered and to provide alternative courses of action or ways in which to determine if changes or adaptations are necessary. This step cannot be executed without the input from the targeted learners themselves through pilot testing, focus groups, and questionnaires. Depending on their input, a preliminary adapted version of the e-learning course could be created and presented to a statistically-valid sampling of the targeted learners. However, the idea behind using the CAP model is to avoid unnecessary or costly adaptations.

Proposed Changes to the Model

The envisioned flow of analytical activities is not optimally represented by the current layout of the model. In revising the model, an attempt will be made to do the following:

1. Show the iterative relationship between describing the characteristics of the course and those of the learners.
    a. Split the model into two equally important, complementary sections, to be conducted simultaneously:
        i.   One section would evaluate the complexity of the proposed e-learning course, perhaps with examples, including critical and assistive dimensions.
        ii. One section would evaluate learner characteristics, actively incorporating seminal cultural research (e.g., Hofstede, Hall, Trompenaars & Hampden-Turner, Gardner, and Henderson) into the model because most users are unfamiliar with these studies.
    b. Design the model to better illustrate the reciprocity between these two concepts.

2. Include steps in the model to insure that a needs assessment is conducted in conjunction with the CAP model, such as the following:

   a. Research the overall educational system. What are attributes of the educational system, such as privileges, class orientation, and values? What are the general demographics and characteristics of learners?

   b. Identify characteristics of the targeted learners. How are they different or similar to the general population or to the culture for which the e-learning course was originally designed?

   c. Describe characteristics of the national culture. What are the known cultural dimensions?

3. Stress focusing on the key needs of the targeted culture, not on the characteristics of the culture that created the e-learning course. This approach avoids making changes that unnecessarily denude the course of all cultural characteristics from the culture for which it was originally designed.

4. Incorporate recent research into the model.

5. The model is missing a practical step at the end, as well. Quantitative evaluation of the effectiveness of the proposed changes should be conducted using either focus groups and pilot tests, as well as qualitative evaluations using surveys to identify learners' preferences for methods and approaches, their use of course features, and other relevant variables (Edmundson, (2004).

6. Show that adaptation solutions go beyond those proposed in the matrix (e.g., translation, localization, RLOs, and origination). Include options (e.g., how the course is marketed); provide supplemental materials (e.g., glossaries), and create supportive activities (e.g., a cooperative discussion group).

7. Generate worksheets or handouts to facilitate the entire process.

Conclusion

This analysis is not as thorough as it would have been in a real situation; instead, it gives the reader an idea about how to proceed with the model, what the terms mean, and how to identify characteristics of the e-learning courses and of the targeted learners. The proposed CAP model merely helps guide explorations of cultural characteristics of the learners and the e-learning course (pre-existing or proposed). One cannot assume this is the end of the process. Instead, users of the model will need to consult targeted learners of that culture; propose logical changes based on existing research and information; and then analyze and pilot test, create and evaluate, and finally perhaps even re-evaluate.

In addition, within the CAP model itself, the critical and assistive cross-cultural dimensions need to be further tested. Do they match, and, if so, to what degree, any of the dimensions described by Hofstede (1997), Trompenaars and Hampden-Turner (1998), and others? Are there differences between educational models that are not reflected in current research and the model? With respect to the characteristics of targeted learners and their preferences, will these learners adopt new educational paradigms? Could learners' preferences for educational paradigms, including techniques and methodologies, change? Are the characteristics and preferences of learners fixed?

The characteristics of a cross-cultural national group are only tendencies and preferences, not absolutes. Preferences can shift with exposure to new types of learning. Learners' tastes and expectations can become more sophisticated. All such changes may take place in slow and perhaps imperceptible ways.

Lastly, the CAP model does not assert that one educational paradigm is better or worse than any other. Instead, does the chosen paradigm accommodate the subject matter or content to be presented, as is usually determined by all good instructional design? Does it accommodate the preferred learning paradigm of the targeted learners, and, if so, does it need to?

The CAP model allows consumers and producers of e-learning for other cultures to do the following:

1. Match an existing course with the cultural profile of targeted learners

2. Adapt an existing course to that profile

3. Create a new course to accommodate a cultural profile

4. Address assumptions about cultural differences in education

5. Generate adaptation strategies that extend beyond those proposed in the model

6. Examine or learn more about one's own culture during the process of learning about another

The CAP model is a simplified process that can be used to analyze and adapt e-learning so it is accessible to other cultures, and so learners in other cultures can achieve equitable outcomes. The CAP model should prove useful to educational researchers, faculty of international educational institutions, corporate educators with outsourced personnel, and instructional designers and producers of e-learning who are expanding their markets globally. In addition, because socioeconomic development is positively correlated with access to education and technology (UNDP, 2001), the creation and dissemination of culturally-viable e-learning contributes to international development efforts. Using the model, or some form of the basic concepts presented within the model, is essential to the successful globalization of e-learning.

References

Cameron, S. (2002). Education in India: A background. *Development in Action*. Retrieved December 5, 2005, from http://www.developmentinaction.org/newspages/index/32.php

Chalofsky, N. (2005, November). Reshaping the way we view the world. *Training and Development (T+D) Magazine, 59,* 54-58.

Country Watch. (n.d.). *Country Review-India.* Retrieved August 25, 2005, from www.CountryWatch.com

Downey, S., Cordova-Wentling, R. M., Wentling, T., & Wadsworth, A. (2004, June 15, 2005). The relationship between national culture and the usability of an e-learning system. *The Knowledge and Learning Systems Group (NLSG), University of Illinois.* Retrieved October 31, 2005, from http://learning.ncsa.uiuc.edu/display-page.cfm?Page=Home

Economist Intelligence Unit. (2004). *Country Profile-Main Report: Asia-India.* Retrieved June 25, 2005, from www.EIU.com

Edmundson, A. L. (2004). *The cross-cultural dimensions of globalized e-learning.* Unpublished doctoral dissertation, Walden University, Minneapolis.

Edmundson, A. L. (2005). The cross-cultural dimensions of globalized e-learning. *International Journal of Information and Communication Technology Education, 1*(2), 47-61.

Hall, E. T. (1981). *Beyond culture: Into the cultural unconscious* (1st ed.). Garden City, NY: Anchor Press.

Henderson, L. (1996). Instructional design of interactive multimedia: A cultural critique. *Educational Technology Research and Development, 44*(4), 85-104.

Hofstede, G. H. (1997). *Cultures and organizations: Software of the mind* (2nd ed.). London; New York: McGraw-Hill.

Jaju, A., Kwak, H., & Zinkhan, G. M. (2002). Learning styles of undergraduate business students: A cross-cultural comparison between the U.S., India, and Korea. *Marketing Education Review, 12*(2).

Macromedia. (1995-2005). Flash Professional (Version 8) [Authorware]. San Francisco: Macromedia, Inc.

Marinetti, A., & Dunn, P. (2002). *Cultural adaptation: Necessity for global e-learning.* Retrieved September 24, 2005, from http://www.linezine.com/7.2/articles/pdamca.htm

Ninthhouse Publishing. (n.d.). *Forging breakthroughs: Module 1-logical thinking.* Retrieved October 29, 2005, from www.ninthhouse.com

Senge, P. M. (1990). *The fifth discipline: The art & practice of the learning organization* (1st ed.). New York: Currency Doubleday.

Smith, M. K., Doyle, M. E., & Jeffs, T. (2005, January 20). *The encyclopedia of informal education (infed).* Retrieved October 31, 2005, from http://www.infed.org/biblio/b-explrn.htm

Trompenaars, A., & Hampden-Turner, C. (1998). *Riding the waves of culture: Understanding cultural diversity in global business* (2nd ed.). New York, London: McGraw Hill.

UNDP. (2001). *Human development report 2001: Making new technologies work for human development.* New York: United Nations Development Programme.

Wikipedia. (n.d.). *Wikipedia, The free encyclopedia.* Wikimedia Foundation, Inc. Retrieved October 28, 2005, from http://en.wikipedia.org/wiki/Indian_English

Wu, K. B., Kaul, V., & Sankar, D. (2005). The quiet revolution: How India is achieving universal elementary education. *Finance and Development, 42*(2). International Monetary Fund. Retrieved June 2005, from http://www.imf.org/external/pubs/ft/fandd/2005/06/wu.htm

Chapter XVII

Communication Barriers and Conflicts in Cross-Cultural E-Learning

Rita Zaltsman
International Center of Modern Education - Prague, Czech Republic

Abstract

The present chapter assesses the key questions of communication barriers in distance learning virtual communities. To examine their cultural aspects, a Web-survey for distance learners has been conducted. The principal areas of interest were a cultural dichotomy of West/East; discrepancies in educational cultures (teacher-centered vs. learner-centered); mismatches in communication and educational traditions in different cultures; conflict paradigm and methods of conflict resolution. The findings of the survey are summarized and interpreted and some implications for further research are discussed.

Communication Barriers and Conflicts in Cross-Cultural E-Learning

Ignoring cultural factors inevitably leads to frustrating and ultimately ineffective learning experiences (Dunn & Marinetti, 2002).

Along with the stunning success, the most striking thing about cross-cultural e-learning is how many initiatives have failed. Dropout rates are as high as 80% ("sources estimate anywhere from a 60 to 80 percent dropout rate for online courses"—Braley-Smith, 2004) resulting not only from terrible content (Dunn, 2003), inefficient instruction (Clay, 1999; Cook, 2001), technological barriers (Mayes, 2001), but also lack of students' motivation (Harasim, 1990; Mehrotra, Hollister, & McGahey, 2001), language barriers (Meierkord, 2000; Young, 2002), cognitive discrepancies (Coomey, Stephenson, 2001) and psychological difficulties (Suler, 2002).

A fundamental reason for this is a poor understanding of how e-learning actually works. The solutions offered to avoid communication pitfalls (Berge, 1998; Mason, 2003) place the main responsibility on online tutors who do not encourage and facilitate collaborative work. The latter seem to be little effective as it is culturally absolutely insensitive (Dunn, et al 2002).

The last two years have produced a growing body of research that studies cultural and cross-cultural dimensions of e-learning (Cook, 2001; Dunn, 2003; Edmundson, 2003; Thorne, 2002) and provides case study analyses with instances of miscommunication between culturally-diverse e-students (Chase, Macfadyen, Reeder, & Röche, 2002; Macfadyen, Chase, Reeder, & Roche, 2003). The Internet is not "a culture-free zone" (Reeder, Macfadyen, Roche, & Chase, 2004), and it influences the whole spectrum of communication on both interpersonal and group level. Accordingly, a conflict in the cyber environment differs greatly from its offline counterpart due to additional barriers such as text-based communication in the absence of visual and auditory cues, the new technology as well as anonymity and invisibility, and others. Still, the cause of most misunderstandings in cross-cultural education stems from differing cultural dimensions.

Goal and Objective of Chapter

In the present chapter, the analysis of cross-cultural communication pitfalls has been extrapolated into the area of distance learning virtual communities. To examine their cultural aspects, a WWW-survey for distance learners has been conducted. The principal areas of interest were the dichotomy of Western vs. Eastern cultures; discrepancies in learning cultures (teacher- vs. learner-centered); mismatches in communicational and educational traditions in different cultures; conflict paradigms and peculiarities of conflict resolution.

It should be noted that for the purpose of this research, the notions of *e-learning, online learning, distance learning, and distance education* denoting the process of learning at a distance on the Internet without face-to-face communication between online students are used interchangeably.

Background

"Culture is always a collective phenomenon ... it is the collective programming of the mind which distinguishes the members of one group or category of people from another...it is learned, not inherited" (Hofstede, 1991, p. 5). G. Hofstede's classical definitions and his comparative cultural analyses remain the benchmark for discussion of national cultures. According to Hofstede, culturally-diverse groups have less similarity than monocultural groups due to different orientations to nature, environment, time, relationships, activities, and so forth. The adaptation of the cross-cultural teams to virtual learning is often accompanied by psychological discomfort, stress, frustration, the feeling of being isolated (Munro, 2002; Suler, 2002). Due to discrepancies in conflict management traditions in different cultures, their inter- and intra-communication sometimes result in intercultural conflicts.

In this chapter, intercultural conflict is defined as the perceived or actual incompatibility of values, norms, processes, or goals between a minimum of two cultural parties over content, identity, relational, and procedural issues. (Ting-Toomey, 1999).

To better understand the nature of communication pitfalls in learning communities, several dimensions for cultural comparison have been offered:

1. Power-distance; collectivism vs. individualism; femininity vs. masculinity; uncertainty avoidance (high vs. low); long-term vs. short-term orientation (Hofstede, 1997).

2. Universalism vs. particularism; achievement vs. ascription; individualism vs. communitarianism; affective vs. neutral cultures; specific vs. diffuse cultures; sequential vs. synchronic cultures (Trompenaars, 1998).

3. High/low context theory (Hall, 1981).

4. Time factor: monochronic/polychronic cultures (Hall & Hall, 1989).

According to Hofstede (1986), Eastern cultures (China, Taiwan, Thailand, etc.) are collectivistic, intuitive, and indirect, traditionally focused on relationships, roles, and status; whereas Western cultures (e.g., U.S., Germany, UK) have a definite orientation towards individualism, are logical, rational, direct, and success-oriented. The opposing cultural distinctions complicate effective communication and learning collaboration within online teams. In addition, Western cultures base their ethics on competitiveness; whereas the ethics of Eastern cultures are based on calmness and humility: Easterners value cooperation and harmony more than competition between individuals. Consequently, the following tactic in offline conflict situations is practiced in Eastern cultures: conflict avoidance as an appropriate behavior which aims at maintaining relational harmony ("lose face" phenomenon); Western cultures favor conflict openness: the Westerners are opened for communicating points of disagreement, and view conflict as an efficient way to solve problems.

There is also a contrast between educational preferences based on the Eastern/Western paradigm: *"listen and reflect," "learn by heart"* (Eastern) vs. *"express a personal opinion," "criticize and discuss"* (Western) (Hofstede, 1986). These preferences generate a conflict potential for online learners as well. To minimize this, some scholars advocate an idea of a constructivist approach to online learning. The term refers to the idea that learners construct knowledge for themselves—each learner individually (and socially) constructs meaning—as he or she learns (Hein, 1991). This is manifested in active dialogues in groups, between learners, tutors, and other actors. A constructivist learning environment presupposes the learners' personal initiative and their responsibility for their own learning. Such learning is not limited to data or facts transfer, when the students are expected only to "digest" knowledge, is directed at solving problems and active collaboration in online communities.

Jin, Mason, and Yim (1998) argue that the Internet can bridge cultural differences and illustrate this with the following example:

Most Chinese, even if they speak English, are much weaker conversationally than in reading and writing. They also are clumsy when put into positions to respond or react publicly, without prior preparation. In contrast, the Americans are generally very good at this. Consequently, if something is written down and a Chinese is given the time to read and to produce a written response, he/she will be able to come up with reasoned, well-thought-out responses. (Jin & Mason, 1998, Language and Interactions with Non-Chinese Section, para. 1)

The time zones difference (12 hours between the U.S. and China) which normally hinders communication plays a positive role here: The Chinese are given additional time to think their answers over. Thus, the Internet turns into an ideal communication setting for these two contextually opposite cultures.

This means that the Internet can play not only *a destructive role* but also *a constructive role*, making online communication across cultures less problematic.

Methodology

The present survey was a part of a doctoral research conducted in 2001-2004 (Zaltsman, 2004) in which the main objective was to investigate and comprehend communication barriers and conflicts in online cross-cultural distance learning communities. The study was based on three research methods: participation-observation, Web-based survey, and case study research (discourse analysis). This combination of methods has provided a more holistic view on the research subject, and contributed to a better understanding of the issues. Consequently, the data validity has been ensured. Some of the research results have already been reported in several print and online publications (Zaltsman, 2005; Zaltsman & Belous, 2004).

The survey was available via the Internet from March to June 2004. Participation in the study was confidential and voluntary. It should be emphasized that global online research is very complex in regard to methodological aspect: The majority of Web surveys attract mostly international students attending one particular university or college. Some researchers, however, through the results obtained from samples of students, make conclusions concerning all representatives of a certain culture, or even generalize them to all cultures. Hence, the findings they obtain may be inaccurate. Second, the present survey, undertaken at the global level, differs from the ones conducted for a certain academic institution: Filling it out was not compulsory, and participants did not benefit from their participation, compared with the University of Windsor survey pretext: "A raffle for a $100 Campus Bookstore gift certificate or University (...) sweatshirt would be offered as an incentive for filling out the survey"—Sloniowski, 1993, Methodology Section, para. 1). This accounted for a relatively limited number of survey participants.

Invitations to complete the survey have been sent to potential respondents over:

1.   Listservs (e.g., ITFORUM@LISTSERV.UGA.EDU);

2.   FIDO newsletters (e.g., psychology, education, instructional psychology);

3.   Online Communication Yahoo Groups: Intercultural Communication, Intercultural Insights, Distance Learning;

4.   Learning communities for intercultural communication: www.dialogin.com, www.sietar-germany.de, www.learningcircuits.org, www.learningtimes.com, etc.

The participants, students, online tutors and PhD learners, psychologists, sociologists, distance learning researchers and administrators, were contacted by email and directed to the www.surveymonkey.com Web site where the survey had been placed.

To gain first-hand information and more understanding of the subject matter, the author has taken part in several distance learning courses designed for cross-cultural virtual learners in the U.S. (Carrollton) and Germany (Saarbrücken). Participants of both programs constituted later the majority of the survey respondents.

1.   **"Distance Learning Certificate Program 10"** (January - June, 2003) conducted by the University of West Georgia, USA (http://distance.westga.edu/) for distance learning tutors and administrators. Conflict paradigm: learning cultures discrepancies (learner vs. teacher-centered) between American and Italian online students.

2.   **"Ikarus: Teaching and Learning in Virtual Learning Environments"** (March - June, 2004) — intercultural online seminar funded by the European Community and conducted by Saarland University, Germany (http://www.online-seminar.net/index.html) together with its partners from European universities and educational research centers in Sweden, Greece and Spain. The entire seminar was concentrated on learning environments based on the Internet. The students were discussing the subject of teaching and debating the issues of learning in the virtual learning

settings. Conflict paradigm: differences in time orientation between Austrian and Chinese students.

Both programs were offered completely online with no residency requirement. The project development was tracked from the inside: The researcher was working alongside with the students. Such field research is known as participant-observation. "The empirical approach to participant observation emphasizes participation as an opportunity for in-depth systematic study of a particular group or activity" (Garson, 2005, Key Concepts and Terms Section, para. 3). This research strategy has contributed to active virtual collaboration with course participants and tutors, direct observation of communication proceeding, and its barriers.

Thus, the data of a relatively neutral online survey were backed up with the researcher's own experiences and impressions. Such an approach, among other things, has led to alterations in objectives and contributed to obtaining valid data.

Survey Results and Discussion

The findings are a result of responses from 91 survey participants (270 invitations to participate have been sent) from 23 countries (response rate: 30.3%). It took each participant an average of 15 minutes to respond to the entire survey. (The obtained results are provided in Appendix A.)

Demographic data. Fifty point seven percent of the respondents were young people between 20 and 40 years old, which coincides with the results obtained by other studies (Hamdorf, 2003). The rest were aged over 40. This indicated that learning in virtual settings is gradually attracting a greater amount of the elderly. The reason for it is that at this age most employees are threatened with unemployment and are forced to continuously update their skills profiles and general abilities. The desire to study on the Internet and the interest in online learning for people over 40 was a predictable parameter (Hamdorf, 2003). However, a high percentage of respondents of this age group was not anticipated.

There was a balance of male and female respondents. Women comprised 51.4% of the total number who took part in the survey. This reflected the standard concept about an equal interest from both genders in e-learning, for example, the gender parameter gave anticipated results. Seventeen persons ignored the question and did not identify their gender.

Cultural profile of the respondents. The results clearly showed that the majority of respondents (66.3%) were Westerners: Out of 68 responses to this question, 35.4% came from European countries with Germany being well represented, more than one third (31%) came from the U.S. and Canada, and the remaining 33.3% came from the rest of the world. Fifty-two point two percent of the participants identified that their cultural values focused on individual's views, decisions, and tasks and, consequently, belonged to individualistic cultures. It is notable, that some respondents did not know what category they should be referred to—individualistic or collectivistic: In their comments, some Easterners indicated that they had been living for years mostly abroad, in the West, under the conditions of a non-native culture. Subsequently, 19.4% of respondents experienced difficulties with this question and either skipped it or have marked a "*don't know*" option.

Online communication issues. The overwhelming majority of respondents were satisfied with communication online indicating that "*it is substantially the same as talking face-to-face to people*" or "*online has its own qualities as has "is-à-vis"*".... Significantly, communication in forum (asynchronous) is more preferable than that in chat (synchronous). The following reasons for that were indicated:

Time Factor

- *[...] I have a chance to carefully consider my responses, as opposed to relying on 'knee-jerk' reactions characteristic of face-to-face interactions.*

- *There is [plenty] of time to work on a response, unlike face-to-face. And my accent does not get in the way.*

- *As a non-native speaker, online communications give me more time to think and write more clearly than communication in a face-to-face environment.*

Decisive Role of Successful Collaboration

- *I find the collaboration and feeling of learning from the whole group to be much more effective than "sage on the stage" teacher-centered learning.*

- *Some students watch rather than participate; class is too lethargic.*

- *It is a matter of context and others' personality more than a stable situation. With some people I feel comfortable, with others not.*

Interestingly, the feeling of being protected (35.4%) or anonymous (25.4%) has been emphasized as criteria for communication comfort and learning success.

Communication barriers. The data suggested that the participants view new technology on the whole as a positive force. Nonetheless, the limitations of e-learning were mentioned; some considered a lack of non-verbal dimension of online communication as the most important barrier:

- *I'm feeling quite comfortable, but I feel it is a very difficult task to avoid misunderstandings—more than in face-to-face (where you can transfer more than words through gestures, mimic etc. and you also receive immediate response via mimic, etc.).*

- *Often the online forms of communication do not offer sufficient richness to communicate as well as in a class. Needs to be even more open.*

In their comments, several respondents advocated the idea that online communication was of inferior quality, and mentioned a perception that online education is too impersonal. Also, the results indicating the attitude to online conflict and conflict resolution revealed dissimilarities: The majority of participants (66.2%) preferred an open dialogue and would rather "*communicate the point of disagreement*," "*share the point of difference*," "*voice out openly*" or "*confront the individual*" as it is practiced in the Western cultures rather than "*keep silent though disagreeing or carry out a public confrontation*." Thus, the Westerners did not feel uneasy sharing their points of difference, whereas the Easterners preferred to avoid conflict "*to save face*."

Other responses included:

- *Tell the person who doesn't agree with me via @-mail.*

- *My response would depend on the nature of the disagreement and the culture within the class and the school. I am not opposed to being forthright, provided I can do it tactfully. Also, my behavior would differ quite a bit depending on whether I were a student or a teacher. As a teacher, I would be less inclined to say, "I disagree." I would need to be much more focused on equanimity and tact.*

The most striking data were a set of figures indicating that every second student (46 out of 91 persons) would need the assistance of the class tutor in case of communication pitfalls. Probably, the idea of asking a tutor to help with conflict resolution was caused by discomfort, frustration, and stress which the participants reported as the predominant feelings experienced by them in e-learning. So, they needed support of a senior person who had much more life experience; many participants were accustomed to this practice in traditional class and felt a lack of it in online settings. The presence of a tutor or a mentor seemed to be an integral part of the educational process for these students, whereas his/her absence turns into a communication barrier.

Learning styles as communication barriers. The question: *Which activity characterizes best the educational tradition in your culture?* has given results which were not anticipated. A high percent (54.3%) of the variant "*listen and reflect*" has shown that in most classrooms (even in Western cultures), a reproductive way of knowledge acquisition through memorizing, listening to instructor, rote learning, and drill testing was being traditionally practiced. It should be noted that there were no more relevant options, for example: "*learning by doing*" which was a limitation of this survey.

- The overwhelming majority (70.6%) of respondents have stated that the educational tradition in their cultures was teacher-centered. Thus, taking into account that most of the responses came from the Westerners, it can be concluded that in the Western classrooms teachers remain the main "source of knowledge," whereas the learners are still unable to confront new challenges and take the responsibility for their learning achievements. Learning process is supposedly only shifting from teacher to learner ("*probably somewhere in the middle at present but moving towards learner-centered*"; "*there seems to be a development towards student-centered*").

Example Excerpts from the Survey Responses:

- *Never considered it a Western or Eastern phenomenon. I encounter both in the States. I think in the U.S., many teachers* pretend *to be learner-centered but are very teacher-centered anyway.*

- Elementary education is learner-centered, secondary and beyond is teacher-centered

- *Given the diffusion of constructivist ideals into the educational system, especially in colleges/universities, I don't think that selecting either teacher-centered or learner-centered would be accurate. It is difficult to know if one style predominates, given by subjective experience at a school of education that emphasizes a learner-centered approach.*

- Combination of both: structured learning through authority as well as critical discussions

- Well, it's worked effectively in many regions (University of London courses in Africa, Indian Open University, United Kingdom Open University, etc.). It's more a matter of appropriate design—and then there's the access problem.

The question of suitability to a greater degree Western or Eastern culture to online learning has resulted in a number (n = 15) of comments. Some respondents did not see any necessity for such a dichotomy, since the choice, in their view, depended on: (a) the age and background of the students; (b) the learning objectives; (c) the purpose of teaching; (d) the individualities of concrete persons. Nevertheless, 43.3% of all participants reported a Western style, 7.8% reported an Eastern style, which clearly indicated that the question was legitimate.

Culture and new technology. The question whether the Internet will dissolve all national differences and create a monolithic modern Internet culture resulted in 54.9% of negative responses; slightly more than 36.3% of participants expressed some level of agreement, with another 8.8% remaining neutral. A clear majority (75.8%) felt that the Internet would stimulate cultural contacts, provide communication, and a cross-cultural dialogue. The students have demonstrated a very thoughtful approach to this issue and showed that they did not view the Internet as a panacea or a machine for learning, but as an environment where various cultures could successfully cooperate to achieve their educational objectives.

Conclusion

The research presented a starting point for exploring the factors inherent in mismatches in intercultural online learning that can affect the success of it. The findings suggested that:

1.   Online learners tend to be older, there is no statistically-significant difference between male and female students

2.   The Western/Eastern division of cultures based on contrasts of communication and educational cultures is quite legitimate

3.   Communication barriers and conflicts in online settings are based on the West vs. East paradigm: Eastern communication is based on conflict avoidance, whereas Western is characterized by the ability to criticize or communicate the point of disagreement

4.   Online communities have an intermediate ("cosmopolitan") group of students who have cross-cultural experiences of living and learning. As such, they can act as conflict mediators along the cultures and help Westerners and Easterners accommodate to cultural diversity of online settings

5.   The majority of respondents feel positive about online communication and perceive it (in spite of the lack of visual and sensitive contact) as an equivalent to face-to-face or not less qualitative

6.   The survey has confirmed that, at present, the teacher occupies a leading position in the virtual class: Most online learning is still teacher-centered

7.   The findings also has suggested that teachers play a more important role in conflict resolution as anticipated

The findings and implications of this study need to be considered in light of their limitations. Unfortunately, no data were collected about the professional background of the respondents. Also, the question about the time of distance learning experience had to be included in the survey; it would have helped us to examine how it could influence the perception of the distance learning.

Furthermore, in order to obtain more exact data, a five-point Likert scale would have been necessary to indicate the extent to which the respondents agreed or disagreed, from strongly disagree to strongly agree.

Additional research is necessary in tracking the dynamics of conflict processes and studying the characteristics of conflict discourse and communication pitfalls between English native and non-native speakers. We are currently conducting a case study research exploring a stress retrieval function of humor in intercultural e-learning conflicts. Some implications that the major findings raise will be discussed and related to a widely-disputed theme of global Internet culture.

References

Allen, I., & Seaman, J. (2004). *Entering the mainstream—The quality and extent of education in the United States, 2003 and 2004.* Needham, MA: Sloan-C. Retrieved September 10, 2005, from http://www.sloan-c.org/resources/entering_mainstream.pdf

Baumeister, H. -P., Williams, J., & Wilson, K. (Eds). (2000). *Teaching across the frontiers. A handbook for international online seminars.* Tübingen: Deusches Institut für Fernstudienforschung an der Universität Tübingen.

Birkenbihl, M. (1990). *Train the trainer: Arbeitsbuch für Ausbilder und Dozenten.* Darmstadt: Moderne Industrie Verlag.

Chase, M., Macfadyen, L., Reeder, K., & Röche, J. (2002). Intercultural challenges in networked learning: Hard technologies meet soft skills. *First Monday, 7*(8). Retrieved September 10, 2005, from http://firstmonday.org/issues/issue7_8/chase/index.html

Correia, A. (2003). *"When differences collide"—Lessons learned from a cross-cultural team.* Retrieved September 10, 2005, from http://www.indiana.edu/~gist/conference2003/Documents/Correia.pdf

Edmundson, A. (2003). *Decreasing cultural disparity in educational ICTs: Tools and recommendations.* Retrieved November 10, 2005, from http://tojde.anadolu.edu.tr/tojde11/articles/edmundson.htm

Garson, G. (2005). *Participant observation (PA 765 research methodology).* Retrieved November 10, 2005, from http://www2.chass.ncsu.edu/garson/pa765/index.htm

Guertler, L. (2003). Conference note: Third workshop "Qualitative psychology: Research questions and matching methods of analysis" (34 paragraphs). *Forum qualitative sozialforschung / forum: Qualitative Social Research (online journal), 4*(1). Retrieved September 10, 2005, from http://www.qualitative-research.net/fqs-texte/1-03/1-03tagung-guertler-e.htm

Hall, E. (2000). *Monochronic and polychronic time.* In L. A. Samovar & R. E. Porter (Eds.), *Intercultural communication: A reader* (9th ed.). Belmont.

Hall, E., & Hall, M. (1989). *Understanding cultural differences.* Yarmouth, ME: Intercultural Press.

Hamdorf, D. (2003). Towards managing diversity: Cultural aspects of conflict management in organizations. *Conflict & Communication Online, 2*(2).

Hein, E. (1991, October 15-22). Constructivist learning theory (The museum and the needs of people). *CECA (International Committee of Museum Educators) Conference,* Jerusalem. Retrieved September 10, 2005, from http://www.exploratorium.edu/IFI/resources/constructivistlearning.html

Hofstede, G. (1986). Cultural differences in teaching and learning. *International Journal of Intercultural Relations, 10*(3), 301-320.

Hofstede, G. (2001). *Culture's consequences: Comparing values, behaviors, institutions, and organizations across nations* (2nd ed.). Thousand Oaks, CA: Sage Publications.

Jin, Z., Mason, R., & Yim, P. (1998). *Bridging USA-China cross-cultural differences using Internet and groupware technologies.* Retrieved September 10, 2005, from http://www.cim-oem.com/bridge_8c18c.html

Macfadyen, L., Chase, M., Reeder, K., & Roche, J. (2003). Matches and mismatches in intercultural learning: Designing and moderating an online intercultural course. In

Proceedings of the UNESCO Conference on International and Intercultural Education, Jyvaskyla, Finland.

Marinetti, A., & Dunn, P. (2002). *Cultural adaptation—A necessity for e-learning.* Retrieved September 10, 2005, from http://www.linezine.com/7.2/articles/ pdamca.htm

Mehrotra, C., Hollister, D., & McGahey, L. (2001). *Distance learning: Principle for effective design, delivery, and evaluation.* London; New Delhi: Sage Publications.

Munro, K. (2002). *Conflict in cyberspace: How to resolve conflict online.* Retrieved September 10, 2005, from http://www.kalimunro.com/article_conflict_online.html

Porter, L. (1997). *Creating the virtual classroom (distance learning with the Internet).* Wiley: Computer Publishing.

Reeder, K., Macfadyen, L., Roche, J., & Chase, M. (2004, May). Negotiating cultures in cyberspace: Participation patterns and problematic. *Language Learning and Technology, 8*(2) 88-105. Retrieved September 10, 2005, from http://llt.msu.edu/ vol8num2/reeder/default.html

Reeves, T. (1997). *Evaluating what really matters in computer-based education.* Retrieved September 10, 2005, from http://www.educationau.edu.au/archives/cp/ reeves.htm

Rösch, O., Loew, R., & Pfeifer, A. (2003). Interkulturelle Kompetenz—heute eine unerlässliche Schlüsselqualifikation. Zwischenbericht zu einem Forschungsprojekt an der TFH Wildau. In: *Wissenschaftliche Beiträge der Technischen Fachhochschule Wildau.*

Schmidt, D., Gruhler, G., & Fearns, A. (Hrsg.) (2003). *E-Learning Experimente und Laborübungen zur Automatisierungstechnik über das Internet: Nutzungsmöglichkeiten, Beispiele und die Simulation am Bildungsmarkt*: Europa-Lernmittel Verlag.

Sloniowski, L. (1993). *Report of findings: Distance education working group student survey project.* Retrieved September 10, 2005, from http://artemis.uwindsor.ca/ kits/gailj/99009a/vck13materials.nsf/0/875ef62fa9e00a5185256e01005aa78a/$FILE/ dereport_of_findings.doc

Suler, J. (2002). The online disinhibition effect. In *The psychology of cyberspace.* Retrieved September 10, 2005, from http://www.rider.edu/~suler/psycyber/dis inhibit.html

Ting-Toomey, S., & Oetzel, J. (2001). *Managing intercultural conflict effectively.* Thousand Oaks, CA: Sage.

Trompenaars, F. (1998). *Riding the waves of culture: Understanding the waves of cultural diversity in global business.* New York: McGraw-Hill.

Zaltsman, R. (2004). *Conflict paradigm in distance learning cross-cultural online settings.* Doctoral dissertation, Academy of Personnel Management, Kiev: IAPM.

Zaltsman, R. (2005, August). The challenge of intercultural electronic learning: English as lingua franca. *Cybercultures: Exploring Critical Issues, 3rd Global Conference,*

Prague, (under review). Retrieved September 10, 2005, from http://www.inter-disciplinary.net/ci/cybercultures/c3/prog.htm

Zaltsman, R., & Belous, A. (2004, June). Considerations to the applications possibilities of E-learning in TRIZ. *QFD-/TRIZ-Kongress,* Kassel, Germany.

Appendix A.
Summary of Survey Results

You're a male/female	Total	Percent
Male	36	48.6%
Female	**38**	**51.4%**
You are		
20-30	18	24.7%
30-40	19	26%
40-55	**27**	**37%**
55+	9	12.3%
What country are you from?		
USA	**27**	**30.9%**
Germany	8	11.8%
Austria, Malaysia, Thailand	à 3	13.5%
Australia, Great Britain, Italy, The Netherlands, Poland, Sweden, Switzerland	à 2	20.4%
Canada, China, Colombia, Egypt, Greece, Venezuela, Mexico, Russia, Spain, Taiwan, Turkey	à 1	23.4%
Do you think your home country is individualistic (focused on individual's views, decisions, tasks, etc.) or rather collectivistic (focused on relationships, roles, status)?		
Individualistic	**24**	**52.2%**
Collectivistic	16	34.8%
Not applicable	1	2.1%
Other (please specify)	5	10.9%
Do you think you belong to the Western cultural tradition?		
Yes	**51**	**70.8%**
No	7	9.7%
Don't know	14	19.4%
Are you comfortable with the communication in your online class? (multiple responses are allowed)		
Yes, absolutely, as I feel anonymous	22	25.4%
Yes, it's just for me absolutely, as I feel protected as compared to face-to-face contacts	**30**	**34.5%**
No, I feel more comfortable when communicating face-to-face	16	18.4%
No, I'm often frustrated: it's stressful to learn in a "global village"	5	5.1%
Don't know	4	4.6%
Other (please specify)	14	12%
What do you think is an ideal medium for communication in an online class? (multiple responses are allowed)		
E-mail	44	62.9%
Voice mail	13	18.6%
Chat	33	47.1%
Video	26	37.1%
Forum	**51**	**72.9%**
Blogs	16	22.9%
Other (please specify)	10	14.3%

Suppose that you feel misunderstood in your online class. Which of the following would you do? (multiple responses are allowed)		
Write an e-mail	**60**	**83.3%**
Use a voice mail	10	13.9%
Chat	18	25%
Meet in video-conference	13	18.1%
Ask for a telephone number	15	20.8%
Meet face-to-face if it's possible	25	34.7%
Other (please specify)	5	6.9%
In case you disagree with somebody in your online class you will:		
Tell the class openly that you don't feel at ease about it	**47**	**66.2%**
Keep silent as confrontation is seen negatively in your culture	14	19.7%
Other (please specify)	10	14.1%
In case you feel misunderstood in your online class, you will apply for help to:		
Your tutor	**46**	**50.5%**
Some student from your class	13	14.3%
The whole group	24	26.4%
Other (please specify)	8	8.8%
Which activity characterizes best the educational tradition in your culture? (multiple responses are allowed)		
Listen and reflect	**38**	**54.3%**
Learn by heart	23	32.9%
Tell your opinion	16	22.9%
Criticize, discuss	24	34.3%
Other (please specify)	10	14.3%
Educational tradition in your culture is:		
Teacher-centered	**49**	**70.6%**
Learner-centered	10	14.3%
Other (please specify)	11	15.1%
Which educational tradition is more appropriate for distance learning?		
Western	**39**	**43.3%**
Eastern	7	7.8%
Don't know	29	32.2%
Other (please specify)	15	16.7%
Do you agree that the Internet is a melting pot - it dissolves all national differences and creates a monolithic modern Internet culture?		
Yes	33	36.3%
No	**50**	**54.9%**
Don't know	8	8.8%
Do you agree that the Internet is an environment where hundreds of national cultures can blossom and enrich each other?		
Yes	**69**	**75.8%**
No	10	11%
Don't know	12	13.2%

Sample Qualitative Comments by Survey Respondents

- I believe that there is an element of trust that is often missing from online instruction. I think building trust is important although difficult.

- I think education, due mainly to technology, must become student centered to be competitive.

- I have both been a student in an online degree program, and am currently involved in creating online higher education. My background is in cultural anthropology and I am interested in your idea that there may be a 'western' vs. 'eastern' methodology for online education—the idea may be too generalized. I don't necessarily see a dichotomy. For US respondents, you should also ask if they're based on the West coast or the East coast of the country—because US Westerners are more influenced by Asian and Native/Hispanic culture, and US Easterners are more influenced by European culture.

- I am fine with online communication but sometimes the lack of proximity is felt.

- Great survey—however, there are still areas that have ambiguous answers and do not fit into choices allowed. Interesting subject. Hope that you get what you need.

- I think that online is a different mode of communication, and as oral or body communication one has to learn the code. I am in the process of learning this code, and as in everything the start is more difficult than the end of the process. I don't think that the distinction Eastern-Western as the role of the teacher concerns is appropriate as there are differentiations in every country (and I find that it indicates a racism).

- These last questions are too narrow, of course Internet and communication technologies have great advantages—but... there are a number of buts

- Cultural aspects do survive, however, some cultures are reticent to get involved fully

- U (you) didn't clarify what u meant by western/eastern tradition; I am Egyptian (eastern, but not like Japan) and educated in UK and U.S. institutions, so I'm eastern relative to U.S. but Western relative to my own country...

- Language barriers can hinder multicultural communications. I only speak and read English. When communicating via the Internet, I am not judged by my ethnicity.

Chapter XVIII

Multi-Cultural E-Learning Teamwork:
Social and Cultural Characteristics and Influence

Datta Kaur Khalsa
University of Maryland, USA

Abstract

Virtual teamwork in the e-learning classroom has provided opportunities for merging social theory and learning theory, mixing technology, culture, identity, and community. Online learning teams have generated attention to the social and cultural characteristics that influence these global interactions. This chapter discusses the prevalence of eight traditional dimensions of culture occurring during online learning team interaction. A study with graduate students, who were experienced in virtual teamwork, provides quotes and examples of experiences, challenges, and suggestions for improvement to the multi-cultural, virtual team experience. The students' suggestions inform guidelines for e-learning faculty and students, while additional study results present understanding of the acculturation process, a process that occurs when diversified social and cultural characteristics come together and form a cultural hybrid to accomplish e-learning team goals.

Introduction

Our team contained a WASP, an Armenian émigré, and a Jewish British ex-Pat on the team. Without being able to be specific, we all brought our differing viewpoints to bear on the problem and each rejoiced in our different ways of looking at things.

For two of us, our diasporas commonalities also gave us strength in the team without being excluding to the third member. Our openness in expressing our differences celebrated and took advantage of our diversity and contributed to our genuine delight in each other and to the team's success. (Online graduate student, 2004)

The increased availability of e-learning has brought convenience and equitable learning possibilities to cross-cultural student populations. The online student classroom may contain diversified student identities: residents from several countries, those who are native to one country, but now living in the U.S., and English as second language learners. Reaching beyond traditional limits of geographical boundaries and time constraints, virtual classrooms provide diversified groups of students with opportunities for discussion, planning, and team projects (Cyrs, 1997; Ess, 2001; Johnson & Johnson, 1994; Ko & Rossen, 2004; Palloff & Pratt, 1999; Rogers, 2002). The online classrooms merge social theory and learning theory, mixing technology, culture, identity, and community (Bandura, 2001; Collins & Berge, 1996; Khalsa & Hildreth, 2000; LaBelle, 2004; Preece, 2000; Wenger, 2004). Traditional team processes take on a new look, as online students are required to adapt and acculturate social and cultural characteristics during virtual teamwork (English-Lueck, Darrah, & Saveri, 2002).

The intentions of this chapter are to present e-learning faculty and students with a practical model for development and support of multi-cultural teamwork in the adult e-learning classroom. The study was designed to answer this question, "Which traditional social and cultural characteristics are important for multi-cultural e-learning team members?" Over a one-year period, 45 graduate students, who had been engaged in teamwork during their online classes, were surveyed and interviewed. The goal was to obtain opinions and suggestions about their general, online team experience, communication, challenges, social and cultural influences, and suggestions for improvement to the virtual team experience. Through description of influential social and cultural characteristics, graduate students provided their top priorities for faculty and fellow students, who will be involved with virtual learning teams. The student suggestions built a guiding framework, and are included in this chapter.

Background

E-learning can benefit from the creation and sharing of knowledge vs. merely long-established knowledge transfer and assimilation. Extending communication and knowledge through collaboration presents opportunities for a collective effort of understanding (Berge, 1998; Bielaczyc & Collins, 1999; Camarinha-Matos & Afsarmanesh, 2004; Dede, 1999; LaBelle, 2004). Online learning teams provide "a dynamic mix of national, geographic, organizational and professional or disciplinary variables in constant inter-action with one another, (changing) according to the context" (Heaton, 2001, p. 220). Online learning that incorporates team-based interactions creates community. It also extends a learning advantage to its adult students, because it mirrors the authentic interaction needed and developing in many educational and organizational settings and practices (Dede, 2001).

E-learning team interactions require intellectual, emotional, and social support, some unlearning, relearning, and deep appreciation for the innovative process and what it will provide team members. Virtual team acculturation is acceptance of another's cultural patterns of behavior (Heusinkveld, 1997) and requires an awareness and interaction of personal social and cultural dimensions in a virtual time, space, and workplace (English-Lueck et al., 2002). The study results provided in this chapter supply verbatim student descriptions and examples related to the adaptation of social and cultural characteristics during multi-cultural team processes (Alexander, 2000; Kezsbom, 2000; Lipnack & Stamps, 2000; Powell, Piccoli, & Blake, 2004; Solomon, 2001; Suchan & Hayzak, 2001). The results of this research created guidelines for the hybrid temporary learning team towards the ultimate goal, efficient and effective achievement of learning goals. This study informs students on how to become more effective team members and helps e-learning teachers become more efficient team guides. An initial examination of general multi-cultural team characteristics creates an awareness of challenges during a virtual team process.

Multi-Cultural Team Characteristics

Teams have been defined as individuals who are interdependent in their tasks, share responsibilities for outcomes, and manage their relationships across organizational boundaries (Cohen & Bailey, 1997; Godar & Ferris, 2004). Global teams within organiza-tions choose members from around the world and rarely meet members face-to-face. They are required to "share information, adapt to time constraints and establish effective relationships at a distance, often under trying political and cultural circumstances" (English-Lueck et al., 2002, p. 92). The same types of conditions exist for diversified online learning teams (Khalsa, 2005).

Short and temporary time frames towards completion of team projects require members to engage in interdependent tasks with common goals and individual competencies, including different levels of technology proficiency (Gibbs, 2002; Godar & Ferris, 2004). Team members represent different cultures, languages, and organizations, as they interact to form and establish common goals. E-learning team endeavors include: diversity of expertise among its members; shared objectives of advancing the collective knowledge and skills; emphasis on learning how to learn; and mechanisms for sharing what is learned (Bielaczyc & Collins, 1999; Johnson & Johnson, 1994). For virtual learning teams to be engaged, motivated, and attain their goals, important considerations need attention.

Overview of E-Learning
Team Considerations

Numerous areas of research provide clarifying information towards proper e-learning team facilitation and sustainability. Andragogy or adult learning theory provides advice on authentic and flexible learning to serve adult career goals and overloaded work schedules (Knowles, 1984). The field of human-computer interaction adds technological suggestions to aid credibility, usability, and dependability of technology (Fogg, 2003; Maloney-Kritchmar & Preece, 2002; Preece, 2000; Shneidermann, 2003). Online community research provides assistance for facilitation, netiquette, lurking, and reciprocity (Nonnecke & Preece, 2003; Preece, 2000; Preece, Sharp, & Rogers, 2002). Research also connects identity, computer-mediated communication, and cross-cultural relationships to social capital and development of trust (Bos, Olson, Gergle, Olson, & Wright, 2002; Cohen & Prusak, 2001; Preece, 2000; Rovai, 2001; Sproull & Kiesler, 1986; Walter, 1996).

Most online team research has emphasized benefits, technological guidelines, processes, and content development with less emphasis on the effects of social and cultural characteristics on team endeavors (Gibbs, 2004). However, online learning team social and cultural influences affect many aspects of teamwork, including roles, activities, expectations, and interpretations of time (Adler & Graham, 1989; Gibbs, 2002; Hall, 1977; Hofstede, 1997; Matei & Ball-Rokeach, 2002; Rheingold, 1993; Walther, 1996). A framework for discussing social and cultural characteristics in online learning teams that will be used here incorporates three key components: social learning theory, identity theory in a collaborative culture, and the acculturation process. Each component adds to the understanding of multi-cultural interaction in online learning teams.

Social Learning Theory

The social learning theory describes a small part of the budding, yet vibrant image of learning in the world today (Bandura, 2001; Wenger, 2004). It explains how thoughts, feelings, and behavior are affected by the presence or implied presence of others (Bandura, 1986). The social and cultural context of the individual, how they perceive and interpret information from others, is the basis of this theory. Simply stated, people observe, imitate, and learn socially. Cognitive skills, attitudes, and behavior impact the environment, and the environment impacts these personal factors (Huitt, 2004; Huitt & Vessels, 2002). This creates an interchange between three variables: overt behavior, personal factors, and environmental factors (Wenger, 2004).

Individuals exist and act within a broad network of environmental structures: imposed, selected, and constructed (Bandura, 2001). The boundaries of influence have been broadened by environmental structures offered by the Internet and technology and as a result, traditional social and cultural characteristics are modified. The socio-structural influences such as roles, rules, and social practices, which normally regulate thought and behavior, exist with broader interpretation. The interplay of social and cultural forces with social learning such as online course discussions and online teamwork enhance course goals, objectives and e-learning possibilities.

By recognizing the power of technology on present-day social and cultural characteristics, one can better understand how team behavior is impacted (Huitt, 2002) and how cognitive skills, attitudes, behaviors, and the environment influence each other (Bandura, 1986). Social learning theory extends relevancy to adult learning needs and provides a description of how intrapersonal and interpersonal information is perceived. "Within this theoretical framework, human functioning is analyzed as socially interdependent, richly contextualized and conditionally orchestrated within the dynamics of various societal subsystems and their complex interplay" (Bandura, 2001, p. 5). Personal identity intersects with the virtual team identity and requires adaptation or acculturation.

Identity in a Collaborative Culture

A personal identity is "a set of attributes, beliefs, desires, or principles of action that a person thinks distinguish her (or him) in socially relevant ways" (Fearon, 1999, p. 2). Personal identity often engulfs group identity, allowing for unique experiences of thought, learning, and action. Identities are shaped through a group experience, built and maintained because of practice and recognized by members in the practice. Thus, characteristics of community become dimensions of identity (Zheng & Storck, 2001). When an individual's identity and perception are verified by a group, then group membership is recognized (Meng & Agarwal, 2005; Polzer, Milton, & Swann, 2002).

"People (interacting) move together in a kind of dance" (Hall, 1997, p. 72). Personal and social identities interact and are sustained through creation and transference of knowledge between community members (Butler, 2001). "Learning is a social becoming, the ongoing negotiation of an identity, that we develop in the context of participation (and non-participation) in communities and their practices" (Wenger, 2004, p. 4). Continual construction and reconstruction of self-identity requires fluidity during virtual interactions. Attention to acculturation or adaptability of self and group identity during e-learning team interactions can help fulfill online student team needs (Meng & Agarwal, 2005; Sudwicks & Ess, 2002).

Acculturation in E-Learning Teams

Virtual team acculturation is an individual's ability to adapt to the cultural behavior patterns of others (Heusinkveld, 1997) and requires shifting interdependence among strangers (English-Lueck et al., 2002). Members intermix, and team member thoughts and actions are usually most affected by ethnicity, social and political circumstances, and physical location. However, because of prevalent technology use, cultural influences have become less stagnant and stereotypical. Individuals are seeing themselves and are seen by others as social entities embedded in larger social systems (Fernandez-Ballesteros,

Diez-Nicolas, Caprara, Barbaranelli, & Bandura, 2002; Powell et al., 2004; Wenger, 2004). The powerful socio-cultural forces that are rooted in social and cultural history, and choices that predate them (Matei & Ball-Rokeach, 2002), now function in an interdependent, ephemeral, virtual, and multi-cultural global team setting (Gibbs, 2002). Considering the complexity of human beings, their multi-faceted identity with many cultures and subcultures, and interactions in e-learning teamwork, it is no longer clear how far native social and cultural characteristics accurately explain human behavior in a virtual world (Sudwicks & Ess, 2002).

Socio-Cultural Constructs in E-Learning Teams

Social and cultural characteristics or constructs, also referred to here as dimensions of culture, describe shared, ethnic, geographic, and collective behaviors and patterns resulting from the fabric of a society. Hall (1977, 1990) researched in detail patterns of different cultures. His findings noted that there are cultural perceptual differences related to time, space, relationships, and materials (Hall, 1977). Hofstede (1984) studied values of people in different cultures, who worked for the same multinational corporation. His results were very similar to a study done 20 years earlier (Inkeles & Levinson, 1969) and resulted in four dimensions:

1.   Power including perceptions of wealth and status

2.   Uncertainty avoidance including perceptions of rules, regulations, and flexibility

3.   Individualism including perceptions on self-reliance, group harmony, and team recognition

4.   Gender including perceptions on competition, assertiveness, and nurturance or support in teamwork

It is also advantageous to note Storti's research (1990, 1998) that built on Hall and Hofstede's work. Storti related culture to business and provided two dimensions, invisible (assumptions, values and beliefs) and visible (behaviors). He described these dimensions as building blocks of socio-cultural differences. His list includes perceptions of self-identity, group identity, time, and power. However, the foundations and practical applications of the more traditional dimension of culture frameworks (Hall, 1977; Hofstede, 2001; Inkeles & Levinson, 1969; Storti, 1990, 1998) require further investigation for determination of relevancy and applicability to multi-cultural e-learning team situations. "(The) traditional notions of culture are becoming less and less applicable in a world where cultures have increasingly permeable boundaries and are blurred and blended through globalization" (Gibbs, 2002, p. 9).

After comparing the socio-cultural constructs or dimensions from the four previously mentioned frameworks (Hall, 1977; Hofstede, 2001; Inkeles & Levinson, 1969; Storti, 1990, 1998), there is strong evidence of the relationship between self-identity, group identity, and group harmony. Individual perceptions related to the following dimensions affect group actions: power, status, recognition, assertiveness, competitiveness, gender, leadership, time, flexibility, support, nurturance, rules, and regulations. These social and cultural characteristics became the base for coding survey and interview text in the online graduate student study described in this chapter.

Online Graduate Student Study

In order to better inform online students, educators, and facilitators, opinions and suggestions from adult online students with virtual team experience were obtained. The research question to be answered was, "Which traditional social and cultural characteristics are important for multi-cultural e-learning team members?" The goal was to obtain opinions and suggestions about student online team experiences, challenges, communication, social and cultural influences, and suggestions for improvement to the virtual team experience.

Participants

The participants for this study were 45 online graduate students (22 females and 23 males) enrolled in two online programs with two universities in the state of California. The researcher of this study (also the author of this chapter) had been teaching in these online programs for over five years, and was familiar with the population of students that these online programs attracted. She describes this sample as a multi-cultural group of adult students with a variety of career goals and experiences including corporate online training, K-12 teaching, university, business and military distance education development, and so forth. Each student's graduate studies was related to technology and learning.

The particular cultural backgrounds of the students had not been specifically determined to protect their privacy. However, the majority is currently located in the U.S. but have a variety of international, native backgrounds. Some did share their native cultural identity, and that information determined multi-cultural backgrounds, which included U.S. citizens living in other countries, natives from a variety of countries including Bangladesh, Oman, Honduras, China, and others. Some students were natives from outside the U.S., but had been living in the U.S. for two to six years. Overall the participants had a fair amount of technology skills and displayed an appreciation for technology-related opportunities shown by their choice of technology-related careers. They had each been involved in virtual teamwork and online learning communities during their online classes and careers.

Methods

Text was acquired from semi-structured and unstructured answers obtained through online surveys and email interviews during a one-year period. The initial interview questions are available in Appendix A. The author coded the interview text using a codebook that contained eight socio-cultural characteristics. These characteristics we all previously determined important by dimension of culture frameworks (Hall, 1977; Hofstede, 2001; Inkeles & Levinson, 1969; Storti, 1990, 1998). The codebook highlights are available in Appendix B.

Results

Dimensions (Appendix B) noted in traditional socio-cultural frameworks by Hall (1977), Hofstede (2001), Inkeles & Levinson (1969), and Storti (1990, 1998), were mentioned as important by graduate students in this study. The frequency of student responses related to socio-cultural constructs during the surveys and interviews is graphically displayed (Figure 1).

Details and interpretations of each dimension are provided next through a summary that connects theory, student suggestions, and quotes. Specific cultural backgrounds of the students are not provided, so generalization of study results to online classrooms and virtual teamwork would assume that student populations have comparatively similar adult demographics.

Figure 1. Percentage of frequency for socio-cultural constructs

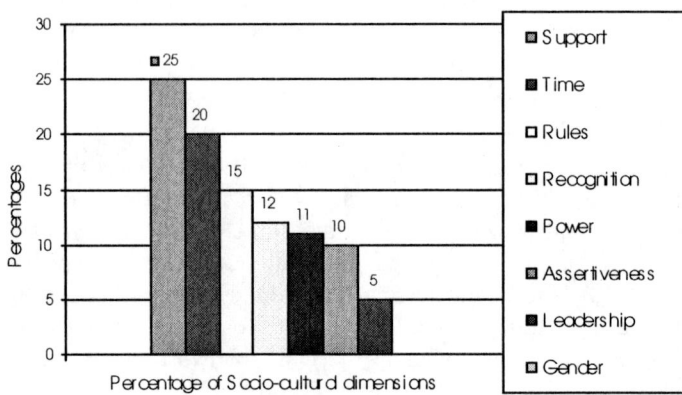

Team Support

According to comments made by the graduate students in this study, team support includes sharing ideas, communicating positively and frequently with constructive criticism, alternative viewpoints, and professionalism. Students, who noted lack of team support, made comments on workload inequality, lack of communication, and noted a particular team member, who did not do their part. Differences of interpretation related to team support often had to do with recognition and respect for what an individual offered the group. This recognition and need for acknowledgment and respect may be tied to original or native social and cultural preferences, but further research would be needed to determine if a particular native culture preferred higher recognition level than others.

These student quotes are good representatives of facets of team support noted by the majority of students in this study. Note the English as a second-language challenge that could easily be misinterpreted by inconsiderate student team members or easily intimidated ESL students.

The team experience was such a joy, the members of the team were able to communicate often, share ideals, set goals and objectives. The team members were extremely knowledgeable in their field of expertise and shared constructive criticism and positive interaction ... (the) team experience was the greatest.

Each person, (whom) I've worked with has been very understanding, helpful, considerate, and focused upon the subject at hand.

These quotes display well lack of team support:

One person did not pull their weight so the remainder of the group simply got on with it without waiting and did the weak person's work as well. We didn't have time to sit around and whine and wait. We just finished it off.

Two of the team members didn't fully participate in the project. One claimed poor English skills, the other personal problems; but it's my grade and so I worked with (R) to produce a good paper!

Recognition

The social learning theory explains how thoughts, feelings, and behavior are affected by the presence or implied presence of others (Bandura, 1986). Often the dimension of recognition was related to individual perceptions of respect. The social and cultural context of the individual, how they perceive and interpret information from others, is the basis of this theory. For example, one team member's assertiveness often resulted in the lack of recognition or perceived respect of another teammate. The representative quotes below display the overlapping effects of three socio-cultural characteristics: power/ status, recognition, and assertiveness. Note the strong emphasis on cultural values in the last quote, as well as the need for definitions and boundaries related to respect.

One member repeatedly edited out another member's contributions to the project ... it was interpreted as disrespect because permission was not sought first ... The hurt party spoke to the other members about the incident, and we in turn encouraged that person to speak with the other team member to resolve the issue personally.

Simply put, if I have respect for you, I will naturally give your ideas and opinions due consideration. If I don't have this respect, it will be easy to disregard your input.

If I feel respected by the rest of the team, I am more likely to be actively participating in the team actions.

But in the end—the individual's perception on what is respectful or disrespectful is going to be the determining factor. And an individual perception is based on their culture of origin, the culture their family of origin and the culture of their community.

Time and Flexibility

Social and cultural influences affect many aspects of teamwork including roles, activities, expectations, and interpretations of time (Adler & Graham, 1989; Gibbs, 2002; Hall, 1977; Hofstede, 1997; Matei & Ball-Rokeach, 2002; Rheingold, 1993; Walther, 1996). Students gave advice towards authentic and flexible learning to serve adult career goals and overloaded work schedules (Knowles, 1984).

These students were engaged in projects with time frames of three months or less and worked virtually. They noted remedies to time challenges, which included acceptance of diversity, time zone differences, tolerance, and a willingness to put forth extra personal effort. The following quotes are representative of diversified students' interpretations of time and flexibility and the general emphases on respect and trust as recommended solutions.

When deadlines approached, and teamwork was needed, the process was clumsy, frustrating, and often times counterproductive. We did not meet our deadline because we had a very difficult time working together. The frustration of the group didn't improve until the topic of respect and trust had been addressed.

I never allowed my personal time limitations (to) affect other members—I worked through entire nights without any sleep, to make sure our group assignments were delivered on time.

(I was) able to jump in and save the day, if needed, to ensure the product would be fine on deadline.

My background helped a lot ... I manage a team that is all virtual—I have staff in California, Utah, Canada, Switzerland, and India ... I am very attuned to different time zones, different cultures, different processes, and different personalities ... I am not afraid to take the lead when I see the group wandering.

Power and Status

When an individual's identity and perception are verified by a group, then group membership is recognized (Meng & Agarwal, 2005; Polzer, Milton, & Swann, 2002). Individual identities often include levels of status or power. Most of the students noted giving up power whenever they are involved in team projects. However, just as many students felt that the quality of the learning experience during teamwork was well worth the extra effort. Note the last quote that mentions the ill effects of humor in virtual teamwork. Many identity references are evident in the quotes below:

With my individual paper, I had greater control (over) the process and outcomes (content, research approach, writing style, editing, etc.). But I did not have input of other ideas or feedback ... With the team paper there was collaboration, brainstorming and more support to write, research, and edit the paper. The challenge was to harmonize different points of view, writing styles and availability schedules. Doing this also trained us to work in groups, to be tolerant and supportive of the group.

Power is also noted from perceptions of status and recognition:

Honestly, I thought my second group was going to be terrible. There was one group member who I thought would not contribute anything. But I was surprised when he brought more to the table than I expected, and the project was improved as a result.

Challenges? Different time zones. Different study skills and habits. Different abilities.

One of the team members thought my idea on the topic as nothing. And I did not want to argue with him. But I was upset and frustrated. So I just followed the team and do my part.

I still cannot melt into the (online) class as a native speaker even though I have been US for 6 years ... I don't get humor or jokes, which is ok. But if our peers' discussion mentions some famous people in this field or other fields, and I have no idea what are they talking about. That's really bad.

Assertiveness

Virtual team acculturation is acceptance of another's cultural patterns of behavior (Heusinkveld, 1997). Personal identity intersects with the virtual team identity and requires adaptation or acculturation. The students in this study reported overall excellent team experiences with no serious complaints about overly assertive team members. Instead, the majority of students seemed to pay special attention to being too assertive and understanding perceptions from each individual in the team.

I also feel that the online environment with educated, empathetic students does hinder full-blooded debate that would be possible in the F2F situation. Without paralinguistic clues we are always second-guessing the emotion of the writer and thus we all try to avoid causing offence. This can, I feel, stifle what could be more interesting debates.

(My biggest challenge is) not taking over everything. Letting other members of the groups get their part done, and trusting that they would do it right.

Unless other members speak out to correct the misbehavior, the community would have been robbed of something very precious—trust—the foundation of Constructivism.

The worse part is when people tend to paraphrase what I mean to help the others get a clearer meaning. I feel insulted ... as if I could not communicate well.

Other students felt comfortable as followers:

I don't have (much) teamwork experience, so I just follow the trend. If I am ready to be a team leader, I think I will make my point clearly in order to avoid conflict or confusing.

I am not sure how to handle the situation if two people are all interested in being the team leaders.

Rules and Guidelines

Extending communication and knowledge through collaboration presents opportunities for a collective effort of understanding (Berge, 1998; Bielaczyc & Collins, 1999; Camarinha-Matos & Afsarmanesh, 2004; Dede, 1999; LaBelle, 2004). Team rules were noted by the majority of students as being important to team project quality and completion. There were many suggestions for initial guidelines and rules that could eliminate confusion and ineffectiveness. The socio-structural influences, such as roles, rules, and social practices that normally regulate thought and behavior, may exist with broader interpretation if initial discussion is prolific, as displayed in these student quotes:

- Suggest a format for members to reintroduce themselves with tombstone data, time zone, industry, restrictions (and/or) other commitments for the period.

- Discuss the topic, workloads, and schedule (of) each team member.

- Common understanding of the requirements of the assignment.

- Maintain good rules of Netiquette.

- Communicate on a daily or at least regular basis

- Trust that the work quality will be high and state those expectations up front.

- Discuss a method of communication. We used too many forms and it caused delays.

- Set up a blog and post ... group guidelines. These expectations kept everyone on track (related to) what was expected of each member.

- Ensure the team members have a similar time frame for working on the course (some prefer early week, some weekends).

- Get the team to choose roles and communicate those roles before the work actually begins.

- Have teams...compile guidelines, but also provide a weekly "report" (to the instructor) of how each of the guidelines is being implemented.

Leadership

"Learning is a social becoming, the ongoing negotiation of an identity, that we develop in the context of participation...in communities and their practice" (Wenger, 2004, p. 4). One form of meaningful identity established in most virtual teamwork is leadership. Leadership and assertiveness often serve each other. Many students noted the need for one main team leader or a plan to alternate the leadership role.

I am very competitive about earning my grades and will do whatever it takes to make a project work ... so when the group wasn't coming together well, I emailed the de facto group leader and we worked it out.

Finding a leader was a challenge in the first teamwork. I tried to instill order but was essentially ignored. Luckily, we are all professional so the task was completed.

The leadership challenge—I have been in situations like this before and tend to try and organize things myself and become the team leader.

Many students also noted their perception of a preferred leader:

I personally prefer the leader to be very formal and directing or even demanding...group project deadlines are always tight. If the leader is very democratic, it will be hard to move on and meet the schedule.

The global thinking sort of leader always plays a great role in inviting all team players to present all ideas on the table. When a great deal of trust is established, the team can then decide which of the ideas are best to work off of.

The leader really can't be VERY democratic or nothing would get done. Instead, the leader needs to listen, evaluate, and decide. The style I prefer in a leader is for him/her to be decisive but not autocratic, taking in information from many or all sources, but not paralyzed or overwhelmed by the weight of decision.

We worked as a self-managing team sharing thoughts and ideas and coming to a consensus rather than as a leader subordinate situation.

Gender

There were 22 females and 23 males in this study. Gender issues were part of the traditional frameworks that were discussed earlier (Hall, 1977; Hofstede, 1984). "(The) traditional notions of culture are becoming less and less applicable in a world where cultures have increasingly permeable boundaries and are blurred and blended through globalization" (Gibbs, 2002, p. 9). However, with this group of students, only two females noted any bias or gender issues. Lack of gender notes may be due to development and emphasis of survey and interview questioning or actual lack of gender bias experiences. More research on this topic is necessary for guidelines to be applied to adult online learners. Here is a sample quote that sums up the opinions of two females who noted gender issues:

(I was in) a forum of members with diverse philosophies ... some of those philosophies were against principles of equality and justice ... I felt not only negativity in these male members ... but also racial and gender biases coming from their own upbringing and socio-cultural environments.

Summary

This study highlights team members' ability to accept diversity with a tolerance and a willingness to put forth extra effort and even take the lead, if the group begins to wander. Comments emphasized respect and trust and not being too assertive. Global thinking that invites all team players to present all ideas can help with the understanding and involvement of students' diversified perceptions.

During this study, each of the eight categories of traditional, socio-cultural dimensions held substantial influence on multi-cultural e-learning teams. The differences between interpretations of these dimensions may be due to participants' cultural backgrounds. Further specific research among additional demographic groups is needed. However, if the following framework of suggestions is applied to adult U.S. online learning programs that incorporate diversified populations of students, virtual teamwork will most likely become more effective and the online educator more efficient.

These graduate students provided their top priorities for faculty and fellow students, who will be involved with virtual learning teams. Their suggestions built this main framework:

- Provide flexibility and democracy for choosing team members, topics, and group roles.

- Each student needs to provide the team tombstone data, time zone, industry, restrictions/other commitments.

- Emphasize the importance of guidelines, which should include team norms and styles, a detailed timeline, a description of the communication process and frequency, rules of cultural etiquette, and division of responsibilities (roles).

- A group leader needs to be clearly named even if the leader rotates from week to week.

Student suggestions also provided an instructor's layer to this framework:

- Give suggestions for communicating better in teams.

- Outline a simple project schedule for teams to adopt.

- Create a strong team self-assessment at the end of the first phase of the teamwork.

- Require a weekly report related to implementation of the team guidelines.

- Require an interim draft of the paper or project.

- Provide a self-assessment inventory, which helps determine teamwork styles and strengths.

- Allow team building to start and continue beyond the limits of one course.

Future Trends

As a result of an expanding global economy, emerging technologies and the popularity of online coursework, opportunities for virtual teamwork will increase. Business and education will find cultural boundaries blurred more frequently, and virtual multi-cultural interactions will become more common. As authentic interaction and application of learning become a more common recommendation for adult online education, e-learning teams will become more necessary. Virtual teamwork provides not only effectiveness in learning, but also authentic application of skills for career choices. If instructors and students use the highlights of this study to create discussion and learning development for their student audiences, multi-cultural e-learning teams can promote extended learning opportunities and objectives.

Conclusions

This chapter has discussed the social learning theory's relationship to multi-cultural e-learning teams, which exist as an intersection of technology, identity, culture, and community. Online graduate students have provided evidence of online learning team effectiveness and challenges. The study informs readers of the necessity of virtual team guidelines and policies that hold respect for diversified opinions and personalities. Virtual teamwork mirrors the authentic interactions required in many educational and organizational settings and practices. The results, thus, add attention to the importance of virtual teamwork.

Virtual communities have expanded the realm of cultural influence and encouraged another look at traditional socio-cultural constructs to determine their importance in the online collaborative classrooms. Comments and suggestions from online graduate students, who were experienced with virtual learning teams, built a framework of suggestions for adult students and faculty, and validated the importance of the traditional dimensions (Hall, 1977; Hofstede, 2001; Inkeles & Levinson, 1969; Storti, 1990, 1998). Finally, we have come full circle, learning that the establishment of personal identity is interwoven and acculturates with group collaborative culture in e-learning teams. Diversified online student populations can balance and intersect many different perspectives through awareness of dominant socio-cultural characteristics in virtual teamwork. Attention to acculturation or adaptability of self and group identity during e-learning team interactions can help fulfill online student team needs (Meng & Agarwal, 2005; Sudwicks & Ess, 2002).

References

Adler, N. J., & Graham, J. L. (1989). Cross-cultural interaction: The international comparison fallacy? *Journal of International Business Studies, 20*(3), 515-537.

Alexander, S. (2000). Virtual teams going global. *InfoWorld, 22*(6), 55-56.

Axelrod, R. (1984). *The evolution of cooperation.* New York: Basic Books.

Bandura, A. (1986). *Social foundations of thought and action: A social cognitive theory.* Englewood Cliffs, NJ: Prentice-Hall.

Bandura, A. (2001). Social cognitive theory: An agentic perspective. *Annual Review of Psychology, 52,* 1-26.

Berge, Z. L. (1998). Differences in teamwork between post-secondary classrooms and the workplace. *Education and Training, 40*(5), 194-201.

Bielaczyc, K., & Collins, A. (1999). Learning communities in classrooms: A reconceptualization of educational practice. In C. Reigeluth (Ed.), *Instructional-design theories and models: A new paradigm of instructional theory* (pp. 169-292). Mahwah, NJ: Lawrence Erlbaum Associates.

Bos, N., Olson, J., Gergle, D., Olson, G., & Wright, Z. (2002, April 20-25). *Effects of four computer-mediated communications channels on trust development.* Paper presented at the proceedings of CHI, Minneapolis, MN.

Butler, B. (2001). Membership size, communication activity, and sustainability: A resource based model of online social structures. *Information Systems Research, 12*(4), 346-362.

Camarinha-Matos, L. M., & Afsarmanesh, H. (2004). *Collaborative networked organizations: A research agenda for emerging business models.* Norwell, MA: Kluwer Academic Publishers.

Cohen, D., & Prusak, L. (2001). *In good company: How social capital makes organizations work.* Boston: Harvard Business School Press.

Cohen, S. G., & Bailey, D. E. (1997). What makes teams work: Group effectiveness research from the shop floor to the executive suite. *Journal of Management, 12*(3), 239-290.

Collins, M., & Berge, Z. (1996, June). *Facilitating interaction in computer mediated online courses.* Background paper for presentation at the FSU/AECT Distance Education Conference, Tallahassee, FL. Retrieved April 16, 2005, from http://www.emoderators.com/moderators/flcc.html

Cyrs, T. (1997). *Teaching and learning at a distance: What it takes to effectively design, deliver, and evaluate programs.* San Francisco: Jossey-Bass.

Dede. C. (1999). *The role of emerging technologies for knowledge mobilization, dissemination, and use in education.* Washington, DC: U.S. Education Department. Retrieved April 10, 2005, from http://www.virtual.gmu.edu/SS_research/cdpapers/mobilpdf.htm

Dede, C. (2001). *Creating research centers to enhance the effective use of learning technologies.* Testimony to the U.S. House of Representatives, Committee on Science, Research Subcommittee, May 10, 2001. Retrieved April 8, 2005, from http://www.house.gov/science/research/reshearings.htm

English-Lueck, J., Darrah, C., & Saveri, A. (2002). Trusting strangers: Work relationships in four-high tech communities. *Information, Communication, & Society, 5*(1), 90-108.

Ess, C. (2001). *Culture, technology, communication: Towards an intercultural global village.* Albany: State University of New York Press.

Fearon, J. (1999). *What is identity (as we now use the word)?* Unpublished manuscript. Stanford University, Stanford, CA (p. 2).

Fernández-Ballesteros, R., Díez-Nicolás J., Caprara, G. V., Barbaranelli, C., & Bandura, A. (2002). Determinants and structural relation of perceived personal efficacy to perceived collective efficacy. *Applied Psychology: An International Review, 51,* 107-125.

Fogg, B. J. (2003). *Persuasive technology: Using computers to change what we think and do.* Boston: Morgan Kaufmann Publishers.

Gibbs, J. (2002, July 15-19). *Loose coupling in global teams: Reconciling cultural tensions across space and time.* Paper presented at ICA Convention, Organizational Communication Division. Seoul, Korea. Retrieved March 19, 2005, at http://www.ohiou.edu/ica-orgcomm/GIBBSPAPER2002.pdf

Godar, S. H., & Ferris, S. P. (Eds). (2004). *Virtual and collaborative teams: Process, technologies, and practice.* Hershey, PA: Idea Group Publishing.

Hall, E. (1959). *The silent language.* Garden City, NY: Doubleday.

Hall, E. (1966). *The hidden dimension.* Garden City, NY: Doubleday.

Hall, E. (1976, 1977). *Beyond culture.* Garden City, NY: Doubleday.

Hall, E. (1990). *Understanding cultural differences.* Yarmouth, ME: Intercultural Press.

Heaton, L. (2001). Preserving communication context: Virtual workspace and interpersonal space in Japanese CSCW. In C. Ess & F. Sudweeks (Eds.), *Culture, technology, communication: Towards an intercultural global village* (pp. 213-240). Albany: State University of New York Press.

Heusinkveld, P. (1997). *Pathways to culture.* Yarmouth, ME: Intercultural Press.

Hofstede, G. (1984, 2001). *Culture's consequences: International differences in work-related values.* London: Sage Publications.

Hofstede, G. (1997). *Cultures and organizations: Software of the mind.* New York: McGraw-Hill.

Huitt, W. (2004). Bloom et al.'s taxonomy of the cognitive domain. *Educational Psychology Interactive.* Valdosta, GA: Valdosta State University. Retrieved April 20, 2005, at http://chiron.valdosta.edu/whuitt/col/cogsys/bloom.html

Huitt, W., & Vessels, G. (2002). Character education. In J. Guthrie (Ed.), *The encyclopedia of education.* New York: Macmillan.

Inkeles, A., & Levinson, D. (1969). National character: The study of modal personality and sociocultural systems. In.G. Lindzey & E. Aronson (Eds.), *The handbook of social psychology* (pp. 311-378). Boston, MA: Addison-Wesley.

Johnson, R., & Johnson, D. (1994). *Creativity and collaborative learning.* Baltimore, MD: Brookes Press.

Kezsbom, D. (2000). Creating teamwork in virtual teams. *Cost Engineering, 42*(10), 33-36.

Khalsa, D. K. (2005, July). *Online learning teams: Impact of socio-cultural dimensions.* Paper presented at the proceedings of Human Computer Interaction International Conference, Las Vegas, NV.

Khalsa, D. K., & Hildreth, S. (2000). *Finding a place for everyone: Creating, maintaining and evolving optimal online learning.* Ithaca, NY: Whole Life Education. Retrieved April 10, 2005, at http://www.wholelifeed.com/placeforeveryone.html

Knowles, M. (1984). *Andragogy in action.* San Francisco: Jossey-Bass.

Ko, S., & Rossen, S. (2004). *Teaching online: A practical guide.* New York: Houghton Mifflin Co.

LaBelle, D. (2004). *Before the team project: Cultivate a community of collaborators.* Proceedings of the 21st Annual Information Systems Education Conference (ISECON 2004). Retrieved August 8, 2005, from http://isedj.org/isecon/2004/0000/index.html

Lipnack, J., & Stamps, J. (2000). *Virtual teams: People working across boundaries with technology.* New York: John Wiley & Sons.

Matei, S., & Ball-Rokeach, S. (2002). Belonging in geographic, ethnic, and Internet spaces. In B. Wellman & C. Haythornwaite (Eds.), *The Internet in everyday life* (pp. 405-427). Malden, MA: Blackwell Publishing.

Meng, M., & Agarwal, R. (in press). Sustaining virtual communities: The role of identity consonance and community artifacts. *Organizational Behavior and Human Decision Processes.*

Nonnecke, B., & Preece, J. (2003). Silent participants: Getting to know lurkers better. In C. Leug & D. Fisher (Eds.), From *Usenet to CoWebs: Interacting with social information spaces* (pp. 110-132). Amsterdam; Holland: Springer-Verlag.

Palloff, R., & Pratt, K. (1999). *Building learning communities in cyberspace: Effective strategies for the online classroom.* San Francisco: Jossey-Bass.

Polzer, J. T., Milton, L. P., & Swann, W. B. (2002). Capitalizing on diversity: Interpersonal congruence in small work groups. *Administrative Science Quarterly, 47*(2), 296-324.

Powell, A., Piccoli, G., & Blake, I. (2004). Virtual teams: A review of current literature and directions for future. *Data Base Advances in Information Systems, 35*(1), 6-36.

Preece, J. (2000). *Online communities: Designing usability, supporting sociability.* New York: John Wiley & Sons.

Preece, J. (Ed.). (2002). Supporting community and building social capital. Special edition of *Communications of the ACM, 45*(4), 37-39.

Preece, J., & Maloney-Krichmar, D. (2003). Online communities. In Jacko & Sears (Eds.), *Handbook of human-computer interaction* (pp. 596-620). Mahwah, NJ: Lawrence Erlbaum Associates Inc.

Preece, J., Sharp, H., & Rogers, Y. (2002). *Interaction design: Beyond human-computer interaction.* New York: John Wiley & Sons.

Rheingold, H. (1993). *The virtual community: Homesteading on the electronic frontier.* Reading, MA: Addison-Wesley.

Rogers, P. (2002). *Designing instruction for technology-enhanced learning.* Hershey, PA: Idea Group Publishing.

Rovai, A. (2001). Classroom community at a distance: A comparative analysis of two ALN-based university programs. *Internet and Higher Education, 4,* 105-118.

Shneiderman, B. (2002). *Leonardo's laptop: Human needs and the new computing technologies.* Cambridge, MA: The MIT Press.

Sproull, L., & Kiesler, S. (1995). Computers, networks, and work. *Scientific American: The Computer in the 21st Century, 6*(1), 116-123.

Storti, C. (1990). *The art of crossing cultures.* Boston: Intercultural Press Inc.

Storti, C. (1998). *Figuring foreigners out.* Boston: Intercultural Press Inc.

Sudweeks, F., & Ess, C. (2002, July). Cultural attitudes towards technology and communication. *Proceedings of the 3rd International Conference on Cultural Attitudes towards Technology and Communication,* Montreal, Canada (pp. 69-88)

Walther, J. (1996). Computer mediated communication: Impersonal, interpersonal, and hyperpersonal interaction. *Communication Research, 23*(1), 3-43.

Wenger, E. (2004). *Learning for a small planet: A research agenda.* Unpublished paper, Institute for Research on Learning, North San Juan, CA. Retrieved April 5, 2004, from http://www.ewenger.com/research

Zhang, W., & Storck, J. (2001). Peripheral members in online communities. *Americas' Conference on Information Systems (AMCIS), 8*(1), 29-38.

Appendix A.
Initial Questions for Graduate Students

- How would you describe each of your team experiences in this online class?

- Were there any surprises related to communication with teams in this online class?

- What was your most challenging factor related to team involvement in this online course?

- What part did your background play in dealing with this challenge?

- What three improvements would you suggest to consolidate the strengths of working in teams?

- How would you contrast your experience of preparing an individual paper with your e-learning team paper?

Appendix B: Socio-Cultural Dimensions

Power/status	Rules/regulations
Recognition	Flexibility/time
Assertiveness/competitiveness	Support/nurturance
Gender issues	Leadership

Chapter XIX

Modern Technology and Mass Education:
A Case Study of a Global Virtual Learning System

Ahmed Ali
University of Wisconsin - LaCrosse, USA

Abstract

This case study examined the effectiveness and significance of the Internet and interactive video broadcasting as instructional and communication media in a global virtual learning system. The study explored how differences in students' technology experiences, curriculum, cultures, and access to technology influence learning and student attitude in a technology-based distance education environment. The research also investigated whether the use of online references and materials is adequate and appropriate for successful distance learning. The setting was a virtual campus that linked universities in the U.S., Australia, and Canada with learning centers in different African countries. E-mail and face-to-face interviews, observations, and Web-based surveys were utilized to collect the data. The study reveals that students had mixed perceptions about the effectiveness of technology, with positive attitudes exhibited towards interactive video and some anxiety and dissatisfaction with the use of the Internet.

Breaking Campus Barriers

Distance learning has been touted as a viable alternative to classroom learning because it allows students to obtain relevant knowledge in their preferred style and time. The existence of various technologies such as interactive video and the Internet facilitate and promote distance education. The Internet, in particular, has become an increasingly important medium for providing instruction in distance education (Simonson, Smaldino, Albright, & Zvacek, 2003). Studies report that traditional teaching and learning may not effectively respond to the learning styles of 21st century students (U.S. Department of Education, 2000). Schools and universities are adopting the Internet as an instructional delivery medium that can complement, and in some circumstances change, traditional classroom instruction.

This change has already begun, propelled by diverse programs ranging from Web-enhanced learning to full-fledged online learning. Virtual schools and colleges have sprung up, and the Web has become an important medium for distance learning. One program with the pseudonym, the Pioneer Global Campus, has created a global virtual learning system that connects universities in developed countries to learning centers in Africa. As a consortium of several universities worldwide, the Pioneer Global Campus is unique in its global focus unlike other major distance education programs that are regional in scope.

Rising educational costs, limited opportunities for qualified students in local universities, and a desire to utilize technology led to the development of the Pioneer Global Campus. This virtual university was created to provide African students with access to education in diverse fields such as science, technology, journalism, languages, and accounting. The university has graduated several thousand students since it was founded during the second half of the nineties.

The university operates by creating partnerships with institutions of higher learning in the United States, Canada, and Australia. The external university partner accredits the programs. Individuals who participate in the program include students pursuing degrees in the receiving country as well as individuals interested in short-term, non-credit courses that do not have entry requirements. This makes the Pioneer Global Campus a mass education institution that caters and appeals to diverse individuals and groups.

Various communication technologies are utilized to deliver content at a distance and to facilitate communication between students and instructors. The Internet and interactive video broadcasting are two common instructional channels. Over 50 learning centers in more than 20 African countries are equipped with satellite and Internet technologies. Students attend the learning centers to receive instruction via video broadcasting and the Internet.

Distance Learning: Use of the Internet

Use of the Internet for education is common in the developed world, though there is increasing need for online education in the developing world (Zembylas & Vrasidas, 2005). In the developed world, educators and students use the Internet to supplement classroom learning. The Internet is also increasingly utilized as a distance education medium.

Whichever way the Internet is used, the potential of the Internet as an instructional tool and instructional medium has been recognized globally. To integrate technology in distance learning, learning experiences should not based on traditional classroom concepts of teacher-directed instruction, but rather should include interactive learning principles that apply student-centered learning styles. Further, it is important to consider the audience for which online education is developed because, "in a global context, online course designers and teachers may face many questions concerning how to design and teach across geographical, social, linguistic, and cultural distances..." (Zembylas & Vrasidas, p. 62)

Scholars and practitioners have talked and written about the application of online learning. Miller, Rainer, and Corley (2003) posit that although Web-based learning has tremendous potential, poor application can be detrimental to effective learning. Poor pedagogical and course management practices can negatively affect learning as traditional classroom techniques do not necessarily work in an online environment. For example, factors such as lack of structure and organization, poor time management on the part of instructors, and lack of interaction can hinder the effectiveness of the online medium as an ideal instructional tool.

Online communication may supplement traditional classroom meetings and discussions. Discussion and dialogue are extended beyond the classroom meeting times through online discussion forums. However, in a study of online discussion boards, Warner (2003) found that online and traditional students were concerned about slow Internet connections, limited computer experience, anxiety about computer skills, and limited Web experience. Warner further reported that course-related concerns raised by the students include: lack of motivation for online discussions and participation, teachers not requiring students to use discussion boards, and lack of interesting discussion topics. Personal concerns raised by the students include time and inconvenience, though Warner stated that both online and traditional students had these similar concerns.

Considerable emphasis has been placed on developing best practices for online teaching. However, in an age when the constructivism mantra is common, considering student learning preferences and technology abilities is crucial. As a student-centered instructional theory, constructivism allows students to construct their own knowledge and meaning.

Methodology

This case study (Stake, 1995) is about the use of technology, particularly the Internet and interactive video broadcasting, for instruction, communication, and interaction in a global virtual learning system. While prior studies about technology and distance education have addressed similar questions, this case is unique because the setting is an inter-continental, cross-cultural system, and the study is meant to shed the spotlight on Africa. Levy (1988) and Tellis (1997) suggest that the single-case, exploratory case study is a preferred and reliable method for examining the use of information technology in higher education.

This study examined the effectiveness and significance of various distance education technologies that are used for content delivery and for communication and interaction across continents. The study explored how differences in students' technology experiences, cultures, and curriculum influence learning and attitude in a technology-based distance education environment. The research also investigated whether the use and content quality of online references and materials is adequate and appropriate for successful learning.

Multiple data collection techniques in case studies contribute to adequate information collection and the validity and reliability of findings (Tellis, 1997). In this study, interviews, observations, and surveys were used for data collection. Over 60 students, instructors, learning facilitators, and administrators participated in the study. All students were of different undergraduate levels and fields of study such as business administration and computer science.

Individual, focus group, and open-ended e-mail interviews were used to collect data about technology and pedagogy in distance education across continents. A learning center in Kenya was observed during different visits over a one-month period. During the visits, some of the activities observed included classroom learning, use of computers (particularly online course management system), use of online libraries, and the role of facilitators.

Conducting a study that spans several countries requires time and resources. In order to obtain adequate data with minimal costs, a Web-based survey was utilized to explore the influence of technology on learning, communication, and interaction. The survey collected information on students' technology skills, attitude towards technology, Internet use in distance education, perceptions regarding the use and quality of online libraries, and use of communication media. Though many of the students who participated in the survey came from Kenya and Ghana, the possibility of other individuals masquerading as students to complete the survey cannot be ruled out, as the Website was not password-protected. However, random follow-up e-mails and triangulation of the data prevented any considerable cause for concern. Further, the survey data was collected over a two-month period during which the administrators and teachers announced to the students the existence of the survey and encouraged participation.

Qualitative data were analyzed by grouping and categorizing the data, and by reducing the information to manageable size (Miles & Hubermann, 1994). Information was coded using common keywords found in the data. A computer software program was used in the analysis of the survey data. Information sources such as interviews, observations, and surveys were triangulated, and member-checking was conducted to improve reliability and trustworthiness of the study.

Instructional Setting and Resources

The Pioneer Global Campus combined face-to-face structure with distance learning. Although this was a distance education program, students collaborated on campus while the course instructor taught from thousands of miles away. This helped students obtain easy access to technology and support from course facilitators. While the distance instructor provided the course content, the local facilitator explained the content. The instructor and the facilitator had complimentary roles, and the facilitator provided students with the support and confidence to enroll in a distance education program as noted in the following observational record:

It is 10:00 am and all students are listening to the facilitator explaining the content of a lesson unit. One would be forgiven for assuming that this is a traditional classroom as the facilitator is using the chalk and board to teach, and room arrangements depict a regular classroom, only that there are computers in this room. Students seem attentive and ask questions which attest to the important role that facilitators play in this distance education program.

...Students are downloading materials placed on WebCT by a distant instructor that they did not meet. Considering the subject the students were learning and lack of prior experience in the course content, it is possible that some of the students in the room would not be present if a facilitator was not here.

The impact of limited interaction between students and the distant course instructor of record was reduced by the presence of course facilitators. Every course had a qualified facilitator that assisted the instructor. This added support was helpful and appropriate, as Dodds (1994) also found out, considering that many of the students were young learners who did not yet have the self-directed and independent-learning attitude and experience of adult learners. In one of the classrooms observed, almost all of the students appeared to be recent high school graduates. From interviews done with the students in the classroom, the facilitator had an indispensable role in guiding students who might otherwise not have had the experience and self-discipline which a distance education course requires. To address concerns about the lack of real-time classroom contacts with the instructor, interactive video conferencing and Web-based communications technologies were used.

To improve learning and facilitate access to learning materials, the Pioneer Global Campus created an online library that students could access at anytime. The library contained academic journals, e-books, and other materials. Although the students appreciated the quality of materials, they expressed concerns about accessibility. They particularly disliked the length of time required to download materials and the fact that the online library materials were text-based only. While their desire for audio and video is understandable, providing materials in these complex formats is not practical considering that students encountered problems with downloading simple text. Scholars outside the African continent produced most of the learning materials available through the online library, though this is not unique to the online library only.

In the online survey, diverse students stated that they visited local libraries because of the limited availability of materials in the online library and the slowness of the Internet. Many of the students reported that they used the local library as their primary source of research because of the variety of materials and easy accessibility.

In interviews, several students complained that sluggish and poor access to the Internet hindered the effective use of the online materials, and this forced them to seek alternative sources for research:

Chris: ... I use it (online library) sometimes. But I use the (local) library more because I can go there anytime without paying and I have many books and materials (to select from).

Irene: I only use it when I am at work because I have a good (fast) computer. Also, at work, I can print. It is expensive to print at the (Internet) cafés. I am a poor student who has part time job.

Michael: Yes, it (Internet) is good but it needs some improvement. When I click (download) a paper I have to wait for a long time.

Mary: Oh my (the rest of the students in the focus group laughing) ... it is as slow as tortoise ... It would have been better if they build a library for our students. It will make it easy for us.

Instructional Media

The Pioneer Global Campus used different media and methods to deliver content to students, including a combination of satellite video broadcasting, Web-based instruction, VHS tapes, CD-ROM, and print. When the program began, interactive one-way and two-way video broadcasting and print materials were mostly used. Because of increased access and development of digital technology and the rising costs of interactive video conferencing, use of the Internet and CD-ROMs gradually increased, eventually surpassing application of satellite video broadcasting. The use of VHS tapes also increased due to their low costs and the students' familiarity with this medium.

The administrators made great efforts to utilize the various media concurrently. However, there is lately more asynchronous learning compared to the beginning years of the program, when real-time communication and interaction was common. Prohibitive costs necessitated a switch from live satellite broadcasting to Web-based learning. Administrators and staff also reported that dwindling donor funding and reduced student enrollment led to a reassessment of the instructional medium.

According to one of the administrators, students and the public had an overwhelming positive reaction when this virtual distance education program started. The administrator stated that one of the reasons for this reaction was that major donors such as the World Bank were supporting the project. A more compelling reason is that many traditional institutions and students were attracted by the use of information and communication technology (ICT). Many people in Africa, particularly Kenya, had not yet used satellite video conferencing and computers and were intrigued by the technology. A combination of all the aforementioned and other factors played a strong role in the initial robust implementation of the program, and this has worked to the advantage of the Pioneer Global Campus.

The Pioneer Global Campus later implemented use of cost-effective and modern instructional media, such as online course management systems. WebCT ™ was selected and utilized to replace the satellite broadcast. The digital technology infrastructure in many African countries is not sufficiently developed to take advantage of the interactivity that WebCT™ allowed. Problems such as slow internet, limited access to Internet facilities and services, and limited technology skills and experience hindered effective use of WebCT ™. As the course management system of choice, WebCT™ was limited to instructors posting lecture notes and students submitting assignments. Most of the valuable interactive technology features of WebCT™ such as chat rooms and discussion forums were rarely utilized.

An advantage of the Web-based learning is the ubiquitous nature of the Internet. Unlike the video broadcasting that confined students to specific centers, the Web allowed students to access learning materials anytime, anywhere. Unfortunately, however, many of the students had no access to a computer at home, and the few students who had computers mostly used them for productivity applications such as word processing to complete assignments. For many, home Internet services were non-existent due to high costs. Several students revealed that they used Internet cafés as they were easily available and less costly:

Peter: *I do not have a computer at a home. I only survive because I used the Internet cafés ... And nowadays, they are so cheap I only pay a shilling (Kenyan currency) for each minute. I can use it for hours and pay peanuts ... I like using it in the morning when there are not many people ... I don't like going to the cafés in the evenings and weekends because I see all this kids playing on the Internet.*

Rose: *... You know what! My father bought a computer for us. We use it to play (video) games. When we tell him we need the Internet, he tells us go to the (Internet) cafés ... I don't like it. But it is very close to our home. I just walk there.*

VHS tapes containing lectures were mailed as an alternative and occasionally to supplement Web-based learning. Students and faculty were overwhelmingly positive about the VHS-taped lectures because the video and audio quality was good and downloading time was not an issue. A limitation was the lack of interactivity; students appeared to be passive learners in the learning process. Students watched the tapes with no inquiry or questioning, discussion, and interaction with instructors and peers.

This study revealed that the level of technological development, accessibility, and cost are important determinants of the instructional medium. More effective technologies such as video conferencing could not be widely adopted because of cost. The Internet was not an appealing alternative because of poor technology infrastructure in the local countries. Recognizing the poor state of the technological development and resources of many African countries such as Kenya and Ghana, one of the brochures of the program stated:

Cognizant of the underdeveloped ICT infrastructure in Africa, the program will use a variety of modes of delivery to include VHS videotaped lectures, CD-ROMs, DVDs, WebCT™ platform with its variety of e-mail, online chat, both synchronous and asynchronous lectures, lecture notes, electronic quizzes, in addition to occasional video conferences. Most materials and different delivery media allows for flexible, mixed-mode of delivery.

Curriculum

The curriculum of the Pioneer Global Campus is strongly influenced by external universities. Instructors and administrators at the external universities played a major role in planning and designing course content and materials, assessment, and teaching styles and schedules. However, the Pioneer Global Campus collaborated with the external universities in implementing the curriculum.

In designing the curriculum and selecting course instructors, it is crucial to consider student learning styles and preferences. Unlike the traditional, face-to-face learning programs where locally-developed curriculum is widely used, several students, though a minority, were of the view that course content and the curriculum were designed for students in developed countries. Some administrators also shared this view. At a presentation at one of the donor conferences, the administrators of the Pioneer Global Campus recognized that one of the challenges they faced was the need to have content developed and delivered by local universities. Locally-developed content has the potential to more effectively relate to student needs and circumstances. For example, students enrolled in business and technology courses revealed that the business portfolios and the software programs that were utilized were widespread in the developed countries, but not common in the local countries. The content appeared to consist of prepackaged materials given to an audience whose needs and preferences had not been taken into consideration. Helen, a second-year student, was occasionally intrigued that some of the notes and programs did not correlate with what she has been learning in high school. She attributed her puzzlement to the way some of the courses were designed, the terminologies used, the examples given, and the general structure of some of the course content that did not naturally flow with what she had become familiar.

On the other hand, several students stated they liked the course content and materials developed by faculty in developed countries because they were getting a "first class" education that their peers in traditional universities were not. Two students, Mary and Michael, underscored such students' sentiments as they used words like "developed," "ahead," "21st century," "leading," "motivated," and "connected (to developed world)."

To illustrate and describe the disparity between educational systems in many African countries and some of the developed world, an American education system comparison may be helpful. In general, American curriculum and pedagogy focuses on student-centered learning. Many courses, instructional strategies, and educational philosophies demonstrate the need to facilitate active student participation in learning. In contrast, curriculum and pedagogical practices in many African countries have the hallmark of a traditional and structured education system within which teachers transmit knowledge to the students. For the most part, in many African countries, education is centralized and curriculum is standardized. Conversely, in America, education is decentralized, and the curriculum is approved at the local level.

Even though considerable efforts have been made to change the curriculum in several African countries such as Kenya, the traditional curriculum and educational system is still dominant. Meanwhile, advocating for curriculum and pedagogical change is not to negate the time-tested, valuable instructional practices traditionally used in classrooms. Nevertheless, as the Pioneer Global Campus is implementing a modern concept of educational delivery, it is appropriate to adopt suitable curriculum and instructional styles that promote and enhance successful learning.

Traditional Differences

Culture and attitude play an important role in distance education. While distance education is increasing in Africa, many people perceive it as an alternative educational program for people who have failed academically and do not qualify for admission to local traditional universities. Use of the Internet for learning is has been suspect to criticism because the Internet is considered by many to be more of a communication and entertainment tool rather than an educational tool. Several students reported that they had initial hesitation when informed that they would use the Internet for learning. Such students held more positive views about video broadcasting because it looked similar to a classroom as a teacher "stood" in front of them while in class. Because of longstanding cultural and educational traditions, some students thought they were missing out on knowledge that came with direct face-to-face instruction. Yolanda, Rose, and Catherine stated that many of their peers in the traditional colleges have a negative attitude towards distance education. Their peers and other members of the community believed that the virtual university (Pioneer Global Campus) was for students who were from wealthy families or those who had no other option for obtaining a college degree.

Displaying displeasure with the attitude of some of the cynics, Rose retorted:

I wish they could understand how much we are far ahead of them (traditional students). We have the best education, we know technology more than them, we will graduate faster than them and our degrees will be from better and world recognized universities...

Some of the criticism stem from the limited technology use in education in Africa because colleges and schools cannot afford them. The technology is new, is generally limited to business and office use, and is used as a communication and entertainment tool by the public. When the Pioneer Global Campus introduced Internet use for education, the concept was alien to many students who, as a result, initially doubted and resented the Internet.

Though not a major issue, two students cited language as an issue that needed to be addressed. A legacy of the British colonial presence in African countries such as Ghana and Kenya is the present-day educational curriculum and the widespread use of the English language. American instructors delivered their lectures in American English, but the students used British English. Two students called attention to the possibility that students could lose points for using British spelling and grammar when being graded by an American instructor. However, these same students added that when watching the VHS tapes, they had no problems understanding the instructor.

Time differences between the external universities and the local countries interfered with real-time learning. Instructors were stationed in the U.S., Canada, and Australia, and this meant that time adjustments had to be made by students to make it easier for the instructors to synchronously interact with their students. According to a member of the teaching staff, the time difference was resolved by scheduling courses during times that were convenient for both students and instructors, such as having classes in the late afternoon in Kenya and morning in the U.S. Some administrators and teaching staff stated that variety and increased access to technology reduced the time difference constraint.

Use of Technology

Experience, skills, access, and attitude played a significant role in Internet use. Students who had more technology skills preferred using the Internet while those with limited technology skills were less inclined to use the Internet for learning. The Web survey revealed that students who had computer experience were more likely to use the Internet and demonstrated greater comfort with it, compared to their counterparts with limited computer technology experience. According to the data, more computer experience translated to increased positive attitude towards computers. With time, the students who initially were not enthusiastic about Internet use changed their perceptions about computers. Meanwhile, several students noted that though they were comfortable with using the Internet for communication and learning, they had reservations abaout using it as the primary learning tool. These students declared preference for the interactive video broadcasting, for it was the closest they could get to a face-to-face classroom learning setting style. They cited the support they obtained from an instructor when using video broadcasting, compared to the Internet lessons where they were literally left on their own.

While appreciating the use and the potential of the Internet, students exhibited negative attitudes toward the use of the Internet as the sole medium of instruction. The problems that plagued the use of the Internet, such as poor accessibility, poor reliability, and limited interactivity, led to some resentment regarding Internet use. In one of the computer-equipped classrooms that was observed, students appeared frustrated in accessing and downloading the course content. In one of the lessons, an Australian university offered the course, and the instructional medium was WebCT. The students had difficulty using the materials because the computers were slow. However, many students and all administrators and facilitators were optimistic and confident that the quality learning eclipsed the technological setbacks which students faced.

Access was another key issue. Students with limited access to the Internet preferred the video broadcasting, and information supplied in VHS tapes and CDs. Difficulty accessing reliable Internet was a recurring issue. A combination of two-way satellite video broadcasting and phone conferencing produced instant and interactive communication between students and the instructor, but the expected increase in interaction and communication through the use of the Internet did not happen.

Students reported in the Web-based survey that they spent an average of twelve hours per week on the Internet, which was not enough time for students taking online classes. The limited Internet use demonstrates the preference the students had for other learning tools and media. While many of the students stated they used Internet cafés for online leaning, they indicated concerns such as noise and lack of privacy which made Internet cafés inconvenient.

Glaring differences in the available Internet services existed. Internet services in South Africa were faster and more reliable than in Ghana and Kenya. An interview with one administrator revealed Internet problems were not caused by the Pioneer Global Campus' failure to provide reliable technology, but by the generally underdeveloped Information Technology of the local countries. The interviewee highlighted the relative success and popularity of the Internet in South Africa with its better infrastructure compared to Kenya. Despite the concerns raised about the use of Internet as a learning tool, there was an encouraging perception that the Internet is an important medium for distance education and a useful learning tool.

Conclusion

This case study reports that distance education programs provide educational opportunities to people who otherwise would not be able to obtain educational or career advancement prospects. A distance education program such as the Pioneer Global Campus is playing an important role in increasing access to education. A significant contribution of the Pioneer Global Campus is the mass education that it provides despite some problems associated with the delivery medium. Although the students were receiving quality education, great strides need to be made towards localizing the curriculum to adapt to student needs and existing educational practices.

The choice of delivery mechanism and instructional medium is critical. As revealed in this case study, cost greatly determines the choice of instructional medium; however, the selection of the instructional medium should prioritize student learning preference and needs. The appropriateness and reliability of the medium is equally worthy of great consideration. The Pioneer Global Campus' combination of interactive video broadcasting, Web, VHS/CD, and print is commendable and appropriate. However, the use of the various instructional media should be complementary and not replace one another. A variety of media would facilitate accessibility and interaction, and would provide students with choices and alternatives.

A thorough needs assessment should be conducted before making major decisions about content delivery media. Access, reliability, and usability of media are important considerations that should not be overlooked. For example, many students could access VHS tapes as they were able to watch the tapes using home video playback machines. In contrast, use of CD-ROMS was found to be inappropriate because many students did not have home computers. Internet cafés, widely used by students, were found to be cumbersome because of noise from other patrons, cost, and lack of privacy. Inadequate and poor technological development leading to slow and unreliable Internet made the use of the Internet as a learning tool less appealing.

Students can learn effectively via distance education if learning structures promote individualized and independent learning. Individualized learning has the added advantage of making students learn at their own pace and styles and according to their abilities. Making students learn in a classroom cohort using traditional teaching and learning strategies undermines the independence and individualized learning that accompanies distance education. If classroom learning becomes necessary, as is the case with the Pioneer Global Campus where facilitators provided tutoring, classroom learning should be supplementary to the distance learning.

Considering some of the issues raised in the study, the selection of the instructional medium should be done carefully when designing courses to ensure successful distance education. Designing a course for distance delivery, particularly one that involves use of technology, should accommodate the flexibility that is traditionally associated with distance education.

Although correspondence study dominated the field of distance education in Africa for decades (Dodds, 1994), the information society of the 21st century calls for an overhaul of the approach, management style, and mode of distance education delivery. Distance education was not initially widely-adopted in Africa because of limited well- organized and independent programs and institutions that focused on distance learning, and the perceptions people held about distance education as a nondescript alternative education. With the inception of the Pioneer Global Campus, the first continent-wide virtual distance education program, a new ground has been broken that will forever alter the distance education landscape in Africa. The use of information technology, as demonstrated by the Pioneer Global Campus, will play a significant role in making distance education a strong competitor to traditional classroom learning in the near future.

References

Dodds, A. (1994). Distance learning for pre-tertiary education in Africa. In M. Thorpe & D. Grugeon (Eds.), *Open learning in the mainstream* (pp. 321-327). Harlow, UK: Longman Group.

Levy, S. (1988). *Information technologies in universities: An institutional case study.* Unpublished doctoral dissertation, Northern Arizona University, Flagstaff.

Miles, M. B., & Huberman, A. M. (1994). *Qualitative data analysis.* Thousand Oaks, CA: Sage Publications.

Miller, M. D., Rainer, R. K., & Corley, J. K. (2003). Predictors of engagement and participation in an online course. *Online Journal of Distance Learning Administration, 6*(1). Retrieved April 15, 2004, from http://www.westga.edu/%7Edistance/ojdla/spring61/miller61.htm

Simonson, M., Smaldino, S., Albright, M., & Zvacek, S. (2003). *Teaching and learning at a distance.* Upper Saddle, NJ: Pearson Education, Inc.

Stake, R. (1995). *The art of case research.* Newbury Park, CA: Sage Publications.

Tellis, W. (1997). Application of a case study methodology. *The Qualitative Report, 3*(3). Retrieved February 10, 2004, from http://www.nova.edu/ssss/QR/QR3-3/tellis2.html

U.S. Department of Education. (2000). E-learning: Putting a world-class education at the fingertips of all children. *The National Educational Technology Plan.* Washington, DC: U.S. Department of Education.

Warner, D. (2003, March 30-April 1). Student recommendations for discussion boards: Conclusions of student problems. *Eighth Annual Mid-South Instructional Technology Conference, Teaching, learning & technology: The Challenge Continues.* Murfreesboro, TN: Middle Tennessee State University.

Zembylas, M., & Vrasidas, C. (2005). Levinas and the "inter-face": The ethical challenges of online education. *Educational Theory, 55*(1), 60-78.

Section V

Conclusion

Chapter XX

The Treasure Trove

Andrea Edmundson
eWorld Learning, USA

Referring back to Gert Jan Hofstede's words in the Foreword, we have a treasure-trove of ideas and concepts to sort through with respect to globalized e-learning cultural challenges. In this book, we have referenced seminal research studies on cultural influences and dimensions, speculated on their potential impact on e-learning, and reviewed examples of empirical research and observations of these cultural challenges. We have explored the potential ramifications of Western-based theories being promulgated in non-Western cultures. We have addressed fresh ideas about the interactions between culture and e-learning, such as paralanguage and cultural learning objects. In addition, we have heard from learners themselves. Lastly, authors have proposed new ways to analyze and/or adapt e-learning for other cultures, based on logical presumptions, on our current experiences, and on existing research.

Where do we stand, then, at this point in time? Imagine the treasure trove, filled with gold, jewels, gems, and other riches. In this book, we have sorted through some of the treasure, initially placing similar items into their unique stacks, gold in one, gems in another, and so on. However, in the near future, with the advent of additional knowledge and experience, we will return to inspect our growing treasure and, subsequently, realize that the initial sorting system was not quite appropriate or, perhaps, not sophisticated enough. Instead, it now makes more sense to sort precious gems by color and metals by type: gold here, silver there; jade here, diamonds there.

In this book, we have completed an initial "sorting" of treasures: We have covered some of what we think we know about globalized e-learning, and what challenges can be anticipated as well as those that have already been recognized. We have speculated on what yet needs to be researched. Thus, what would we like to see when we reexamine our treasure trove in the future? We hope to find:

1.   A deeper understanding of educational paradigms, theories, and philosophies from non-Western entities;

2.   Expanded use of new tools and concepts, such as cultural learning objects (CLOs) and the use of communication technologies such as instant messaging, blogs, podcasting, and so forth;

3.   Deeper exporation of online communications across cultures, such as conflict resolution online and e-teamwork;

4.   Expanded information about other cultures' educational systems, cultural values, ICT usage, and learning preferences;

5.   Reports on:

   a.   Empirically-tested methods of e-instructional design for different cultures, including localization and adaptation techniques, instructional strategies, instructional activities, language, and semiotics;

   b.   Changes that have occurred as a result of closer contact between cultures;

   c.   The impact of increasing exposure to other cultures, such as changes in perceptions, acceptance of different learning styles and different pedagogies, discoveries of new theories and philosophies, and/or potential alteration of learning styles or preferences;

   d.   The successes generated by the globalization of e-learning, such as improved technical literacy, improved understanding and tolerance of other cultures, and the proliferation of open source education for all areas of the world; and

6.   Broadened perspectives of the challenges generated by globalized e-learning documented by other cultures—Indian, African, Asian, European, Latin American, and so forth—not just Western ones.

And the list goes on! This book provides an introduction, and new perspectives, for educators from, and of, all cultures; for producers of e-learning, such as instructional designers; for consumers of e-learning, such as multinational corporations and online universities; and, of course, the learners. The intention of this book was to raise the consciousness of these stakeholders; we hope we have succeeded. More riches await us. Happy treasure hunting!

About the Authors

Andrea Edmundson, PhD, (educational technology) is the CEO of eWorld Learning (www.eWorldLearning.com), USA, which provides educational and consulting services for corporations, online universities, and other educational organizations that are expanding their e-learning investments beyond local markets. She has been an educator, corporate trainer, business owner, and consultant for 20 years, working in more than 15 countries throughout Africa, Eastern Europe, Asia, the Pacific, and the Caribbean. She was also the professional development manager of a multinational medical software company, responsible for training and educating 1,200+ employees in five countries, as well as clients, extensively using educational ICTs. Her research and work led her to publishing the book, *Globalized E-Learning Cultural Challenges*. Her expertise in educational technology, adult learning, training, and international development make her uniquely qualified to guide eWorld Learning towards its mission: promoting global convergence through e-education by facilitating increased access, equitable learning outcomes, and better technical education for all online learners.

* * *

Ahmed Ali (ali.ahme@uwlax.edu), PhD, is an assistant professor of instructional technology at the University of Wisconsin - La Crosse, USA. Ali's teaching and research interests focus on technology and pedagogy, instructional design, Web and multimedia developments, and online learning. He has published and presented at national and international conferences.

David Catterick is a lecturer in applied languages at the University of Dundee, Scotland. His research interests include the support of international students in online learning, and he is currently undertaking a longitudinal study of the support needs of international students on an online MBA program. David currently teaches on a master's in international professional communication and contributes to an MSc in the globalization program. He is also partnering in a transnational project focusing on the design of professional English training for online delivery being funded by the European Union.

Marcus D. Childress is associate professor and chair of the Instructional Design & Technology Department in The Teachers College at Emporia State University, USA, where he directs an online graduate degree program in instructional design & technology. Dr. Childress teaches courses in instructional/multimedia design and online learning. Research interests include distance education, massively multiplayer online games in training/education, and using technology integration as a catalyst for school reform. Dr. Childress serves as a senior trainer for the Intel Teach to the Future program and is past president of the Research and Theory Division of the Association for Educational Communications and Technology.

Caroline M. Crawford (Crawford@uhcl.edu), EdD, is an associate professor of instructional technology at the University of Houston - Clear Lake in Houston, Texas, USA. At this point in Dr. Crawford's professional career, her main areas of interest focus upon the appropriate and successful integration of technologies into the learning environment.

Patrick Dunn has worked in educational and training technology for 15 years, mainly with large organizations in the public and private sectors. He is currently an independent consultant working with a number of UK-based providers of e-learning services. He specializes in two areas: the effects of cultural difference on learning design processes, and cultivating creative practice and innovation in meeting learning design challenges. He has worked with some of the most significant players in the e-learning and knowledge management industry, including DigitalThink and PricewaterhouseCoopers. He holds an MA from Oxford University and an MBA from Warwick Business School.

Jane Eberle is an assistant professor of instructional design and technology in the Teachers College at Emporia State University, USA. She teaches technology in the classroom to undergraduate education majors and online graduate courses in Web training and assistive technology and universal design for learning. She has 15 years of elementary classroom teaching experience in which she incorporated many uses of technology into her teaching. Her research interests include effective uses of technology in the classroom, universal design, and assistive technology.

Ruth Gannon Cook, EdD, is an assistant professor at DePaul University in Chicago, USA. Dr. Gannon Cook earned her doctorate from the University of Houston (2003); further, she earned a certificate for advanced studies from Queens College, Cambridge, UK, with an emphasis in change diffusion and technology integration. Her MSEd in educational administration and BA in business are both from Loyola University, New Orleans. She currently serves on the board of trustees for the Cordell Hull Foundation for International Education, New York, and is a judging panel coordinator for the International Student Media Festival of AECT.

Lyn Henderson, PhD, is an associate professor in the School of Education, James Cook University, Australia. Her undergraduate and postgraduate teaching, research, and publications target mental models and other thinking processes when learning and teaching with information communication technologies. Instructional design of online learning and teaching and blended teaching examines the role of multiple cultures and internationalization of e-courses. Teenagers' thinking skills when playing recreational computer games is a further focus. Henderson is building a research hub with national and international scholars and research students utilizing stimulated recall methodologies and mental models.

Gert Jan Hofstede (gertjan.hofstede@wur.nl) is an associate professor in information management at Wageningen University, Social Science Group, and a regular guest lecturer at many places, a.o. London School of Economics and ETH Zürich. He holds an MSc in biology and a doctorate in production planning, and teaches database design. Gert Jan started to use his father Geert's work on national cultures in the mid-nineties to create simulation games, and has since become a well-known speaker, consultant, and author about cross-cultural communication. He is first author of *Exploring Culture* (2002), a book with practical exercises on cross-cultural communication, and co-author of *Cultures and Organizations 2nd ed.* (2005).

Datta Kaur Khalsa, PhD, is a long-time educator, educational technologist, teacher trainer and core faculty for California State University's East Bay graduate program in online teaching and learning. She also owns her own business, Khalsa & Associates, which develops curriculum for educational programs, conducts research focusing on ESL, social computing, online communities, virtual teamwork as well as the policy, training and organizational structure related to application of cross-cultural communication to multidisciplinary K-12 curriculum. Her publication titled include *Support for Global Project Based Learning: U.S. Teacher Motivation, Online Training, Virtual Teamwork, Trust and Identity* (2005), *Online Learning Teams: Impact of Socio-Cultural Dimensions* (2005), and *Breathing Heritage and Equality into the Curriculum* (2005).

Wanjira Kinuthia is an assistant professor at Georgia State University, USA, where she teaches courses in instructional design and technology. Prior to that, she worked as an instructional designer in higher education and business. She has a PhD in instructional design and development, a master's degree in international affairs focusing on African studies and women's studies, and a master's degree in computer education and technology. She also has a bachelor's degree in international business. Wanjira has a special interest in international and comparative education. Her research focuses on socio-cultural factors influencing e-learning in developing countries.

Mimi Miyoung Lee (mlee7@uh.edu) is an assistant professor of curriculum and instruction at University of Houston in Texas, USA. She earned her doctorate in 2004 from Indiana University, Bloomington. Her research interests include cross-cultural and multicultural aspects of education, theories of representation, discourse analysis, and instructional theories. She has a background in literary criticism and critical theory.

Meng-Fen (Grace) Lin (grace.mf.lin@gmail.com) earned her doctorate in 2006 from the University of Houston in Texas, USA. Her research interests include online community, open education resources (OER), and social learning theories.

Youmei Liu (EdD, University of Houston, USA) works as a senior instructional designer in the office of Educational Technology and University Outreach. She is also an adjunct faculty member teaching an advanced Web technology course at UH. She provides faculty training and support related to online course design and instructional delivery. Her research interests include faculty development, online assessment, cross-cultural online education, and integration of multimedia components and learning objects in course design.

Alessandra Marinetti has been involved in adult education for over 10 years, in academia, as well as in the public and in the private sector. She currently works as a learning specialist for The Global Fund to Fight AIDS, Tuberculosis & Malaria, Switzerland, and is responsible for the planning and development of all learning programs and activities for the Fund's Secretariat. Before the Global Fund, Ms. Marinetti worked as an instructional design consultant with the UNHCR's Staff Development Section in Geneva, providing instructional design support to the organization's training officers. She also gained extensive experience in the e-learning arena while working as learning strategist for U.S. e-learning provider DigitalThink, designing custom e-learning courseware chiefly for private sector customers. Ms. Marinetti has also worked as a lecturer at several schools and universities in the U.S. and in Germany. She holds an MA in instructional technologies from San Francisco State University and an MA in German studies from "La Sapienza" University in Rome.

Steve McCarty is a professor at Osaka Jogakuin College, Japan. He is the elected president of the World Association for Online Education, an NPO registered in the U.S. (1998-2007). He teaches English as a foreign language (EFL) through topics such as current events, human rights, and bilingualism. His online library of publications, with English and Japanese annotated versions, has received a 4-star rating, very useful for research, in 1997, 2001, and 2005 from the Asian Studies WWW Virtual Library. His online spoken library is the podcasting blog "Japancasting." For additional information, visit www.waoe.org/steve.

Catherine McLoughlin is associate professor at the School of Education, Australian Catholic University, Canberra, Australia, where she teaches at undergraduate and postgraduate levels. Dr. McLoughlin is the author and co-author of more than 120 refereed publications, including journal articles, book chapters, and conference papers on a wide range of topics in education, such as teaching quality, e-learning, design of culturally-sensitive learning environments, metacognition, evaluation of learning technologies, online assessment, and learner engagement. Dr. McLoughlin describes her philosophy of teaching as learner-centered, and that effective teaching is about using diverse strategies and resources to meet learner needs, engaging them in authentic real-life tasks and enabling them to become independent learners who enter the workforce with skills in self-management, literacy, problem solving, and other generic skills. Dr. McLoughlin is editor of the *Australian Journal of Educational Technology* and a member of the program committee of the World Conference on Educational Multimedia and Hypermedia, organized by the Association for Advancement of Computing in Education. In addition, she is on the editorial boards of a number of leading international journals in the field of learning technology.

Bolanle Olaniran (Olaniran@ttu.edu) (PhD, University of Oklahoma, 1991) is a professor at Texas Tech University in the Department of Communication Studies (USA). His research interests have been in the area of computer-mediated communication and specifically exploring the role and effects of communication technologies in organizations and student learning. His works have appeared in varieties of communication several book chapters along with other interdisciplinary journals at regional, national, and international arena. He attempts to bring a multidisciplinary approach to his teachings and classrooms. His interest in communication technology has received recognition and consulting from both private and government agencies, including the assessment of videoconferencing at the Department of Commerce - U.S. Census Bureau. Other areas of teaching and research interests include cross-cultural and communication and diversity in workplaces.

Nektaria Palaiologou (npal@unipi.gr) holds a bachelor's, master's and doctoral degree in education (University of Athens) and has followed post-doctoral studies in education and culture (University of London). Until now, Dr. Nektaria Palaiologou has taught at the Department of Pre-Primary Education-Democritus University, Department of Special Needs Education-University of Thessaly, Marasleion Didaskaleion-University of Athens and at Higher Police Academy. Since 2002, Dr. Nektaria Palaiologou is affiliated with the Department of Technology Education and Digital Systems of the University of Piraeus, Greece, where she is teaching the pedagogical and assessment modules as a visiting lecturer. She is the co-writer of three books in Greek (1. *Intercultural Pedagogy;* 2. *Designing and Implementing Educational Programmes;* 3. *School Attainments of Immigrant Pupils in Greece*) as well as author and co-author of published papers in international journals in the broader field of education with intercultural dimensions.

Thomas C. Reeves is a professor in the Department of Educational Psychology and Instructional Technology at The University of Georgia, USA, where he teaches evaluation, research, and instructional design. His research interests include evaluation and assessment methods; cognitive tools and mental models; socially-responsible research; authentic tasks for online learning; and instructional technology in developing countries. He has been an invited speaker in 22 countries. In 2003, he was the first person to receive the AACE Fellowship Award from the Association for the Advancement of Computing in Education. For additional information, visit http://it.coe.uga.edu/~treeves/.

Martin Schell was born in New York City and has spent the last 20 years in Japan, Thailand, and Indonesia. He has taught English in each of those countries, rewritten Japanese-to-English translations, designed distance learning materials in Thailand, and prepared cost-of-living surveys in Indonesia. He is currently a freelance Web designer and editor, serving academic authors who are native to South America, Europe, and Asia. He also teaches an online course in business writing for NYU's Stern School of Business. Based in his wife's hometown in central Java, he hosts an online discussion group about Asia that he founded in 1996.

Chun-Min Wang (flat@uga.edu) is a doctoral student in the Department of Educational Psychology and Instructional Technology in the College of Education at The University of Georgia, USA. A native of Taiwan, his research interests include cultural issues in online education; design-based research; evaluation of instructional technology; and creativity in instructional design. His PhD research is focused on the intersection of cultural dimensions in online learning environments with a special interest in Chinese international students studying in the United States. He is also involved in the evaluation of digital libraries funded by the National Science Foundation.

Katherine Watson teaches French, English, linguistics, anthropology, and English as a second language. She did undergraduate work at Mount Holyoke College and California State University, Fullerton, receiving degrees in anthropology and French; graduate work led her to Indiana University, the Université d'Aix-Marseille, the University of Connecticut, and Nova University, specializing in zoosemiotics and French linguistics, theoretical linguistics and applied linguistics; historical linguistics, prosody, and metrics, and the acquisition and loss of language comprised her various thesis topics. Recent publications include papers on secondary language acquisition, learning among older adults, and online learning, generally concentrating on French and English. Dr. Watson has remained active in translation and interpretation as well; she served as an interpreter-trainer and an interpreter for the United States Olympic Committee and for the World Cup Organizing Committee, and her literary translations of the Marquis de Sade's political and philosophical works are to be published shortly.

Rita Zaltsman, PhD, has worked for years in education, both in the private and academic sectors. After settling down in Germany, she graduated from Reutlingen Technical University and worked in a software firm in Stuttgart. Both interests, teaching and computers, led her to The State University of West Georgia (USA) where she specialized in distance learning instruction. Her dissertation theme was: "Conflict Paradigm in Cross-Cultural Distance Learning Settings." She is a freelancer, currently developing e-learning courses on cross-cultural communication for the International Center of Modern Education in Prague, Czech Republic, publishing articles on e-learning issues and contributing to German and international conferences. Her main research interests are Web-based discourse analysis, cross-cultural e-learning, conflicts in e-learning communities and psycholinguistics.

Index

cultural diversity 66, 132, 224
cultural etiquette 321
cultural experience 66
cultural identity 313
cultural inclusion 67
cultural inclusivity 70, 235
cultural influence 62, 308
cultural learning 84
cultural learning object (CLO); cultural LO
    85, 270
cultural pluralism 132
cultural sensitivity 7, 10
cultural value system 35, 36
cultural values 51, 52, 54
cultural variables 62
cultural Web 80
culturally blind 132
culturally sensitive 3
culture 1, 3, 4, 6, 7, 20, 21, 22, 23, 24,
    27, 28, 40, 43, 60, 61, 76, 84, 132,
    140, 225, 255, 270, 308
culture and learning 20
culture, definitions of 76
culture dimensions 4
culture switching 140
curricula 132
curriculum design 41
custom 132
cyber-culture 77, 79
cyberspace 79

D

de Saussure, Ferdinand 191
deductive 214
definition of culture 62
democracy 321
design and delivery of instruction 61
digital divide 64
dimension 20, 312, 314
dimension of culture frameworks 312
dimension of cultural variability 20
dimension of culture 78, 312
discipline 140
discussion forum 133
distance education 1, 189, 251, 335
distance education courses 251

distance learning 1, 36, 240, 331
distributed cognitive environment 143
diversified online learning team 308, 309
diversified perception 320
diversified student 316
diversity 320
diversity of expertise 309
domestic violence 140
dominant culture 138

E

e-activity 143
e-apprenticeship 145
e-conference 147
e-courses 133
e-education 138
e-instructional design 132
e-learning 18, 19, 21, 22, 23, 24, 25,
    26, 28, 31, 65, 68, 130, 183, 224,
    255, 268, 269, 292
e-learning course 268
e-learning, examples of successful integra-
    tion 68
e-learning resource 130
e-mail 143, 252, 314
e-mail interviews 314
e-materials 133
e-paper 147
e-partner 143
e-professional development 131
e-quiz 143
e-teaching 130
e-tutorial 139
Eastern culture 36, 46
Eastern Europe 133
Easterner 36, 42, 52
eclectic pedagogic paradigm 141
eclectic pedagogy 143
economic 131
economically-developed country (EDC)
    22, 25
economy 131
EDC (see economically-developed country)
education 62, 63, 103, 110, 133, 188
education for all (EFA) 63
education model 62

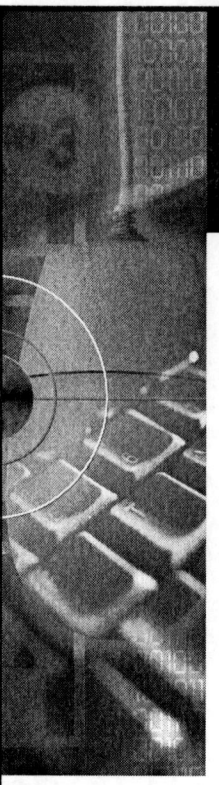
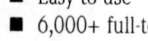